THE QUEEN'S KNIGHT

The Queen's Knight Volume 9
Created By Kim Kang Won

Translation - Sora Han
English Adaptation - Kara Stambach
Retouch and Lettering - Star Print Brokers
Production Artist - Bowen Park
Graphic Designer - Monalisa De Asis

Editor - Hyun Joo Kim
Digital Imaging Manager - Chris Buford
Pre-Production Supervisor - Erika Terriquez
Art Director - Anne Marie Horne
Production Manager - Elisabeth Brizzi
Managing Editor - Vy Nguyen
VP of Production - Ron Klamert
Editor-in-Chief - Rob Tokar
Publisher - Mike Kiley
President and C.O.O. - John Parker
C.E.O. and Chief Creative Officer - Stuart Levy

A **TOKYOPOP** Manga

TOKYOPOP and are trademarks or registered trademarks of TOKYOPOP Inc.

TOKYOPOP Inc.
5900 Wilshire Blvd. Suite 2000
Los Angeles, CA 90036

E-mail: info@TOKYOPOP.com
Come visit us online at www.TOKYOPOP.com

ISBN: 978-1-59532-265-4
First TOKYOPOP printing: August 2007
10 9 8 7 6 5 4 3 2 1
Printed in the USA

THE QUEEN'S KNIGHT

VOLUME 9

BY KIM KANG WON

HAMBURG // LONDON // LOS ANGELES // TOKYO

LAST TIME IN...

THE QUEEN'S KNIGHT

Yuna is a normal girl who visits her mother in Germany and befalls a terrible disaster. After she returns home from her accident, she begins to have strange dreams. In her dream, a knight who calls himself "Rieno" tells Yuna that she is his Queen and that he is her knight. Yuna's brothers send her back to Germany, where she meets the knight from her dreams--who then promptly kidnaps her, taking her to Phantasma.

Phantasma is a world covered entirely with snow, and Yuna is forced to live with Rieno. But just when Yuna was getting used to being with him, spring arrives, and Yuna is taken to Elysian to be properly installed as the Queen of Phantasma. Once there, Yuna befriends the Queen's Guardian Knights, Ehren, Leon and Schiller, the hateful Chancellor Kent, as well as the Queen's rival, Princess Libera.

Yuna almost immediately begins to shake things up, as she not only repeals the taxes and declares slavery illegal, but insists on creating new policies and institutions like schools and hospitals.

As she settles into her new gig as the queen, she discovers that the queen's main duty is to maintain springtime in Phantasma and that can only be done if she's happily in love. As all her predecessors had fallen for Rieno, who would never reciprocate the sentiment, spring had all eventually come to an end...till now. Speculators, and even Yuna herself, are convinced that Yuna's object of amore is Ehren and that this is fantastic news for Phantasma as spring can be eternal again.

Later, Yuna learns of the doomed romance between Rieno and Eli, the Queen before her. At the same time, Ehren gets a brief history lesson of Phantasma and how Rieno, when he reaches age nineteen, will come to rule the land as lord of darkness. In order to prevent such travesty, Ehren is entrusted with a critical assignment: He must persuade Queen Yuna to drive the Mistletoe Wooden Dagger into Rieno's heart...

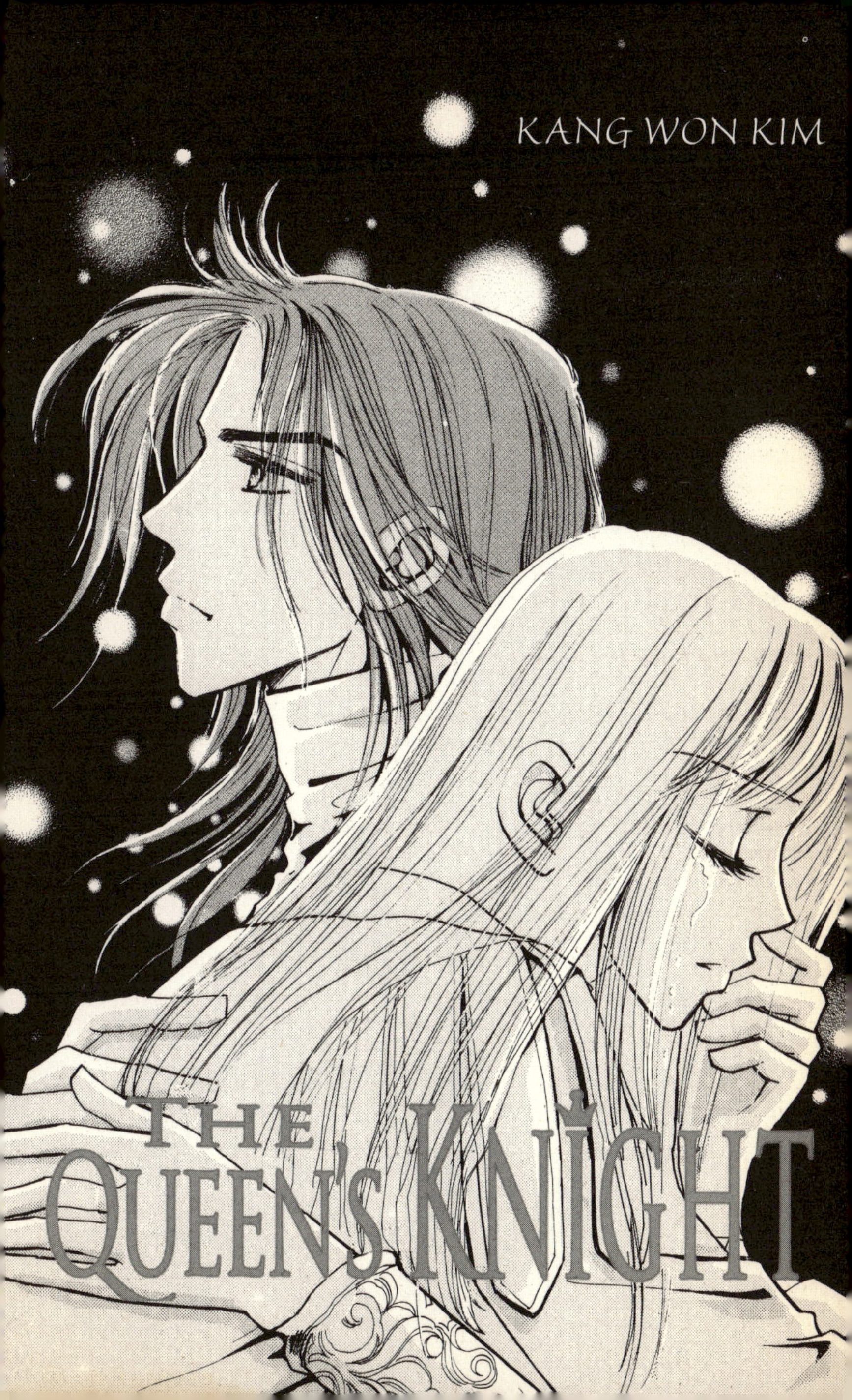
KANG WON KIM
THE QUEEN'S KNIGHT

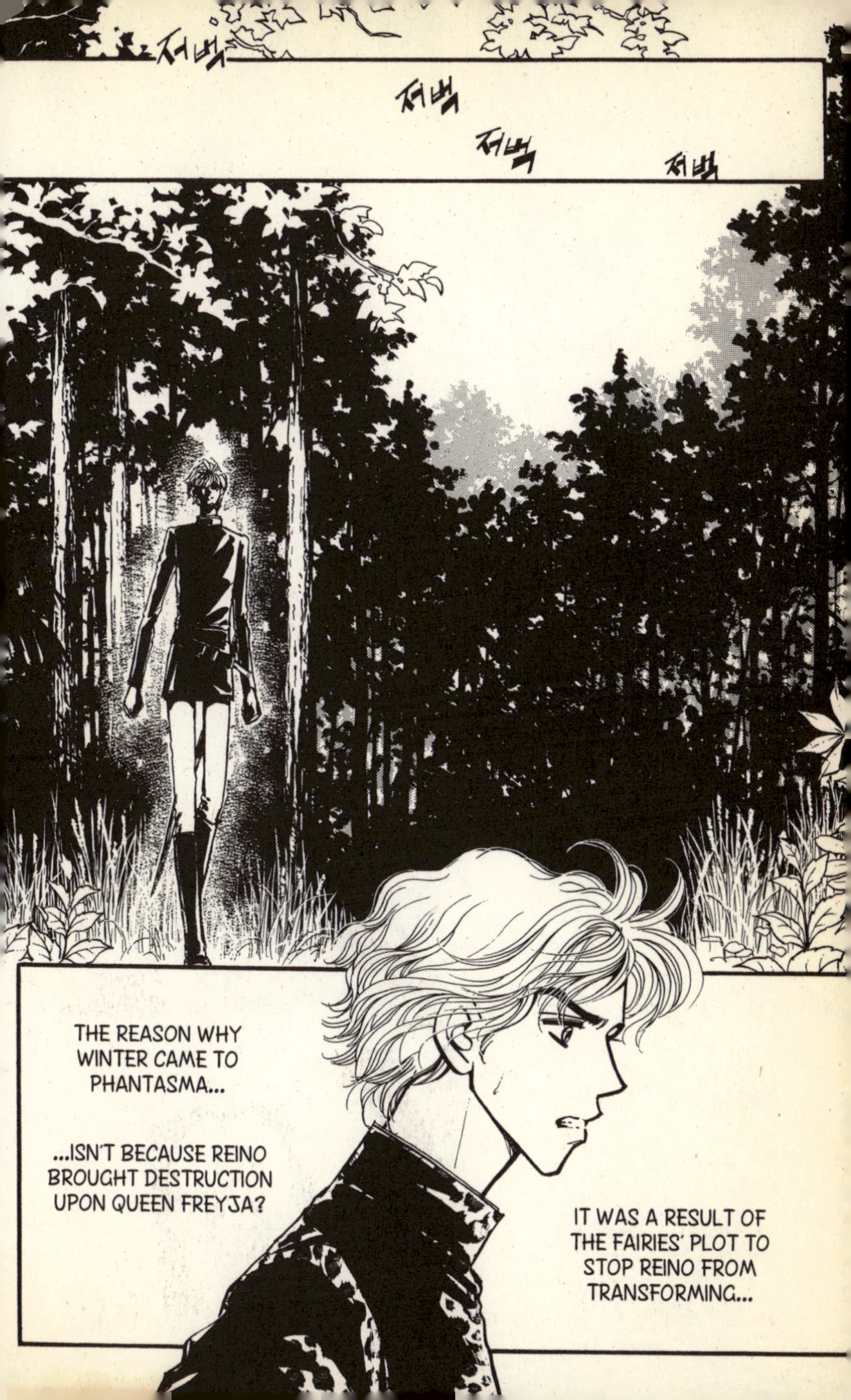

저벅
저벅
저벅
저벅
THE REASON WHY WINTER CAME TO PHANTASMA...
...ISN'T BECAUSE REINO BROUGHT DESTRUCTION UPON QUEEN FREYJA?
IT WAS A RESULT OF THE FAIRIES' PLOT TO STOP REINO FROM TRANSFORMING...

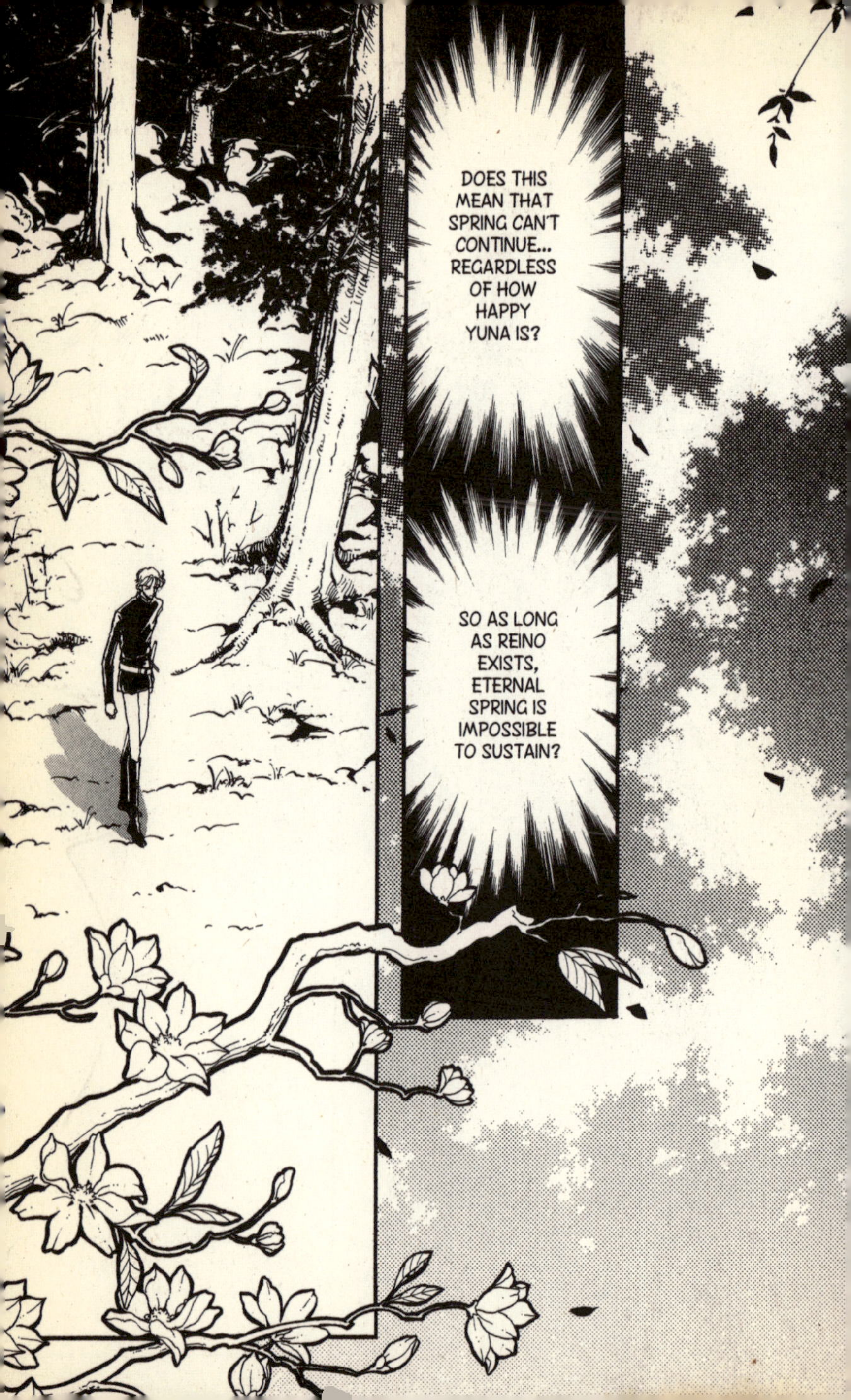
DOES THIS MEAN THAT SPRING CAN'T CONTINUE... REGARDLESS OF HOW HAPPY YUNA IS?
SO AS LONG AS REINO EXISTS, ETERNAL SPRING IS IMPOSSIBLE TO SUSTAIN?

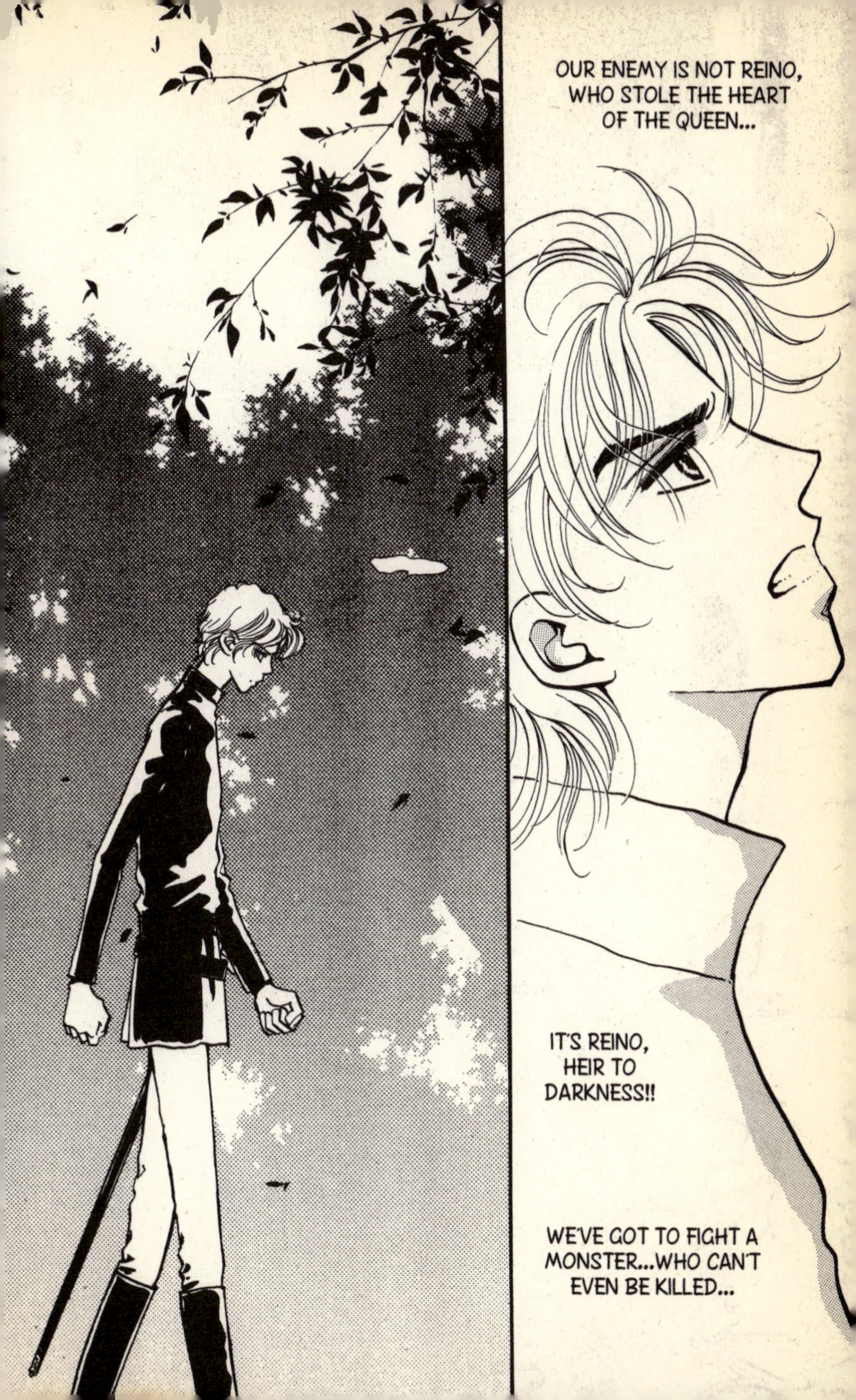
OUR ENEMY IS NOT REINO, WHO STOLE THE HEART OF THE QUEEN...
IT'S REINO, HEIR TO DARKNESS!!
WE'VE GOT TO FIGHT A MONSTER...WHO CAN'T EVEN BE KILLED...

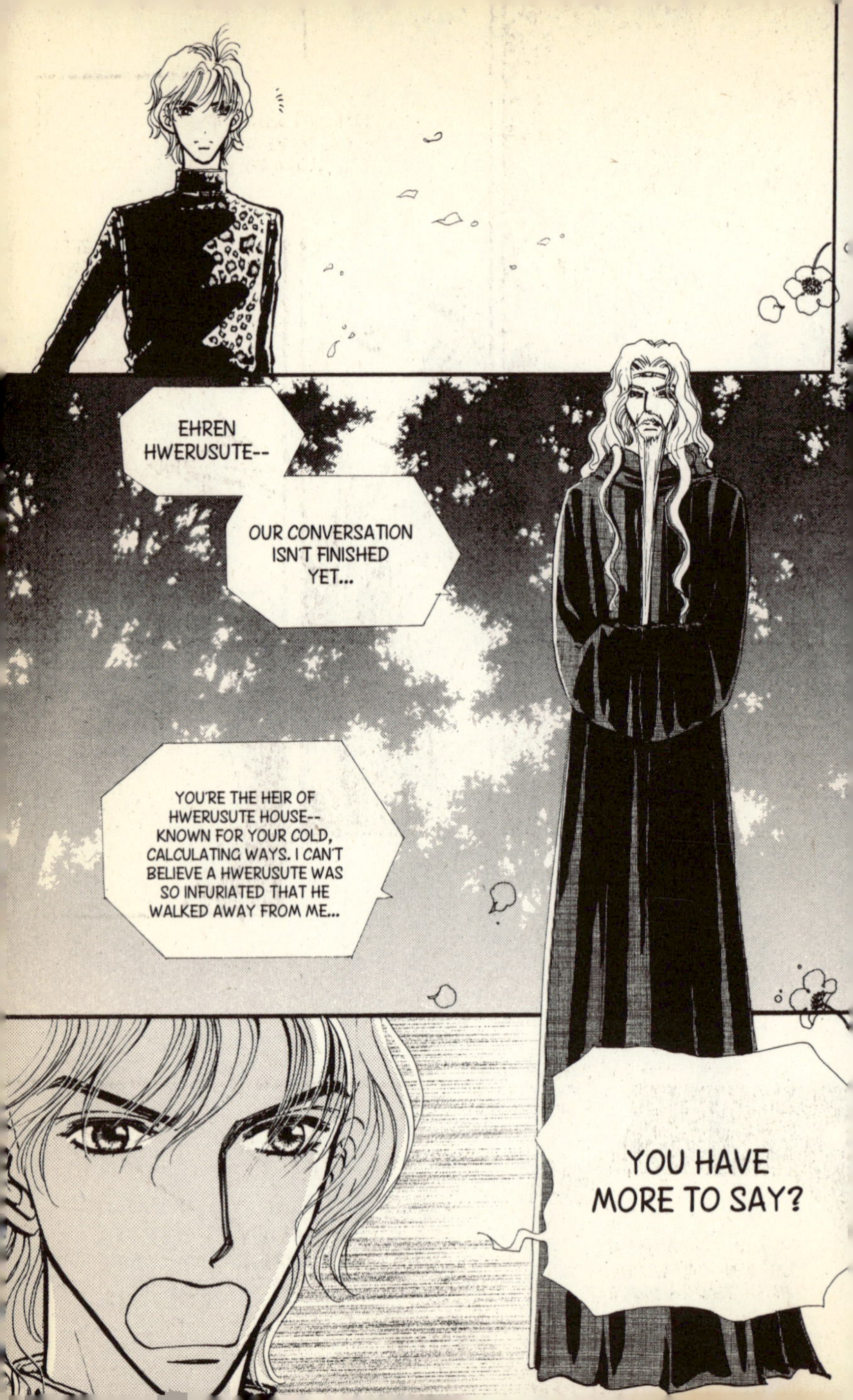
EHREN HWERUSUTE--
OUR CONVERSATION ISN'T FINISHED YET...
YOU'RE THE HEIR OF HWERUSUTE HOUSE-- KNOWN FOR YOUR COLD, CALCULATING WAYS. I CAN'T BELIEVE A HWERUSUTE WAS SO INFURIATED THAT HE WALKED AWAY FROM ME...
YOU HAVE MORE TO SAY?

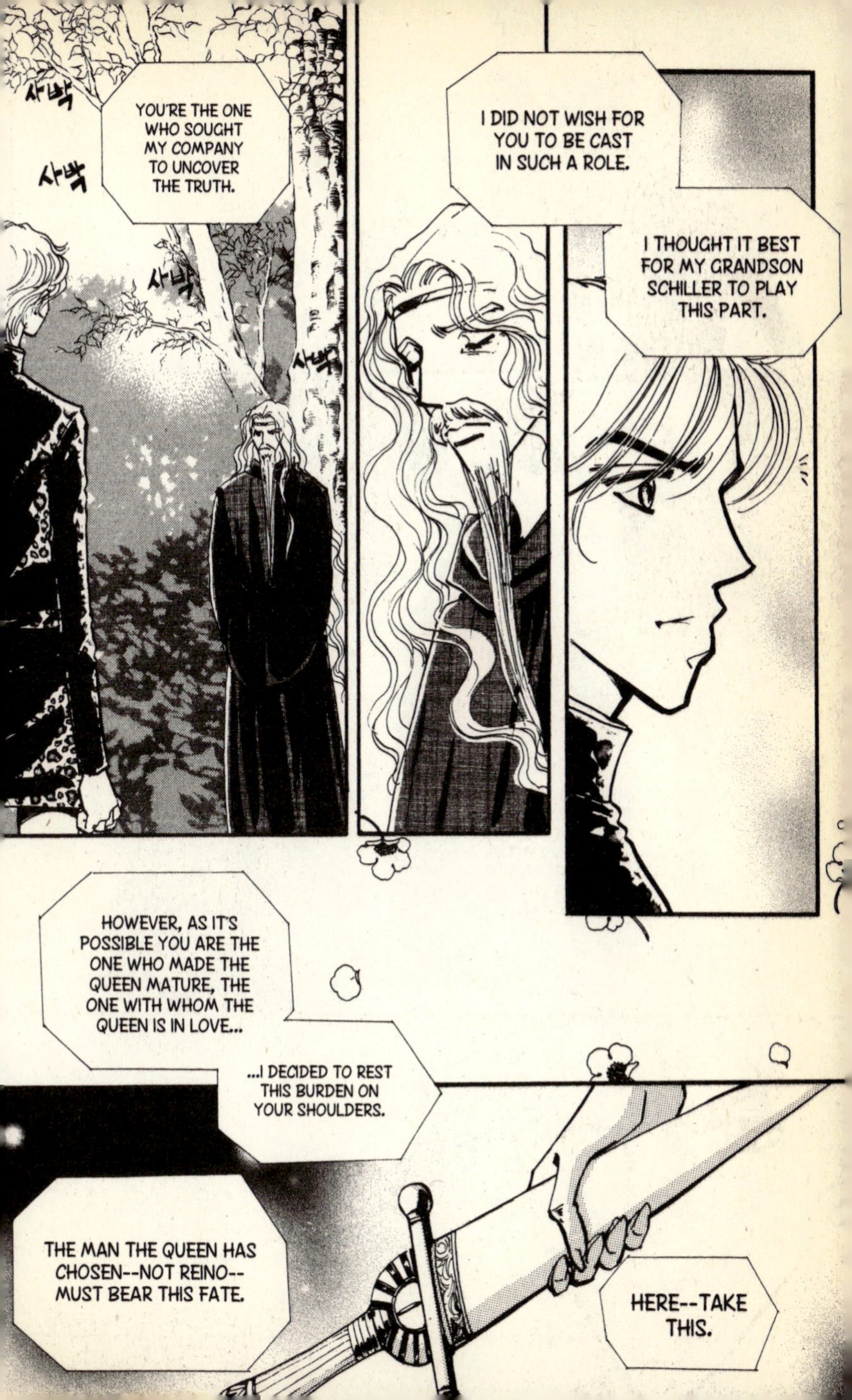
사박
YOU'RE THE ONE WHO SOUGHT MY COMPANY TO UNCOVER THE TRUTH.
사박
사박
사박
I DID NOT WISH FOR YOU TO BE CAST IN SUCH A ROLE.
I THOUGHT IT BEST FOR MY GRANDSON SCHILLER TO PLAY THIS PART.
HOWEVER, AS IT'S POSSIBLE YOU ARE THE ONE WHO MADE THE QUEEN MATURE, THE ONE WITH WHOM THE QUEEN IS IN LOVE...
...I DECIDED TO REST THIS BURDEN ON YOUR SHOULDERS.
THE MAN THE QUEEN HAS CHOSEN--NOT REINO--MUST BEAR THIS FATE.
HERE--TAKE THIS.

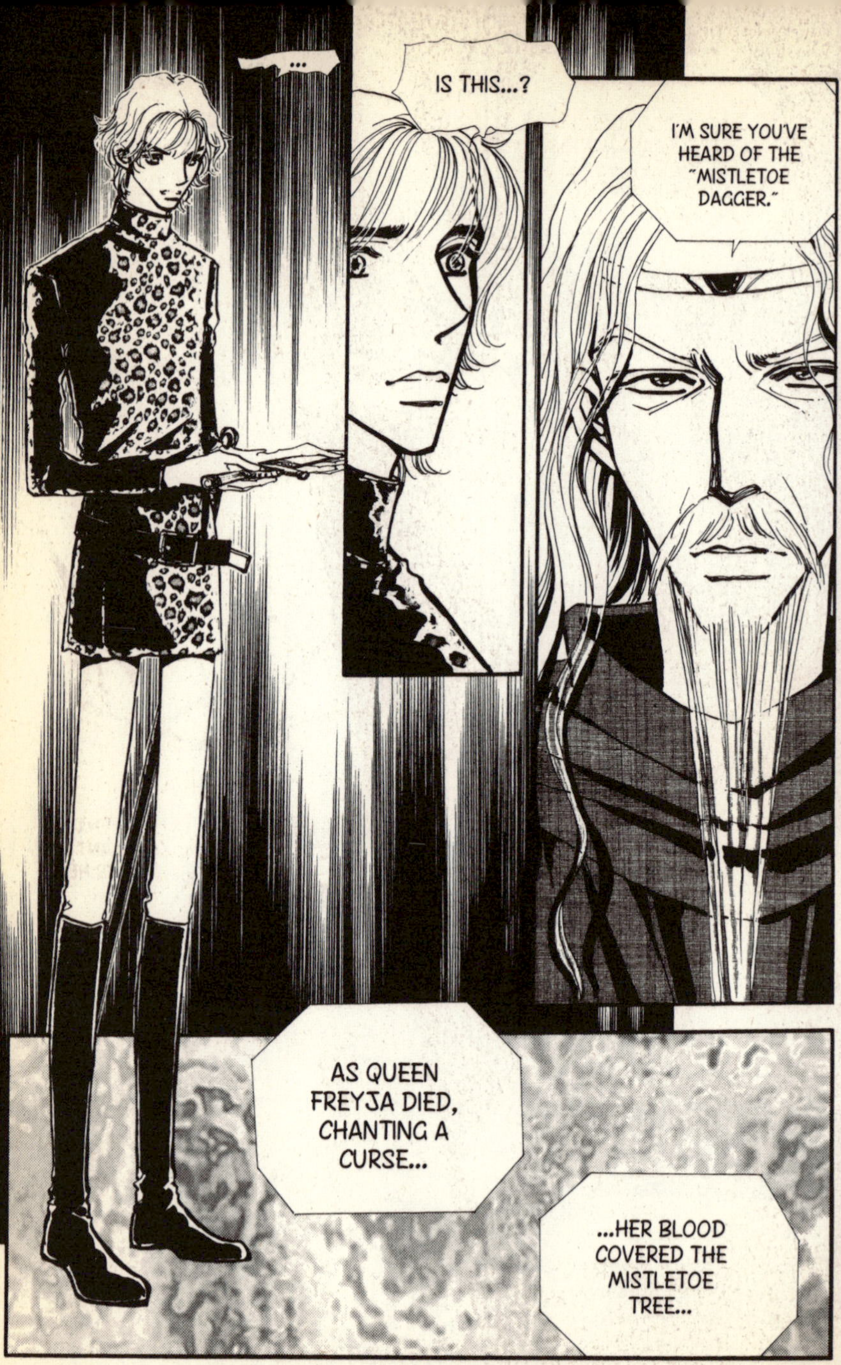
...
IS THIS...?
I'M SURE YOU'VE HEARD OF THE "MISTLETOE DAGGER."
AS QUEEN FREYJA DIED, CHANTING A CURSE...
...HER BLOOD COVERED THE MISTLETOE TREE...

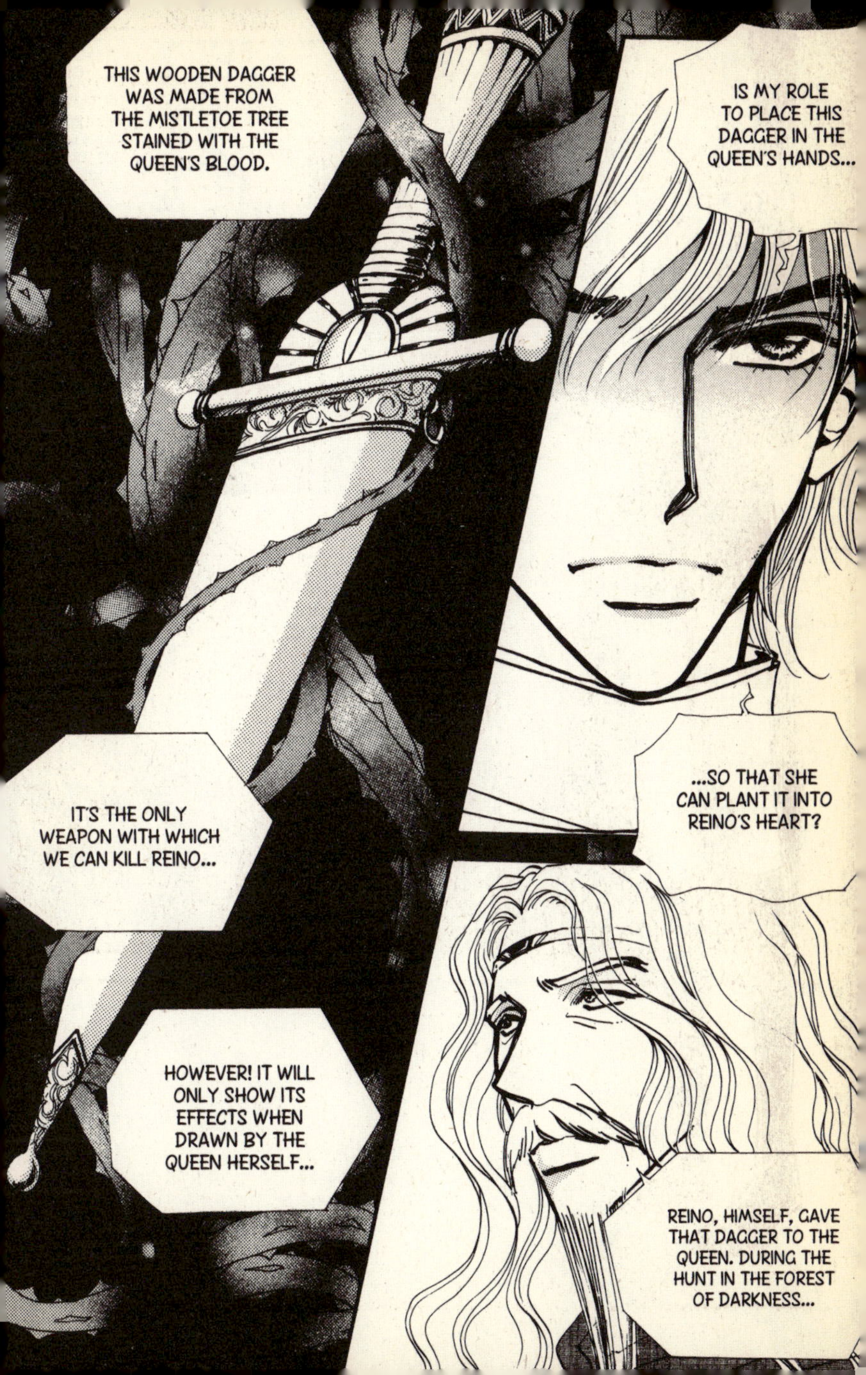

THIS WOODEN DAGGER WAS MADE FROM THE MISTLETOE TREE STAINED WITH THE QUEEN'S BLOOD.
IS MY ROLE TO PLACE THIS DAGGER IN THE QUEEN'S HANDS...
IT'S THE ONLY WEAPON WITH WHICH WE CAN KILL REINO...
...SO THAT SHE CAN PLANT IT INTO REINO'S HEART?
HOWEVER! IT WILL ONLY SHOW ITS EFFECTS WHEN DRAWN BY THE QUEEN HERSELF...
REINO, HIMSELF, GAVE THAT DAGGER TO THE QUEEN. DURING THE HUNT IN THE FOREST OF DARKNESS...

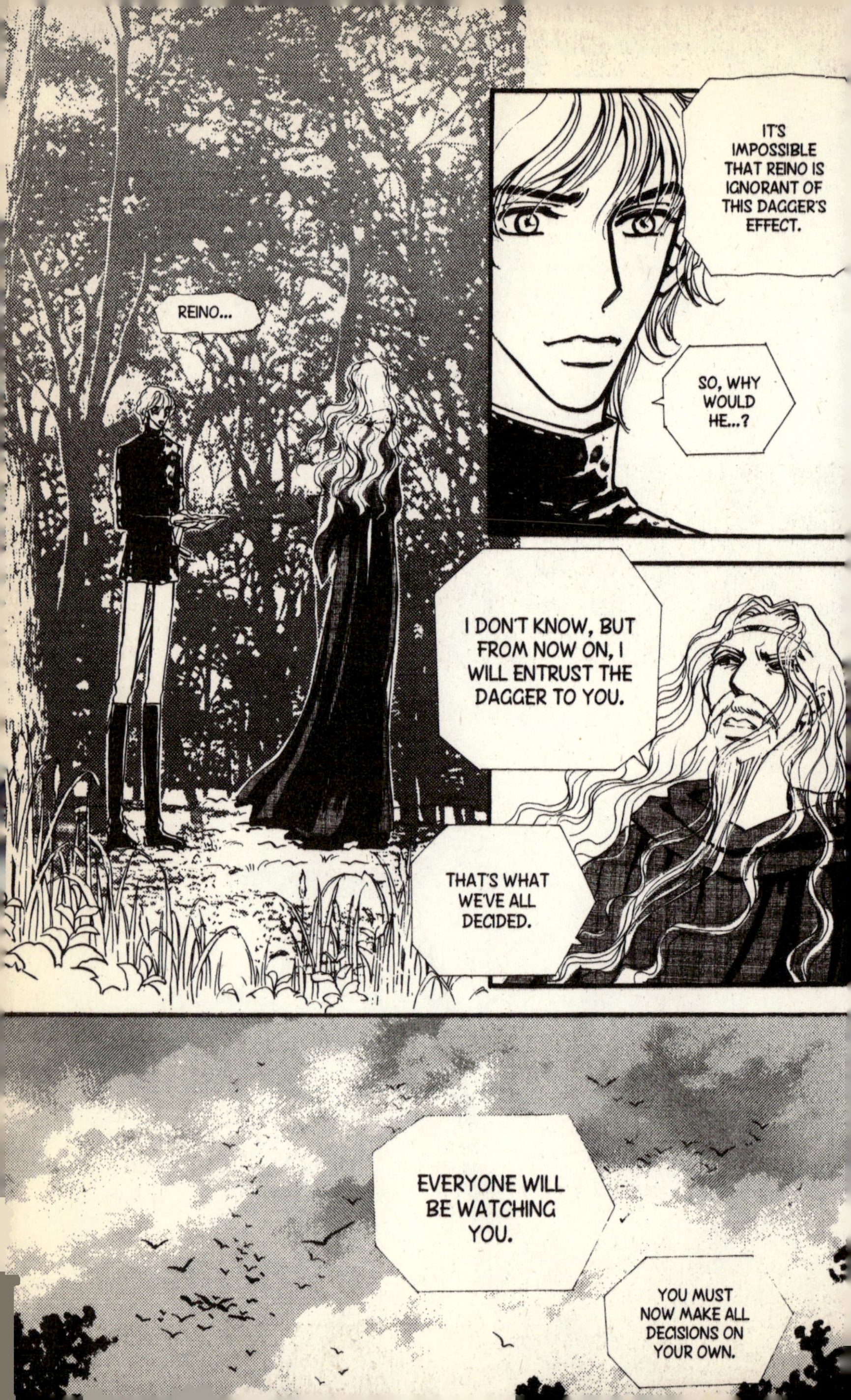
REINO...
IT'S IMPOSSIBLE THAT REINO IS IGNORANT OF THIS DAGGER'S EFFECT.
SO, WHY WOULD HE...?
I DON'T KNOW, BUT FROM NOW ON, I WILL ENTRUST THE DAGGER TO YOU.
THAT'S WHAT WE'VE ALL DECIDED.
EVERYONE WILL BE WATCHING YOU.
YOU MUST NOW MAKE ALL DECISIONS ON YOUR OWN.

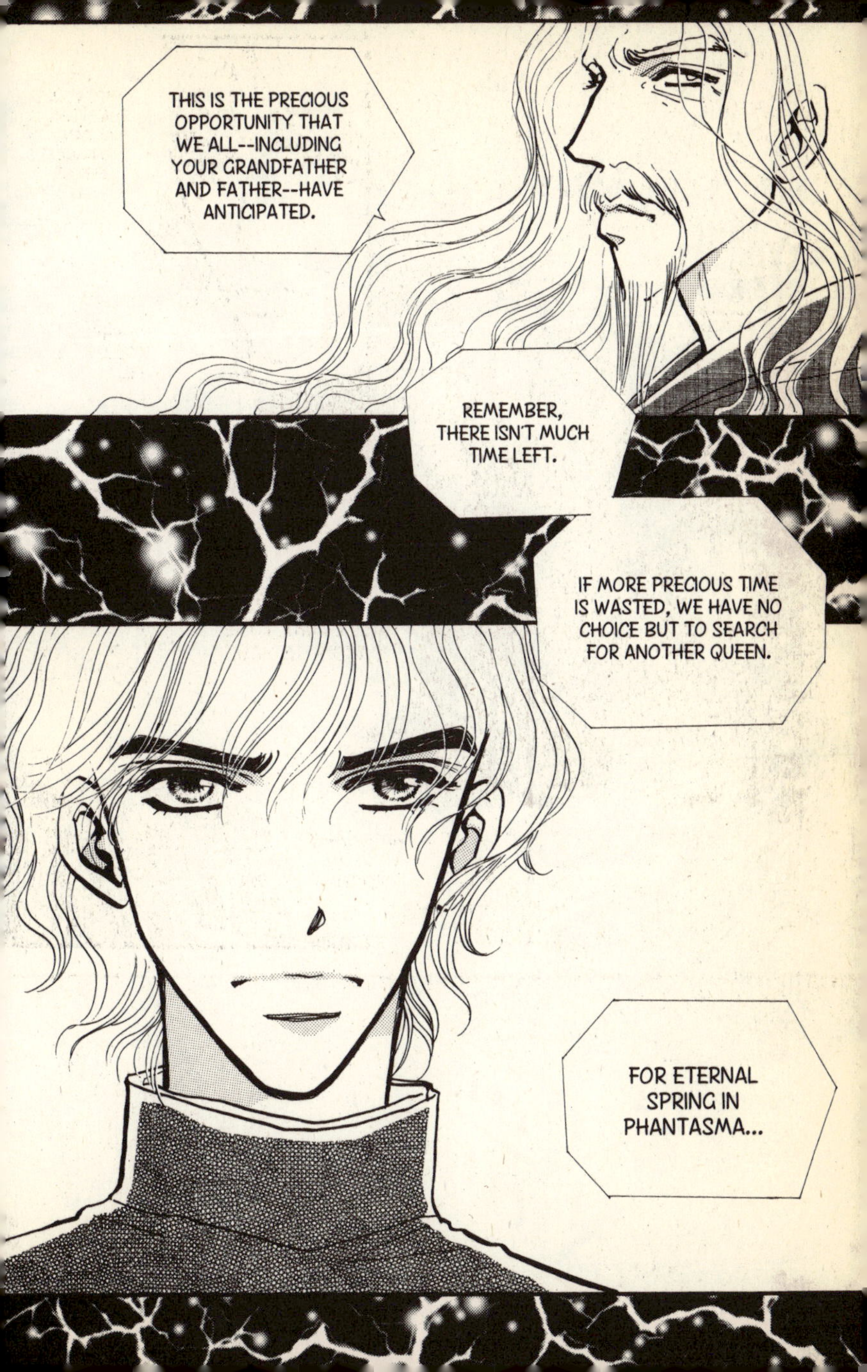
THIS IS THE PRECIOUS OPPORTUNITY THAT WE ALL--INCLUDING YOUR GRANDFATHER AND FATHER--HAVE ANTICIPATED.
REMEMBER, THERE ISN'T MUCH TIME LEFT.
IF MORE PRECIOUS TIME IS WASTED, WE HAVE NO CHOICE BUT TO SEARCH FOR ANOTHER QUEEN.
FOR ETERNAL SPRING IN PHANTASMA...

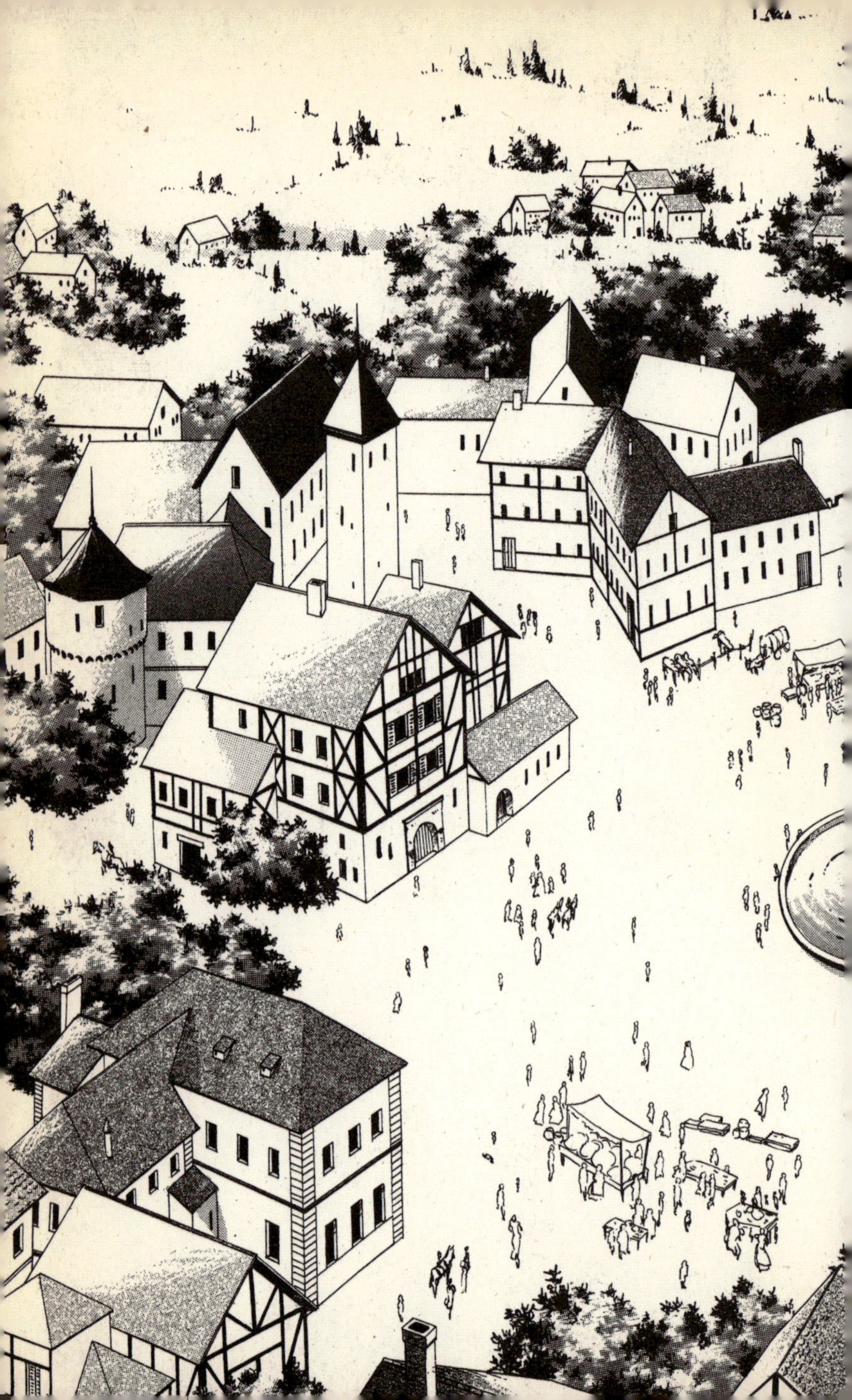

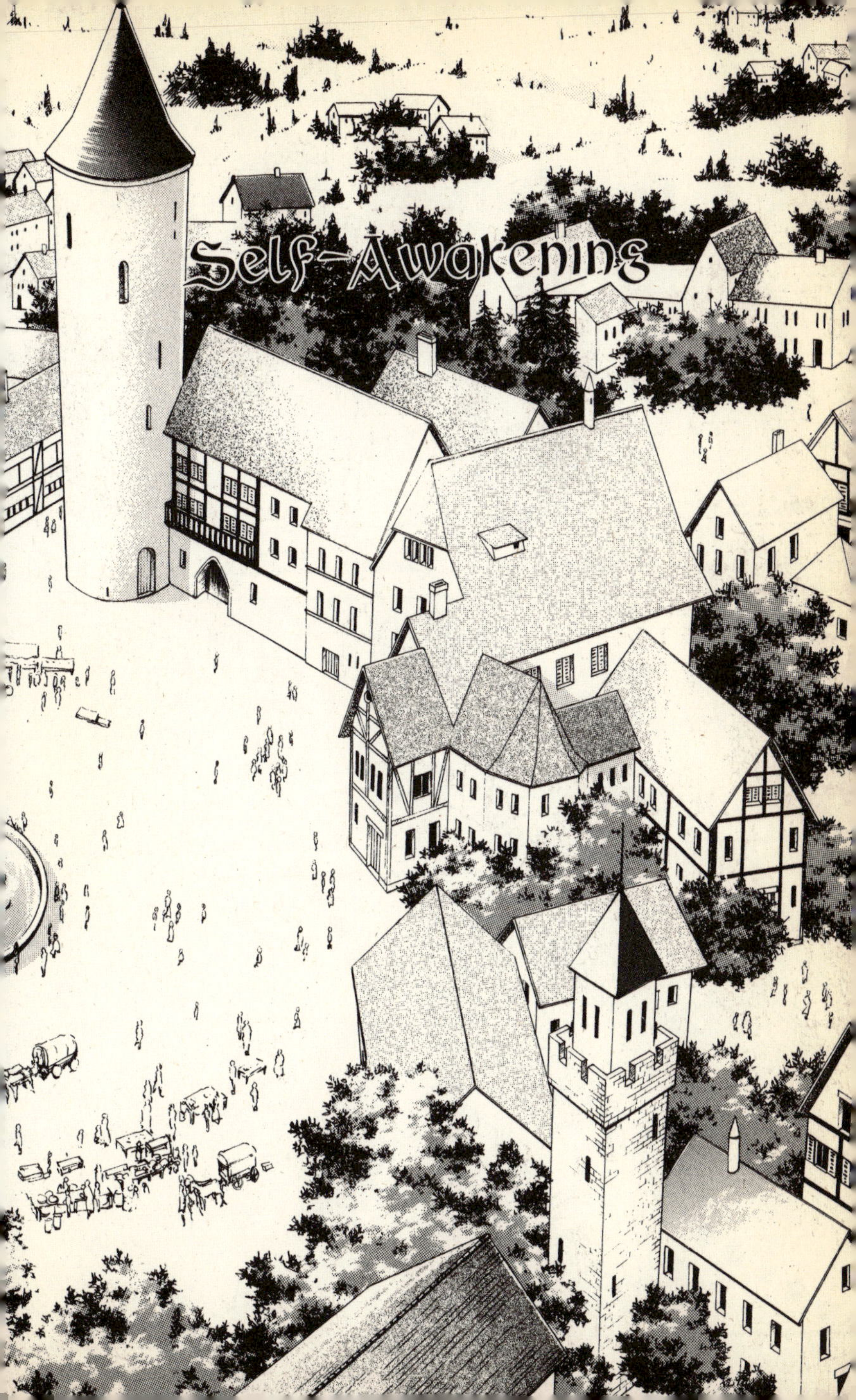
Self-Awakening

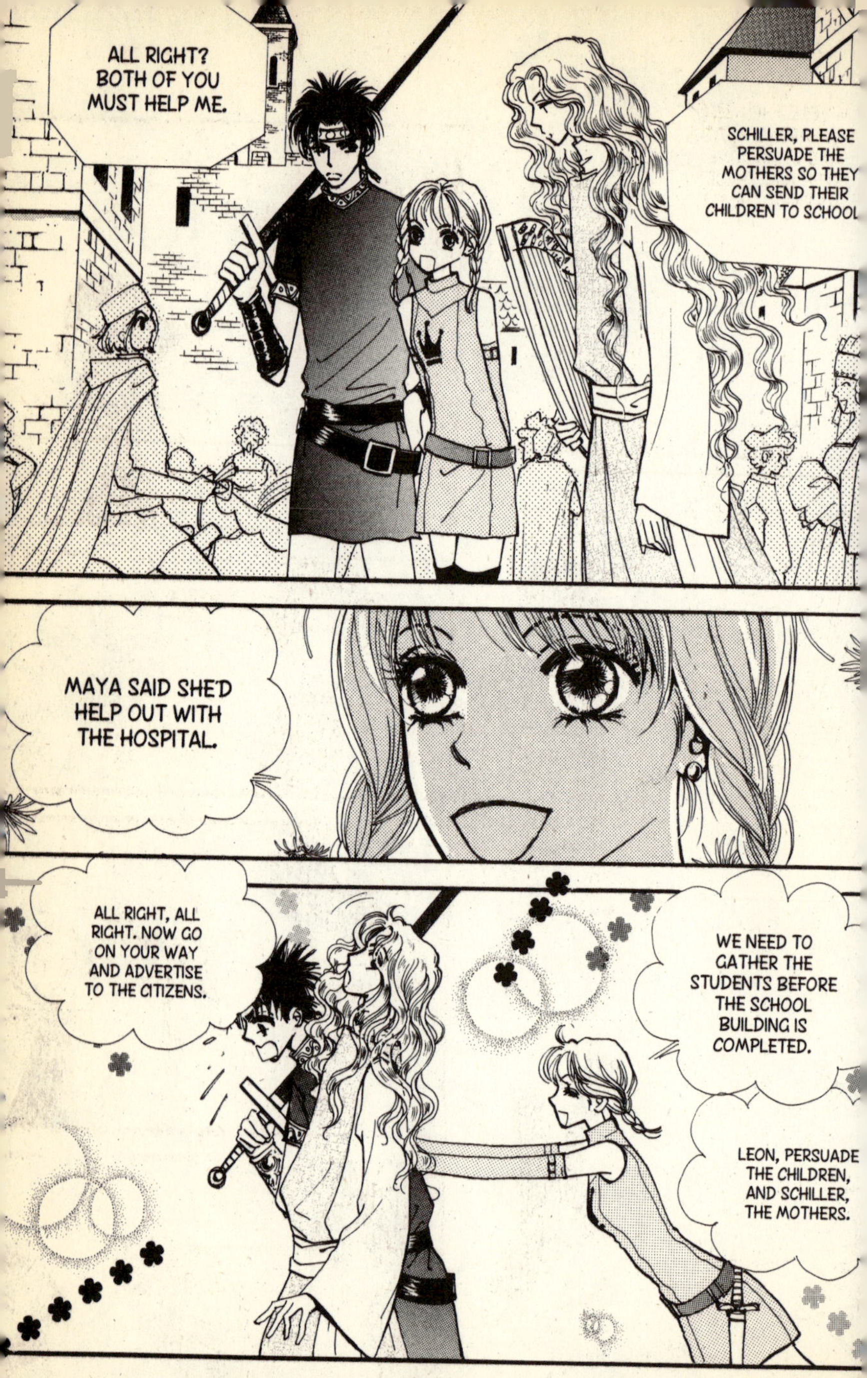
ALL RIGHT? BOTH OF YOU MUST HELP ME.
SCHILLER, PLEASE PERSUADE THE MOTHERS SO THEY CAN SEND THEIR CHILDREN TO SCHOOL
MAYA SAID SHE'D HELP OUT WITH THE HOSPITAL.
ALL RIGHT, ALL RIGHT. NOW GO ON YOUR WAY AND ADVERTISE TO THE CITIZENS.
WE NEED TO GATHER THE STUDENTS BEFORE THE SCHOOL BUILDING IS COMPLETED.
LEON, PERSUADE THE CHILDREN, AND SCHILLER, THE MOTHERS.

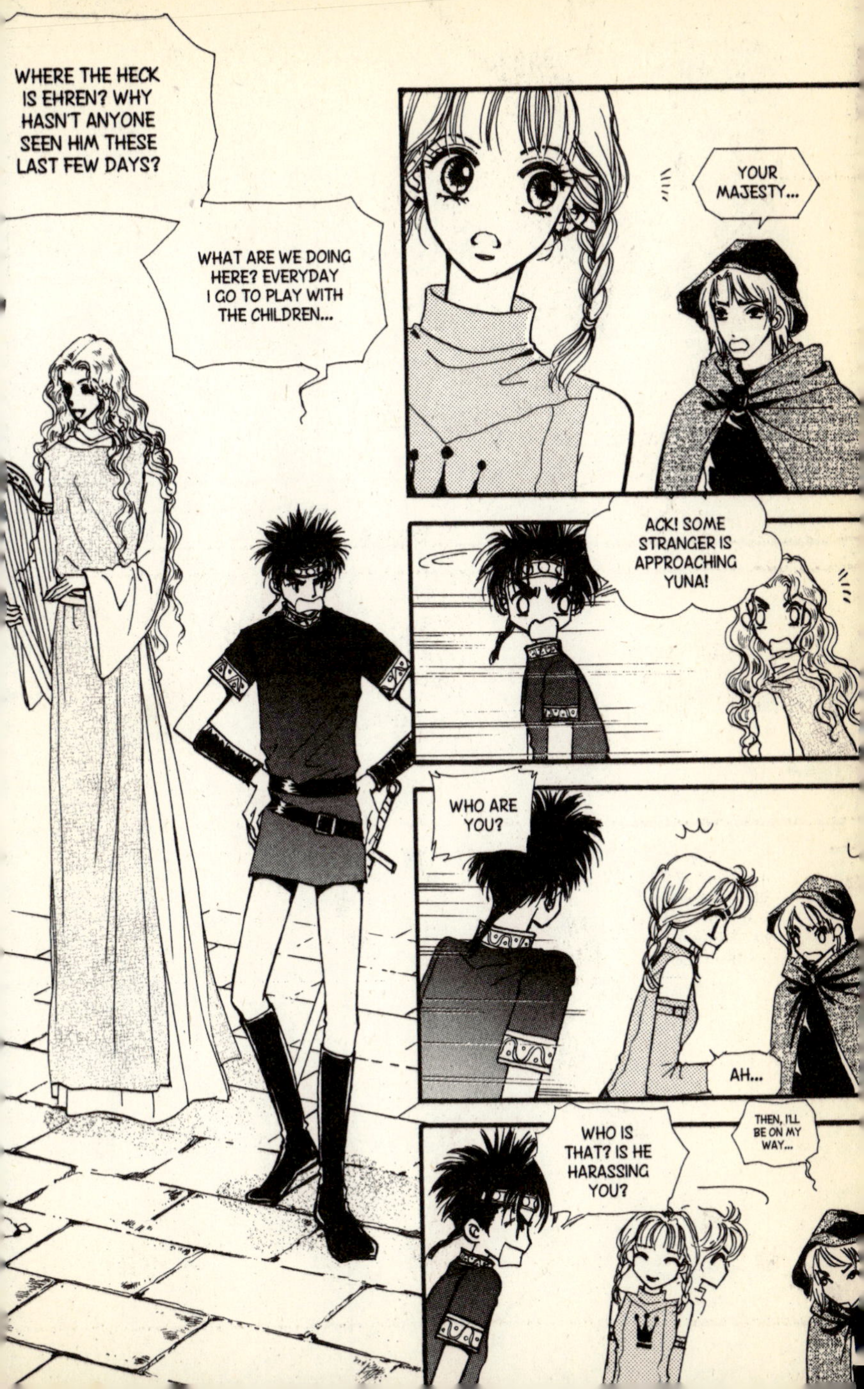

WHERE THE HECK IS EHREN? WHY HASN'T ANYONE SEEN HIM THESE LAST FEW DAYS?
WHAT ARE WE DOING HERE? EVERYDAY I GO TO PLAY WITH THE CHILDREN...
YOUR MAJESTY...
ACK! SOME STRANGER IS APPROACHING YUNA!
WHO ARE YOU?
AH...
WHO IS THAT? IS HE HARASSING YOU?
THEN, I'LL BE ON MY WAY...

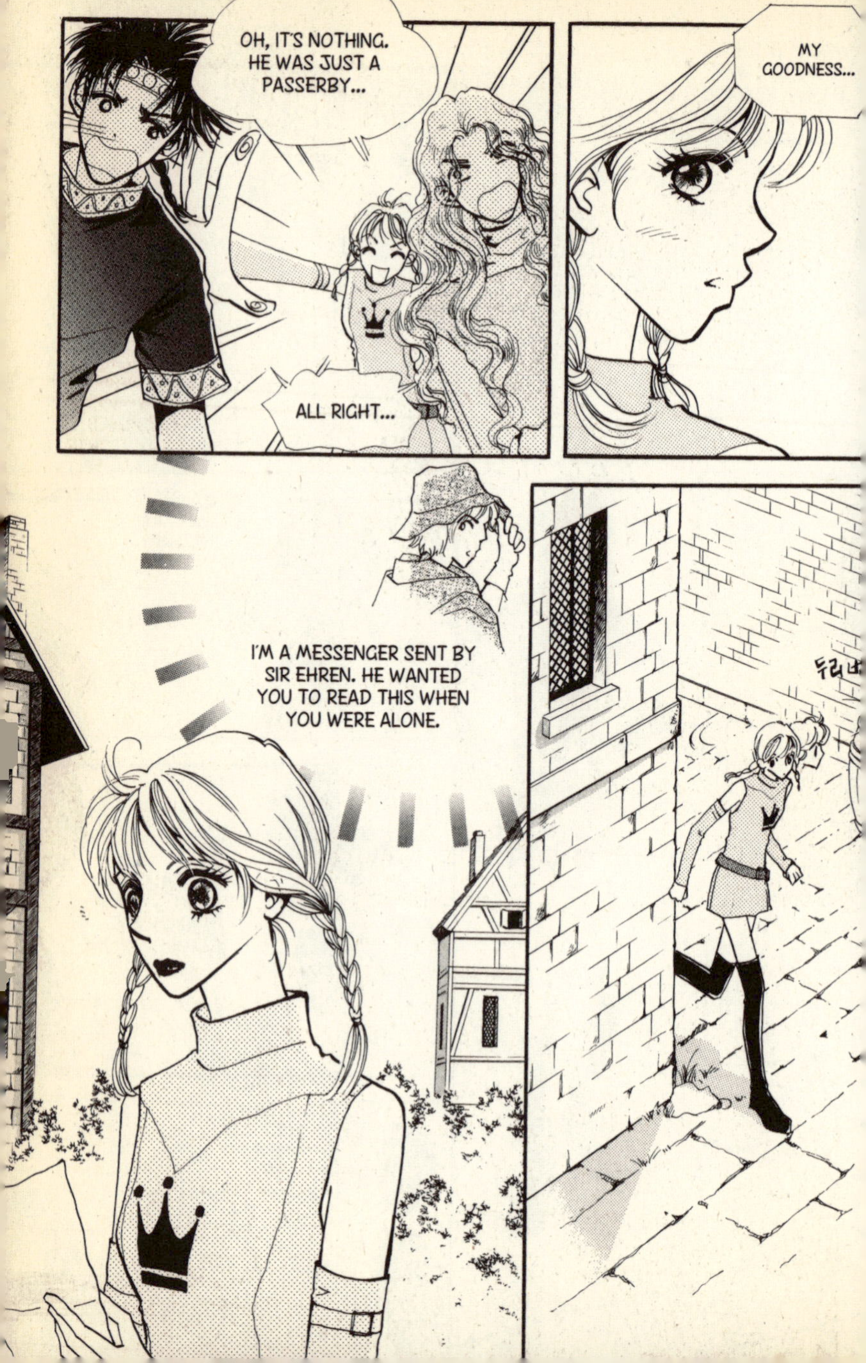
OH, IT'S NOTHING. HE WAS JUST A PASSERBY...
ALL RIGHT...
MY GOODNESS...
I'M A MESSENGER SENT BY SIR EHREN. HE WANTED YOU TO READ THIS WHEN YOU WERE ALONE.

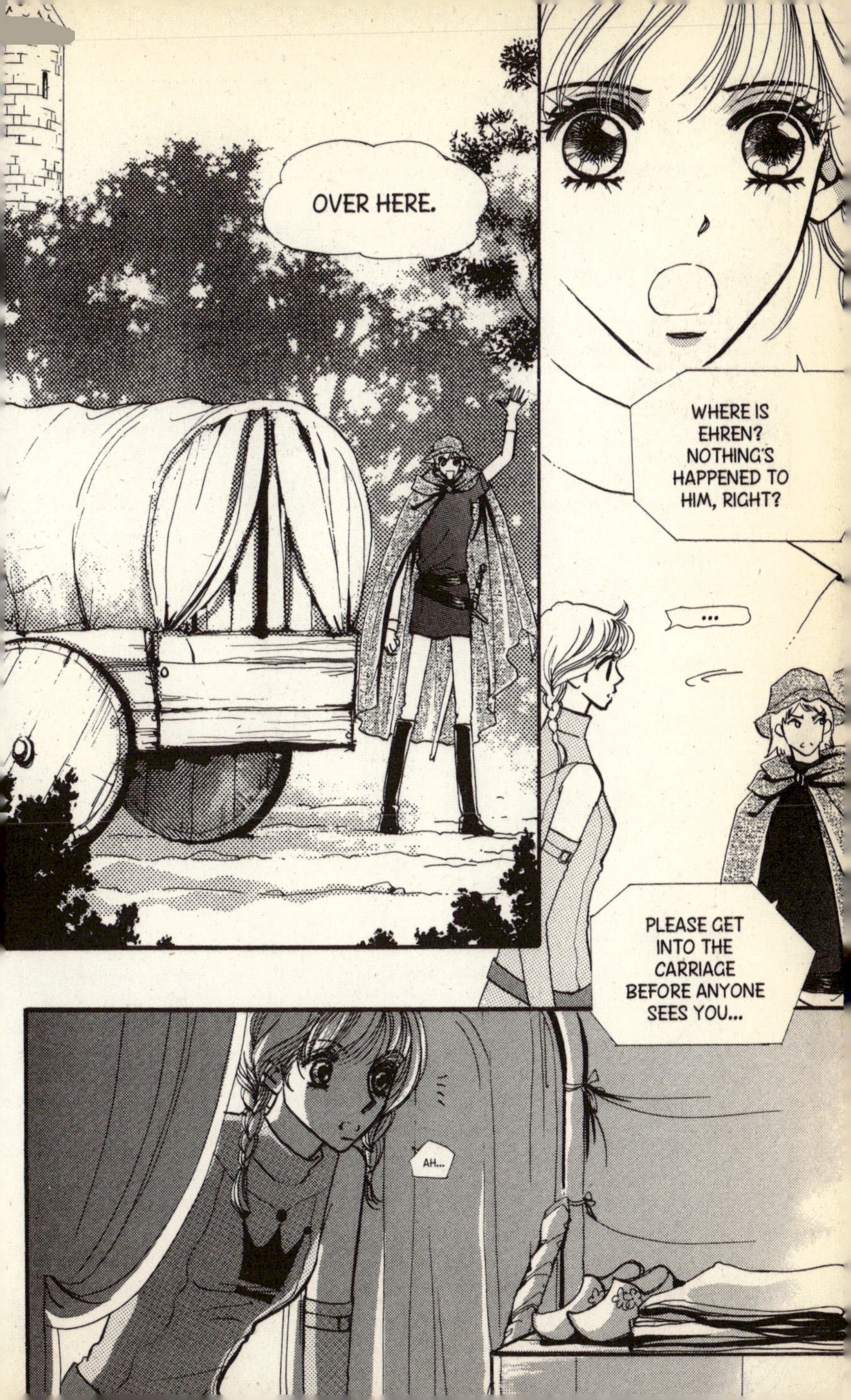
OVER HERE.
WHERE IS EHREN? NOTHING'S HAPPENED TO HIM, RIGHT?
...
PLEASE GET INTO THE CARRIAGE BEFORE ANYONE SEES YOU...
AH...

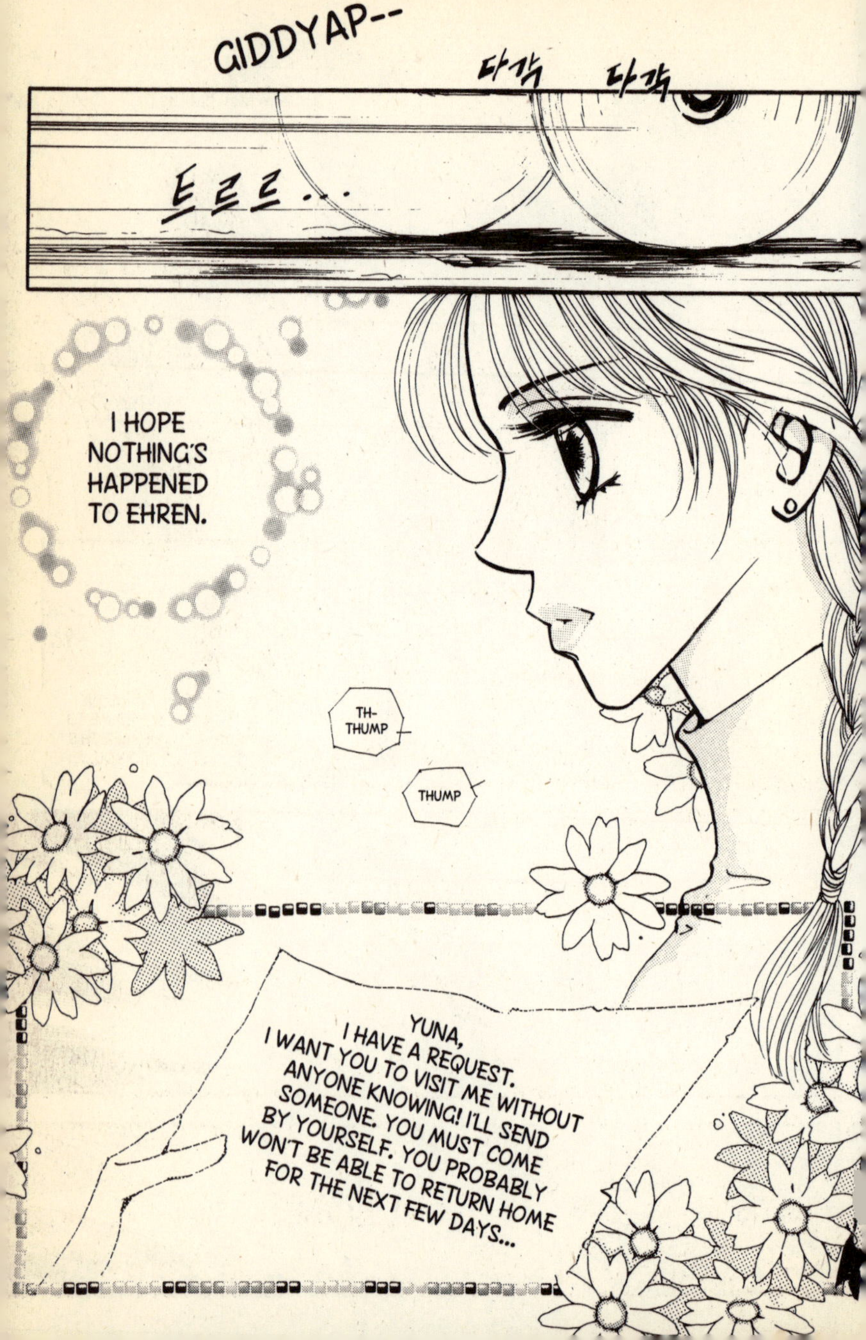
GIDDYAP--
다각 다각
트르르...
I HOPE NOTHING'S HAPPENED TO EHREN.
TH-THUMP
THUMP
YUNA, I HAVE A REQUEST. I WANT YOU TO VISIT ME WITHOUT ANYONE KNOWING! I'LL SEND SOMEONE. YOU MUST COME BY YOURSELF. YOU PROBABLY WON'T BE ABLE TO RETURN HOME FOR THE NEXT FEW DAYS...

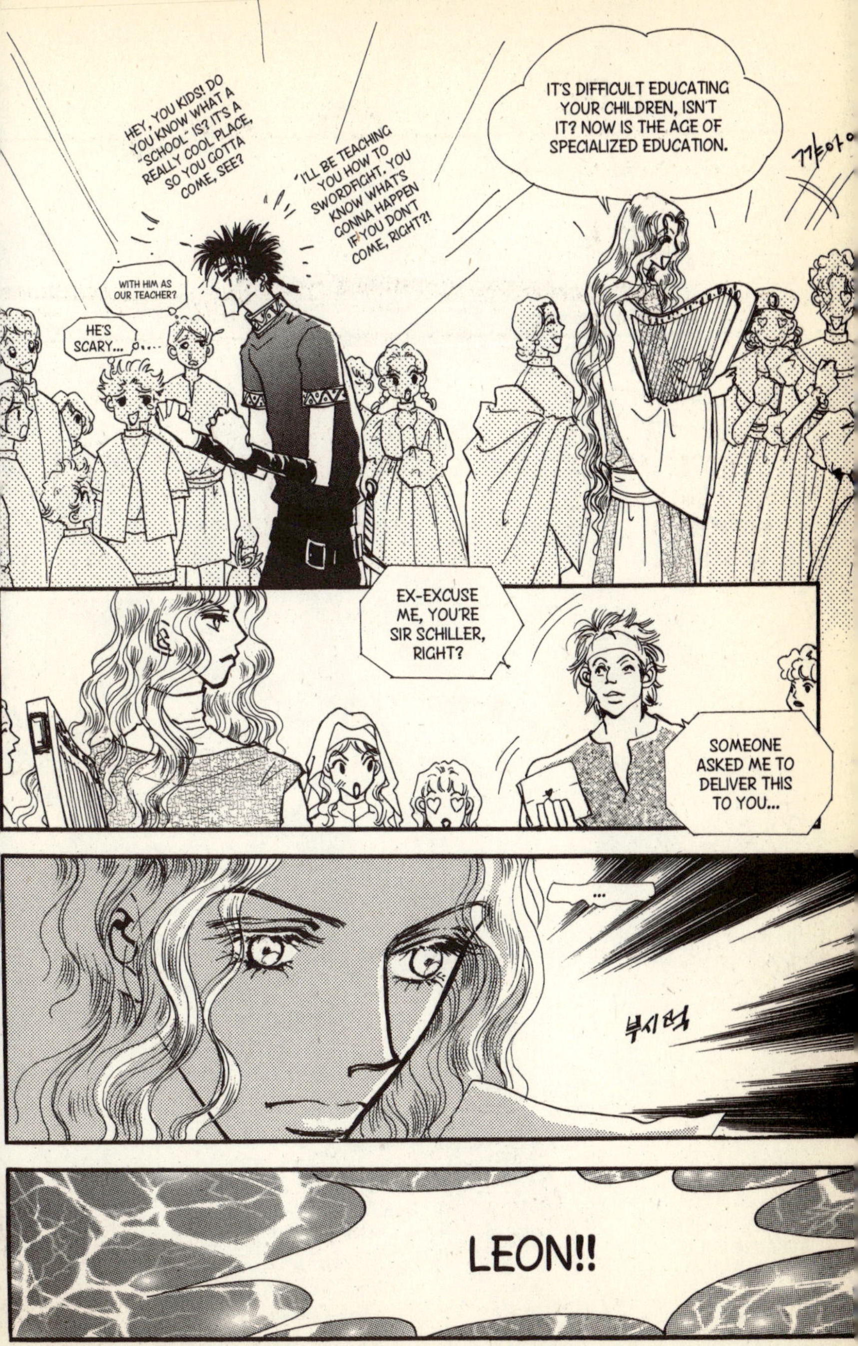

HEY, YOU KIDS! DO YOU KNOW WHAT A "SCHOOL" IS? IT'S A REALLY COOL PLACE, SO YOU GOTTA COME, SEE?
WITH HIM AS OUR TEACHER?
HE'S SCARY...
I'LL BE TEACHING YOU HOW TO SWORDFIGHT. YOU KNOW WHAT'S GONNA HAPPEN IF YOU DON'T COME, RIGHT?!
IT'S DIFFICULT EDUCATING YOUR CHILDREN, ISN'T IT? NOW IS THE AGE OF SPECIALIZED EDUCATION.
EX-EXCUSE ME, YOU'RE SIR SCHILLER, RIGHT?
SOMEONE ASKED ME TO DELIVER THIS TO YOU...
...
부시럭
LEON!!

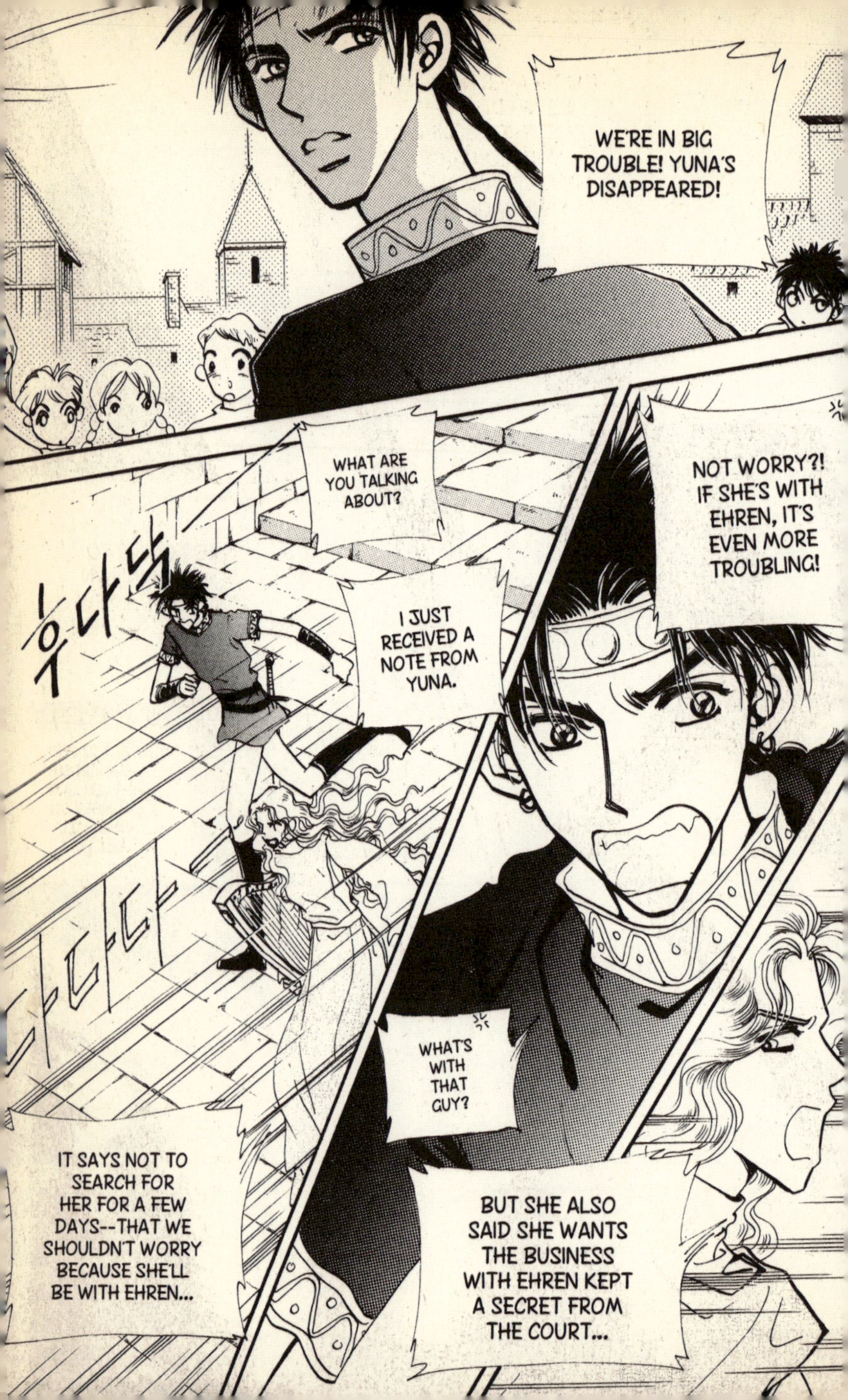
WE'RE IN BIG TROUBLE! YUNA'S DISAPPEARED!
우다닥
WHAT ARE YOU TALKING ABOUT?
I JUST RECEIVED A NOTE FROM YUNA.
다다다
IT SAYS NOT TO SEARCH FOR HER FOR A FEW DAYS--THAT WE SHOULDN'T WORRY BECAUSE SHE'LL BE WITH EHREN...
NOT WORRY?! IF SHE'S WITH EHREN, IT'S EVEN MORE TROUBLING!
WHAT'S WITH THAT GUY?
BUT SHE ALSO SAID SHE WANTS THE BUSINESS WITH EHREN KEPT A SECRET FROM THE COURT...

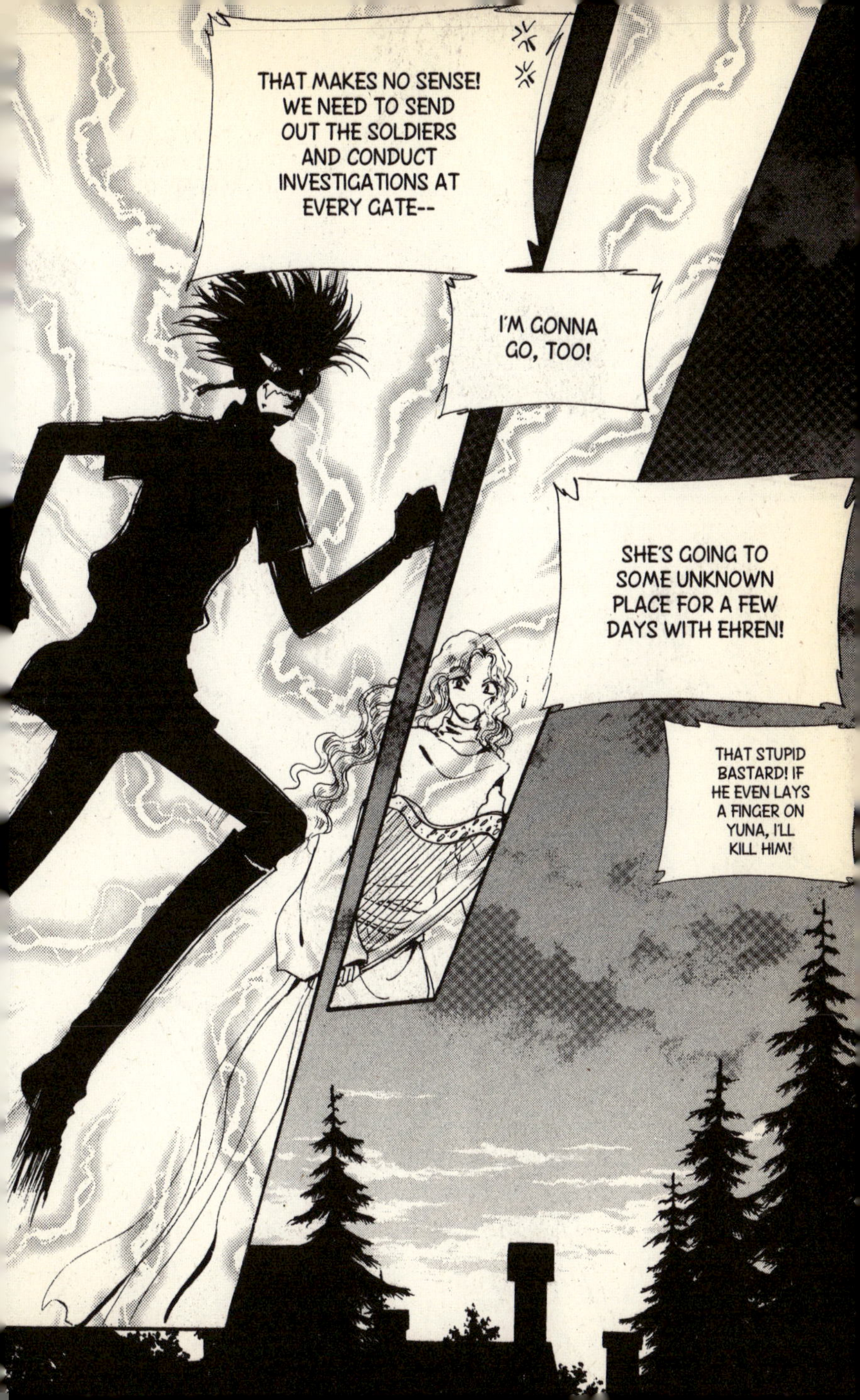
THAT MAKES NO SENSE! WE NEED TO SEND OUT THE SOLDIERS AND CONDUCT INVESTIGATIONS AT EVERY GATE--
I'M GONNA GO, TOO!
SHE'S GOING TO SOME UNKNOWN PLACE FOR A FEW DAYS WITH EHREN!
THAT STUPID BASTARD! IF HE EVEN LAYS A FINGER ON YUNA, I'LL KILL HIM!

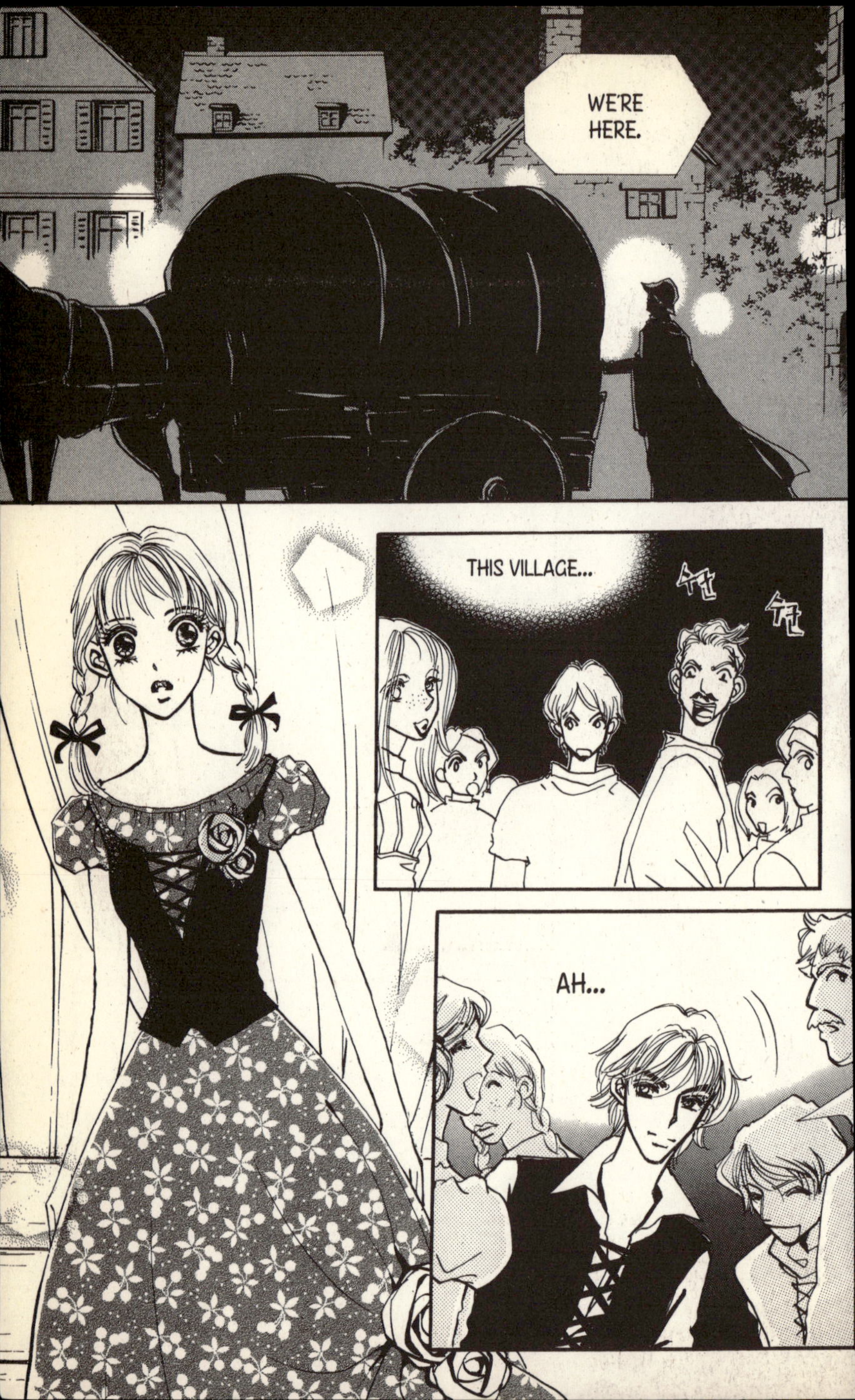
WE'RE HERE.
THIS VILLAGE...
AH...

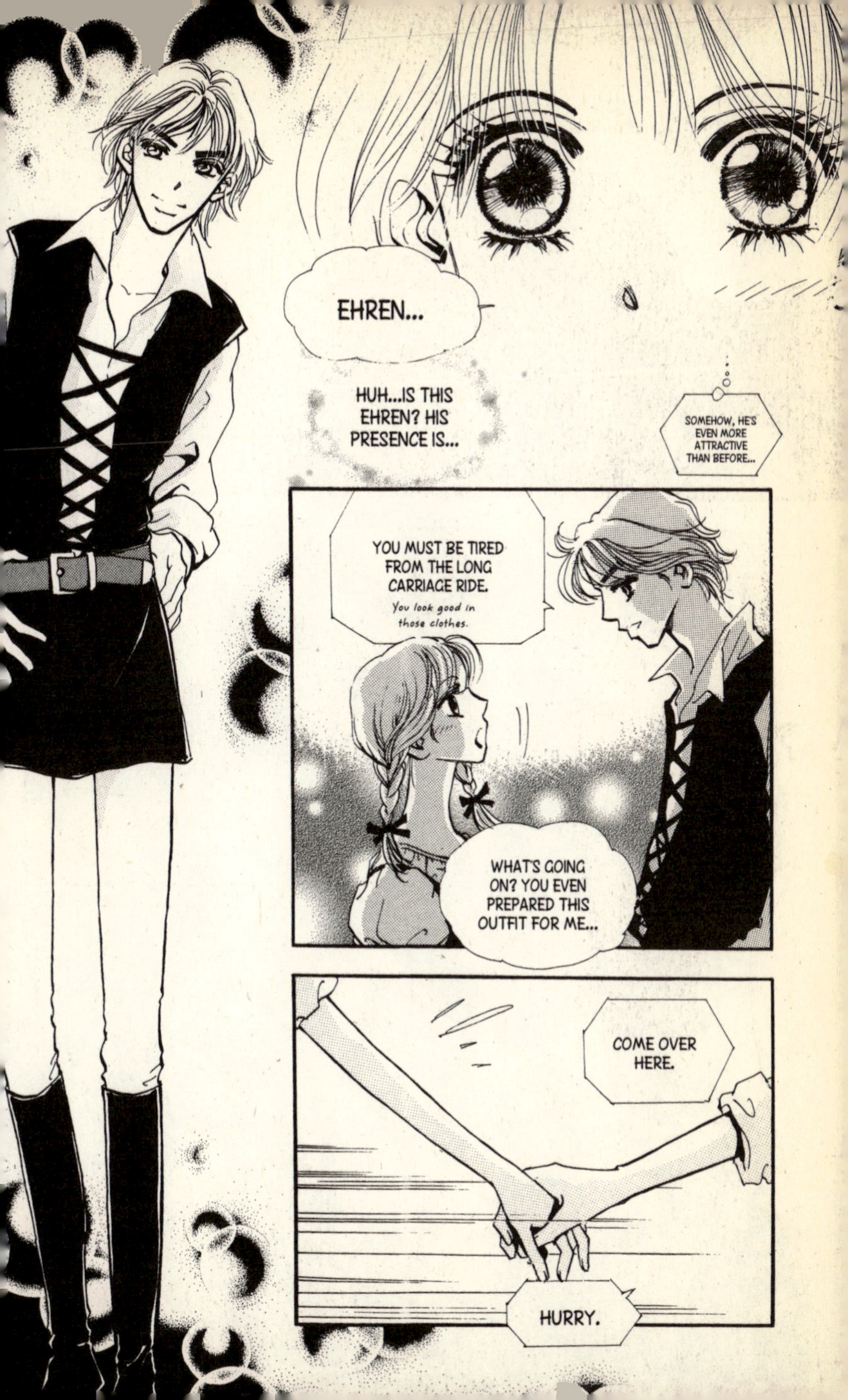
EHREN...
HUH...IS THIS EHREN? HIS PRESENCE IS...
SOMEHOW, HE'S EVEN MORE ATTRACTIVE THAN BEFORE...
YOU MUST BE TIRED FROM THE LONG CARRIAGE RIDE.
You look good in those clothes.
WHAT'S GOING ON? YOU EVEN PREPARED THIS OUTFIT FOR ME...
COME OVER HERE.
HURRY.

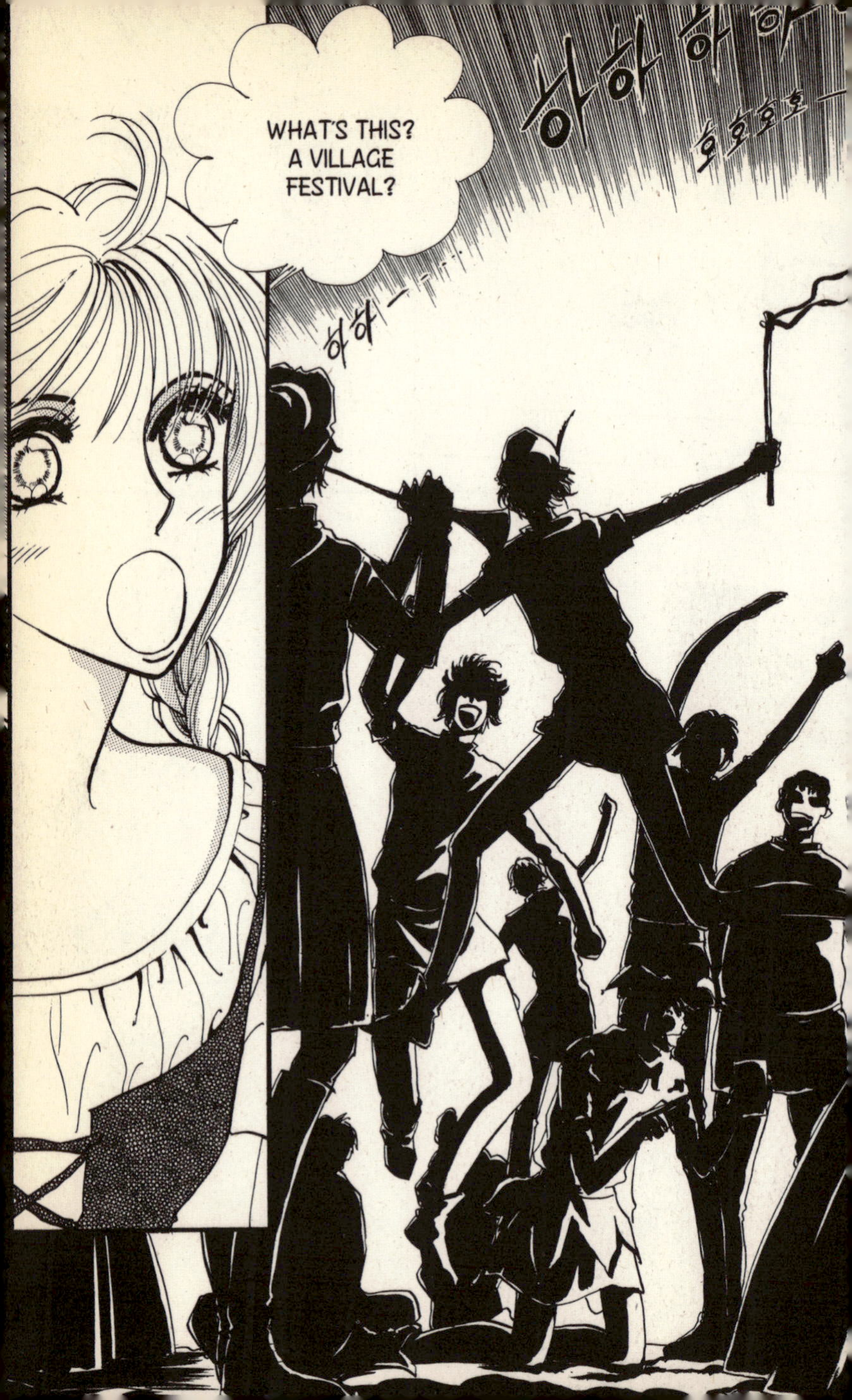
WHAT'S THIS? A VILLAGE FESTIVAL?
하하 하하
호호호호ー
하하ー...

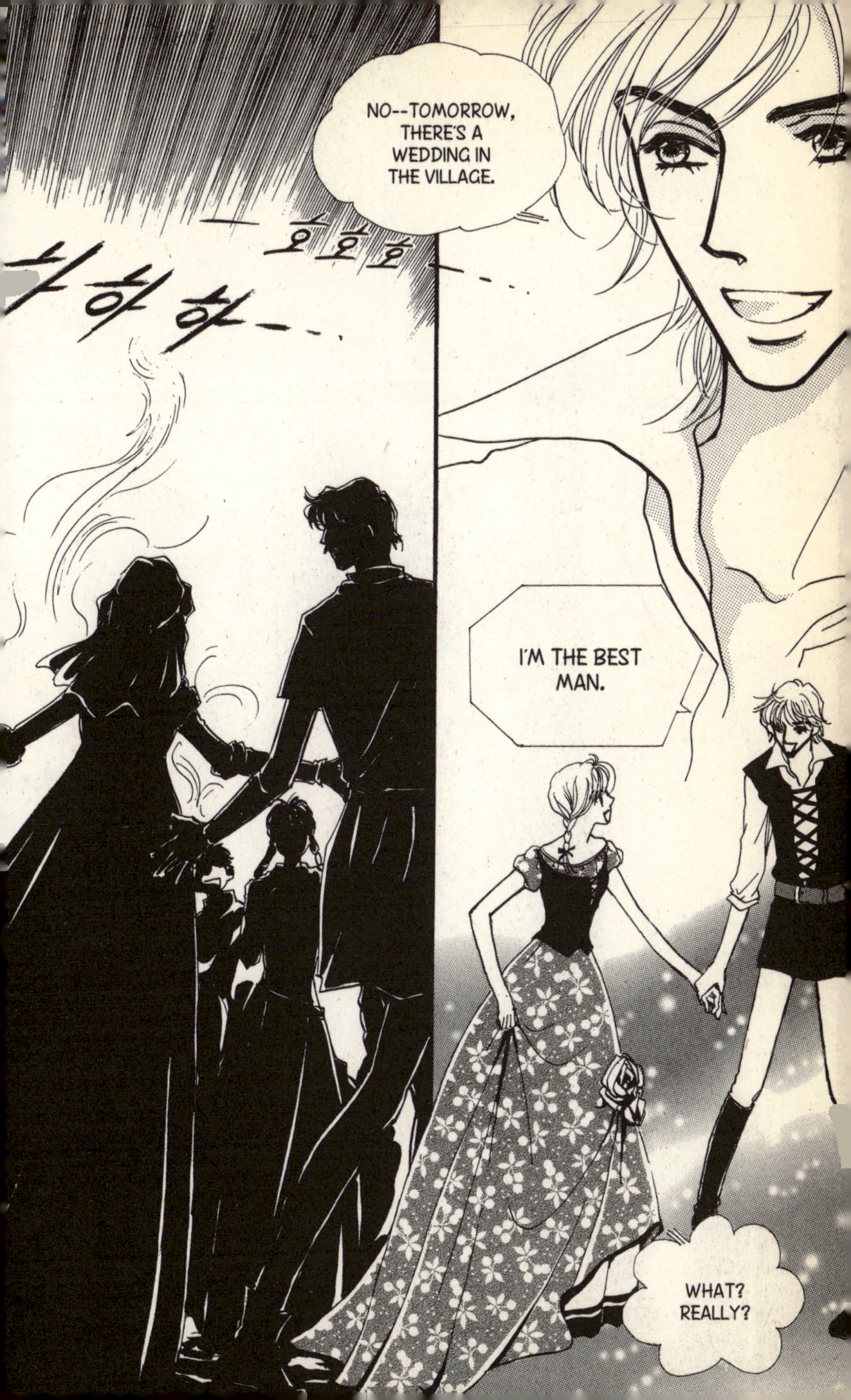
NO--TOMORROW, THERE'S A WEDDING IN THE VILLAGE.
호호호—
하하—
I'M THE BEST MAN.
WHAT? REALLY?

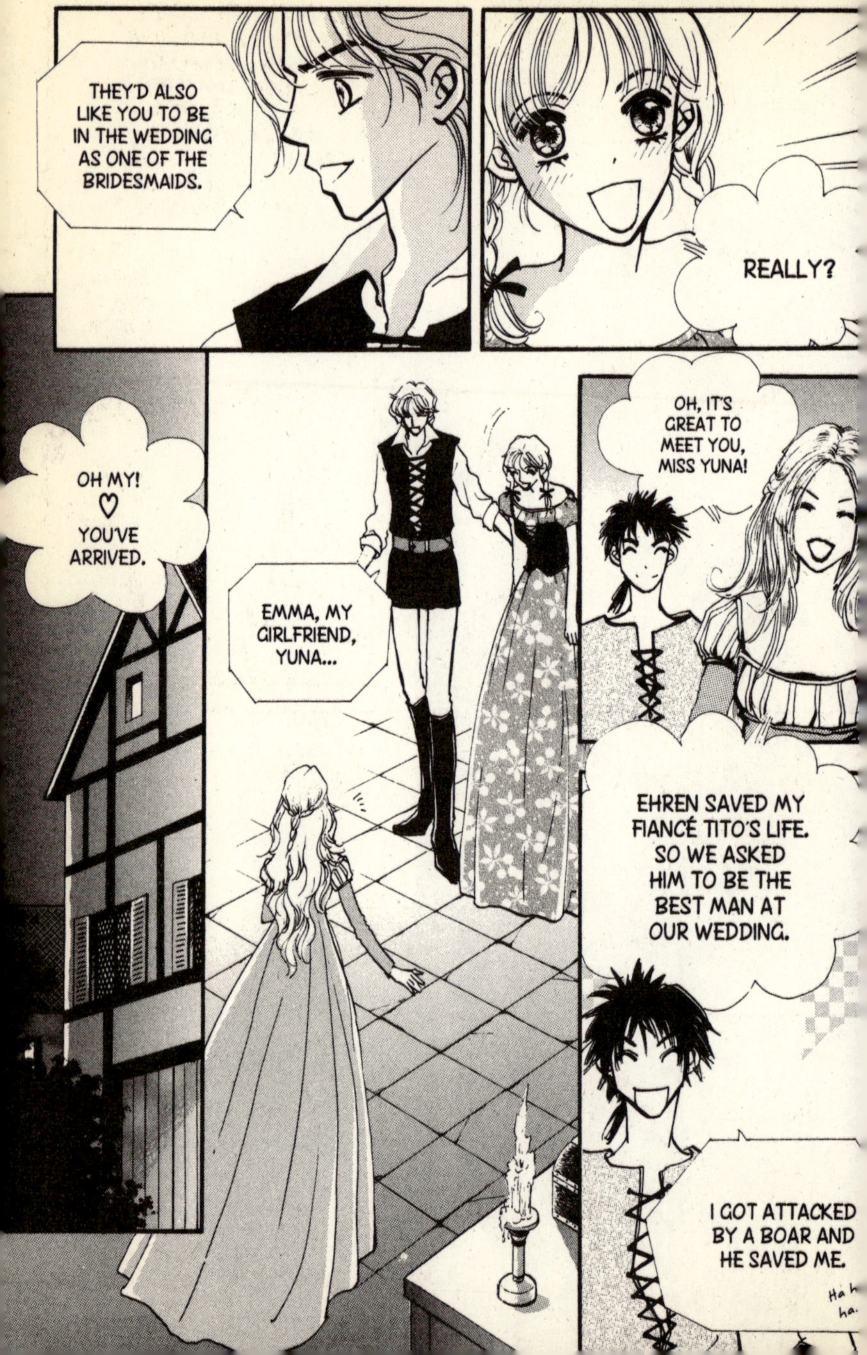
THEY'D ALSO LIKE YOU TO BE IN THE WEDDING AS ONE OF THE BRIDESMAIDS.
REALLY?
OH MY! ♡ YOU'VE ARRIVED.
EMMA, MY GIRLFRIEND, YUNA...
OH, IT'S GREAT TO MEET YOU, MISS YUNA!
EHREN SAVED MY FIANCÉ TITO'S LIFE. SO WE ASKED HIM TO BE THE BEST MAN AT OUR WEDDING.
I GOT ATTACKED BY A BOAR AND HE SAVED ME.

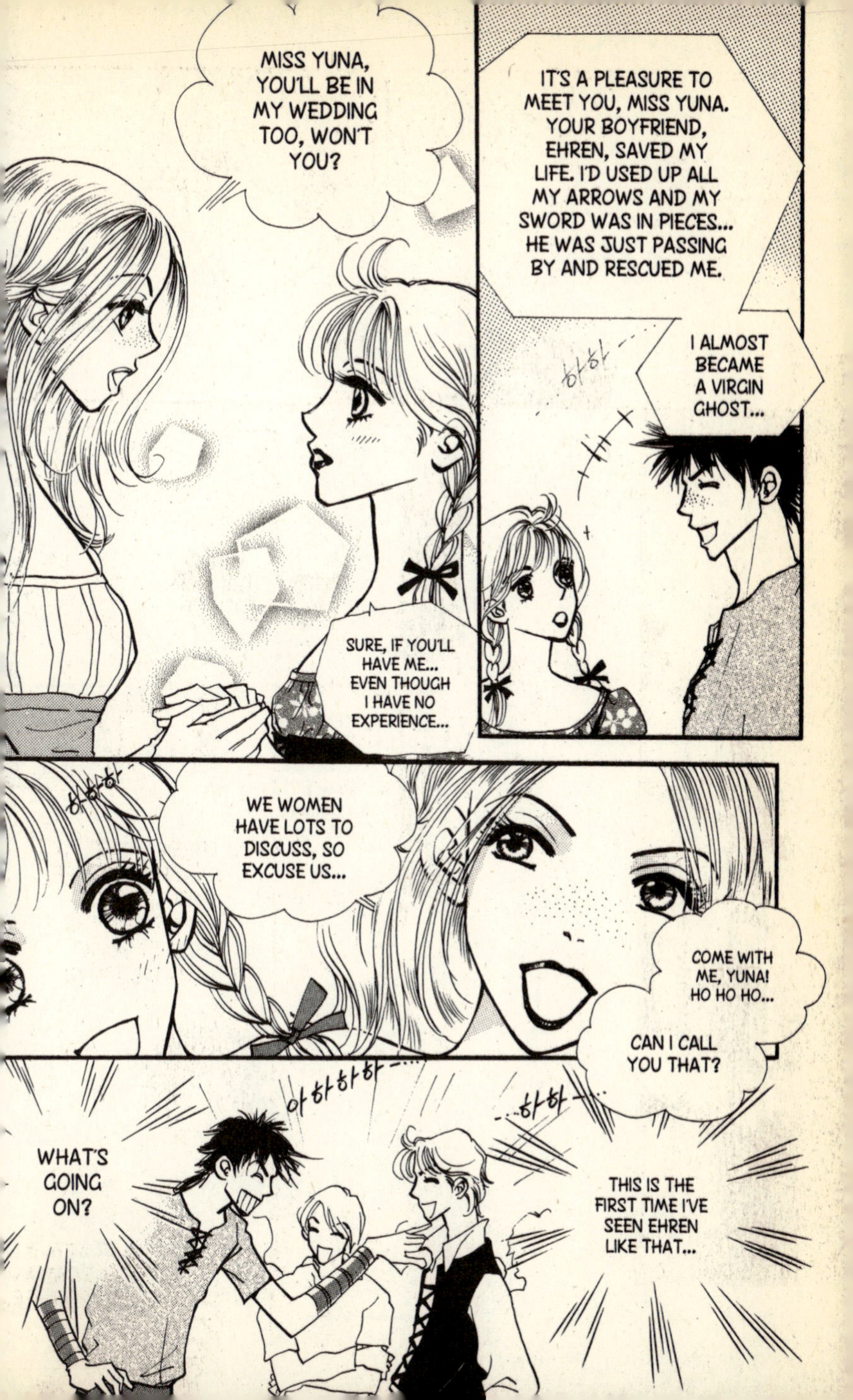
MISS YUNA, YOU'LL BE IN MY WEDDING TOO, WON'T YOU?
SURE, IF YOU'LL HAVE ME... EVEN THOUGH I HAVE NO EXPERIENCE...
IT'S A PLEASURE TO MEET YOU, MISS YUNA. YOUR BOYFRIEND, EHREN, SAVED MY LIFE. I'D USED UP ALL MY ARROWS AND MY SWORD WAS IN PIECES... HE WAS JUST PASSING BY AND RESCUED ME.
하하...
I ALMOST BECAME A VIRGIN GHOST...
하하하
WE WOMEN HAVE LOTS TO DISCUSS, SO EXCUSE US...
COME WITH ME, YUNA! HO HO HO...
CAN I CALL YOU THAT?
아하하하-...
...하하-
WHAT'S GOING ON?
THIS IS THE FIRST TIME I'VE SEEN EHREN LIKE THAT...

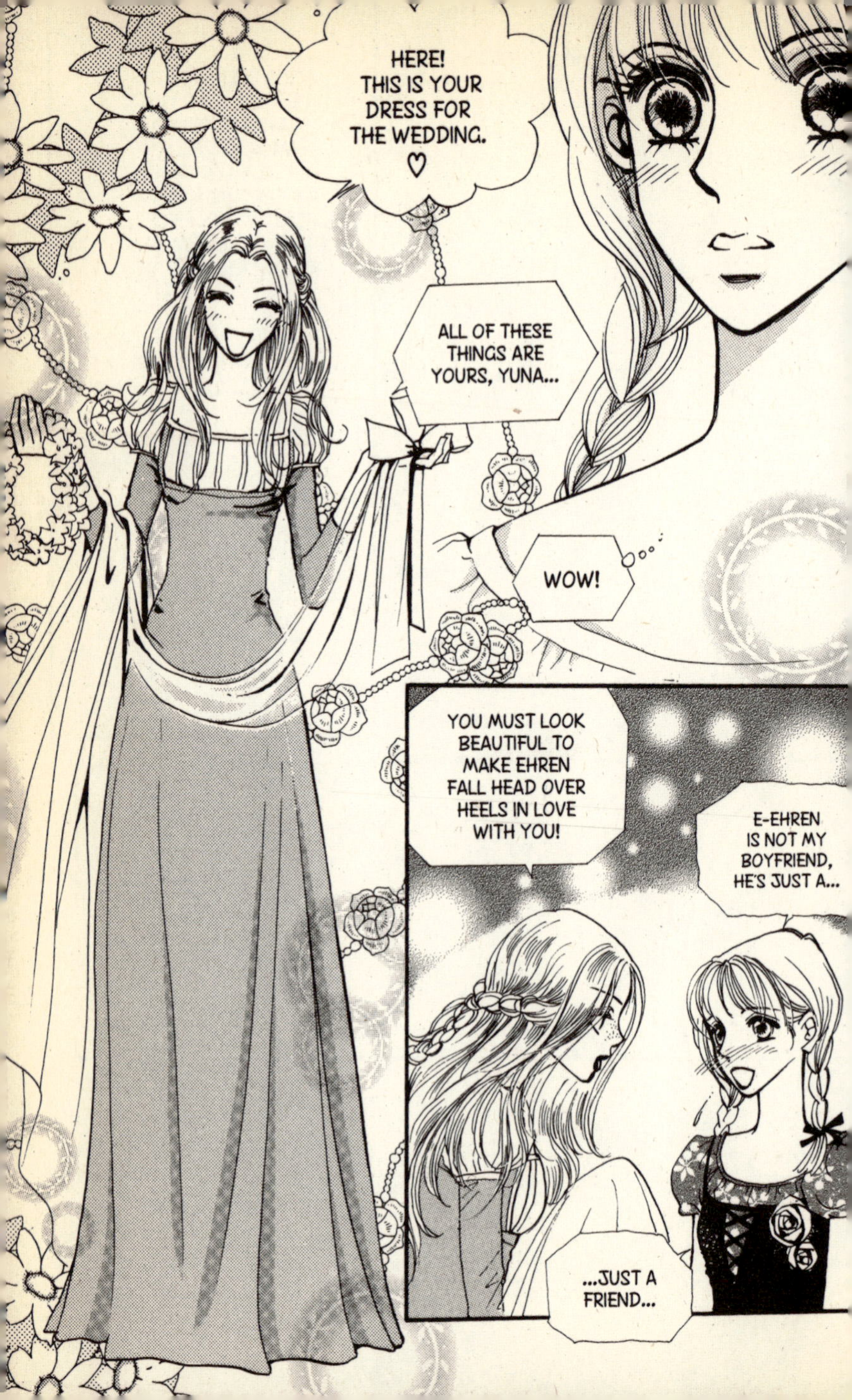
HERE! THIS IS YOUR DRESS FOR THE WEDDING. ♡
ALL OF THESE THINGS ARE YOURS, YUNA...
WOW!
YOU MUST LOOK BEAUTIFUL TO MAKE EHREN FALL HEAD OVER HEELS IN LOVE WITH YOU!
E-EHREN IS NOT MY BOYFRIEND, HE'S JUST A...
...JUST A FRIEND...

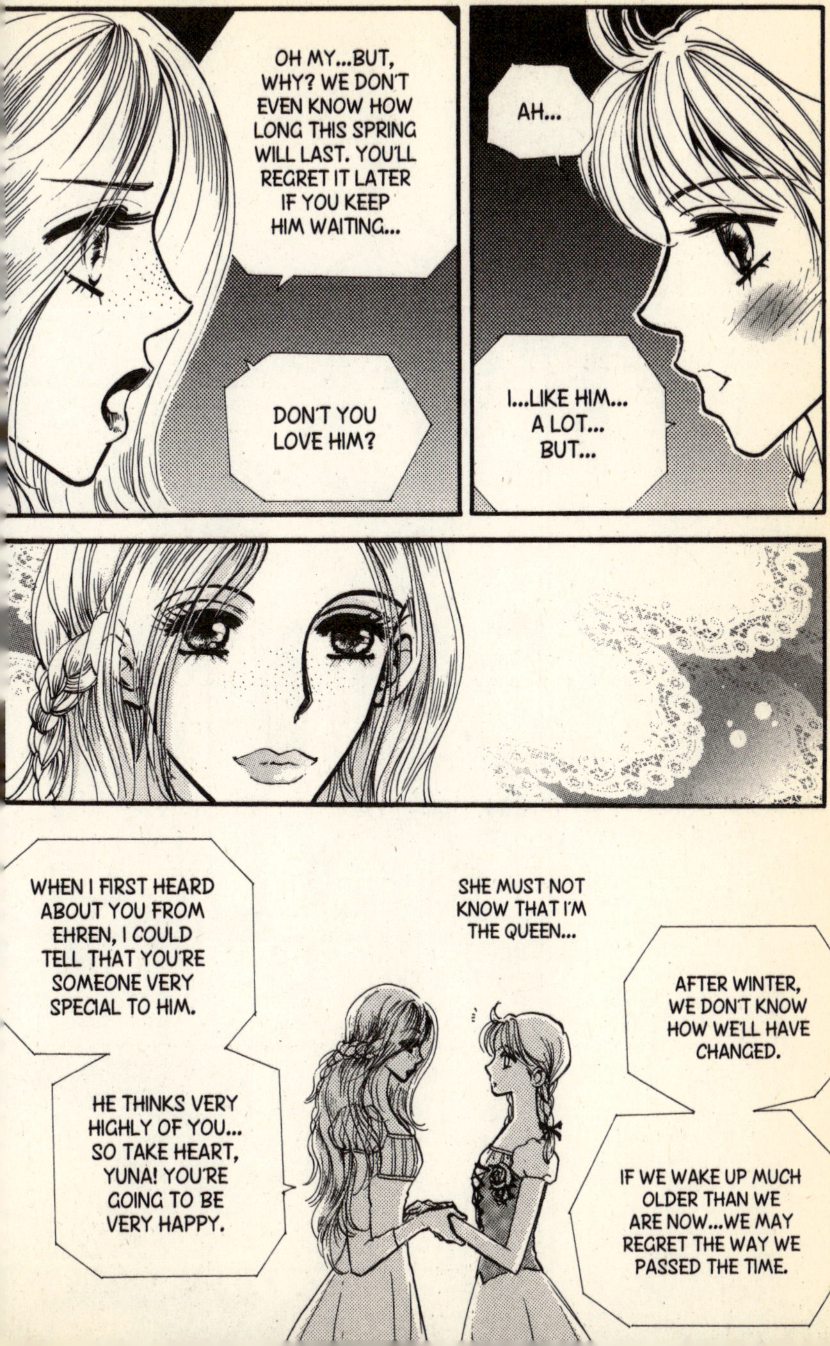
OH MY...BUT, WHY? WE DON'T EVEN KNOW HOW LONG THIS SPRING WILL LAST. YOU'LL REGRET IT LATER IF YOU KEEP HIM WAITING...
DON'T YOU LOVE HIM?
AH...
I...LIKE HIM... A LOT... BUT...
WHEN I FIRST HEARD ABOUT YOU FROM EHREN, I COULD TELL THAT YOU'RE SOMEONE VERY SPECIAL TO HIM.
HE THINKS VERY HIGHLY OF YOU... SO TAKE HEART, YUNA! YOU'RE GOING TO BE VERY HAPPY.
SHE MUST NOT KNOW THAT I'M THE QUEEN...
AFTER WINTER, WE DON'T KNOW HOW WE'LL HAVE CHANGED.
IF WE WAKE UP MUCH OLDER THAN WE ARE NOW...WE MAY REGRET THE WAY WE PASSED THE TIME.

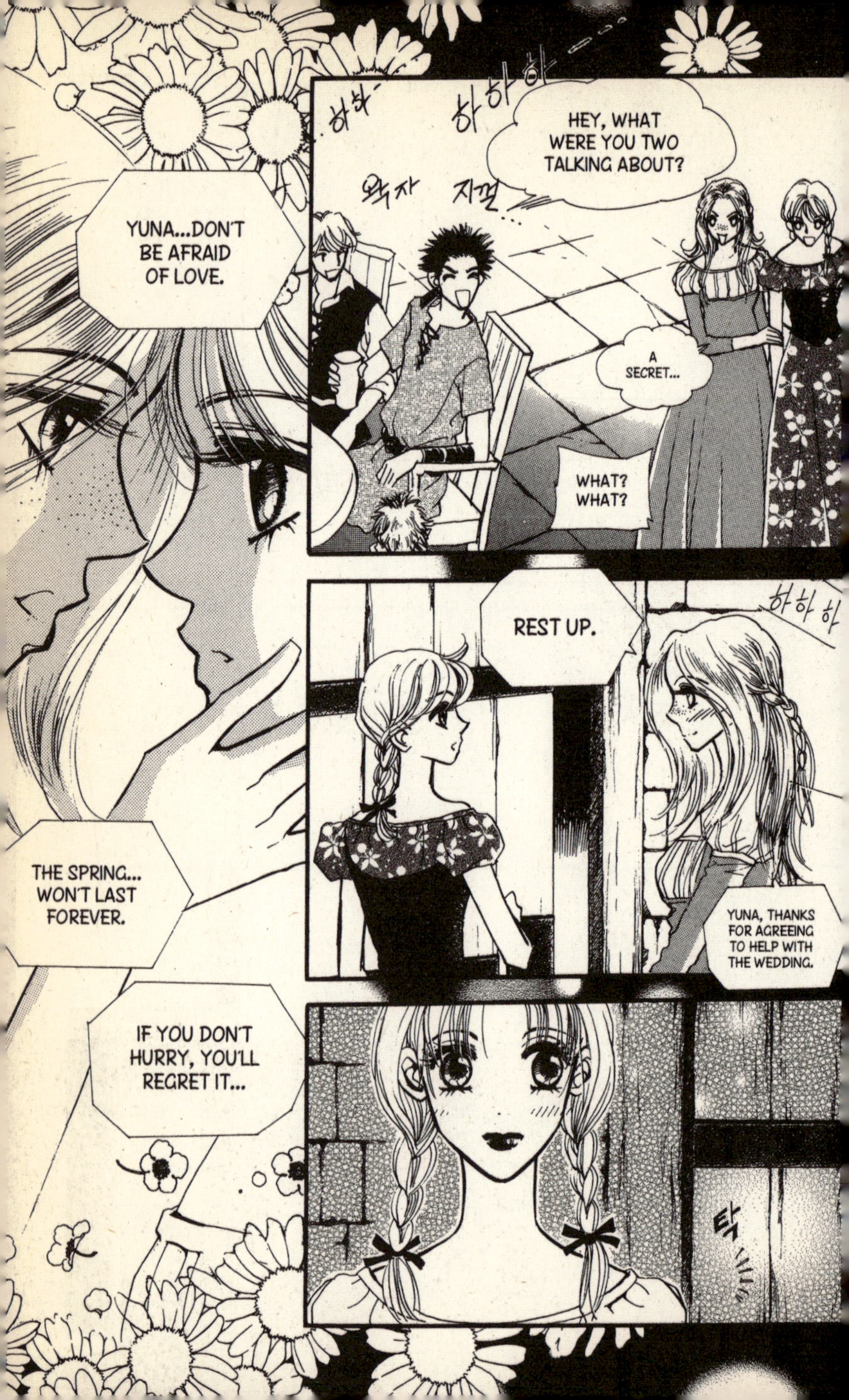
YUNA...DON'T BE AFRAID OF LOVE.
THE SPRING... WON'T LAST FOREVER.
IF YOU DON'T HURRY, YOU'LL REGRET IT...
하하
하하하
HEY, WHAT WERE YOU TWO TALKING ABOUT?
왁자 지껄...
A SECRET...
WHAT? WHAT?
REST UP.
하하하
YUNA, THANKS FOR AGREEING TO HELP WITH THE WEDDING.
탁

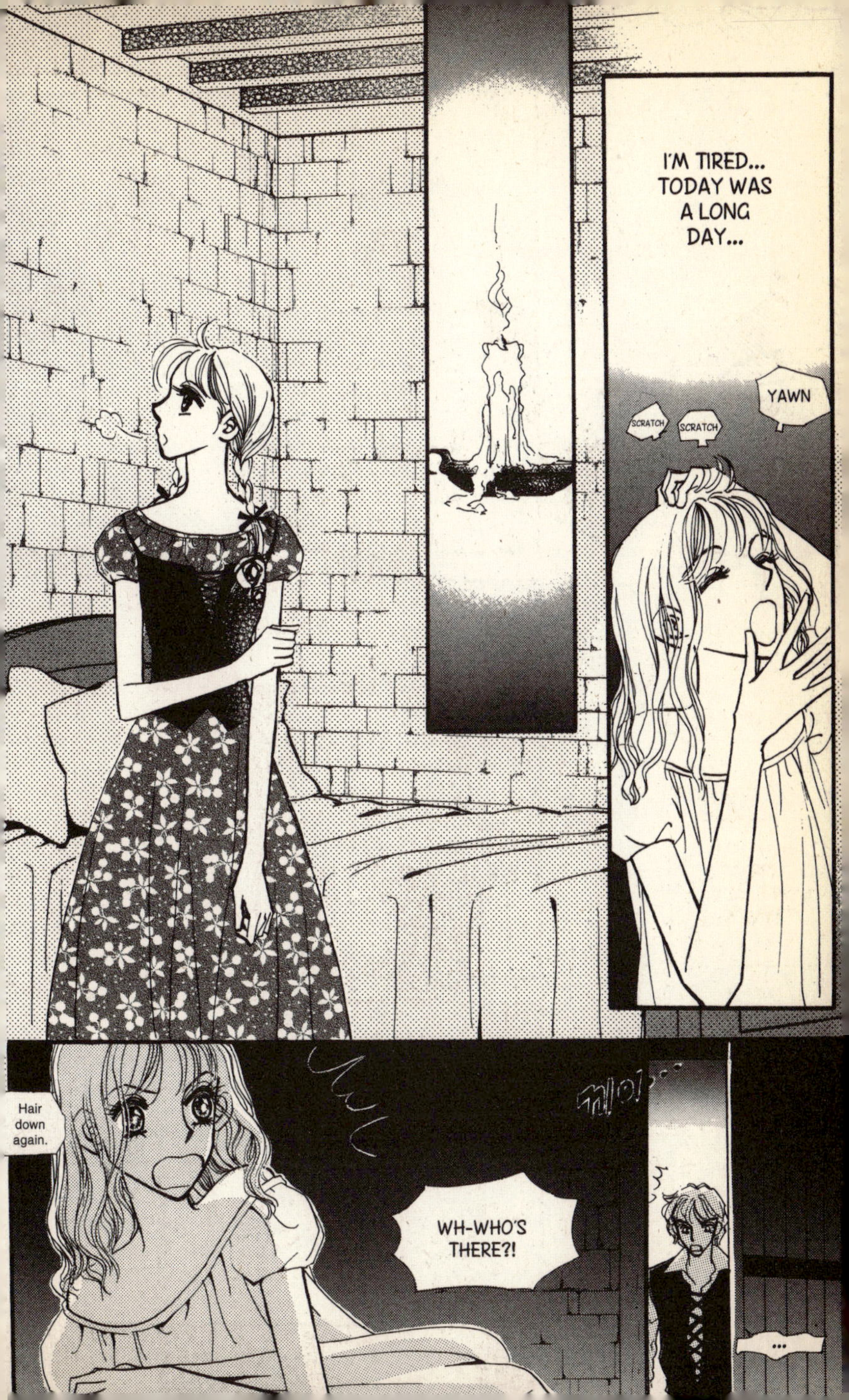
I'M TIRED... TODAY WAS A LONG DAY...
SCRATCH
SCRATCH
YAWN
Hair down again.
WH-WHO'S THERE?!
...

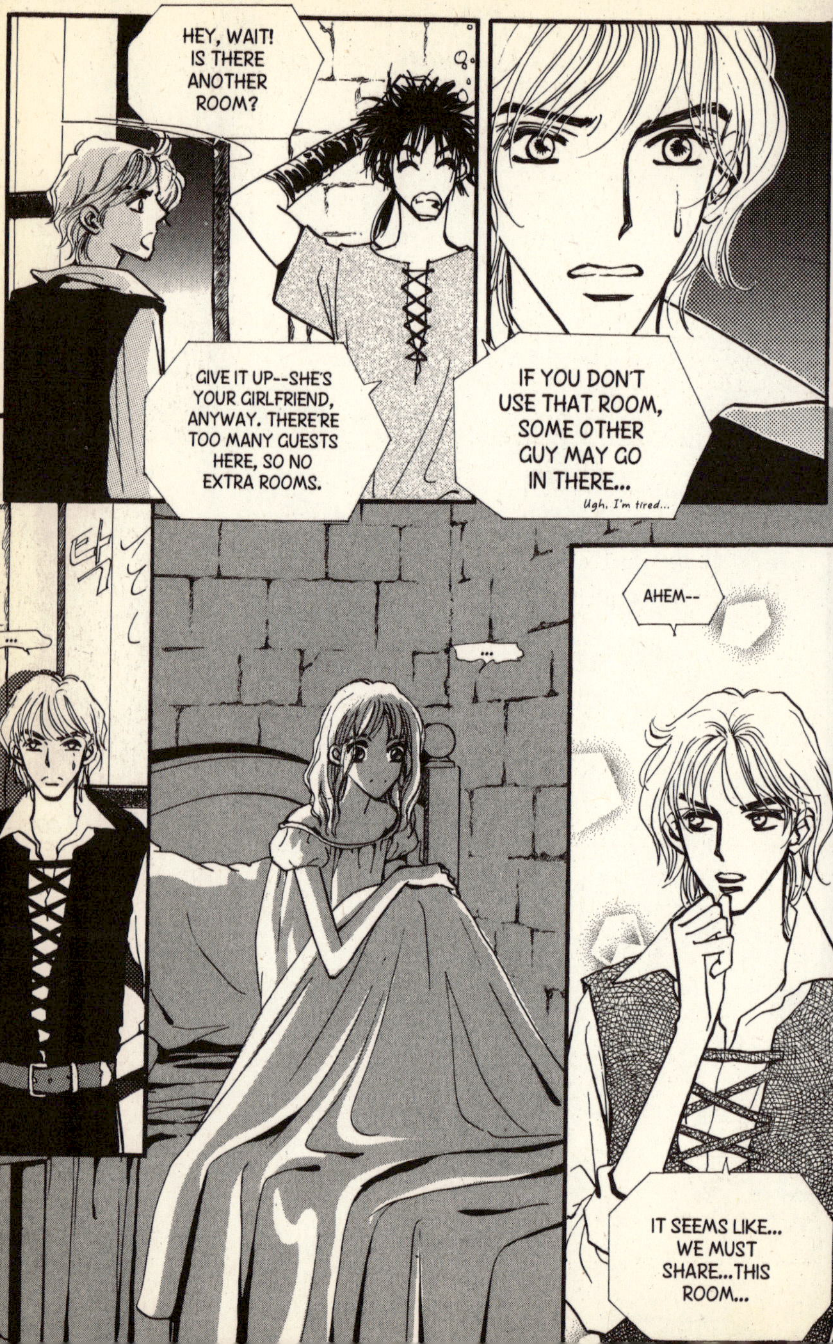
HEY, WAIT! IS THERE ANOTHER ROOM?
GIVE IT UP--SHE'S YOUR GIRLFRIEND, ANYWAY. THERE'RE TOO MANY GUESTS HERE, SO NO EXTRA ROOMS.
IF YOU DON'T USE THAT ROOM, SOME OTHER GUY MAY GO IN THERE...
Ugh, I'm tired...
탁
...
...
AHEM--
IT SEEMS LIKE... WE MUST SHARE...THIS ROOM...

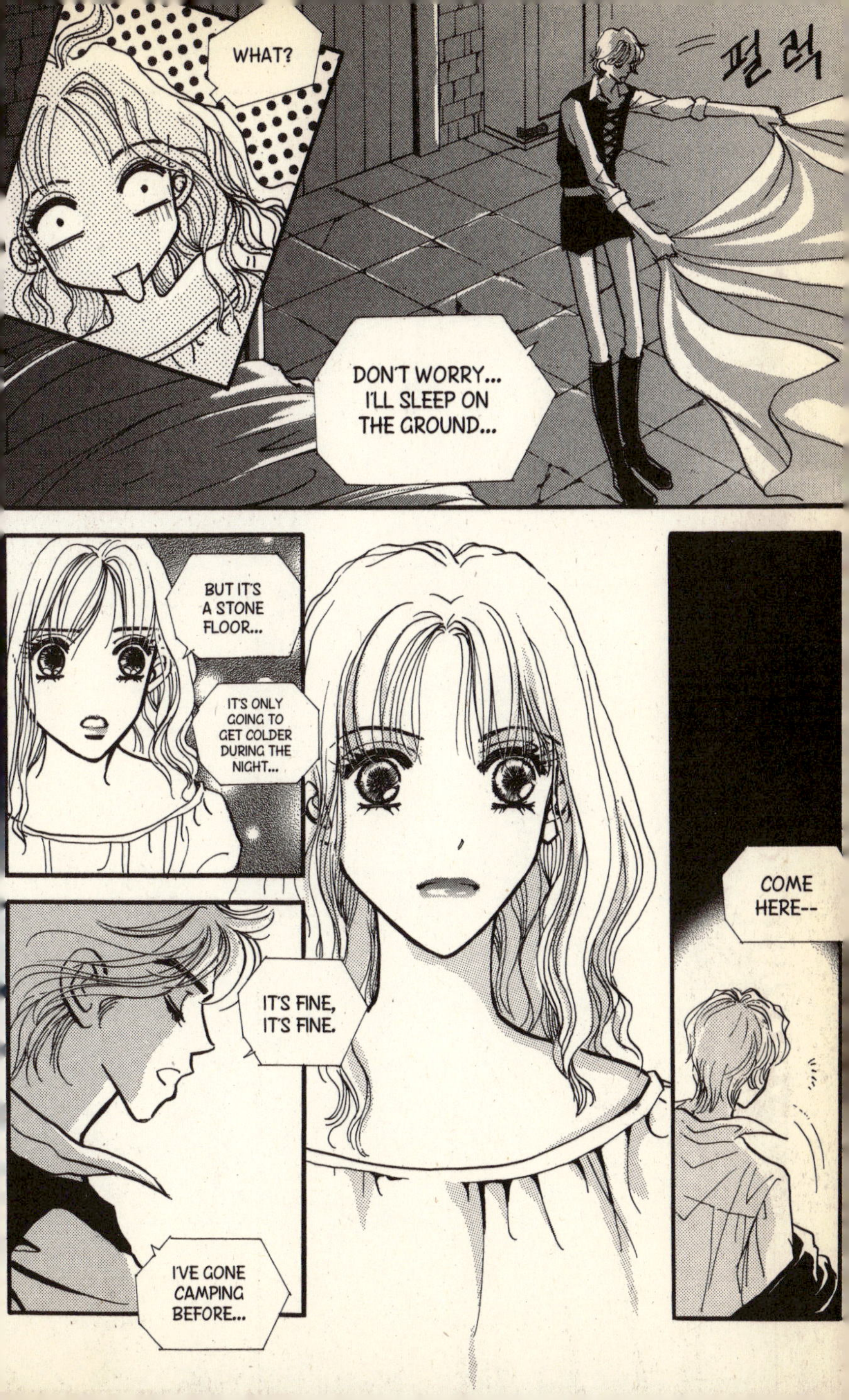
WHAT?
펄럭
DON'T WORRY... I'LL SLEEP ON THE GROUND...
BUT IT'S A STONE FLOOR...
IT'S ONLY GOING TO GET COLDER DURING THE NIGHT...
IT'S FINE, IT'S FINE.
I'VE GONE CAMPING BEFORE...
COME HERE--

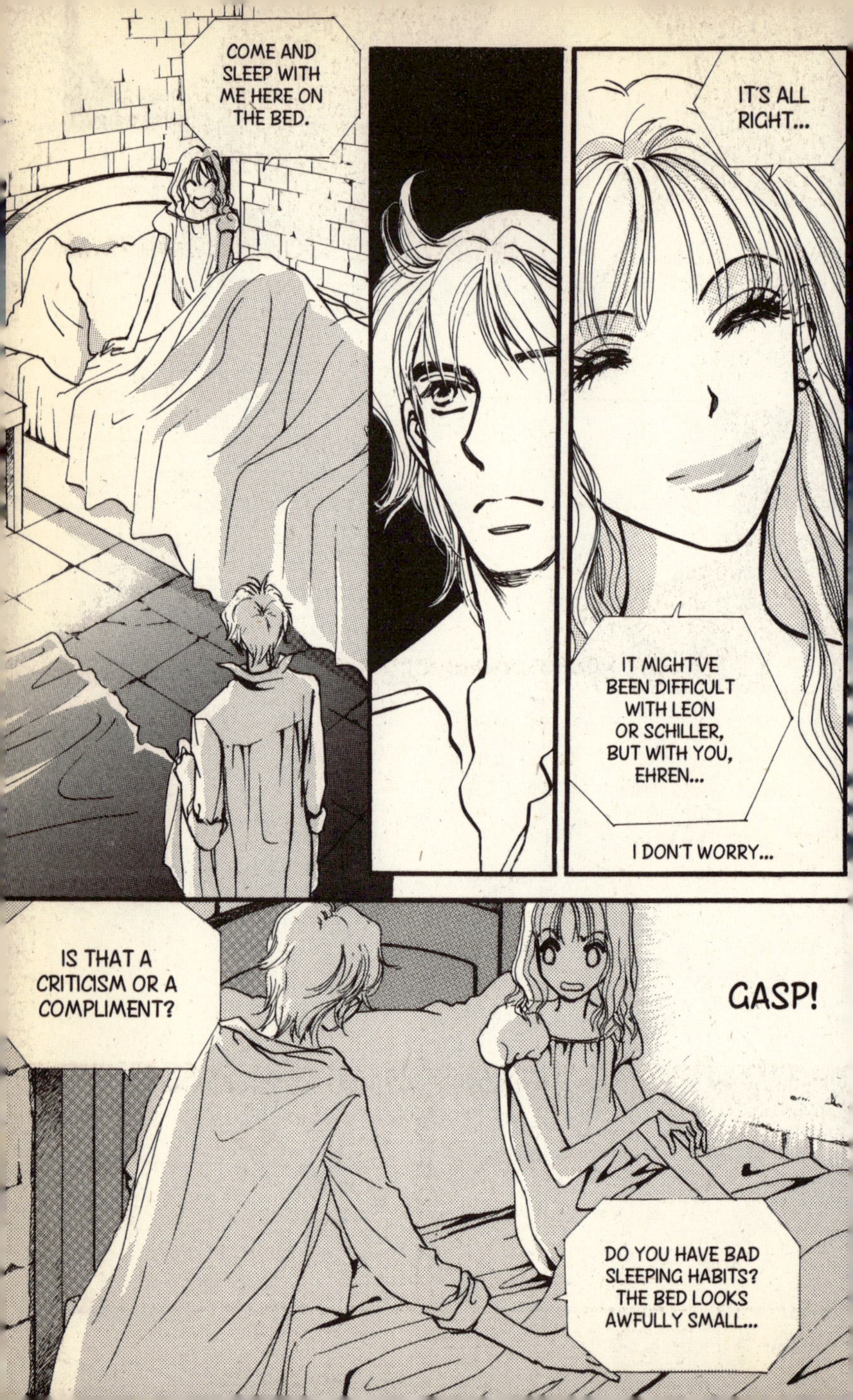
COME AND SLEEP WITH ME HERE ON THE BED.
IT'S ALL RIGHT...
IT MIGHT'VE BEEN DIFFICULT WITH LEON OR SCHILLER, BUT WITH YOU, EHREN...
I DON'T WORRY...
IS THAT A CRITICISM OR A COMPLIMENT?
GASP!
DO YOU HAVE BAD SLEEPING HABITS? THE BED LOOKS AWFULLY SMALL...

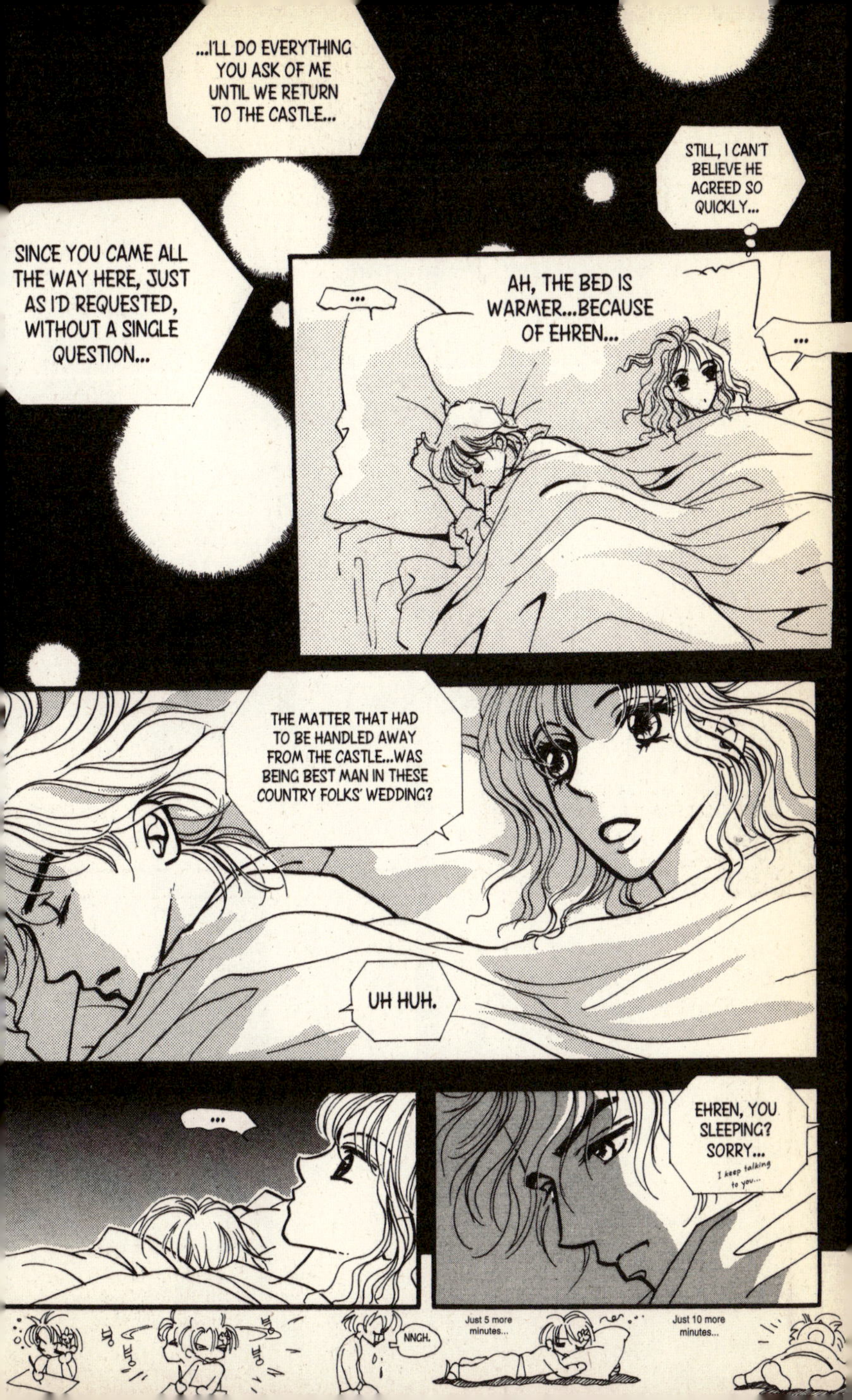

SINCE YOU CAME ALL THE WAY HERE, JUST AS I'D REQUESTED, WITHOUT A SINGLE QUESTION...
...I'LL DO EVERYTHING YOU ASK OF ME UNTIL WE RETURN TO THE CASTLE...
STILL, I CAN'T BELIEVE HE AGREED SO QUICKLY...
...
AH, THE BED IS WARMER...BECAUSE OF EHREN...
...
THE MATTER THAT HAD TO BE HANDLED AWAY FROM THE CASTLE...WAS BEING BEST MAN IN THESE COUNTRY FOLKS' WEDDING?
UH HUH.
...
EHREN, YOU SLEEPING? SORRY...
I keep talking to you...
NNGH.
Just 5 more minutes...
Just 10 more minutes...

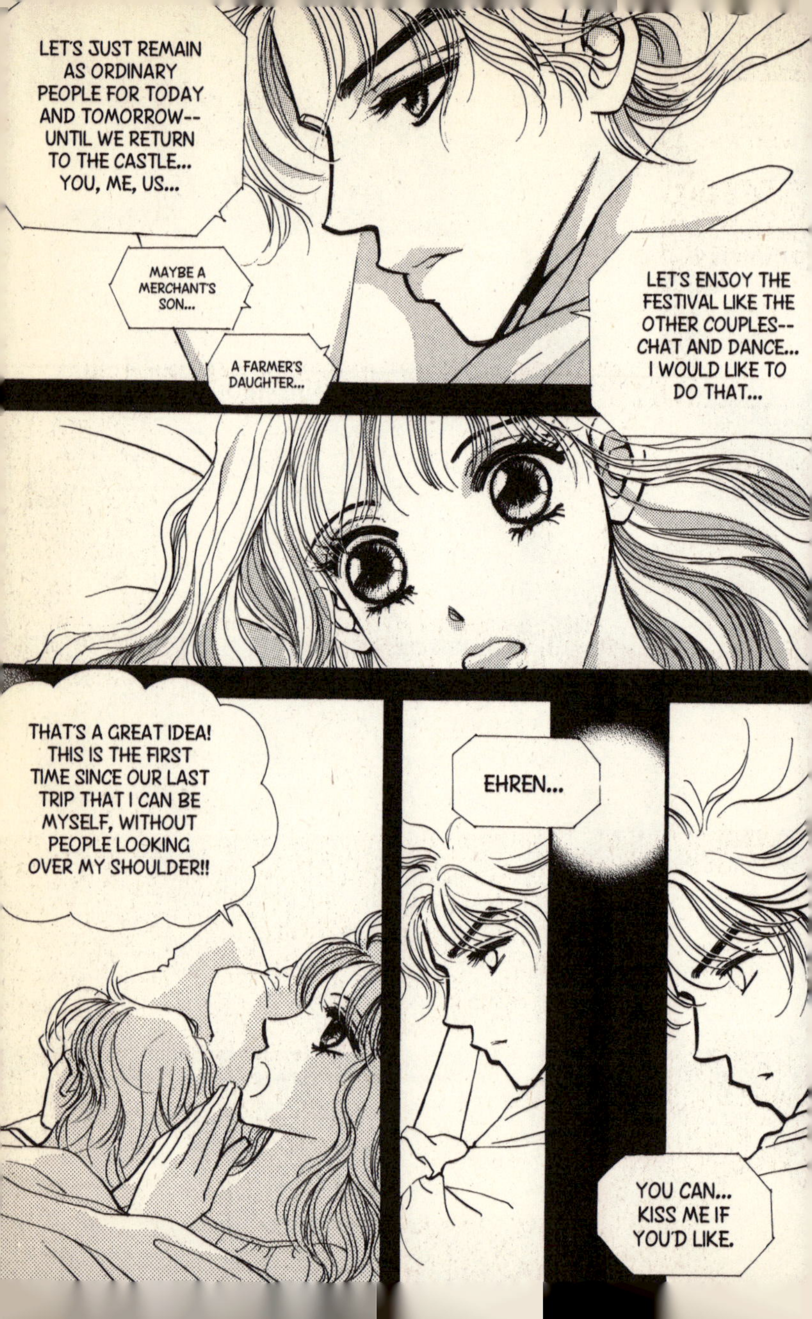
LET'S JUST REMAIN AS ORDINARY PEOPLE FOR TODAY AND TOMORROW-- UNTIL WE RETURN TO THE CASTLE... YOU, ME, US...
MAYBE A MERCHANT'S SON...
A FARMER'S DAUGHTER...
LET'S ENJOY THE FESTIVAL LIKE THE OTHER COUPLES-- CHAT AND DANCE... I WOULD LIKE TO DO THAT...
THAT'S A GREAT IDEA! THIS IS THE FIRST TIME SINCE OUR LAST TRIP THAT I CAN BE MYSELF, WITHOUT PEOPLE LOOKING OVER MY SHOULDER!!
EHREN...
YOU CAN... KISS ME IF YOU'D LIKE.

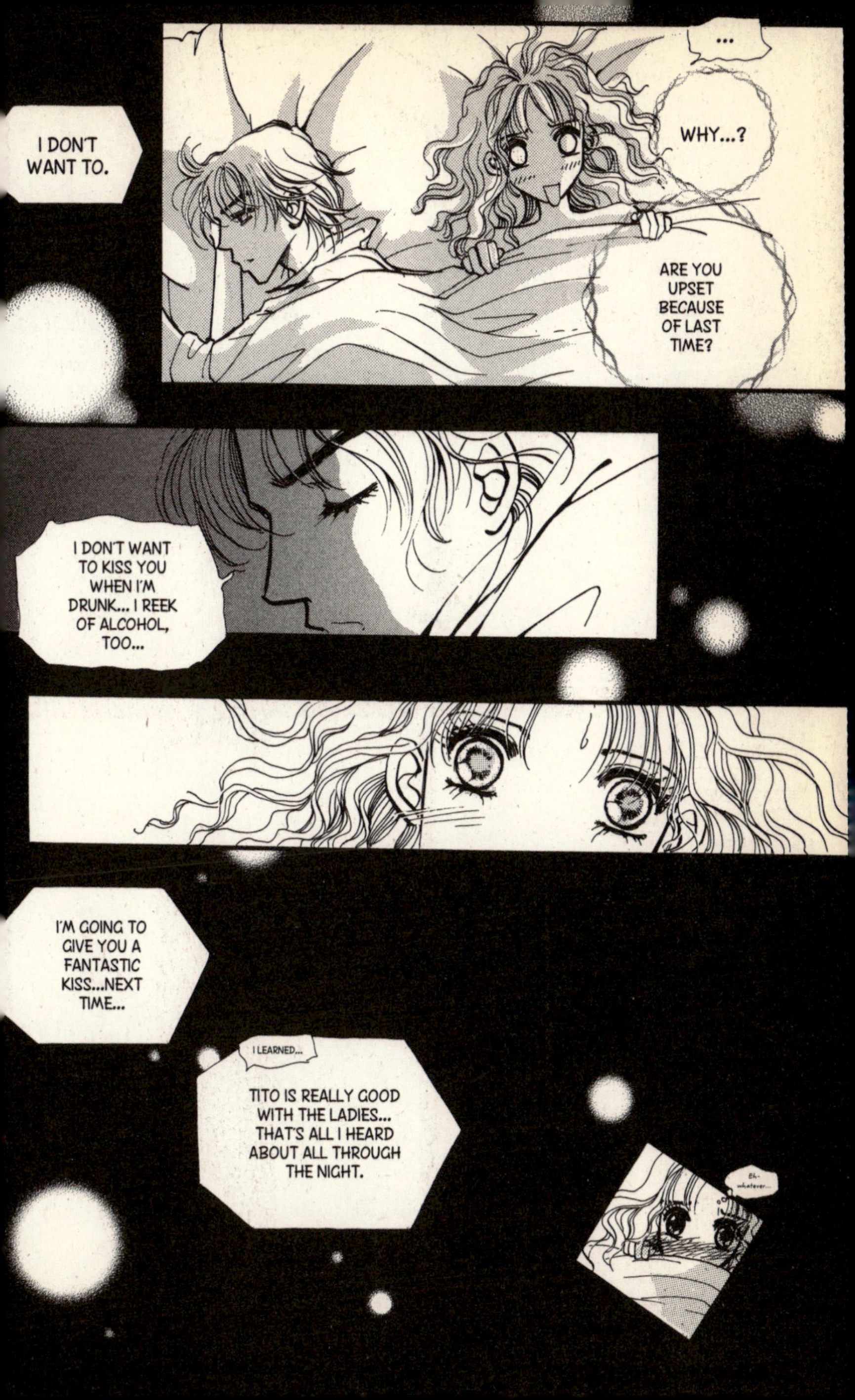
I DON'T WANT TO.
...
WHY...?
ARE YOU UPSET BECAUSE OF LAST TIME?
I DON'T WANT TO KISS YOU WHEN I'M DRUNK... I REEK OF ALCOHOL, TOO...
I'M GOING TO GIVE YOU A FANTASTIC KISS...NEXT TIME...
I LEARNED...
TITO IS REALLY GOOD WITH THE LADIES... THAT'S ALL I HEARD ABOUT ALL THROUGH THE NIGHT.
Eh- whatever...

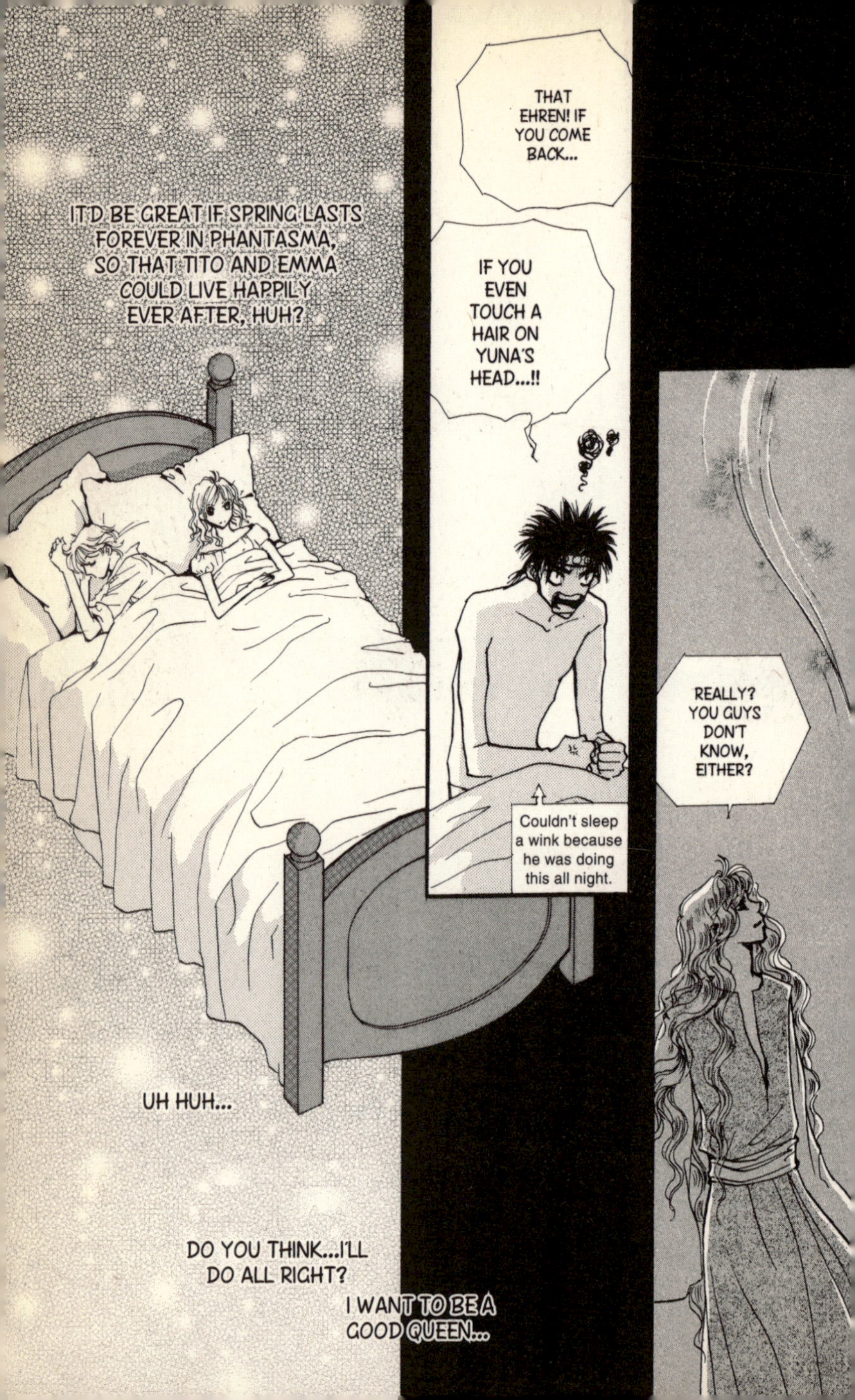
IT'D BE GREAT IF SPRING LASTS FOREVER IN PHANTASMA, SO THAT TITO AND EMMA COULD LIVE HAPPILY EVER AFTER, HUH?
UH HUH...
DO YOU THINK...I'LL DO ALL RIGHT?
I WANT TO BE A GOOD QUEEN...
THAT EHREN! IF YOU COME BACK...
IF YOU EVEN TOUCH A HAIR ON YUNA'S HEAD...!!
Couldn't sleep a wink because he was doing this all night.
REALLY? YOU GUYS DON'T KNOW, EITHER?

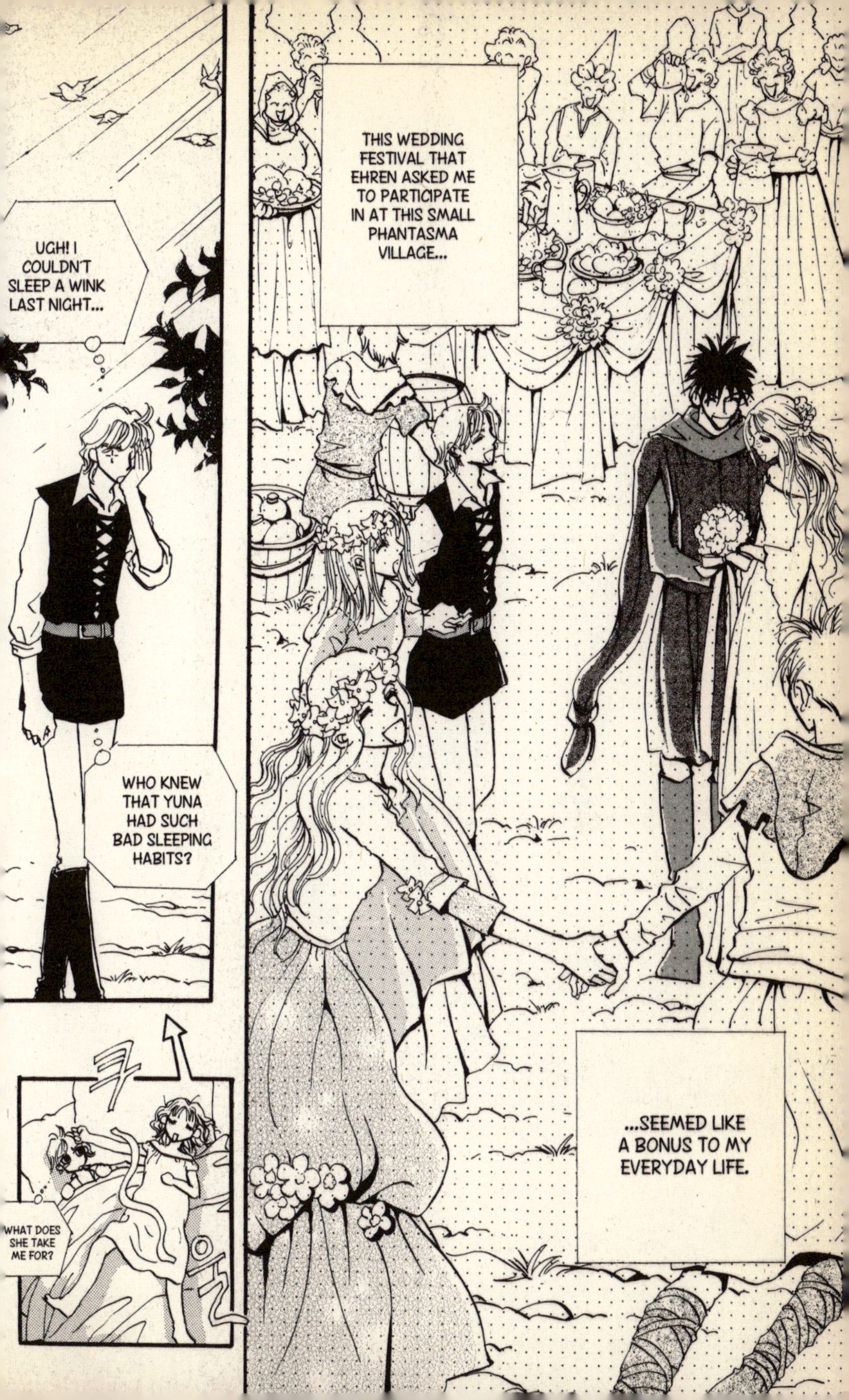
UGH! I COULDN'T SLEEP A WINK LAST NIGHT...
WHO KNEW THAT YUNA HAD SUCH BAD SLEEPING HABITS?
WHAT DOES SHE TAKE ME FOR?
THIS WEDDING FESTIVAL THAT EHREN ASKED ME TO PARTICIPATE IN AT THIS SMALL PHANTASMA VILLAGE...
...SEEMED LIKE A BONUS TO MY EVERYDAY LIFE.

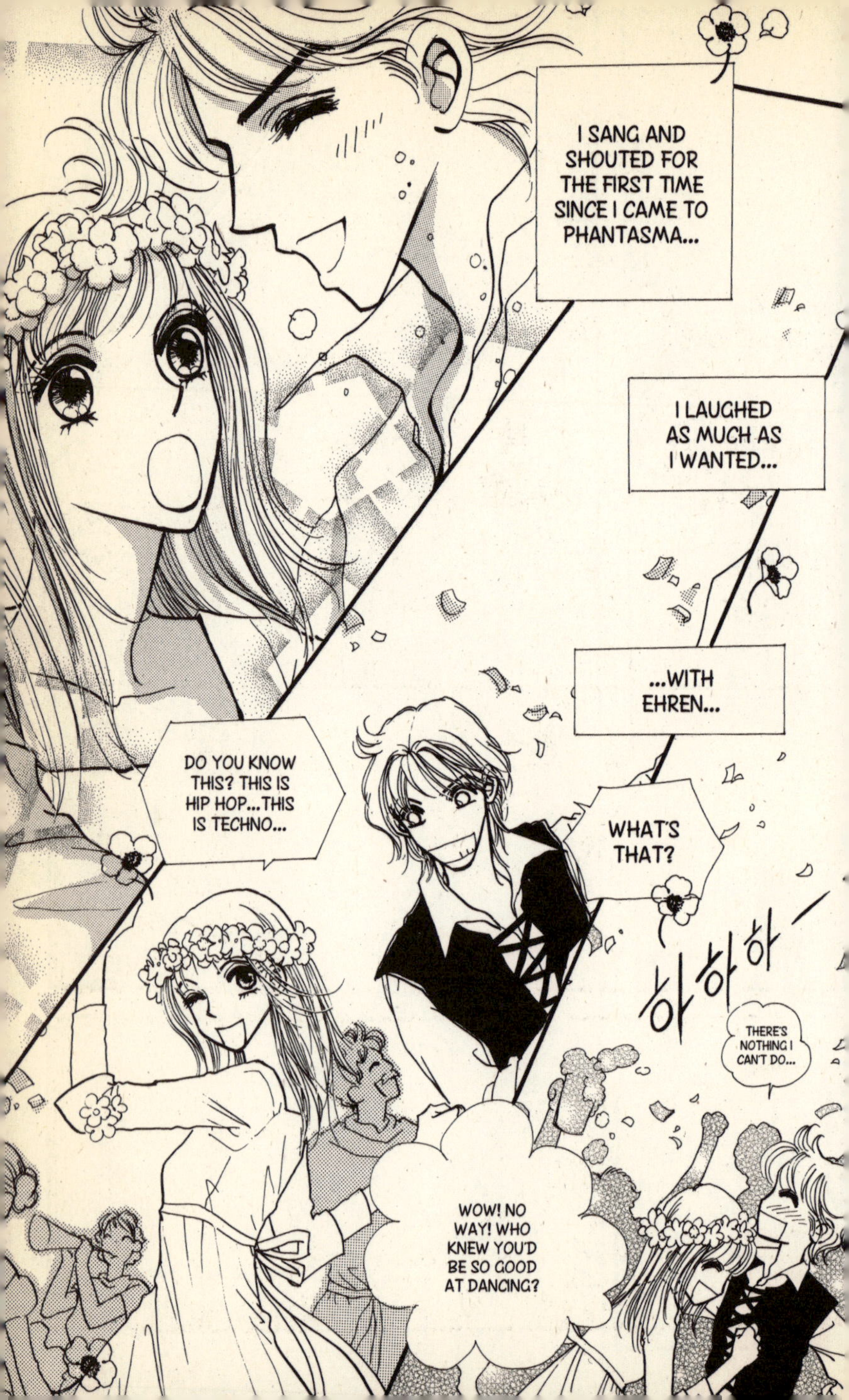
I SANG AND SHOUTED FOR THE FIRST TIME SINCE I CAME TO PHANTASMA...
I LAUGHED AS MUCH AS I WANTED...
...WITH EHREN...
DO YOU KNOW THIS? THIS IS HIP HOP...THIS IS TECHNO...
WHAT'S THAT?
하하하
THERE'S NOTHING I CAN'T DO...
WOW! NO WAY! WHO KNEW YOU'D BE SO GOOD AT DANCING?

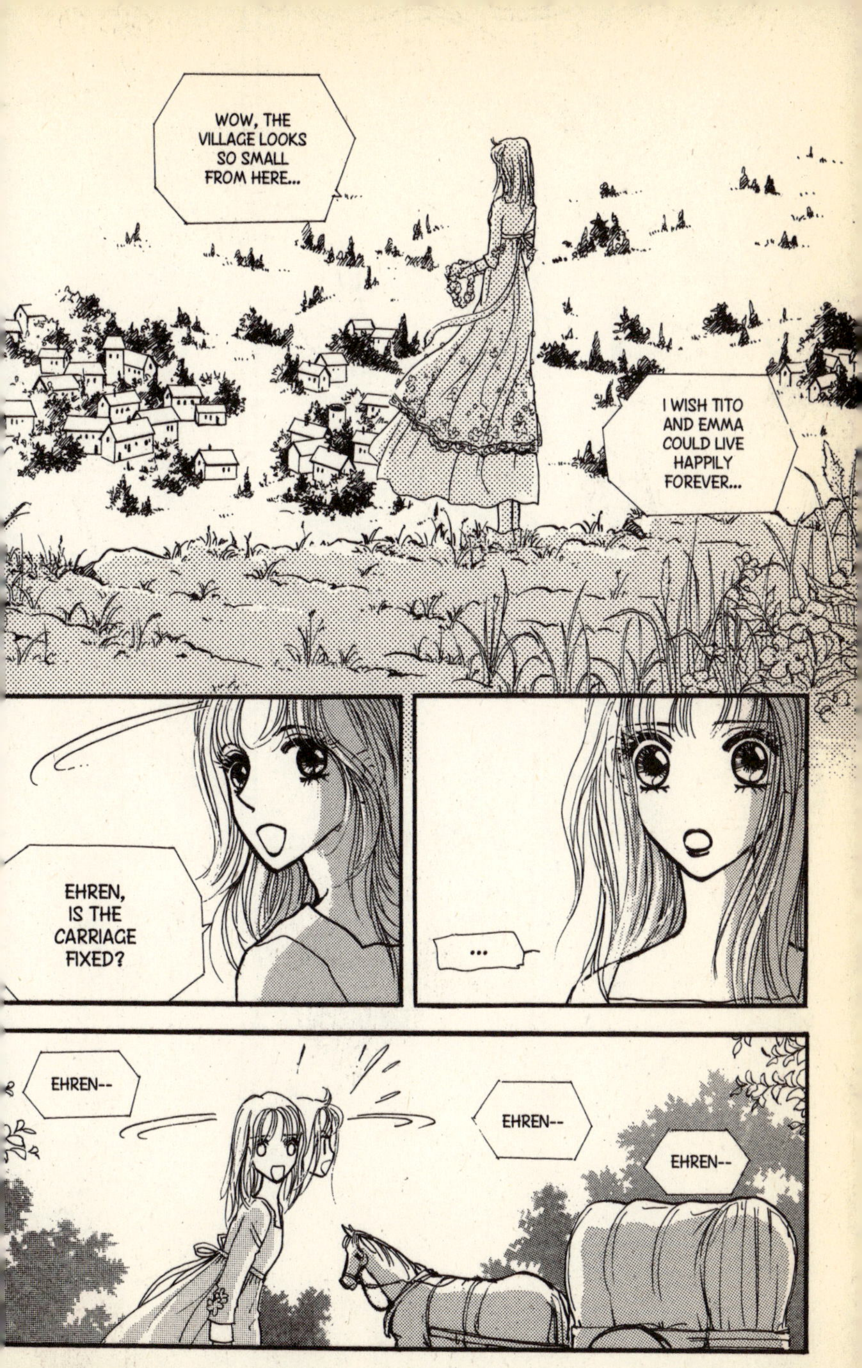
WOW, THE VILLAGE LOOKS SO SMALL FROM HERE...
I WISH TITO AND EMMA COULD LIVE HAPPILY FOREVER...
EHREN, IS THE CARRIAGE FIXED?
...
EHREN--
!
!
EHREN--
EHREN--

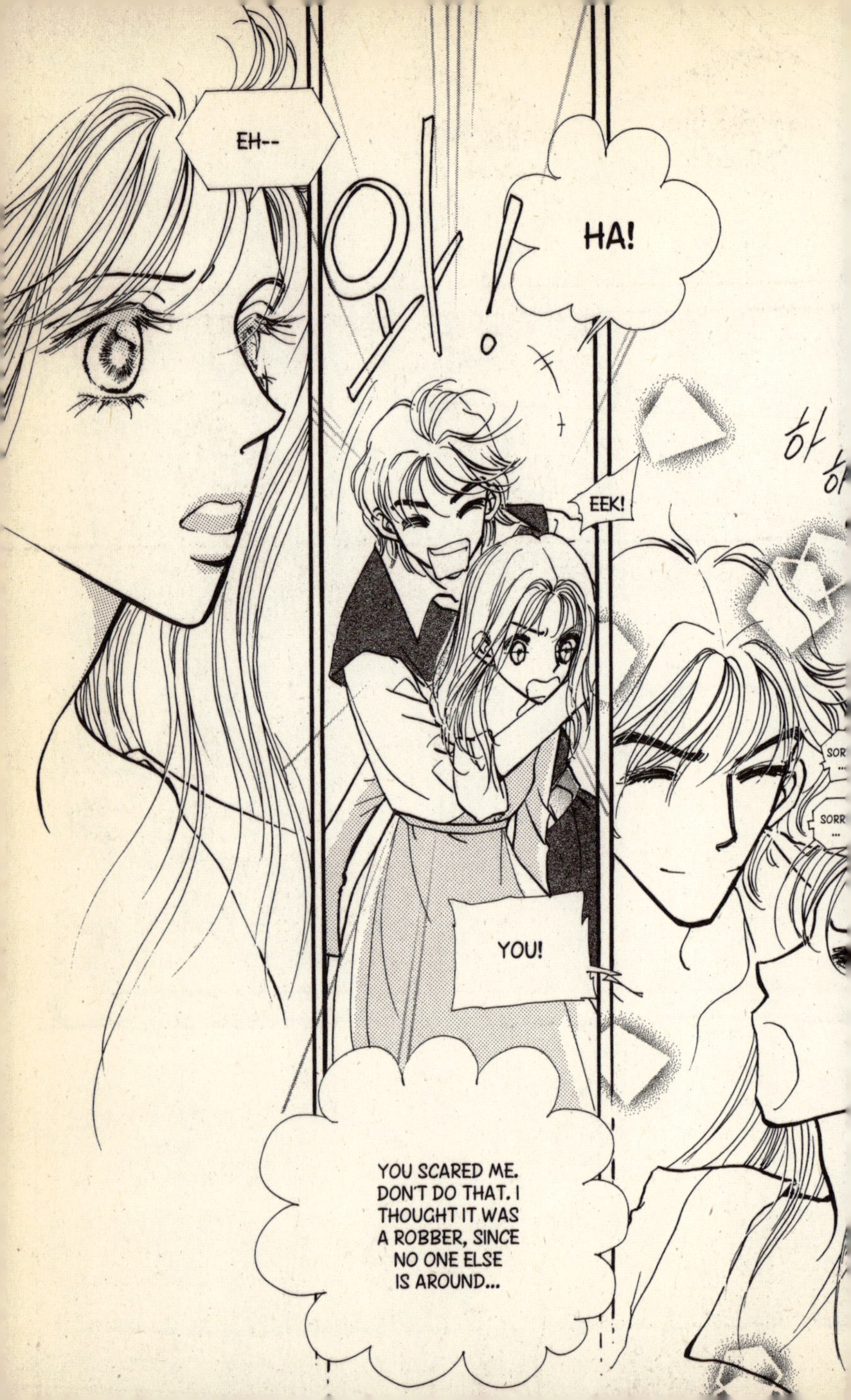
EH--
앗!
HA!
EEK!
YOU!
YOU SCARED ME. DON'T DO THAT. I THOUGHT IT WAS A ROBBER, SINCE NO ONE ELSE IS AROUND...
하 하
SORR ...
SORR ...

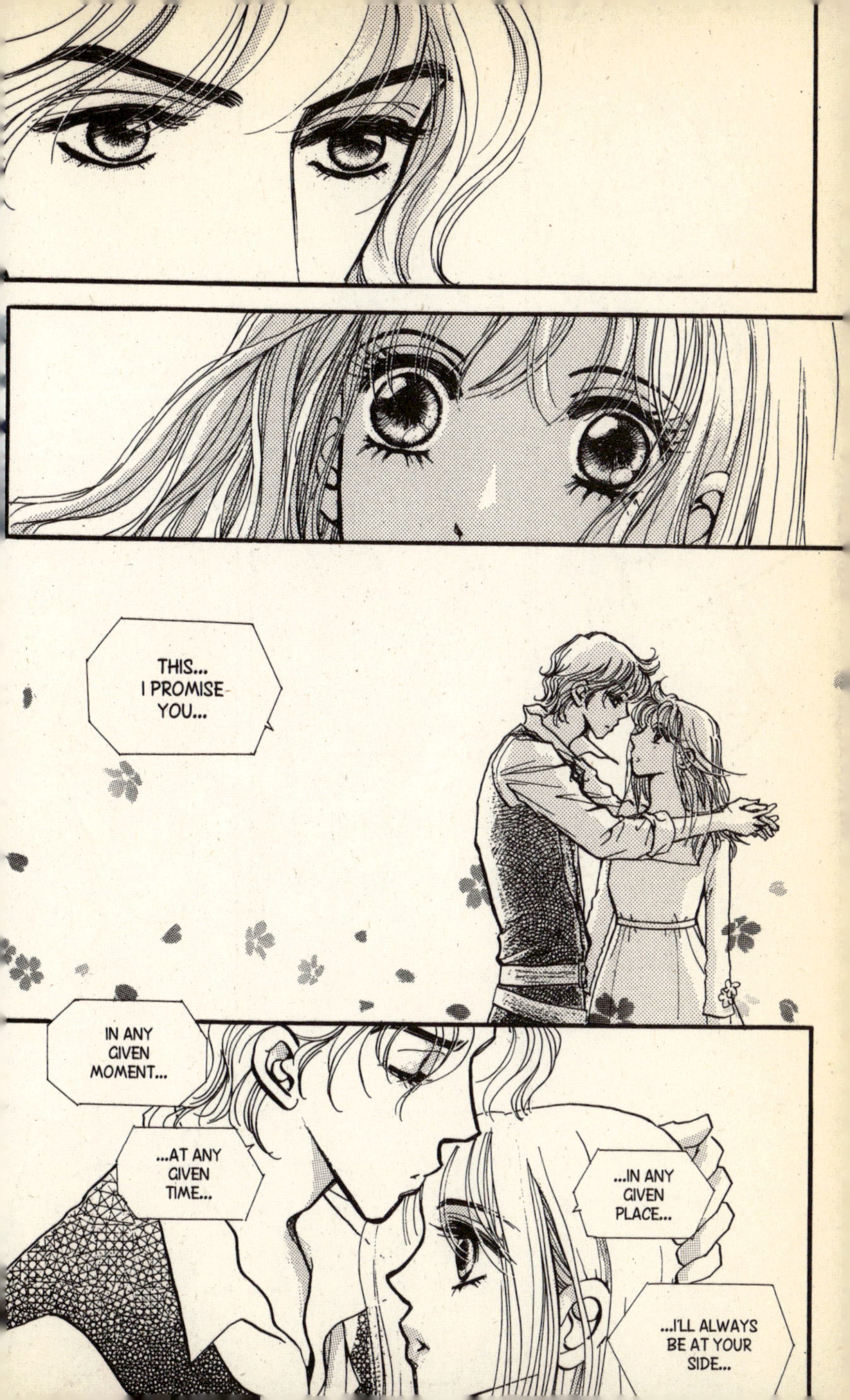
THIS... I PROMISE YOU...
IN ANY GIVEN MOMENT...
...AT ANY GIVEN TIME...
...IN ANY GIVEN PLACE...
...I'LL ALWAYS BE AT YOUR SIDE...

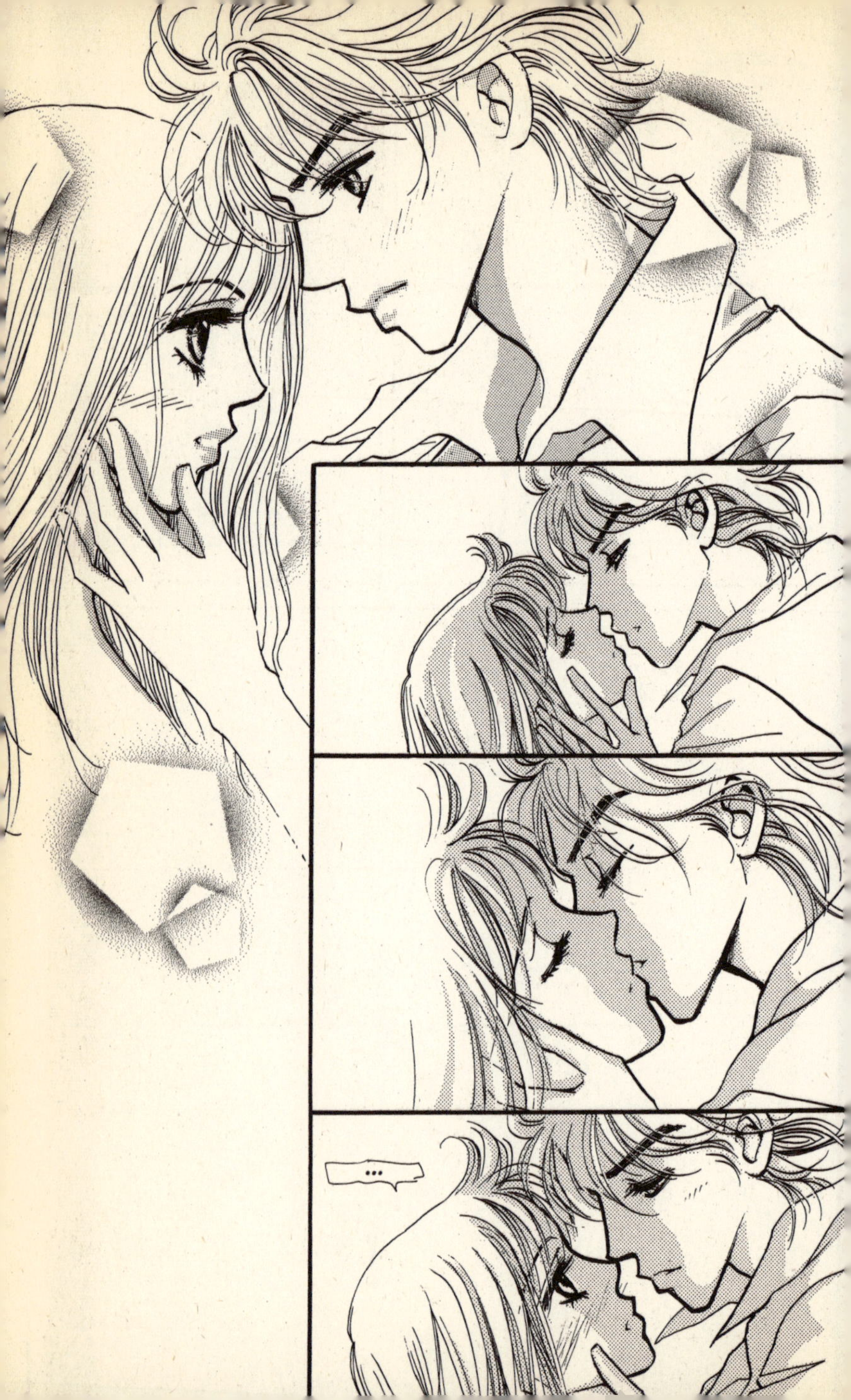
...

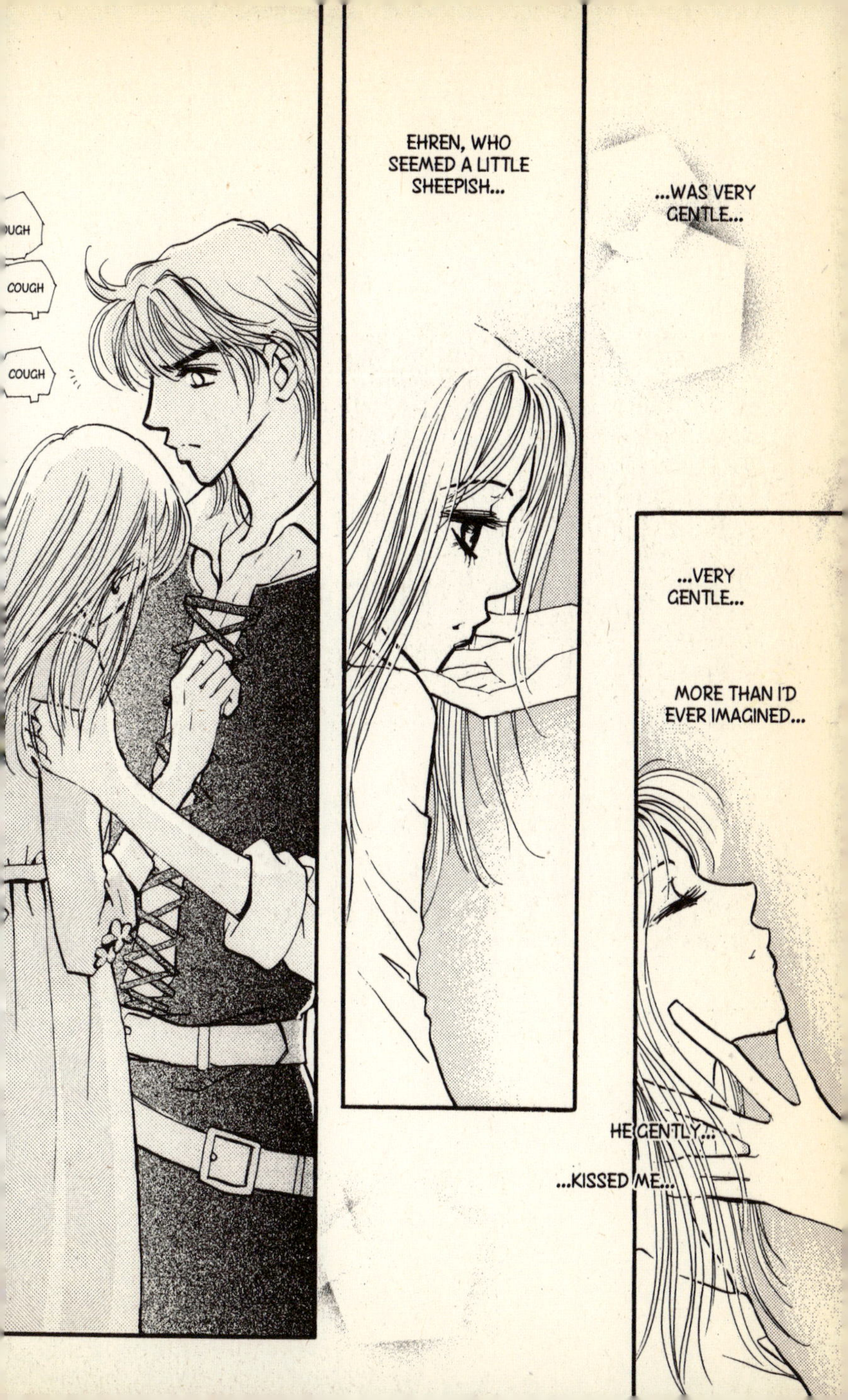

OUGH
COUGH
COUGH
EHREN, WHO SEEMED A LITTLE SHEEPISH...
...WAS VERY GENTLE...
...VERY GENTLE...
MORE THAN I'D EVER IMAGINED...
HE GENTLY...
...KISSED ME...

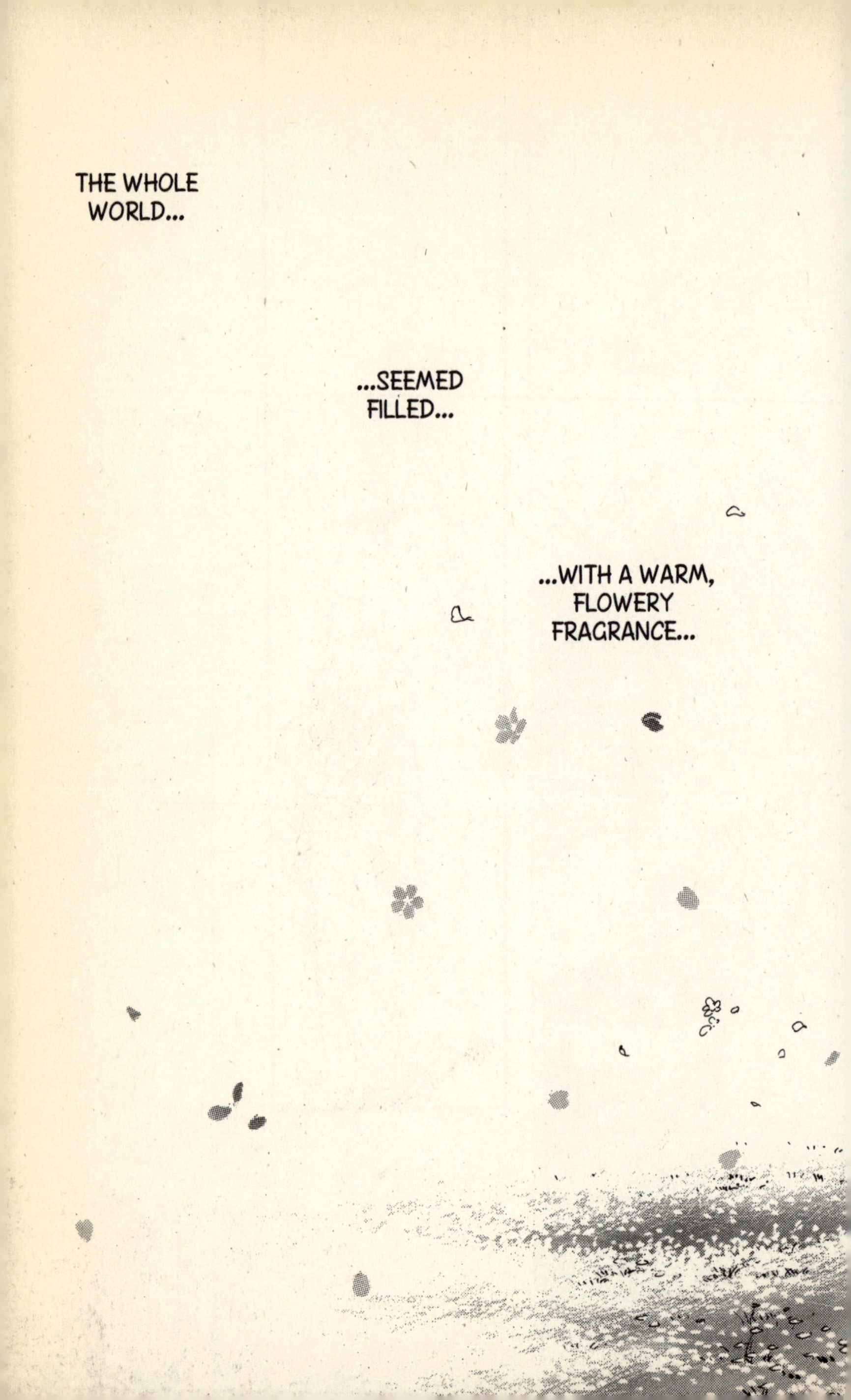
THE WHOLE WORLD...
...SEEMED FILLED...
...WITH A WARM, FLOWERY FRAGRANCE...

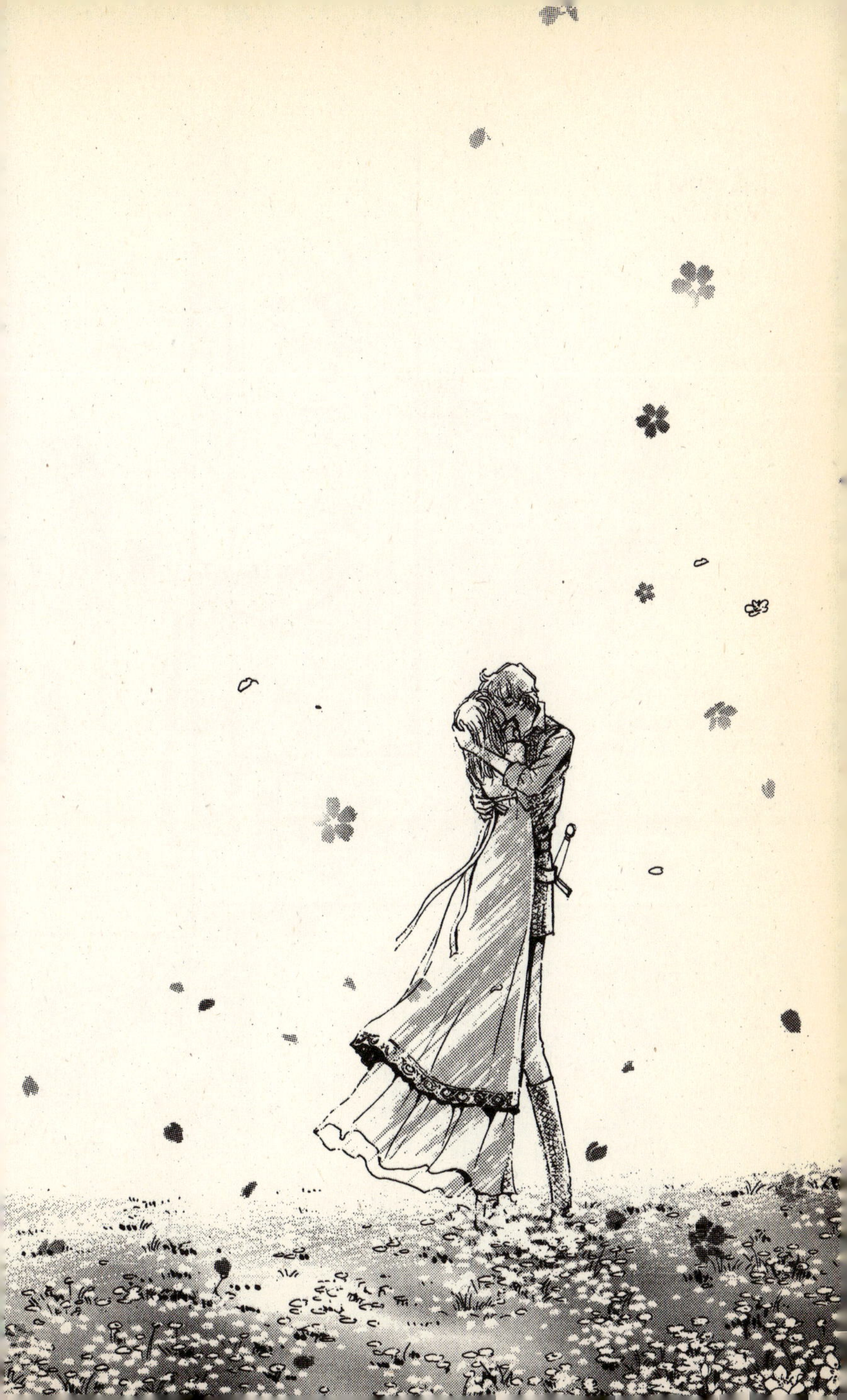

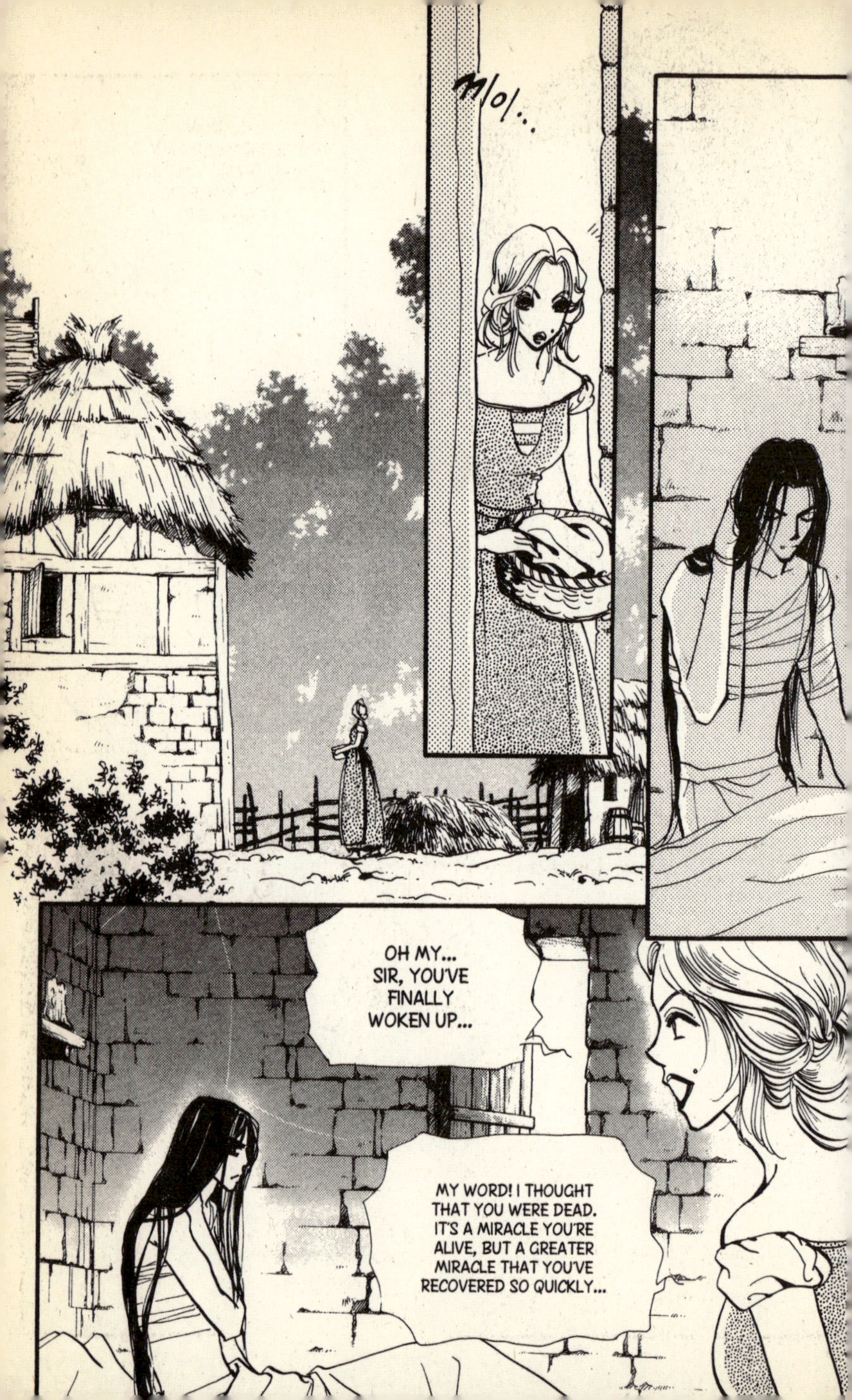
OH MY... SIR, YOU'VE FINALLY WOKEN UP...
MY WORD! I THOUGHT THAT YOU WERE DEAD. IT'S A MIRACLE YOU'RE ALIVE, BUT A GREATER MIRACLE THAT YOU'VE RECOVERED SO QUICKLY...

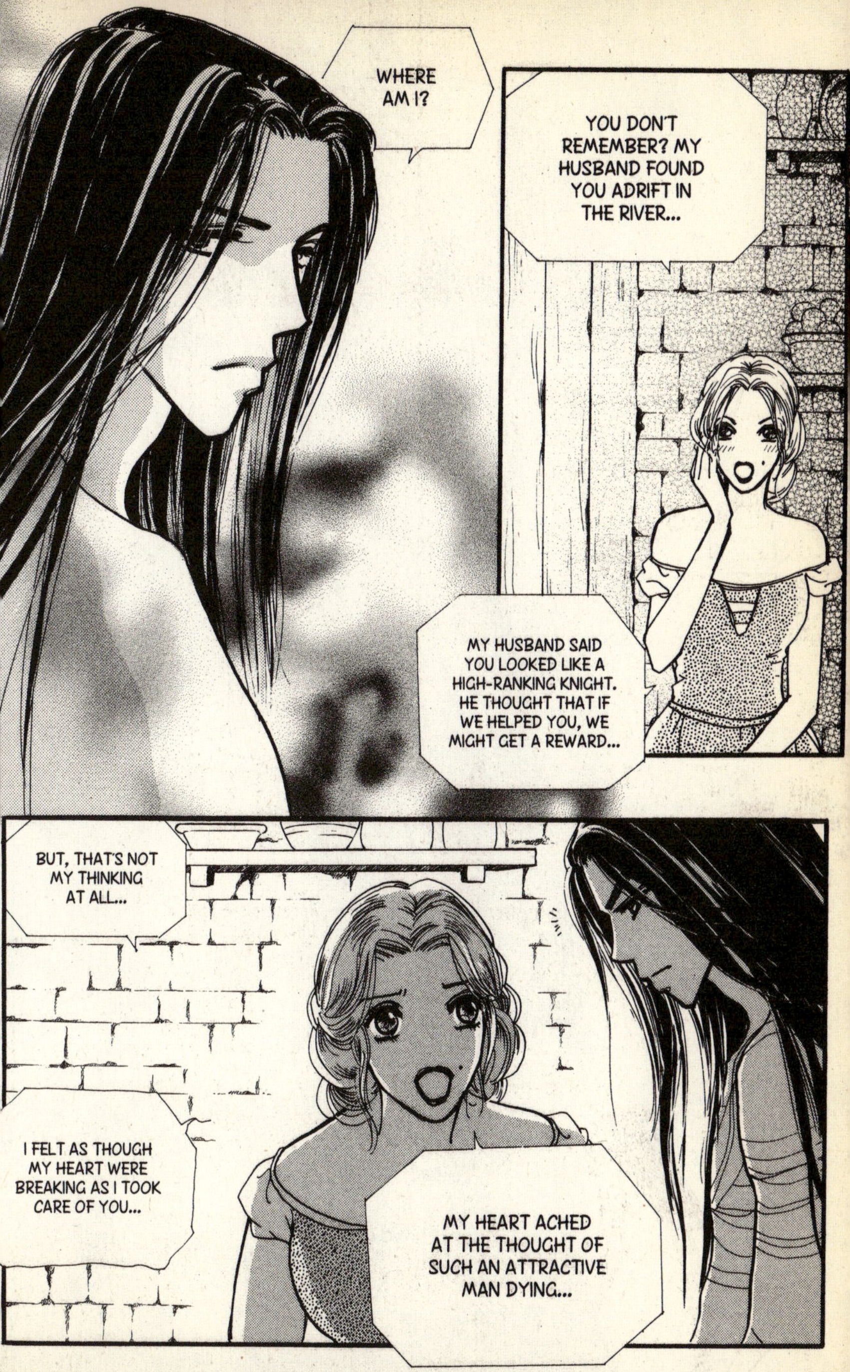
WHERE AM I?
YOU DON'T REMEMBER? MY HUSBAND FOUND YOU ADRIFT IN THE RIVER...
MY HUSBAND SAID YOU LOOKED LIKE A HIGH-RANKING KNIGHT. HE THOUGHT THAT IF WE HELPED YOU, WE MIGHT GET A REWARD...
BUT, THAT'S NOT MY THINKING AT ALL...
I FELT AS THOUGH MY HEART WERE BREAKING AS I TOOK CARE OF YOU...
MY HEART ACHED AT THE THOUGHT OF SUCH AN ATTRACTIVE MAN DYING...

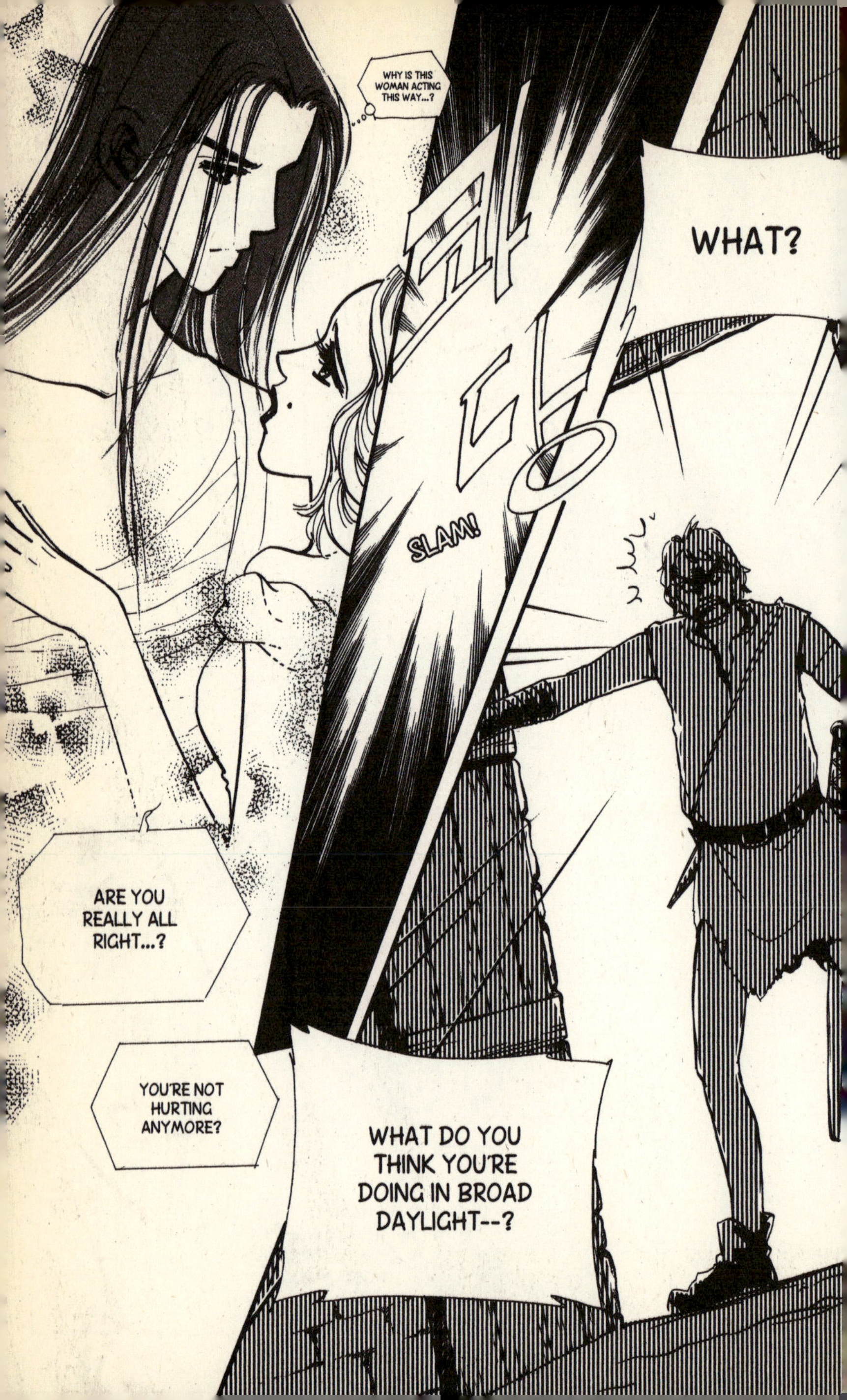
WHY IS THIS WOMAN ACTING THIS WAY...?
ARE YOU REALLY ALL RIGHT...?
YOU'RE NOT HURTING ANYMORE?
SLAM!
WHAT?
WHAT DO YOU THINK YOU'RE DOING IN BROAD DAYLIGHT--?

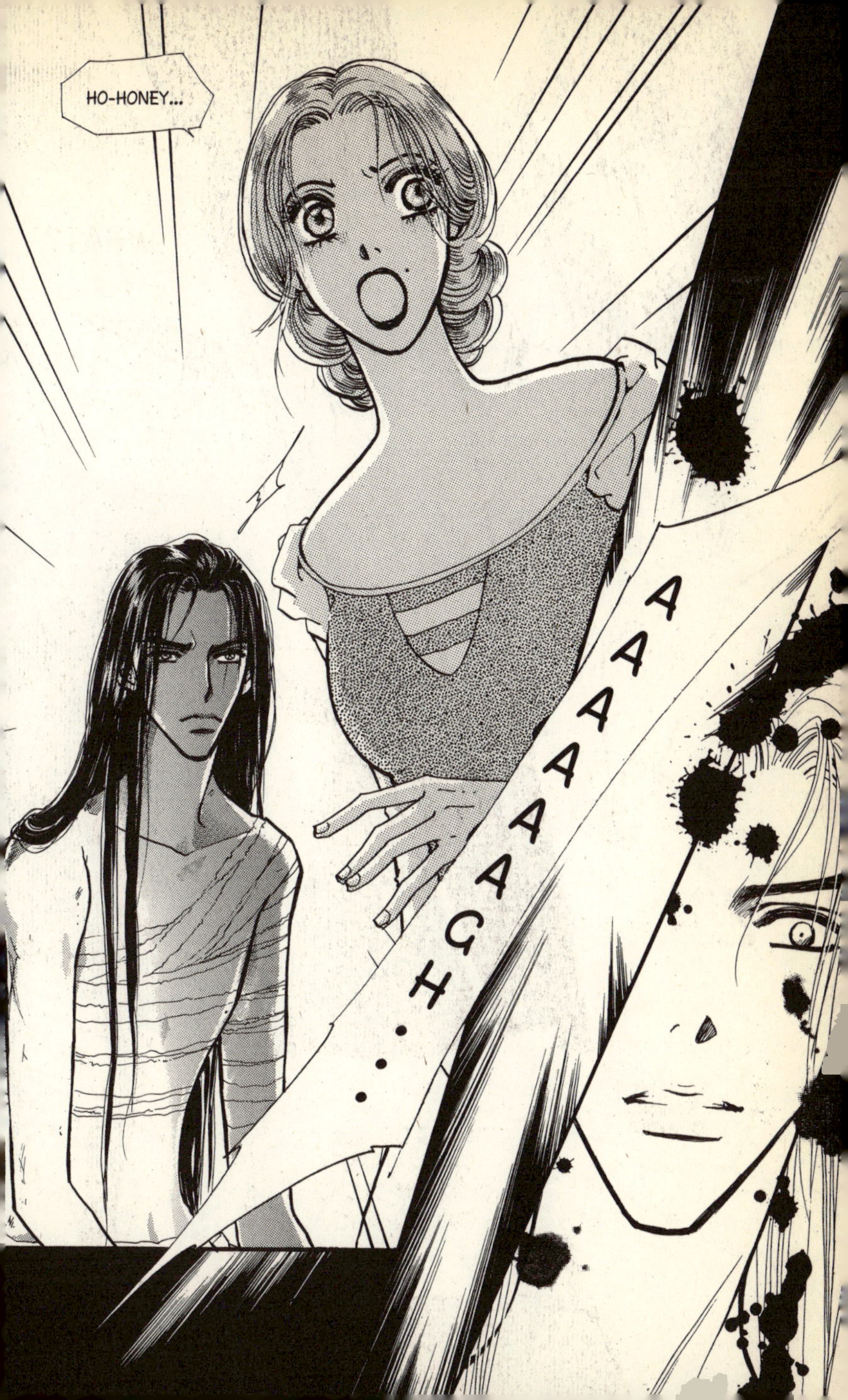
HO-HONEY...
AAAAAAAGH...

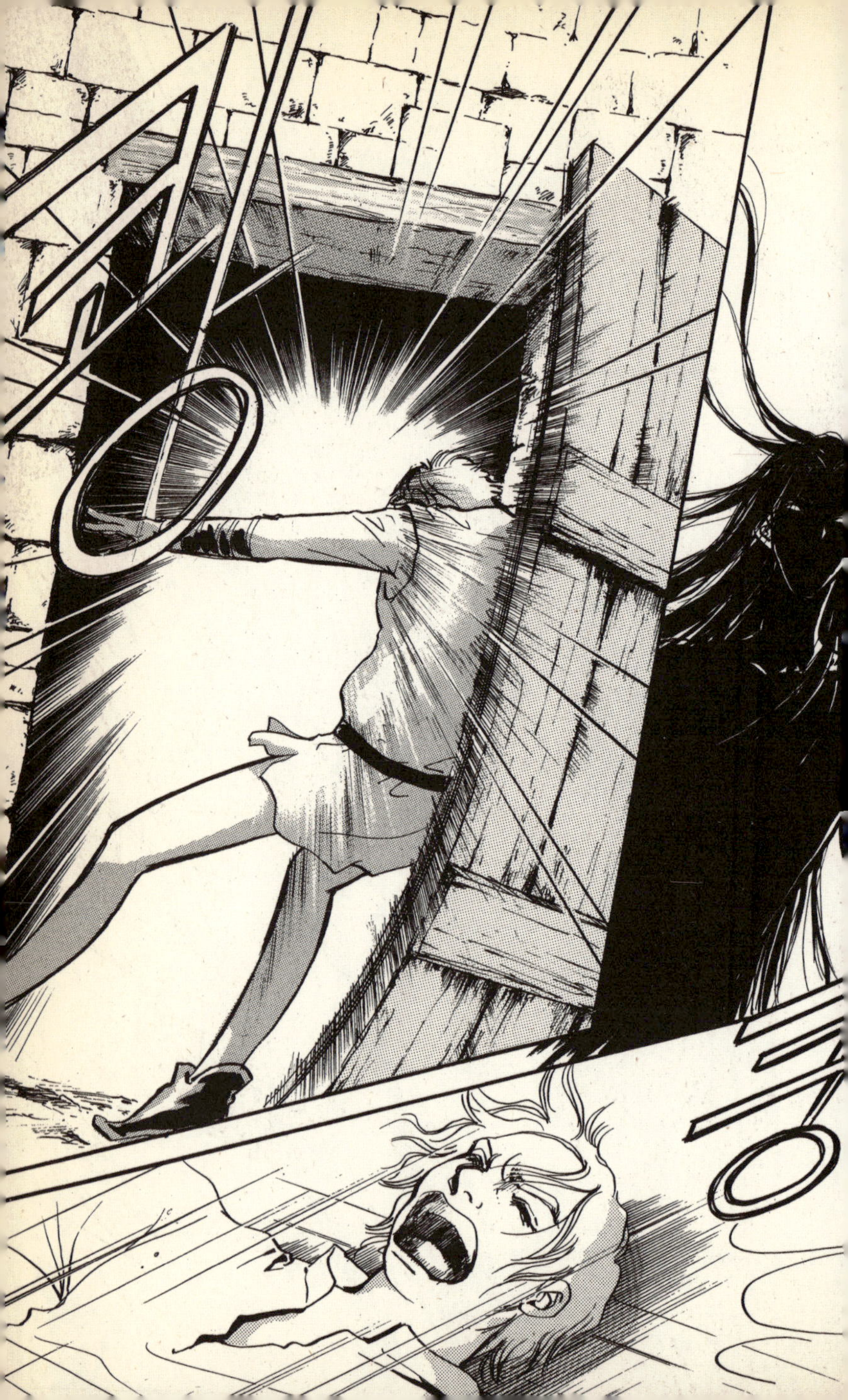

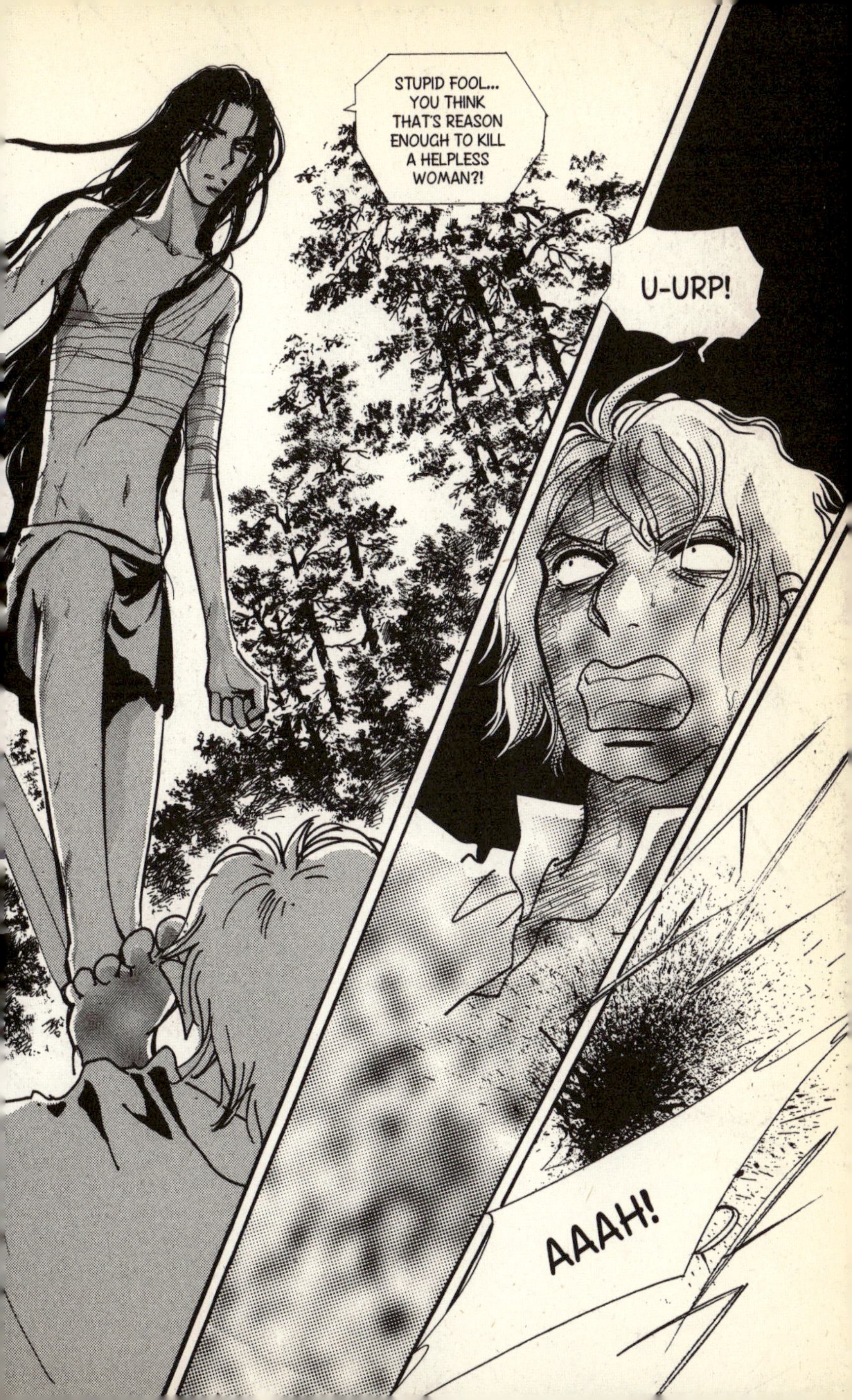
STUPID FOOL... YOU THINK THAT'S REASON ENOUGH TO KILL A HELPLESS WOMAN?!
U-URP!
AAAH!

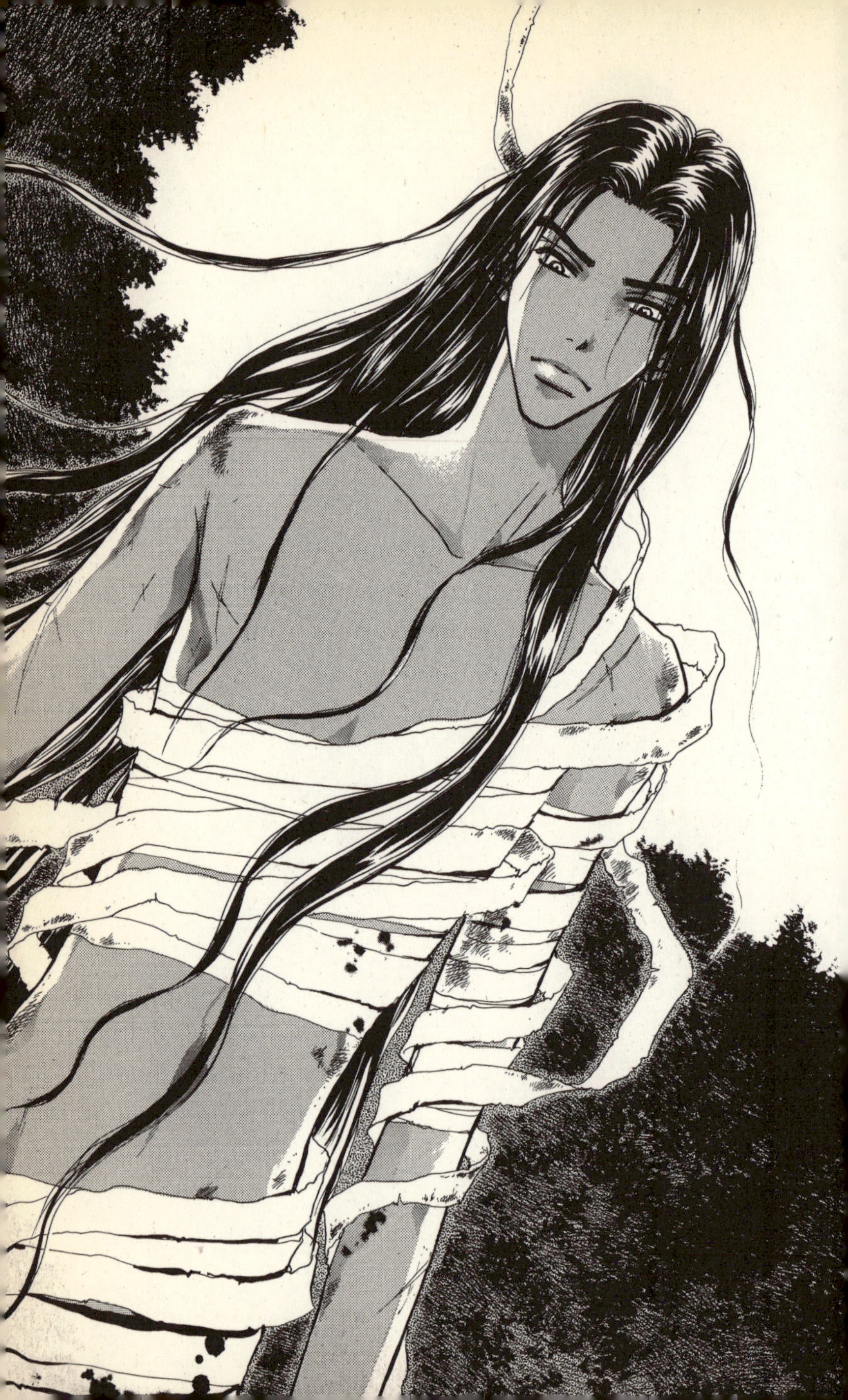

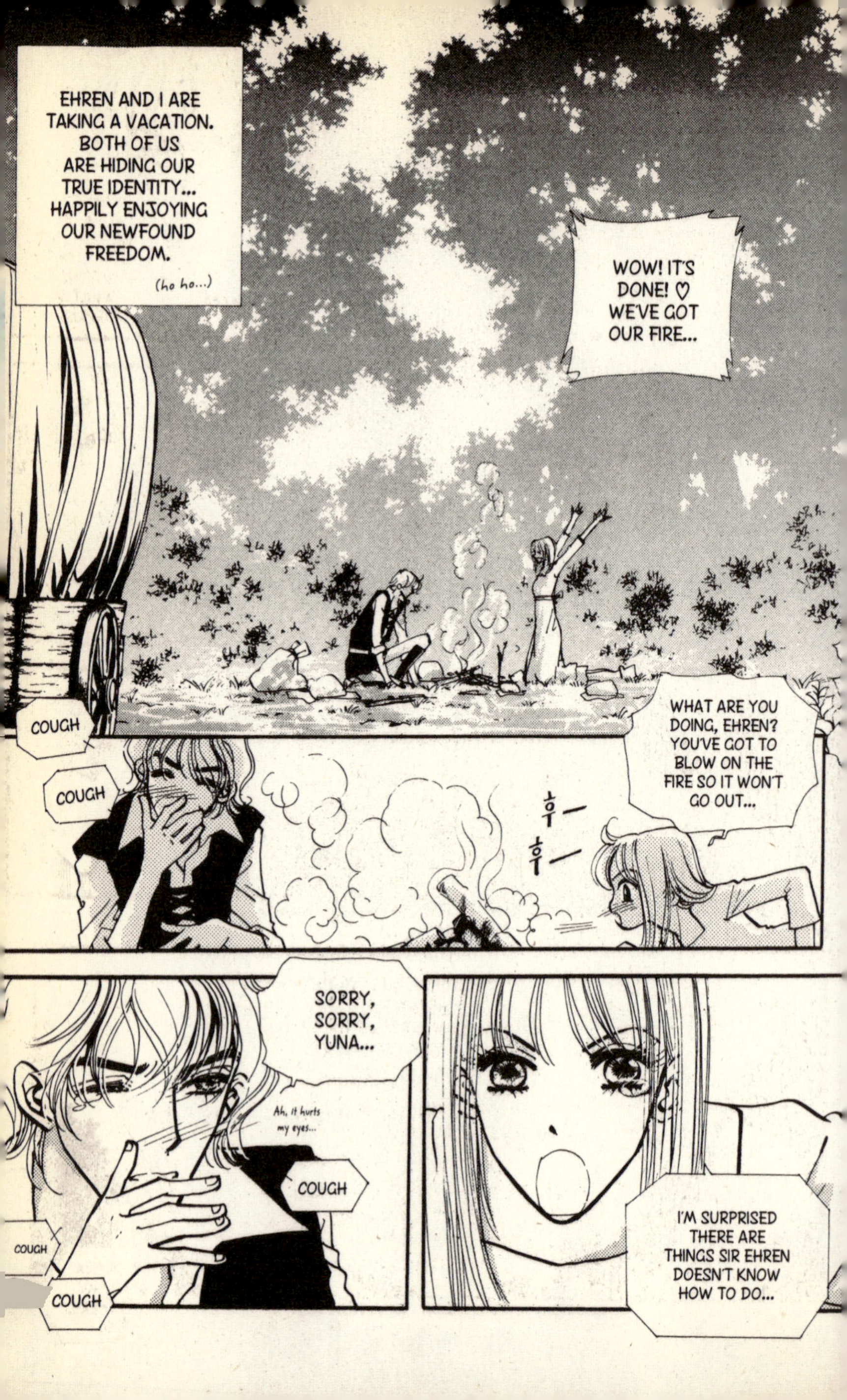
EHREN AND I ARE TAKING A VACATION. BOTH OF US ARE HIDING OUR TRUE IDENTITY... HAPPILY ENJOYING OUR NEWFOUND FREEDOM.
(ho ho...)
WOW! IT'S DONE! ♡ WE'VE GOT OUR FIRE...
COUGH
COUGH
WHAT ARE YOU DOING, EHREN? YOU'VE GOT TO BLOW ON THE FIRE SO IT WON'T GO OUT...
후—
후—
SORRY, SORRY, YUNA...
Ah, it hurts my eyes...
COUGH
COUGH
COUGH
I'M SURPRISED THERE ARE THINGS SIR EHREN DOESN'T KNOW HOW TO DO...

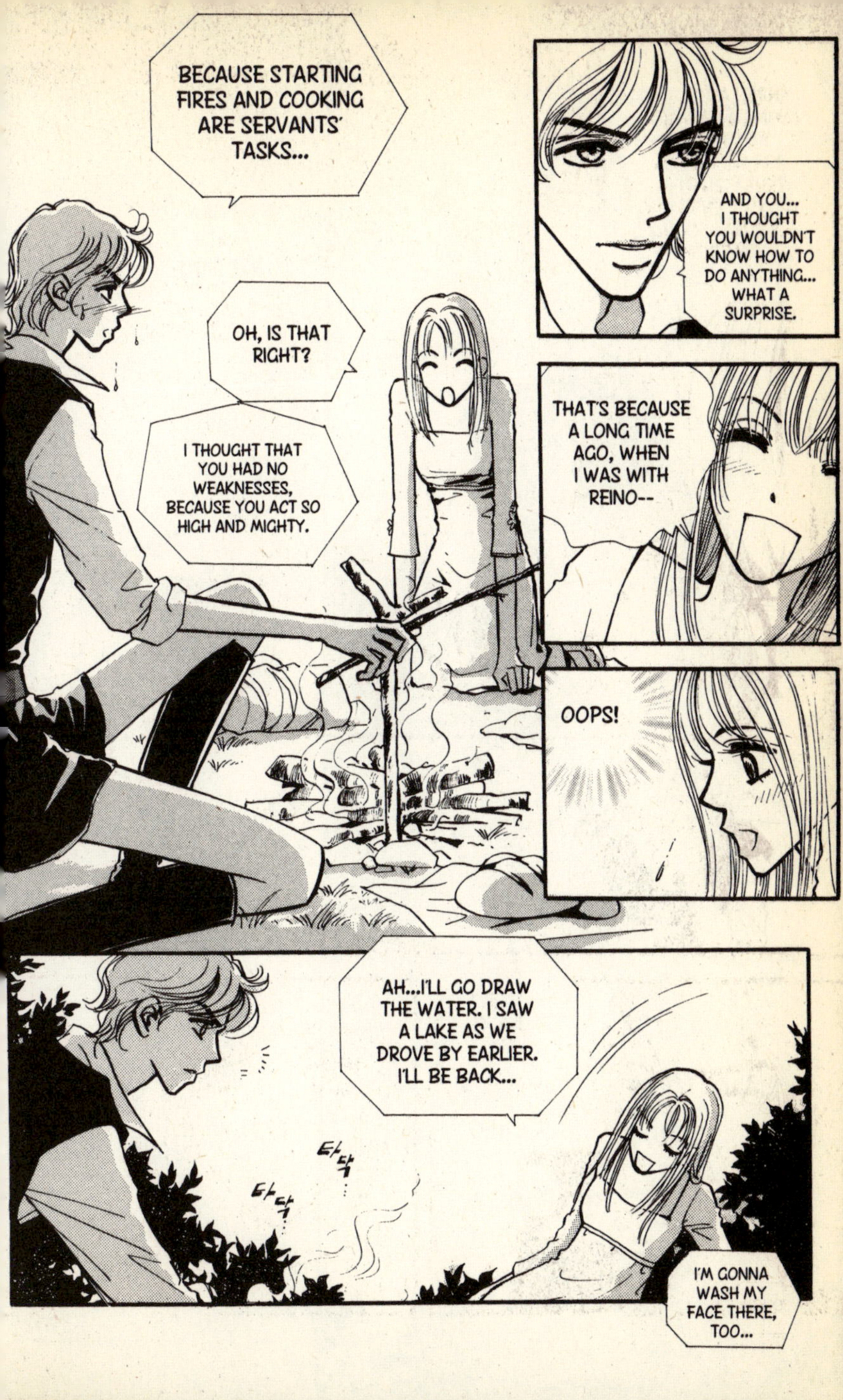
BECAUSE STARTING FIRES AND COOKING ARE SERVANTS' TASKS...
OH, IS THAT RIGHT?
I THOUGHT THAT YOU HAD NO WEAKNESSES, BECAUSE YOU ACT SO HIGH AND MIGHTY.
AND YOU... I THOUGHT YOU WOULDN'T KNOW HOW TO DO ANYTHING... WHAT A SURPRISE.
THAT'S BECAUSE A LONG TIME AGO, WHEN I WAS WITH REINO--
OOPS!
AH...I'LL GO DRAW THE WATER. I SAW A LAKE AS WE DROVE BY EARLIER. I'LL BE BACK...
타닥...
타닥...
I'M GONNA WASH MY FACE THERE, TOO...

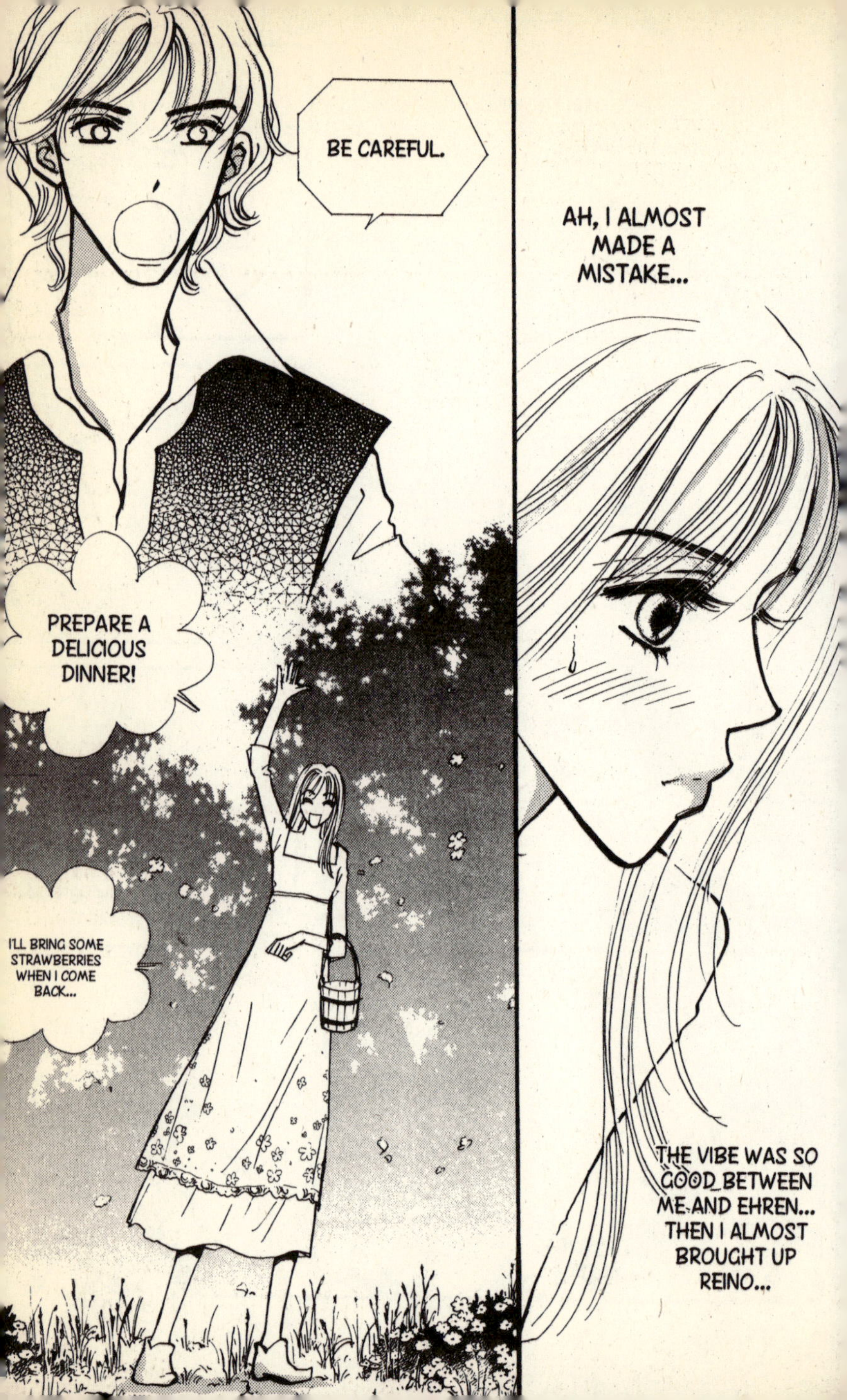
BE CAREFUL.
PREPARE A DELICIOUS DINNER!
I'LL BRING SOME STRAWBERRIES WHEN I COME BACK...
AH, I ALMOST MADE A MISTAKE...
THE VIBE WAS SO GOOD BETWEEN ME AND EHREN... THEN I ALMOST BROUGHT UP REINO...

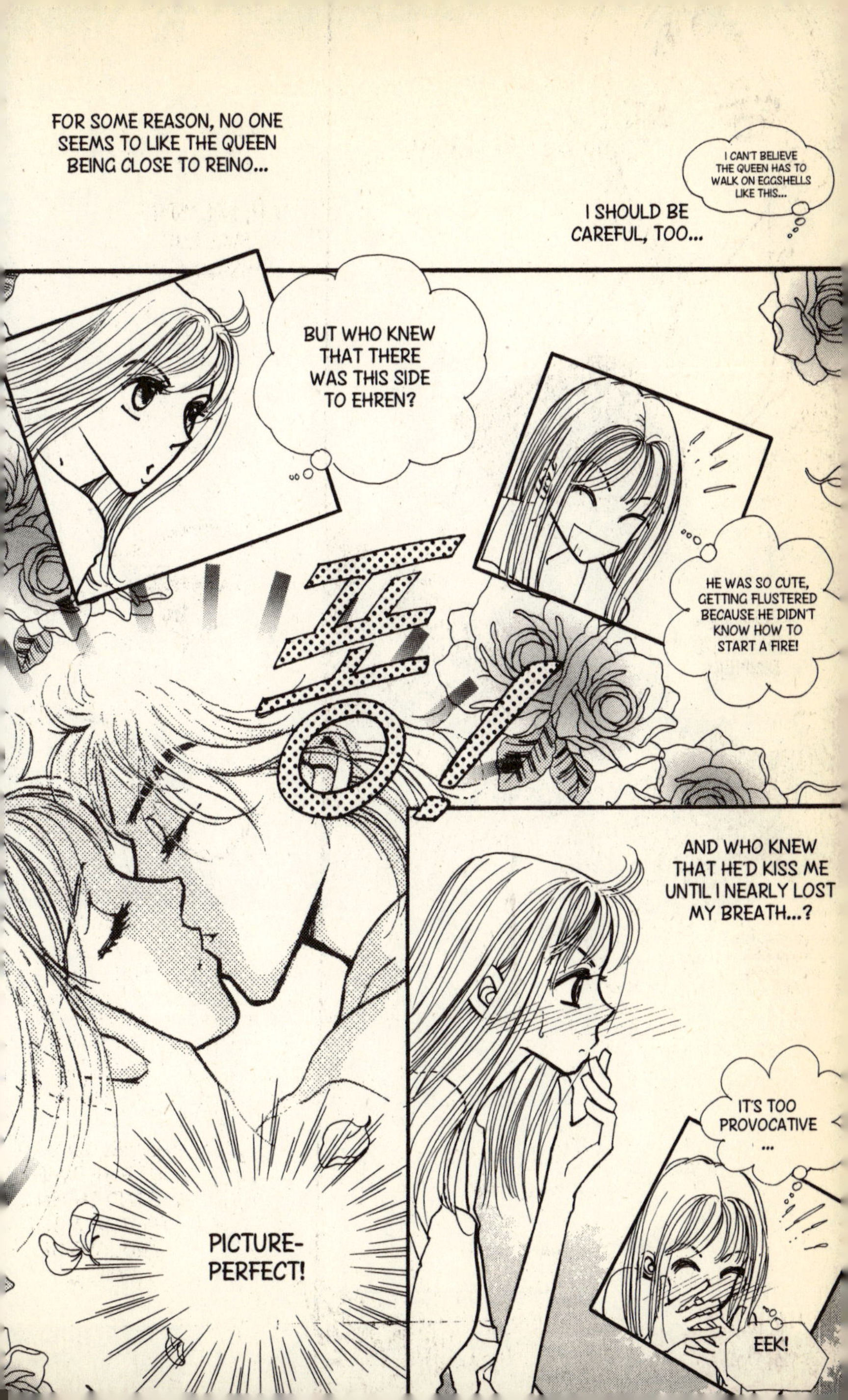
FOR SOME REASON, NO ONE SEEMS TO LIKE THE QUEEN BEING CLOSE TO REINO...
I CAN'T BELIEVE THE QUEEN HAS TO WALK ON EGGSHELLS LIKE THIS...
I SHOULD BE CAREFUL, TOO...
BUT WHO KNEW THAT THERE WAS THIS SIDE TO EHREN?
HE WAS SO CUTE, GETTING FLUSTERED BECAUSE HE DIDN'T KNOW HOW TO START A FIRE!
PICTURE-PERFECT!
AND WHO KNEW THAT HE'D KISS ME UNTIL I NEARLY LOST MY BREATH...?
IT'S TOO PROVOCATIVE ...
EEK!

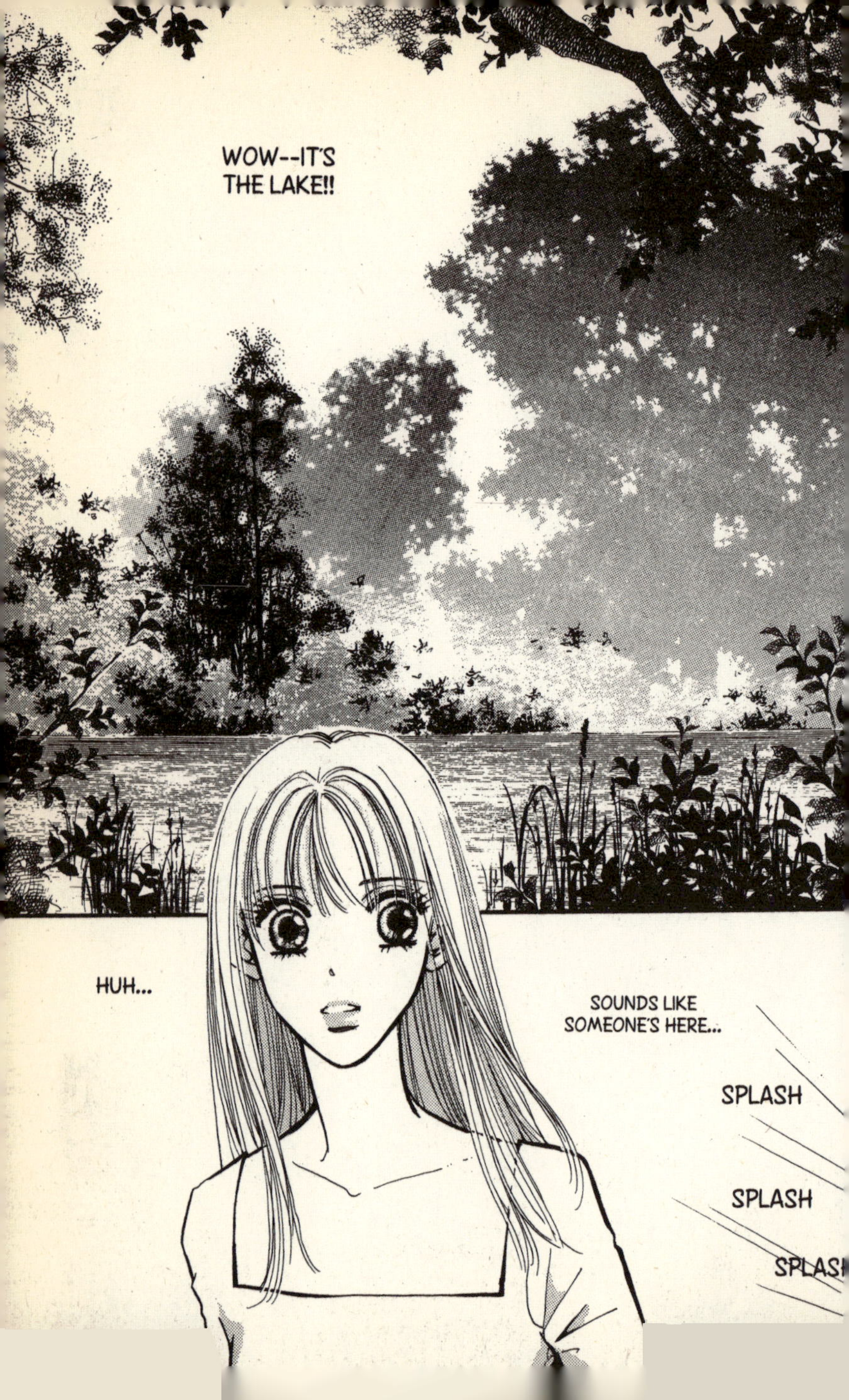
WOW--IT'S THE LAKE!!
HUH...
SOUNDS LIKE SOMEONE'S HERE...
SPLASH
SPLASH
SPLAS

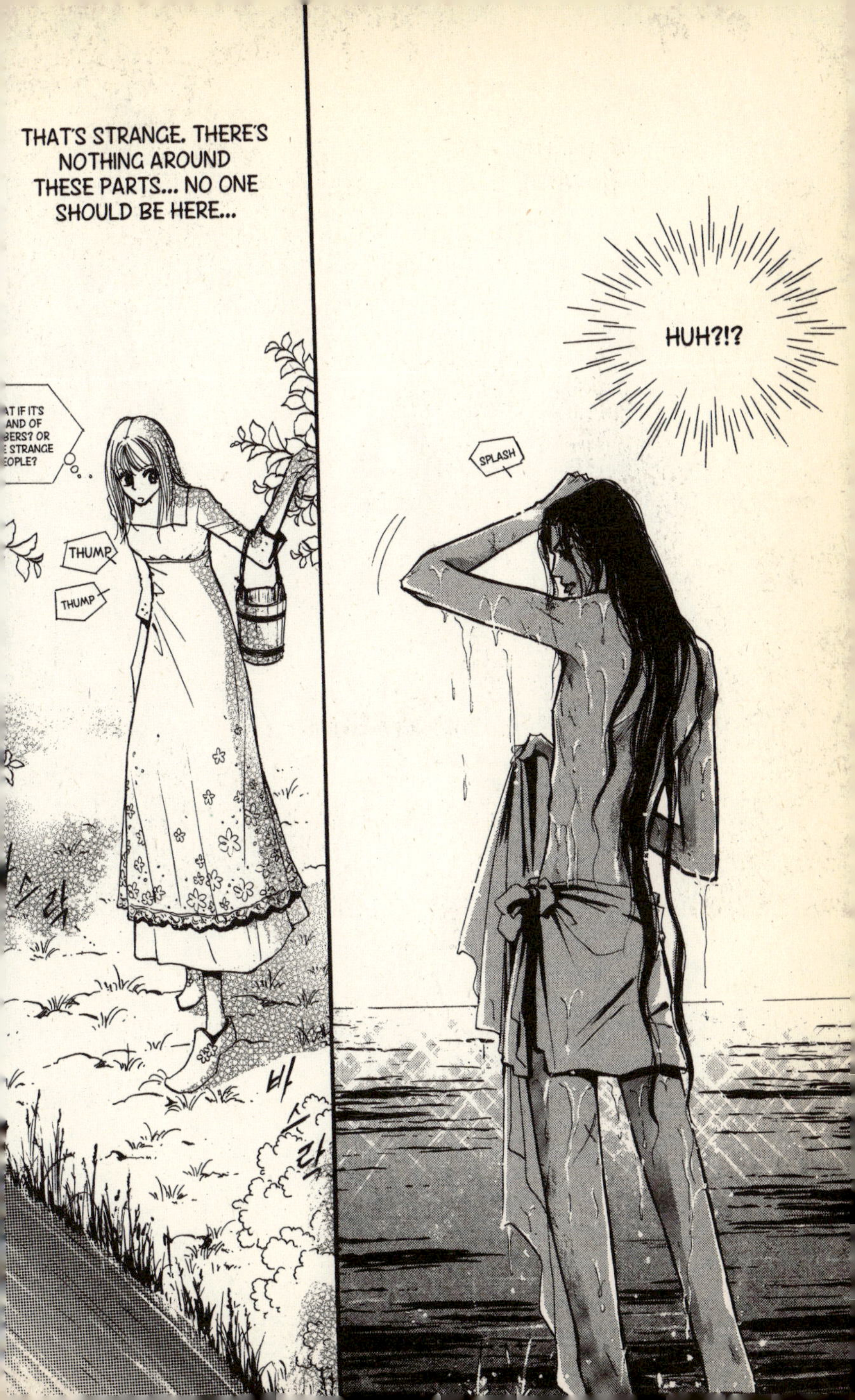
THAT'S STRANGE. THERE'S NOTHING AROUND THESE PARTS... NO ONE SHOULD BE HERE...
AT IF IT'S AND OF BERS? OR E STRANGE EOPLE?
THUMP
THUMP
바스락
HUH?!?
SPLASH

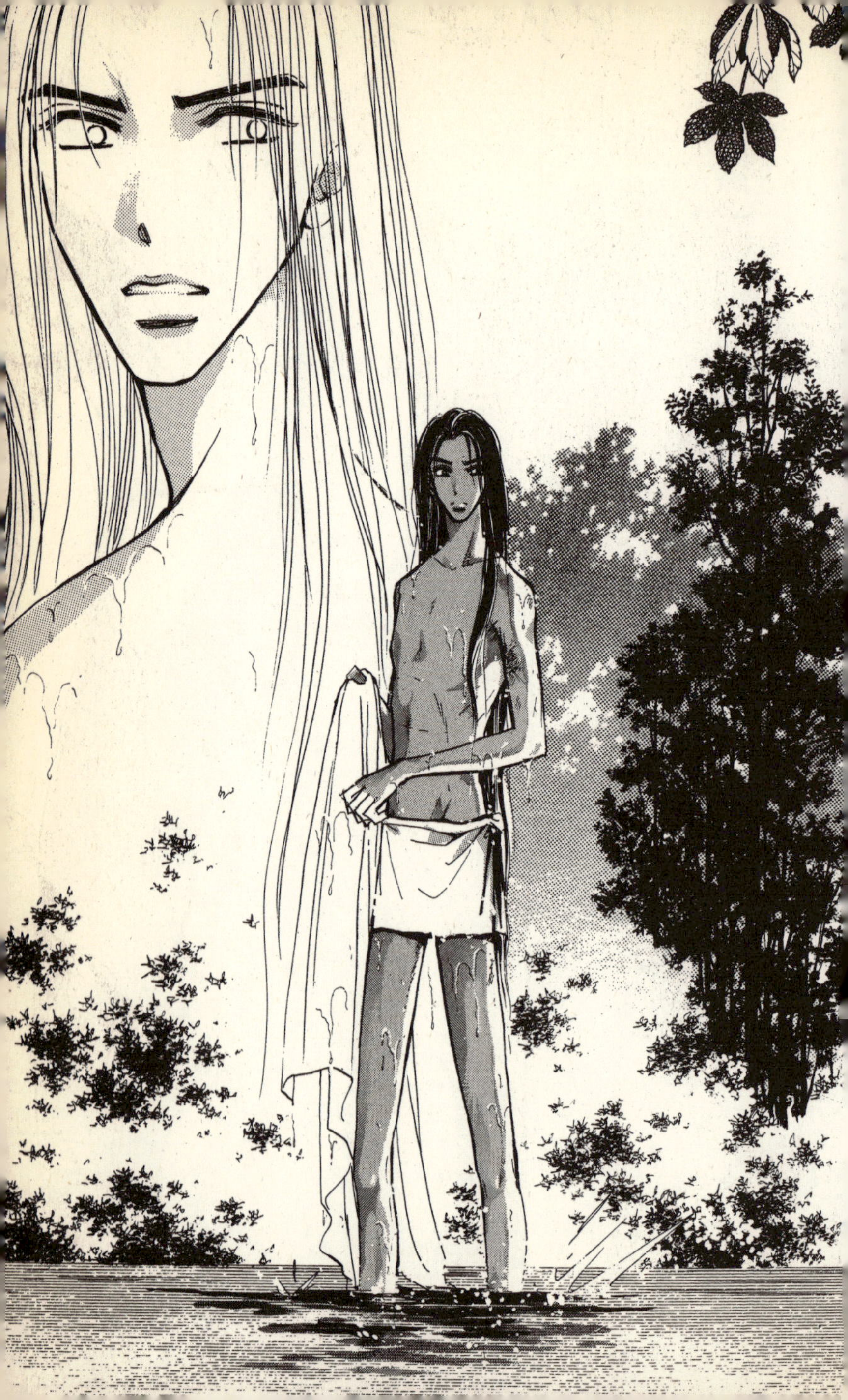

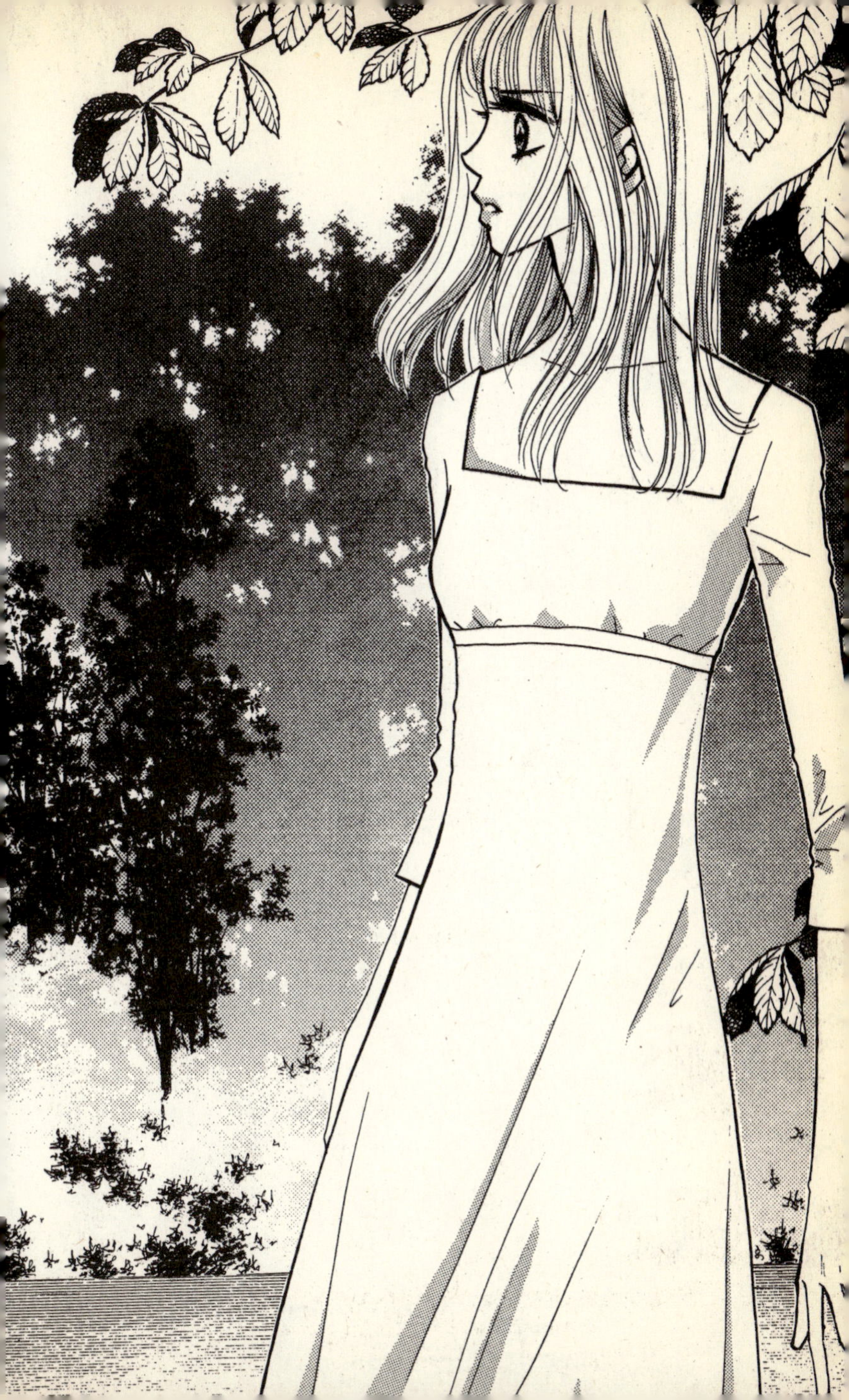

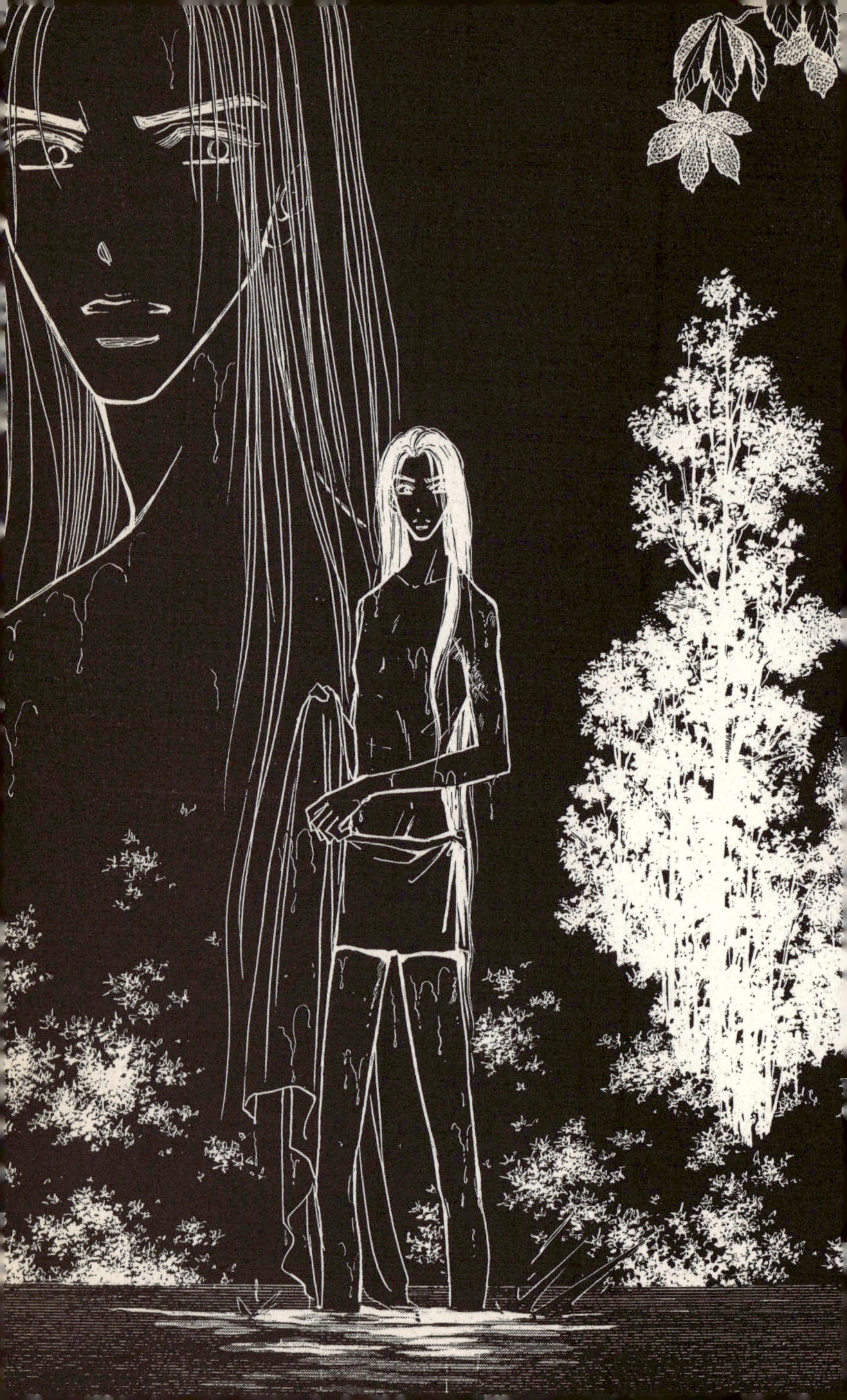

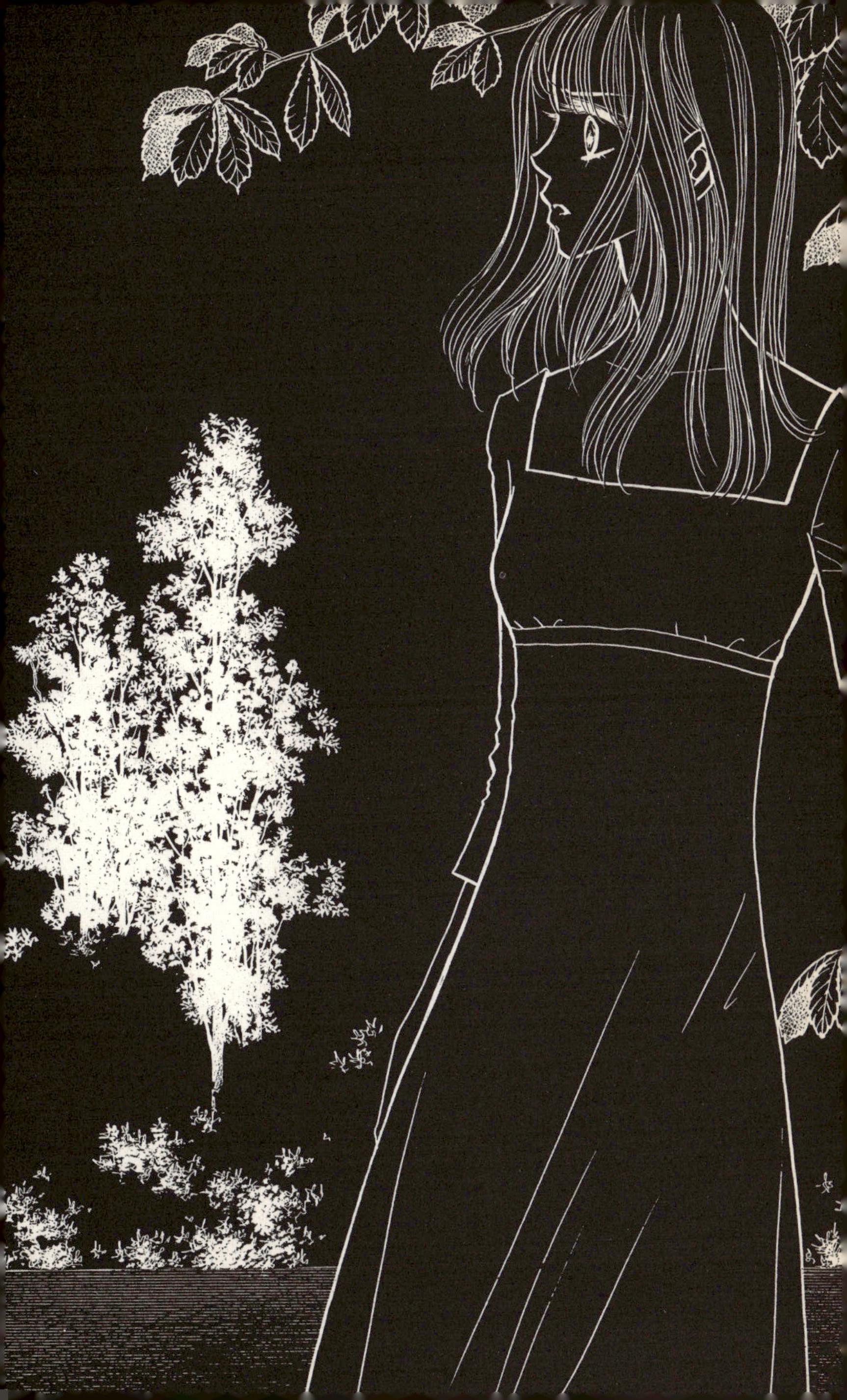

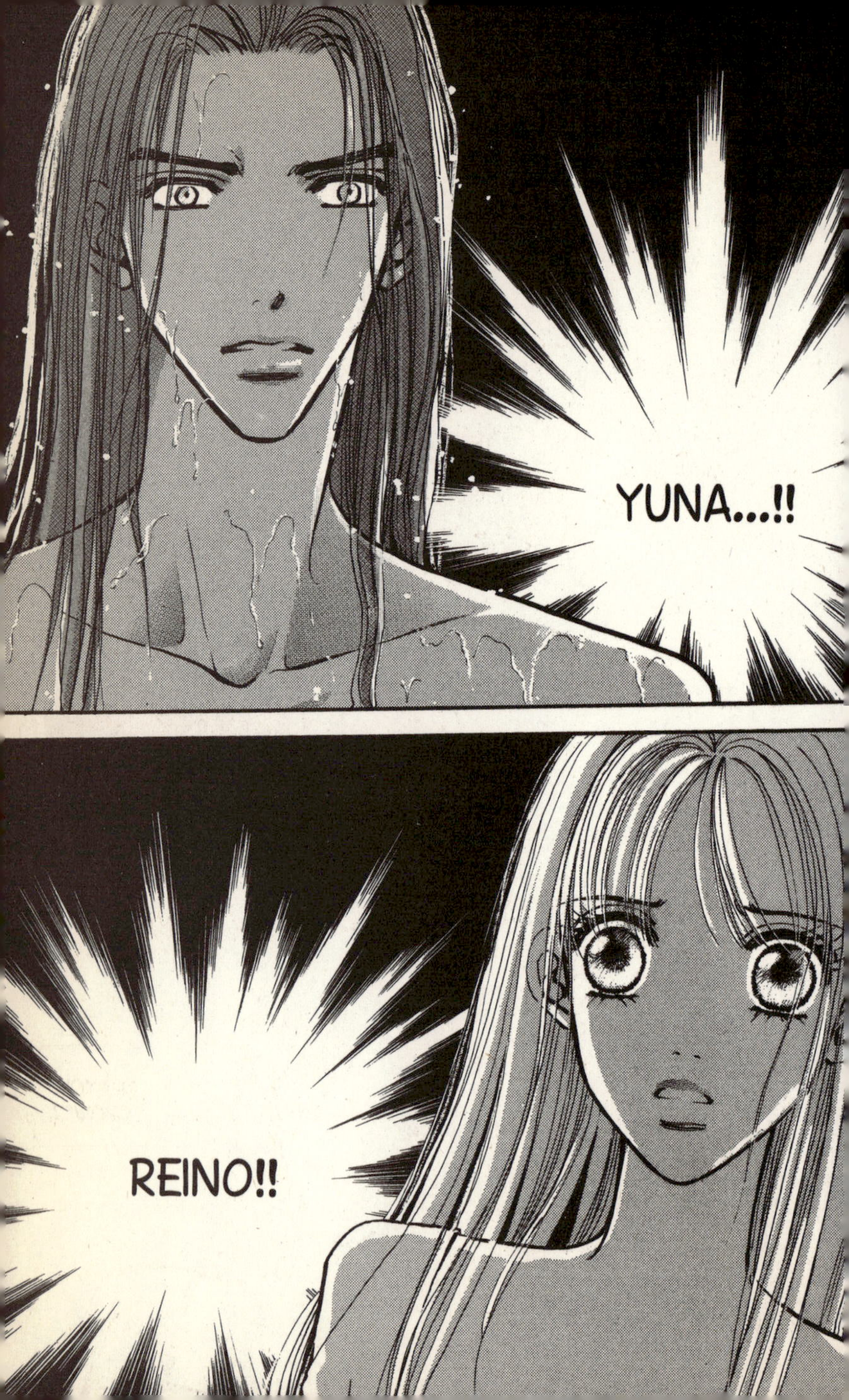
YUNA...!!
REINO!!

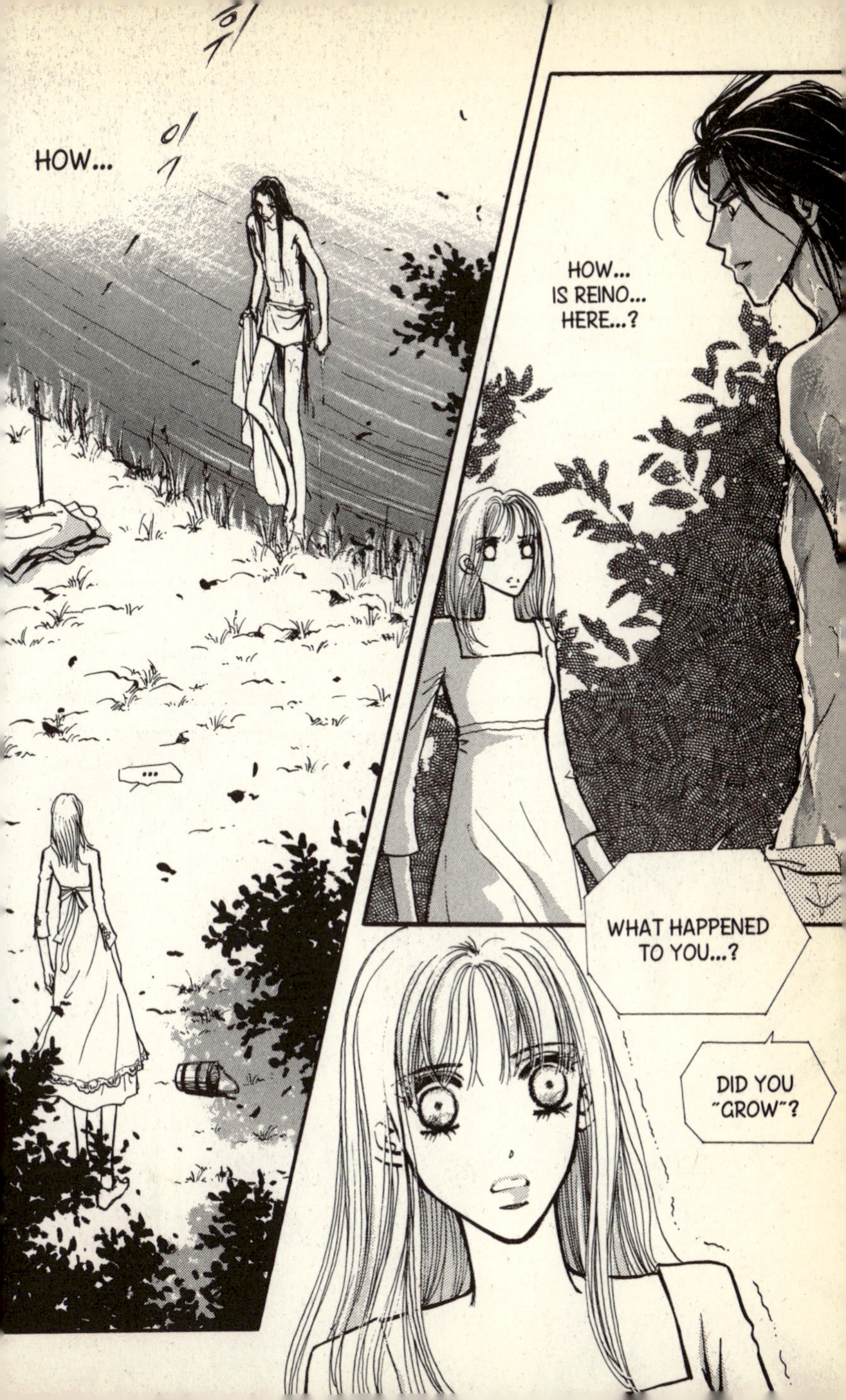
히
이
HOW...
...
HOW... IS REINO... HERE...?
WHAT HAPPENED TO YOU...?
DID YOU "GROW"?

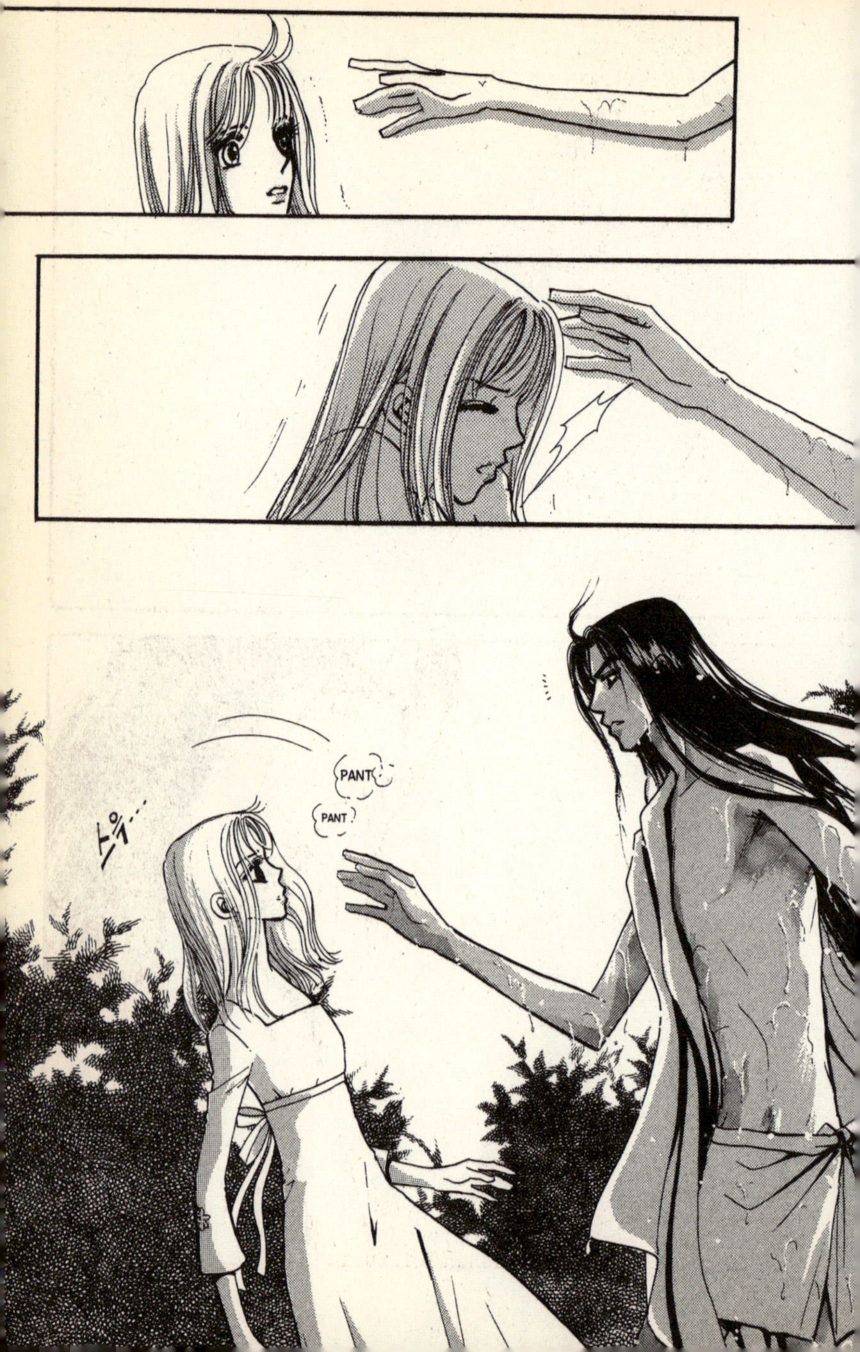
PANT
PANT

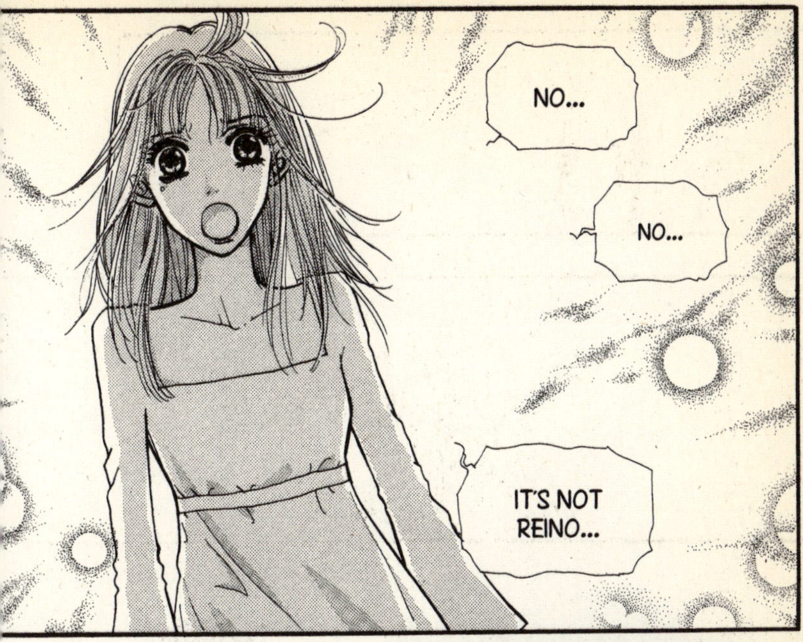
NO...
NO...
IT'S NOT REINO...

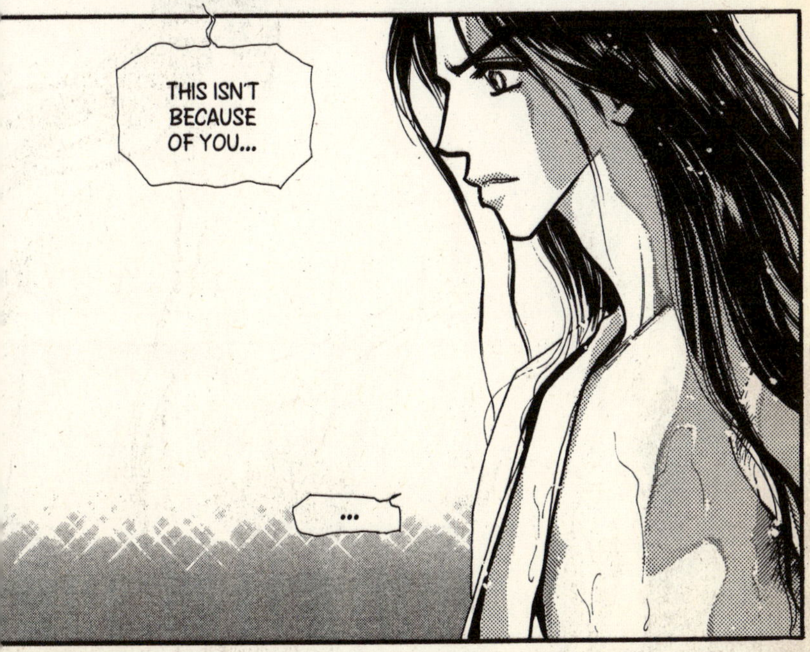
THIS ISN'T BECAUSE OF YOU...
...

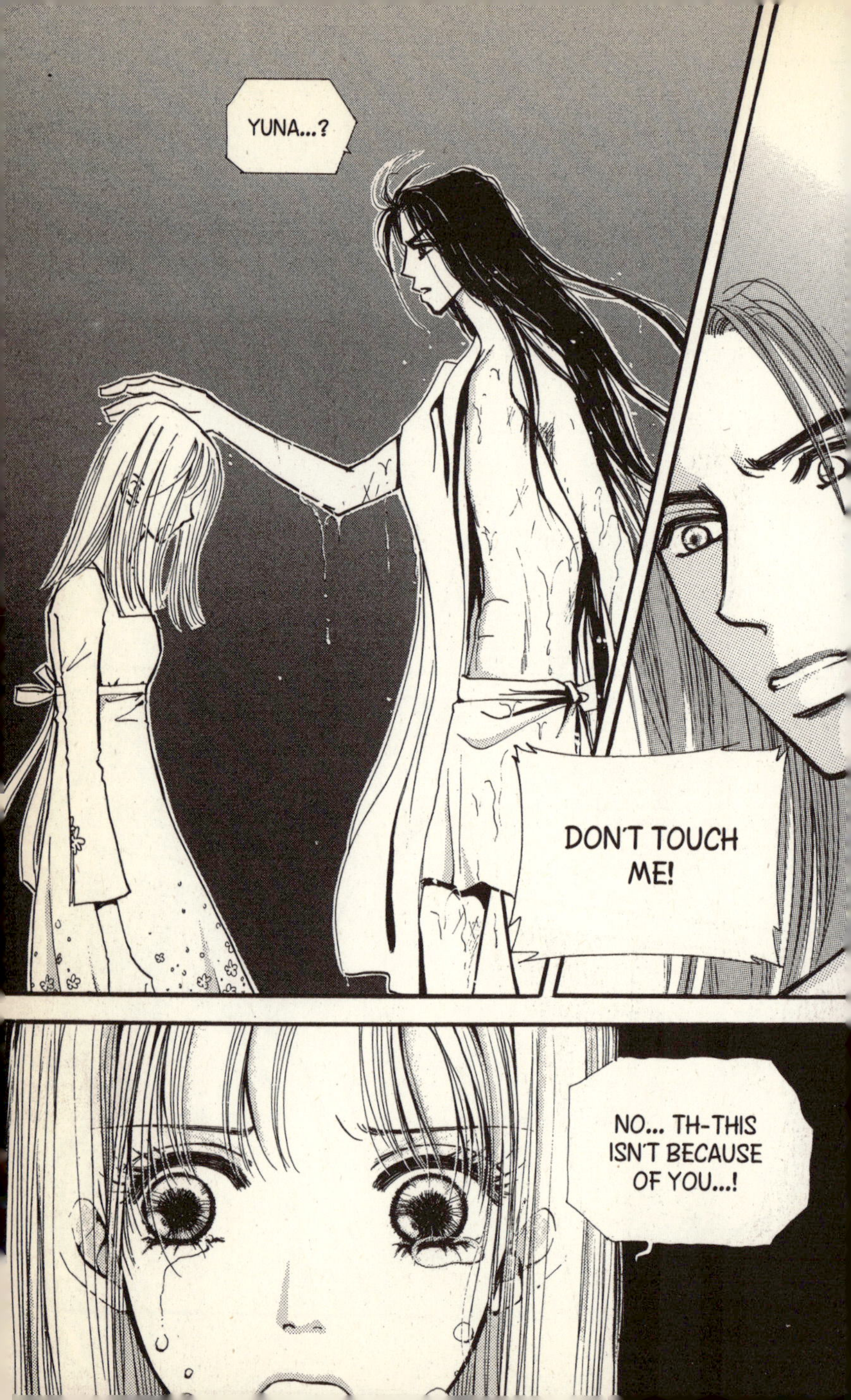
YUNA...?
DON'T TOUCH ME!
NO... TH-THIS ISN'T BECAUSE OF YOU...!

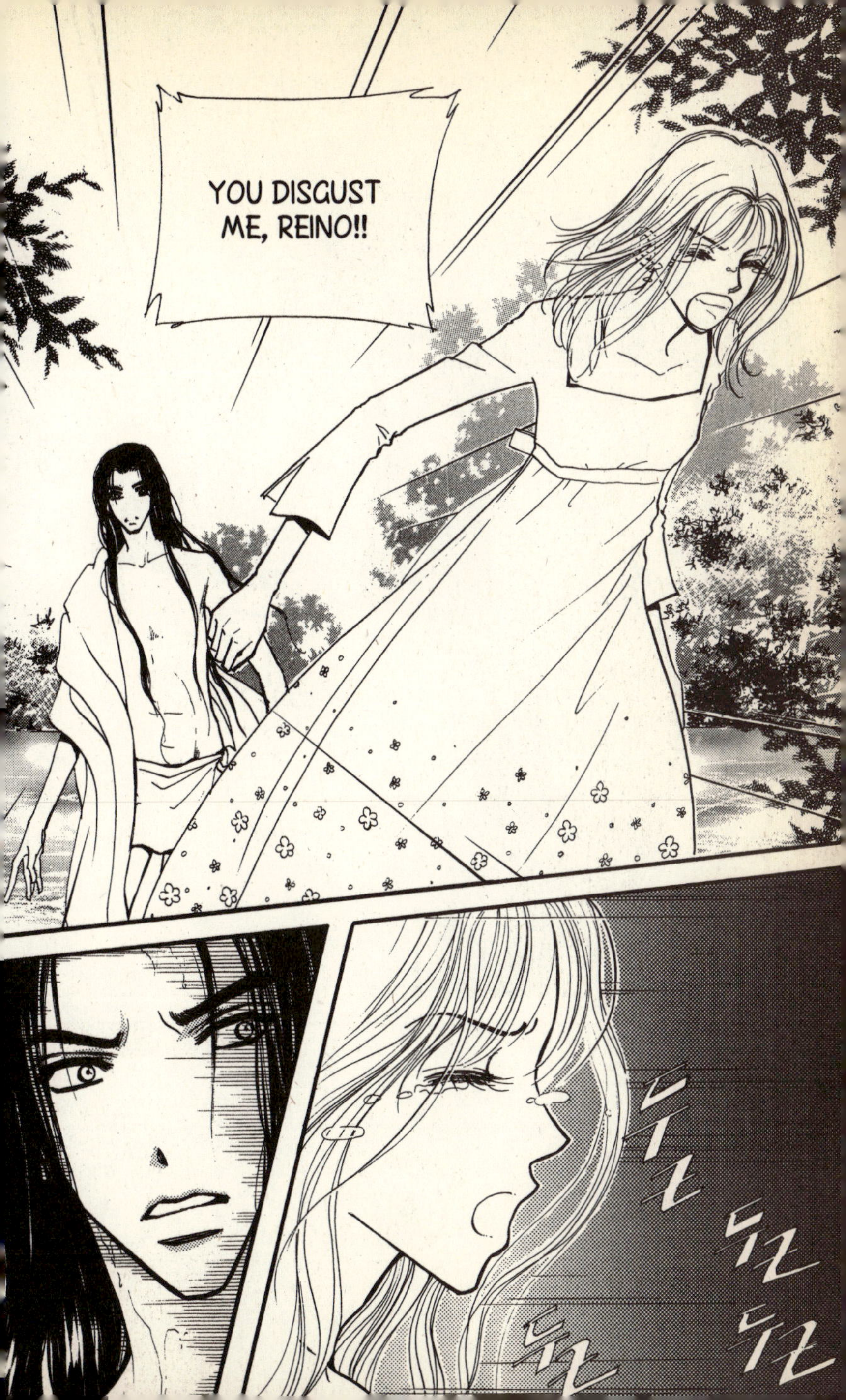
YOU DISGUST ME, REINO!!

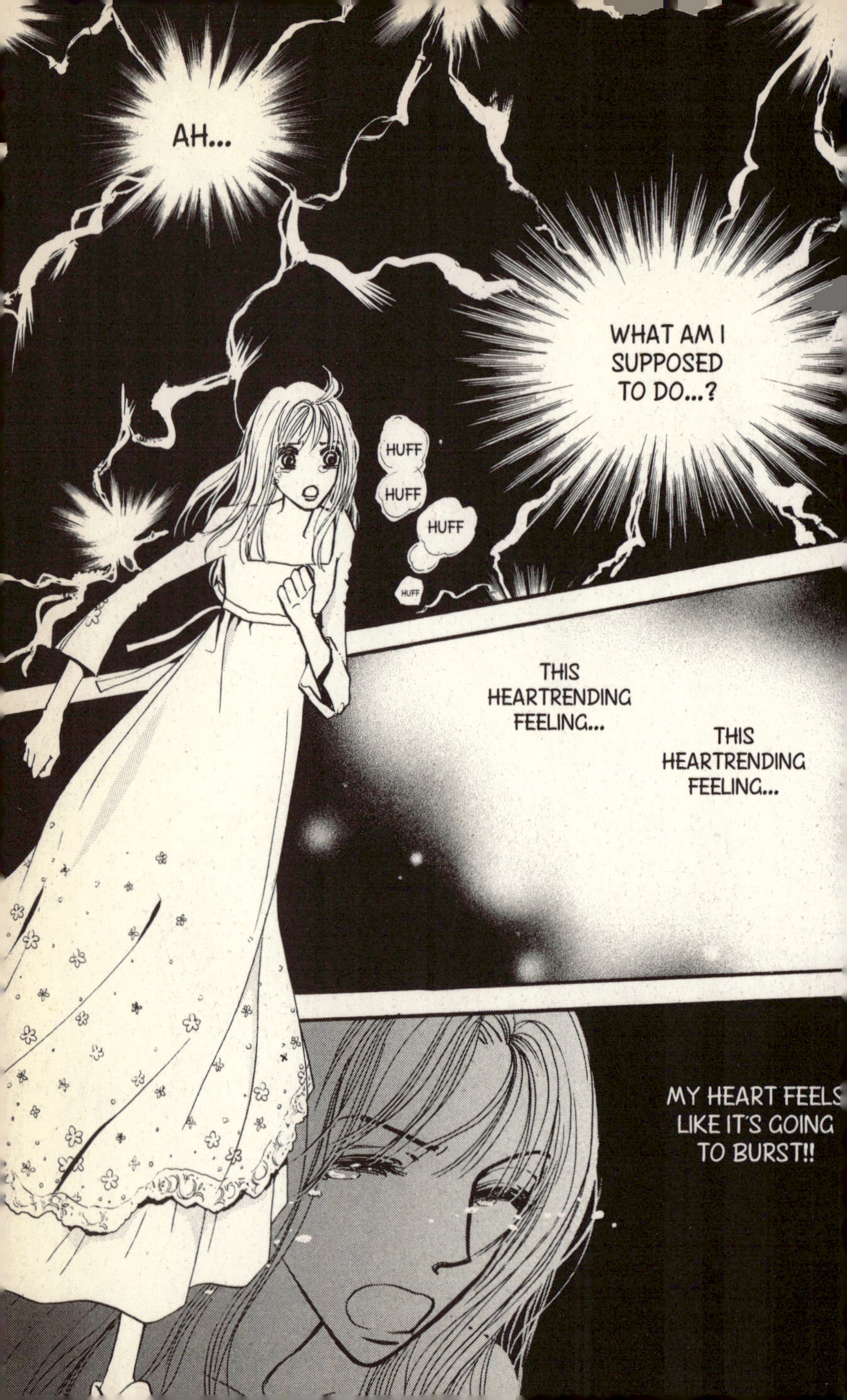
AH...
WHAT AM I SUPPOSED TO DO...?
HUFF
HUFF
HUFF
HUFF
THIS HEARTRENDING FEELING...
THIS HEARTRENDING FEELING...
MY HEART FEELS LIKE IT'S GOING TO BURST!!

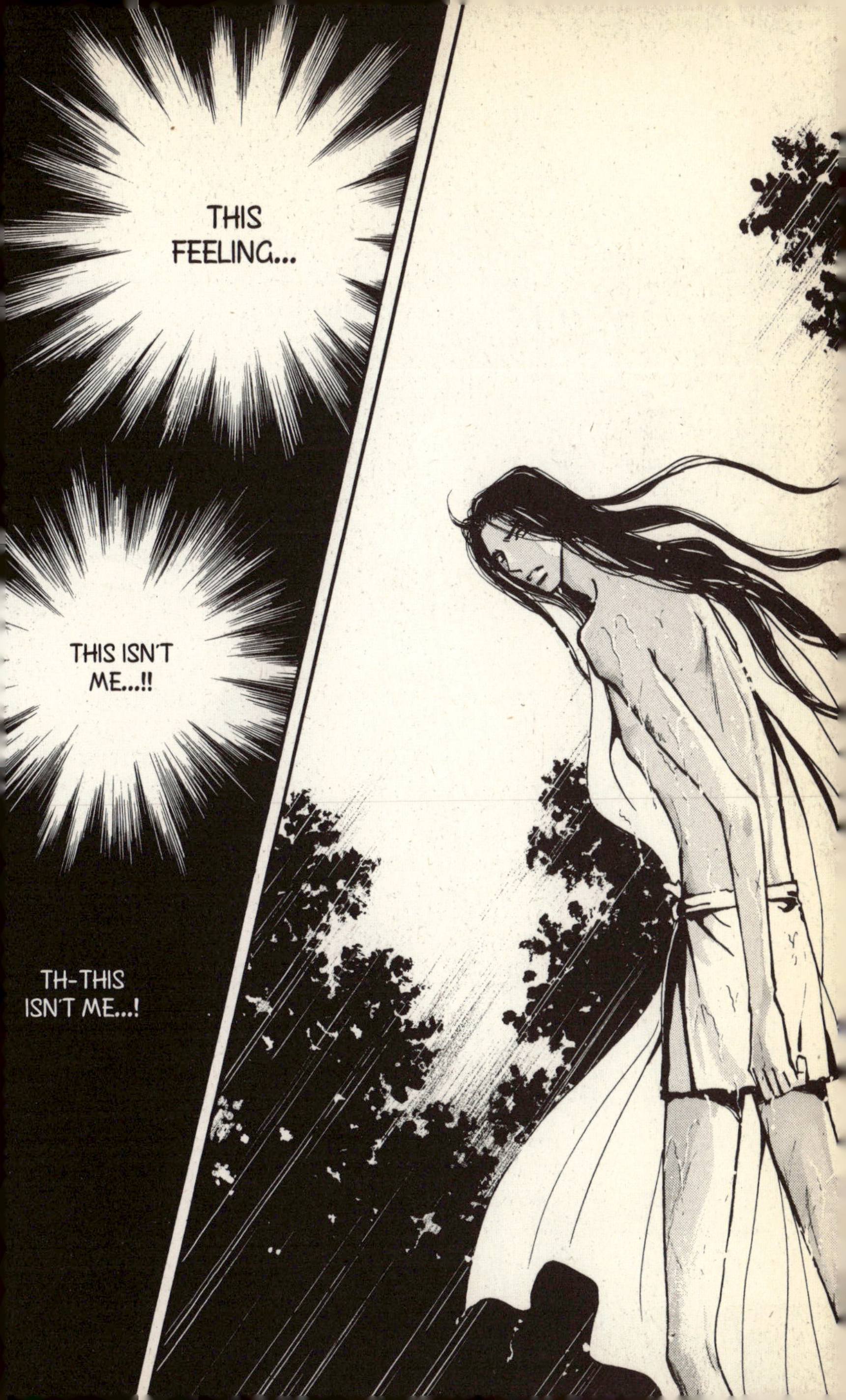
THIS FEELING...
THIS ISN'T ME...!!
TH-THIS ISN'T ME...!

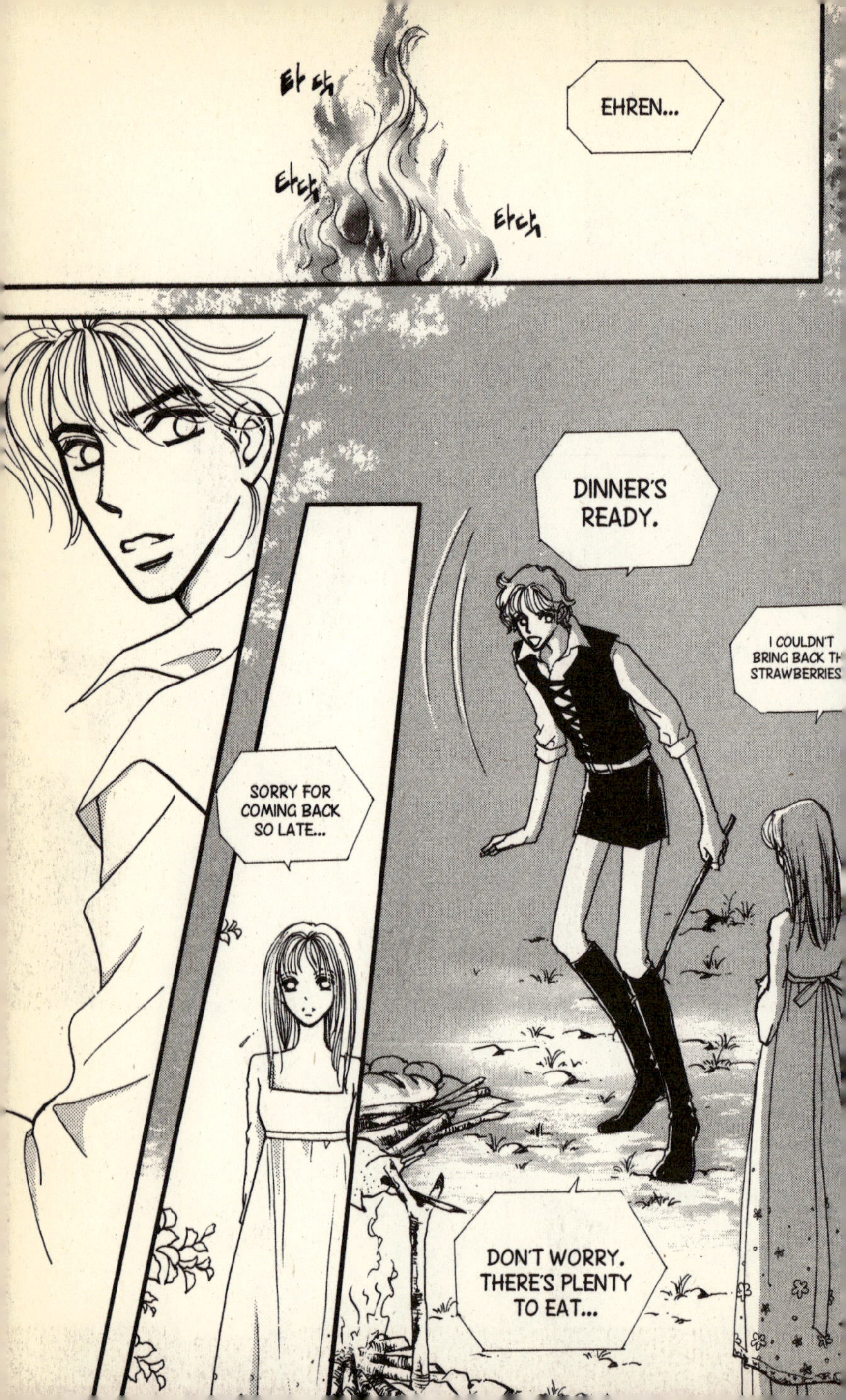
타닥
타닥
타닥
EHREN...
SORRY FOR COMING BACK SO LATE...
DINNER'S READY.
I COULDN'T BRING BACK TH STRAWBERRIES
DON'T WORRY. THERE'S PLENTY TO EAT...

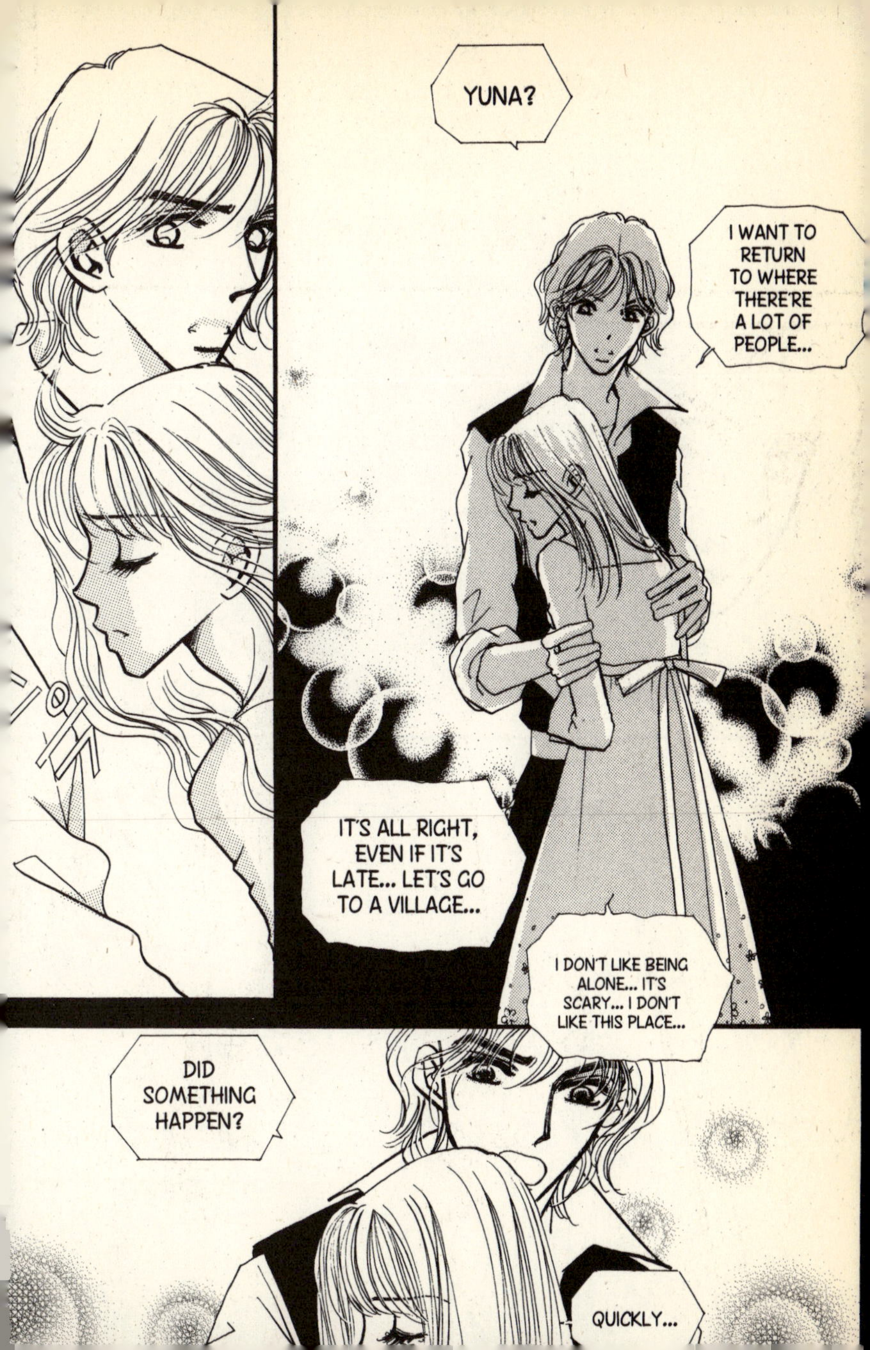
YUNA?
I WANT TO RETURN TO WHERE THERE'RE A LOT OF PEOPLE...
IT'S ALL RIGHT, EVEN IF IT'S LATE... LET'S GO TO A VILLAGE...
I DON'T LIKE BEING ALONE... IT'S SCARY... I DON'T LIKE THIS PLACE...
DID SOMETHING HAPPEN?
QUICKLY...

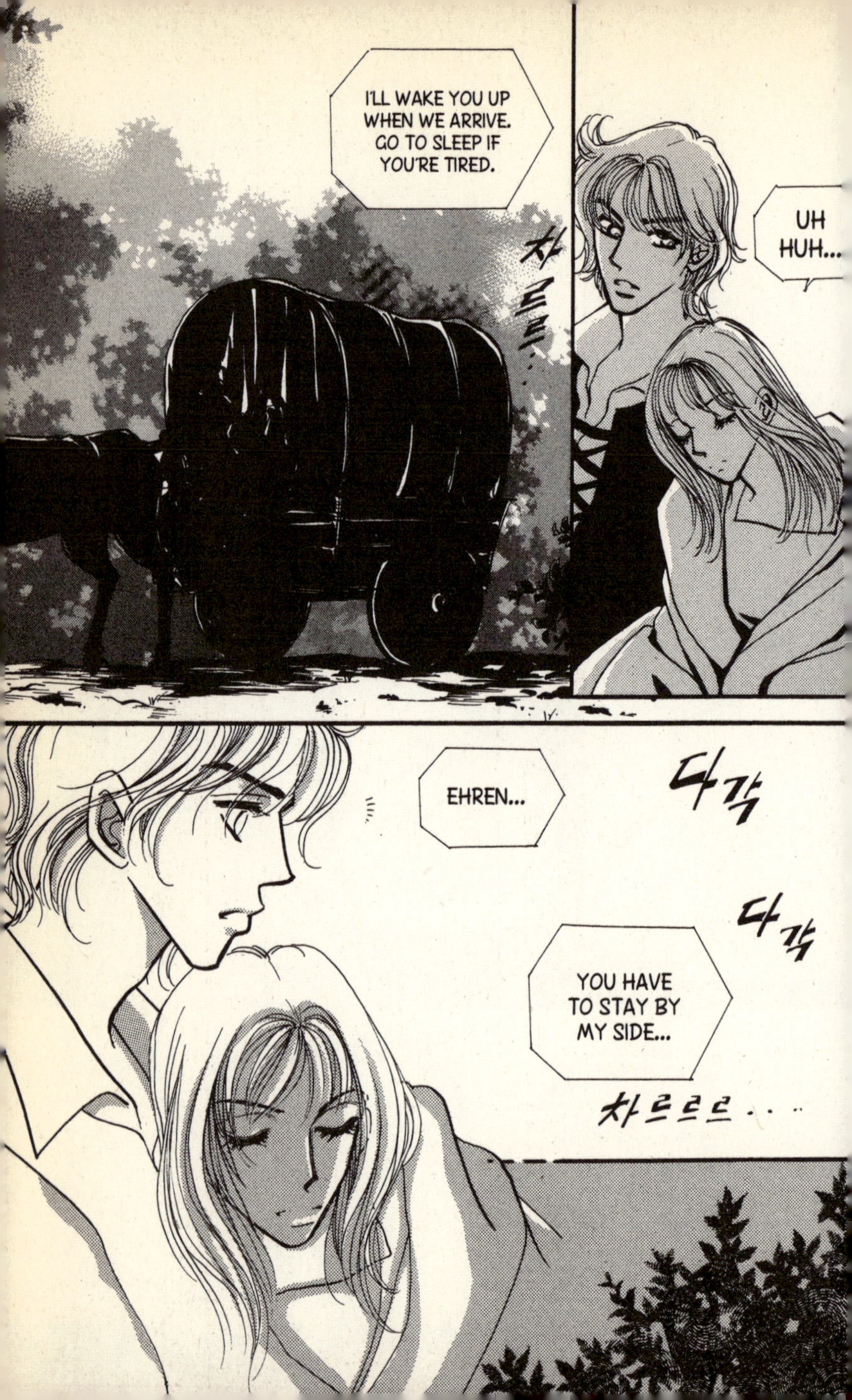
I'LL WAKE YOU UP WHEN WE ARRIVE. GO TO SLEEP IF YOU'RE TIRED.
차르르...
UH HUH...
EHREN...
다각
다각
YOU HAVE TO STAY BY MY SIDE...
차르르르...

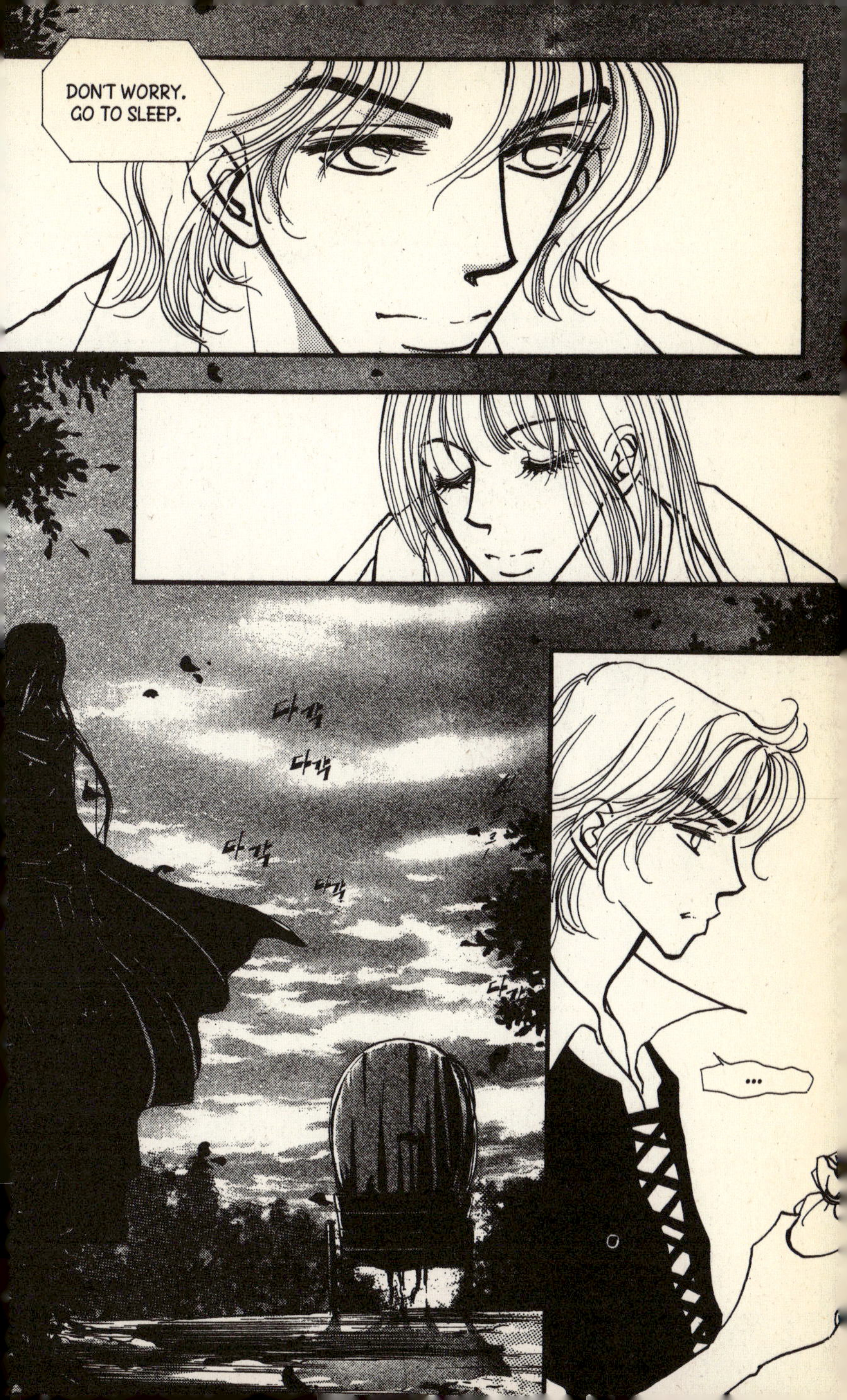
DON'T WORRY.
GO TO SLEEP.
다각
다각
다각
다각
...

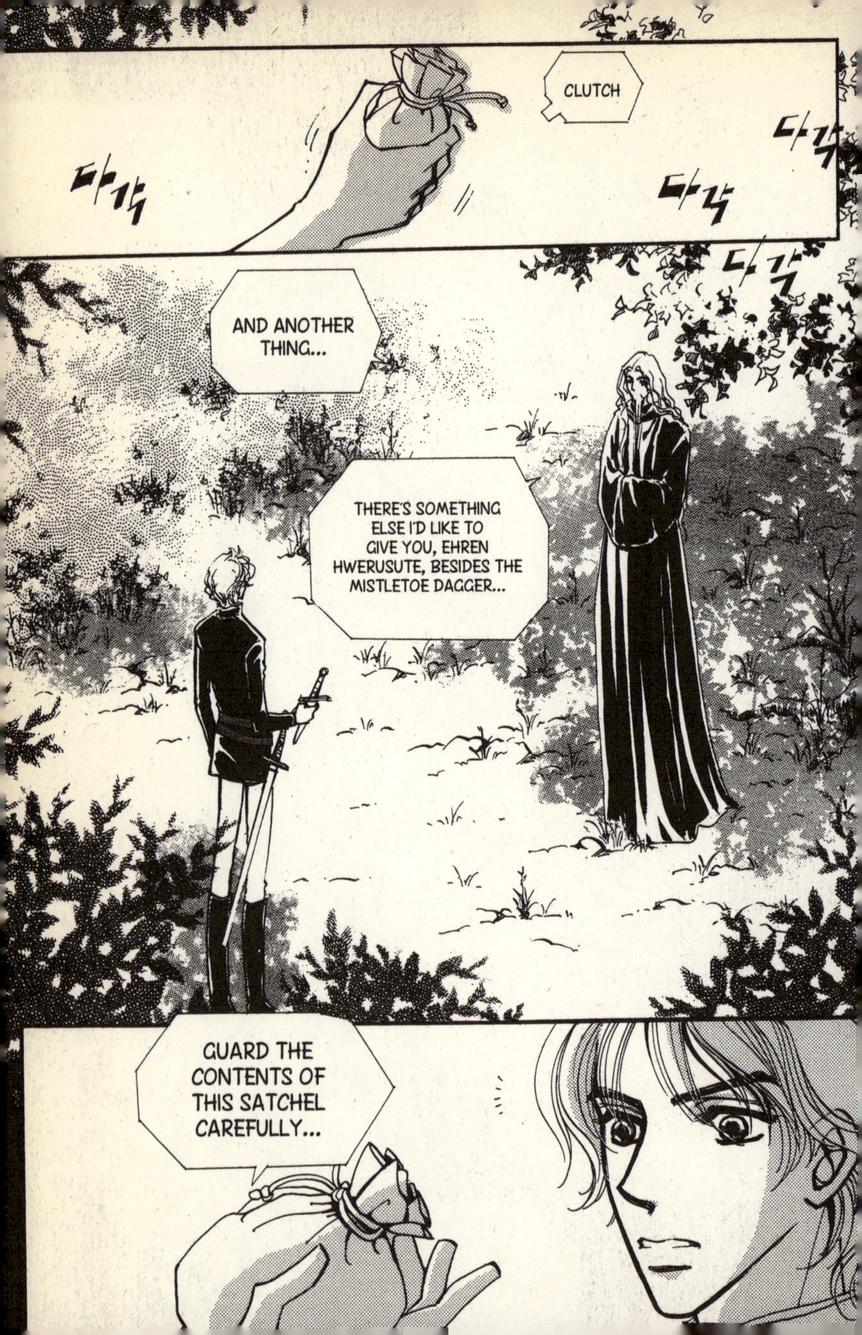
CLUTCH
다각
다각
다각
다각
AND ANOTHER THING...
THERE'S SOMETHING ELSE I'D LIKE TO GIVE YOU, EHREN HWERUSUTE, BESIDES THE MISTLETOE DAGGER...
GUARD THE CONTENTS OF THIS SATCHEL CAREFULLY...

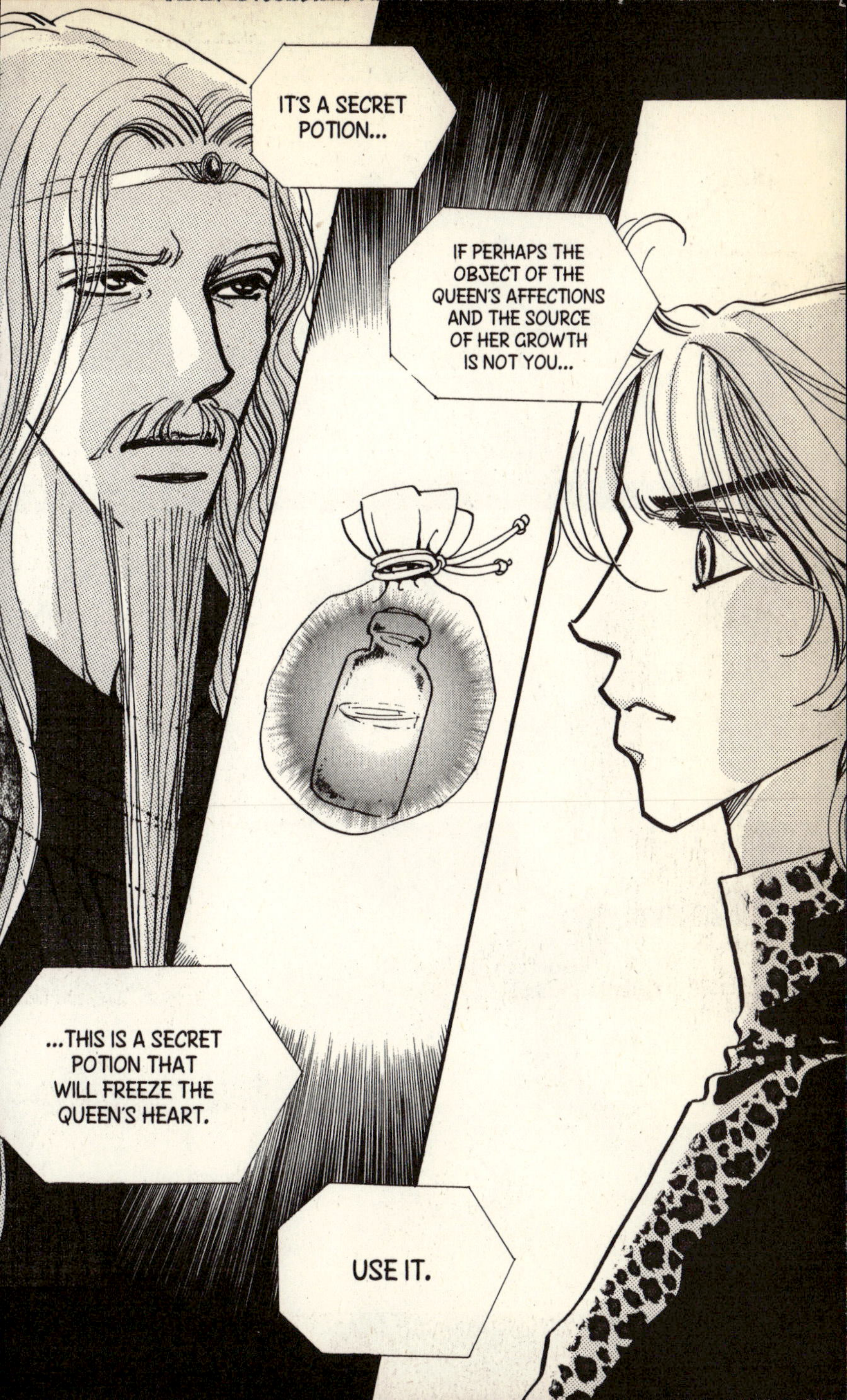
IT'S A SECRET POTION...
IF PERHAPS THE OBJECT OF THE QUEEN'S AFFECTIONS AND THE SOURCE OF HER GROWTH IS NOT YOU...
...THIS IS A SECRET POTION THAT WILL FREEZE THE QUEEN'S HEART.
USE IT.

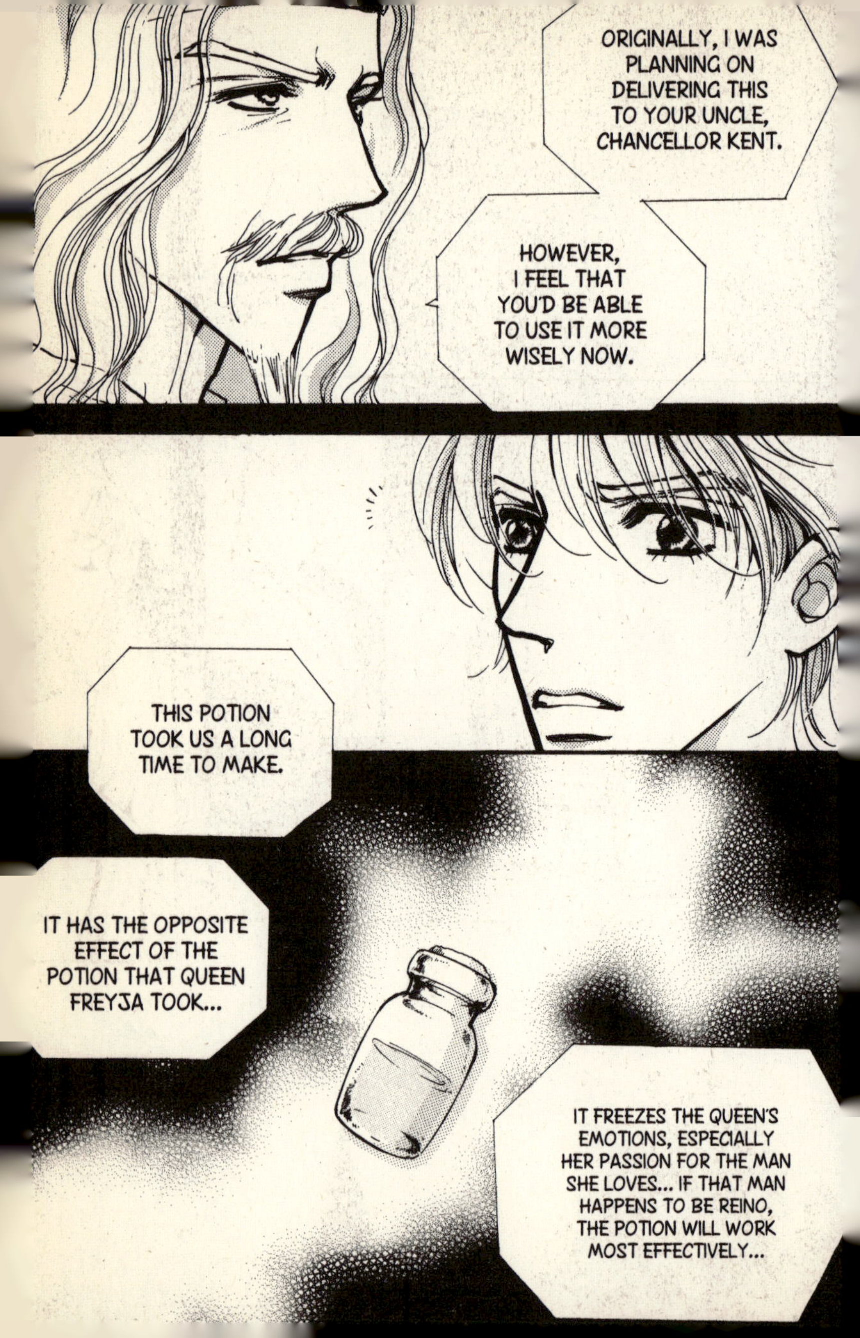
ORIGINALLY, I WAS PLANNING ON DELIVERING THIS TO YOUR UNCLE, CHANCELLOR KENT.
HOWEVER, I FEEL THAT YOU'D BE ABLE TO USE IT MORE WISELY NOW.
THIS POTION TOOK US A LONG TIME TO MAKE.
IT HAS THE OPPOSITE EFFECT OF THE POTION THAT QUEEN FREYJA TOOK...
IT FREEZES THE QUEEN'S EMOTIONS, ESPECIALLY HER PASSION FOR THE MAN SHE LOVES... IF THAT MAN HAPPENS TO BE REINO, THE POTION WILL WORK MOST EFFECTIVELY...

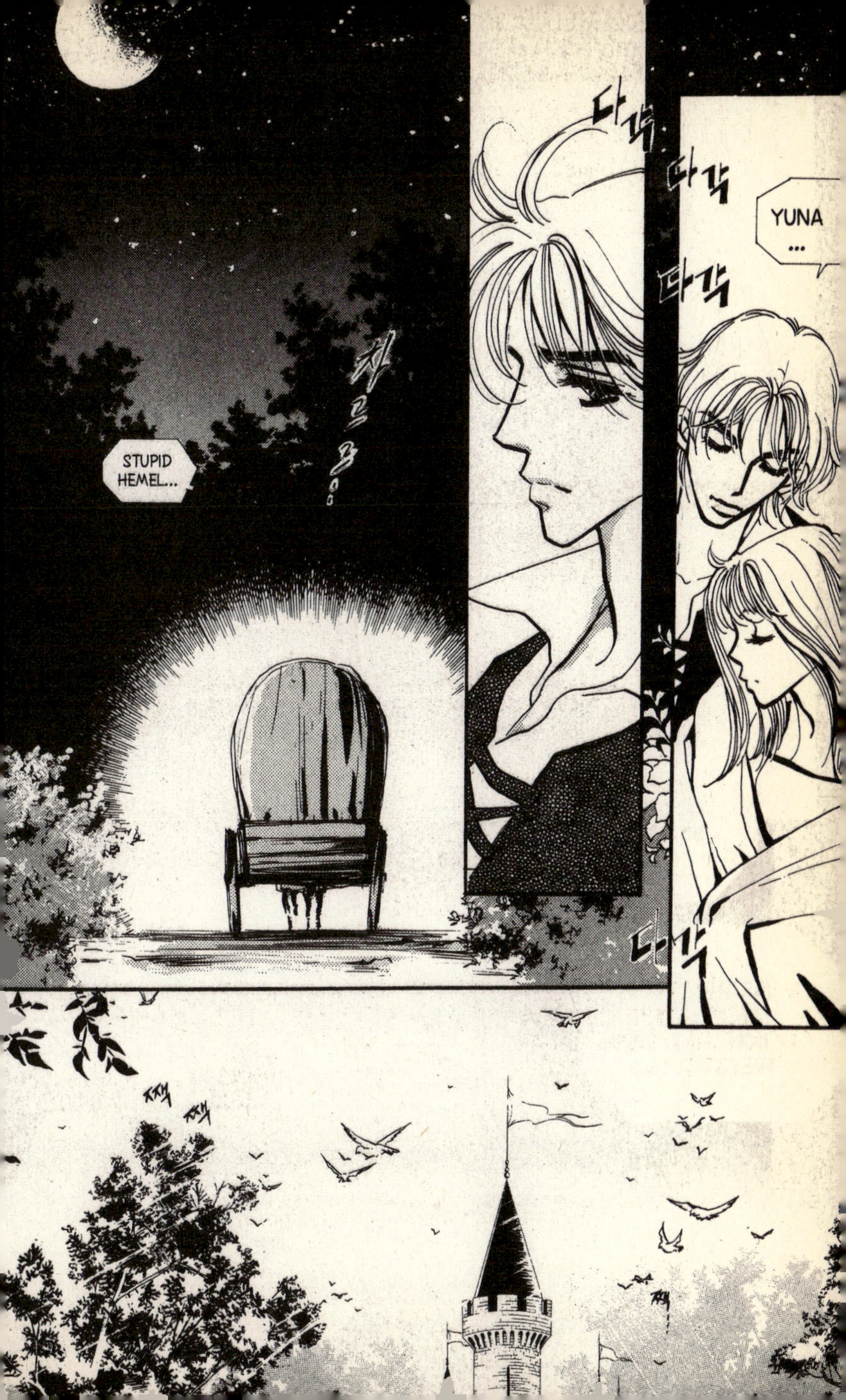
STUPID HEMEL...
처르릉..
다각
다각
다각
YUNA ...
다각
짹
짹

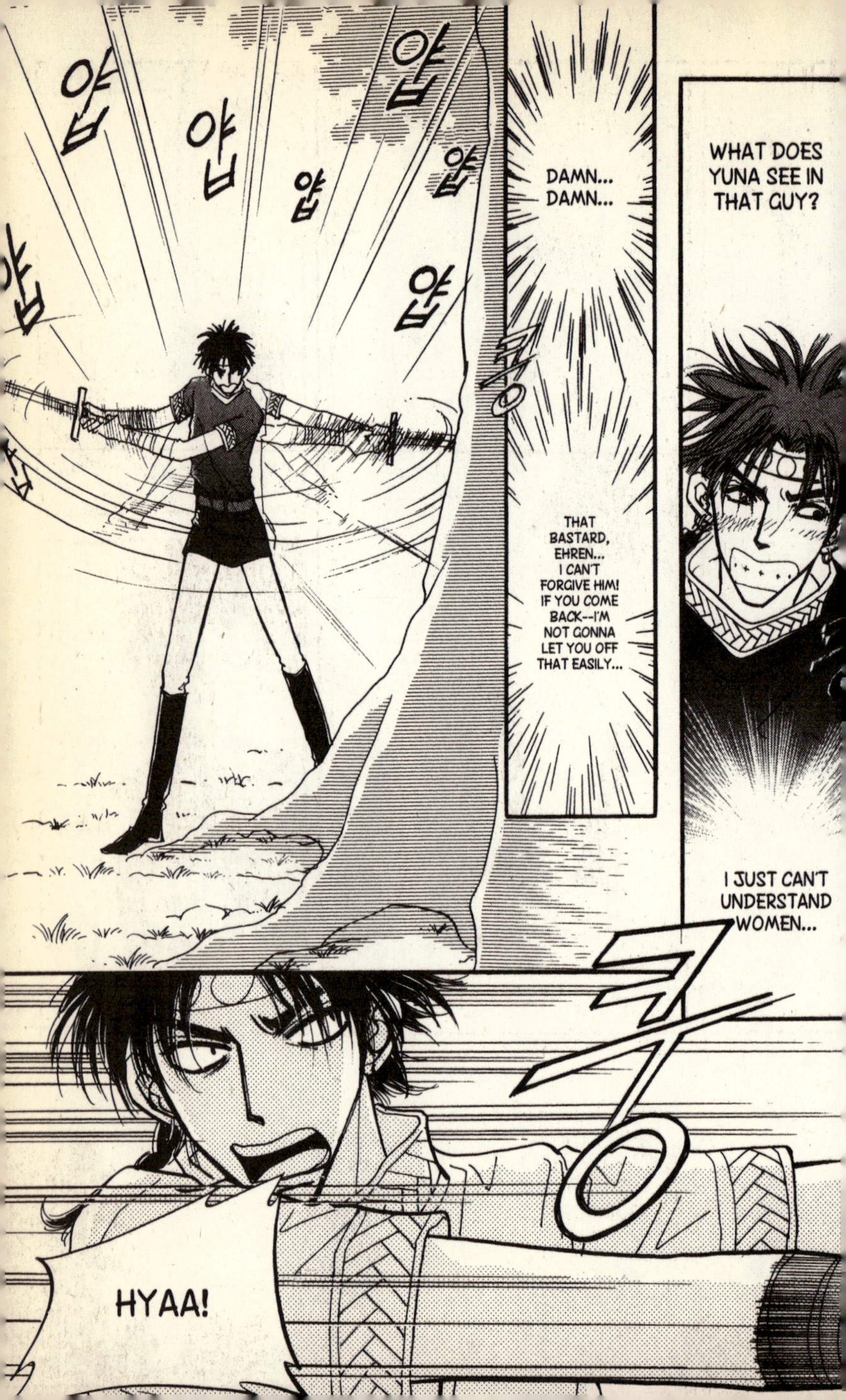
얍
얍
얍
얍
얍
얍
쿵
DAMN... DAMN...
THAT BASTARD, EHREN... I CAN'T FORGIVE HIM! IF YOU COME BACK--I'M NOT GONNA LET YOU OFF THAT EASILY...
WHAT DOES YUNA SEE IN THAT GUY?
I JUST CAN'T UNDERSTAND WOMEN...
HYAA!
크

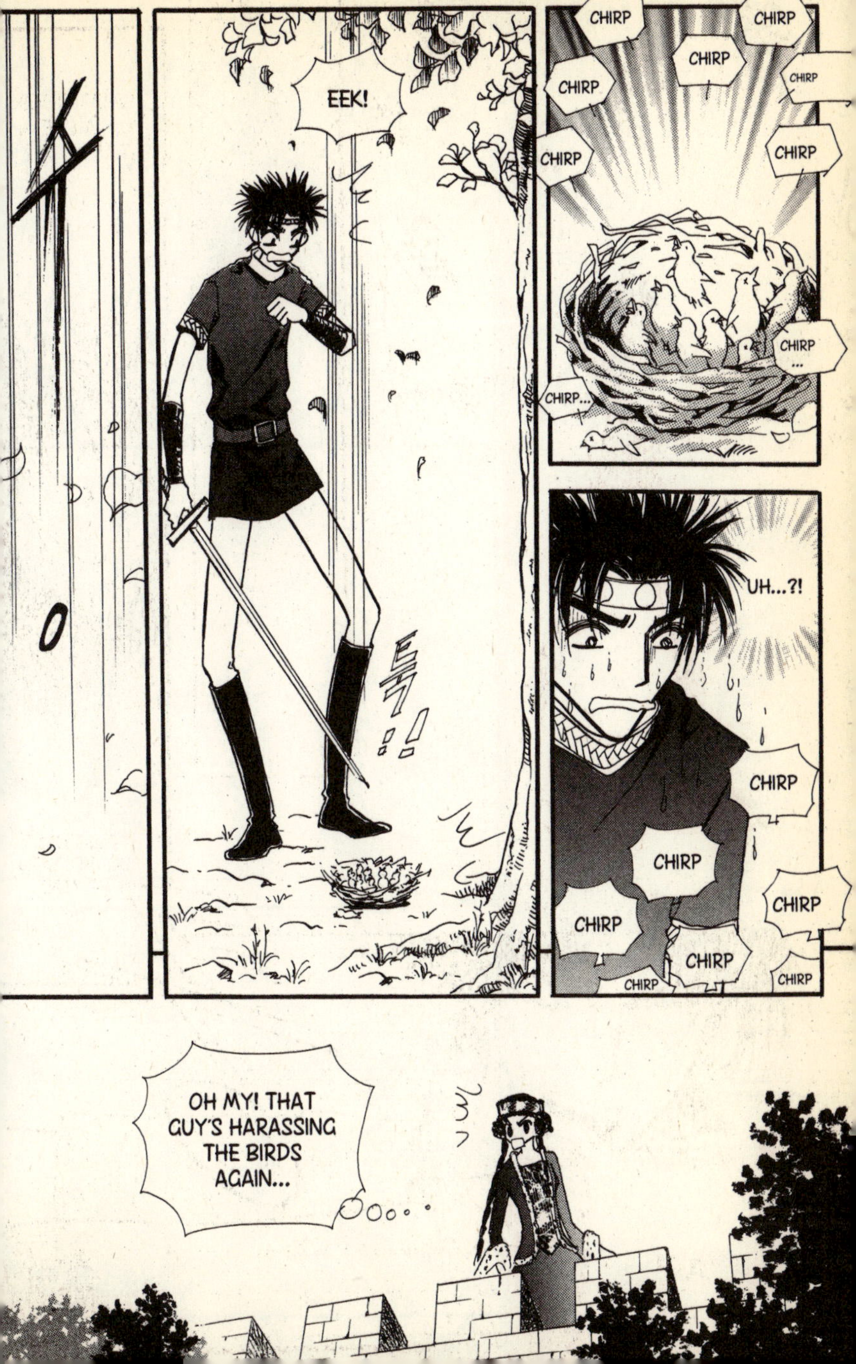
EEK!
CHIRP
CHIRP
CHIRP
CHIRP
CHIRP
CHIRP
CHIRP
CHIRP...
CHIRP...
UH...?!
CHIRP
CHIRP
CHIRP
CHIRP
CHIRP
CHIRP
CHIRP
OH MY! THAT GUY'S HARASSING THE BIRDS AGAIN...

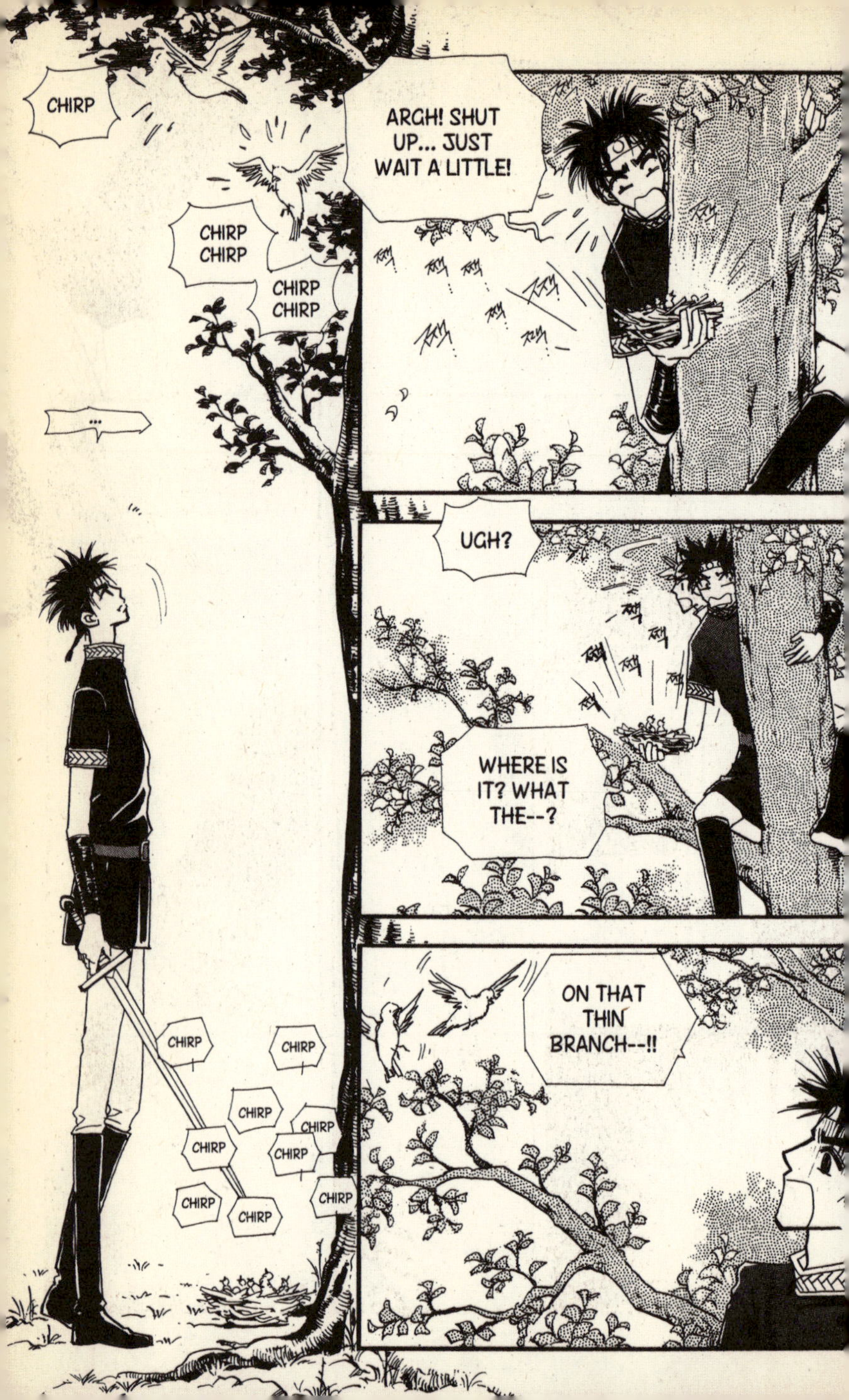
CHIRP
CHIRP CHIRP
CHIRP CHIRP
...
CHIRP
CHIRP
CHIRP
CHIRP
CHIRP
CHIRP
CHIRP
CHIRP
CHIRP
ARGH! SHUT UP... JUST WAIT A LITTLE!
UGH?
WHERE IS IT? WHAT THE--?
ON THAT THIN BRANCH--!!

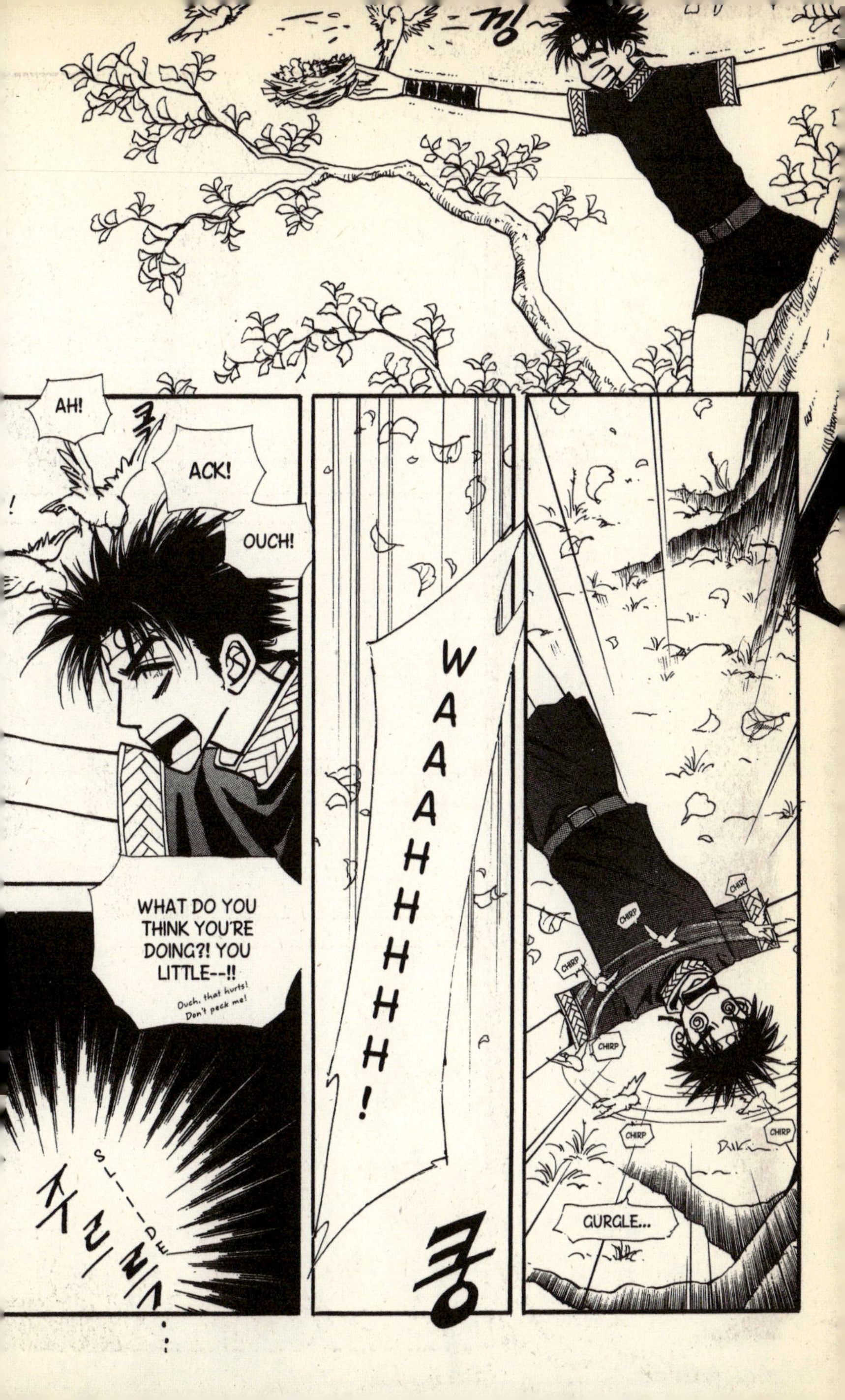
찡
AH!
ACK!
OUCH!
WHAT DO YOU THINK YOU'RE DOING?! YOU LITTLE--!!
Ouch, that hurts! Don't peck me!
S-L-I-I-DE
WAAAHHHHHH!
쿵
CHIRP
CHIRP
CHIRP
CHIRP
CHIRP
CHIRP
GURGLE...

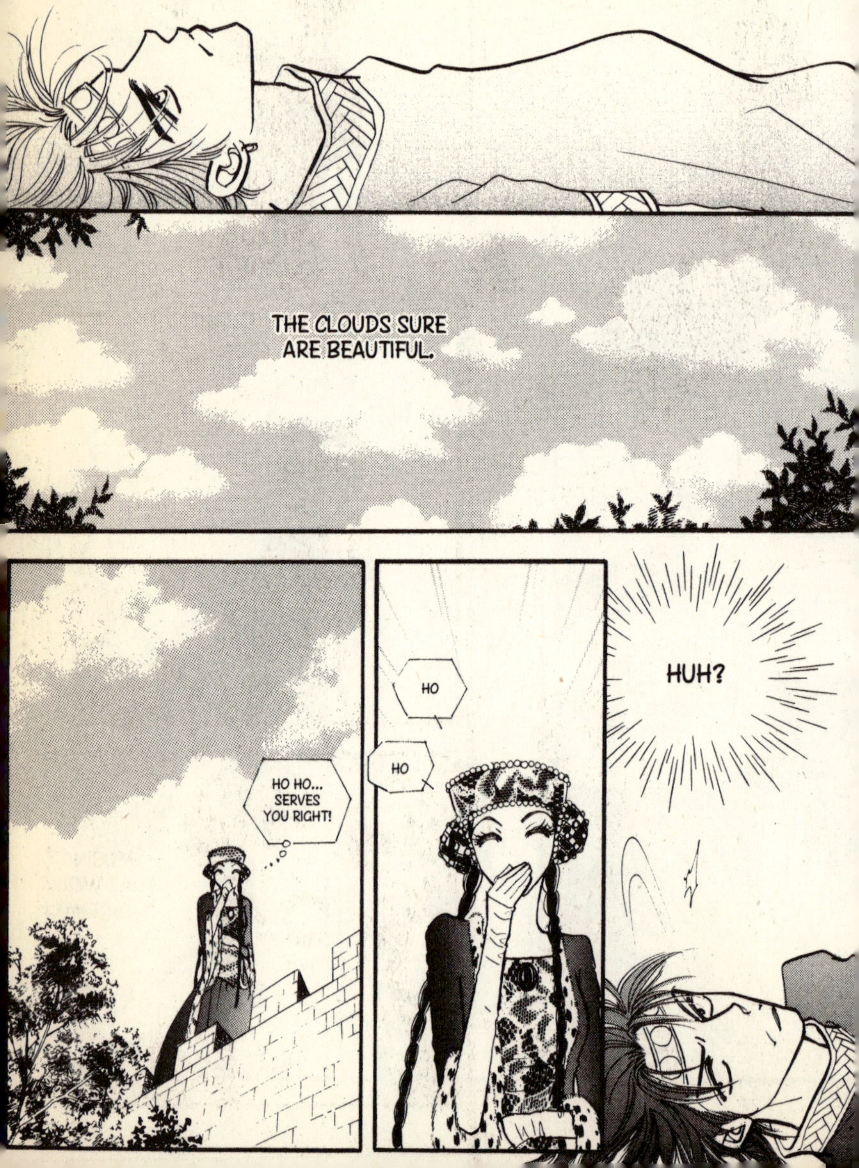
THE CLOUDS SURE ARE BEAUTIFUL.
HO HO... SERVES YOU RIGHT!
HO
HO
HUH?

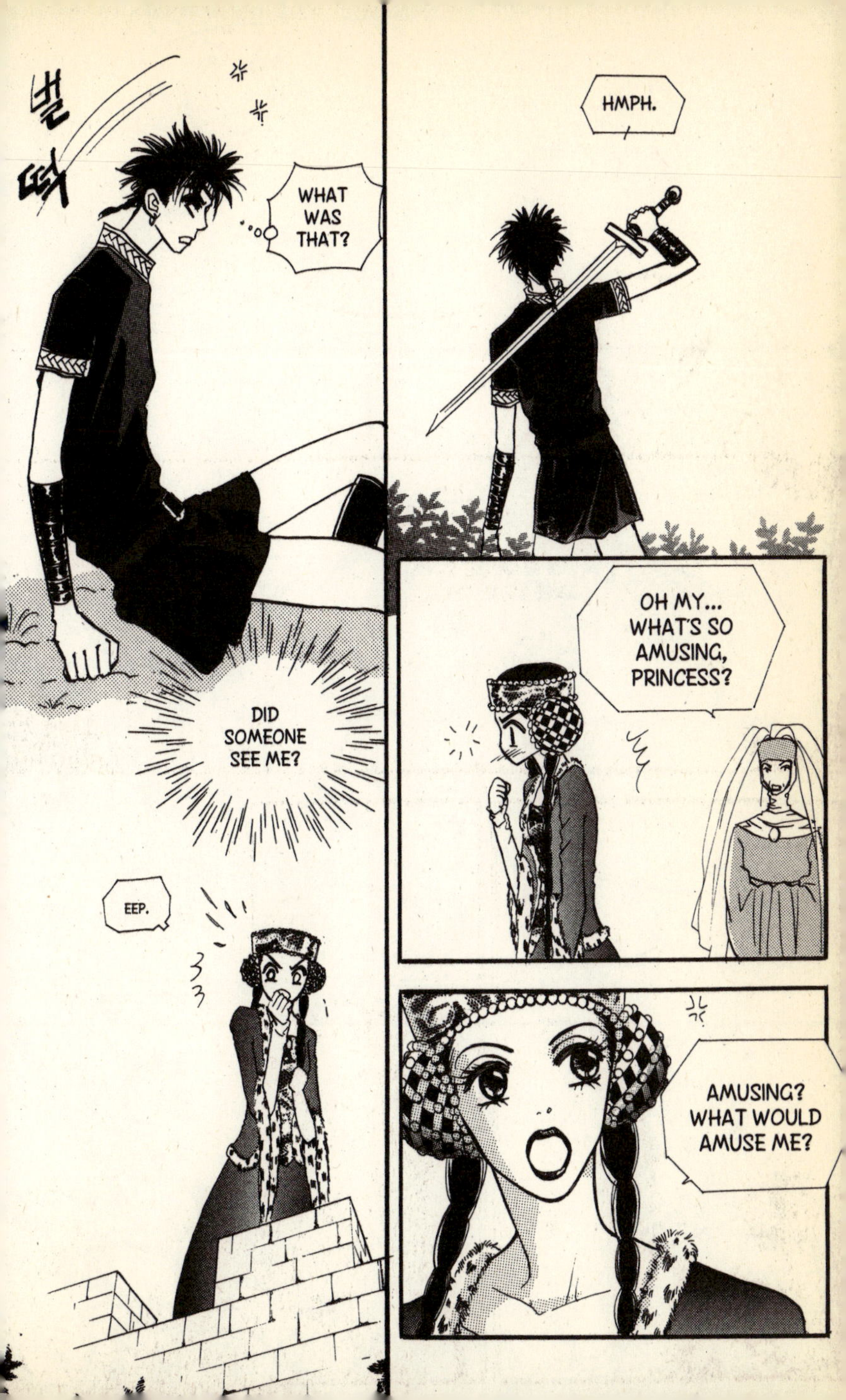
벌떡
WHAT WAS THAT?
DID SOMEONE SEE ME?
EEP.
HMPH.
OH MY... WHAT'S SO AMUSING, PRINCESS?
AMUSING? WHAT WOULD AMUSE ME?

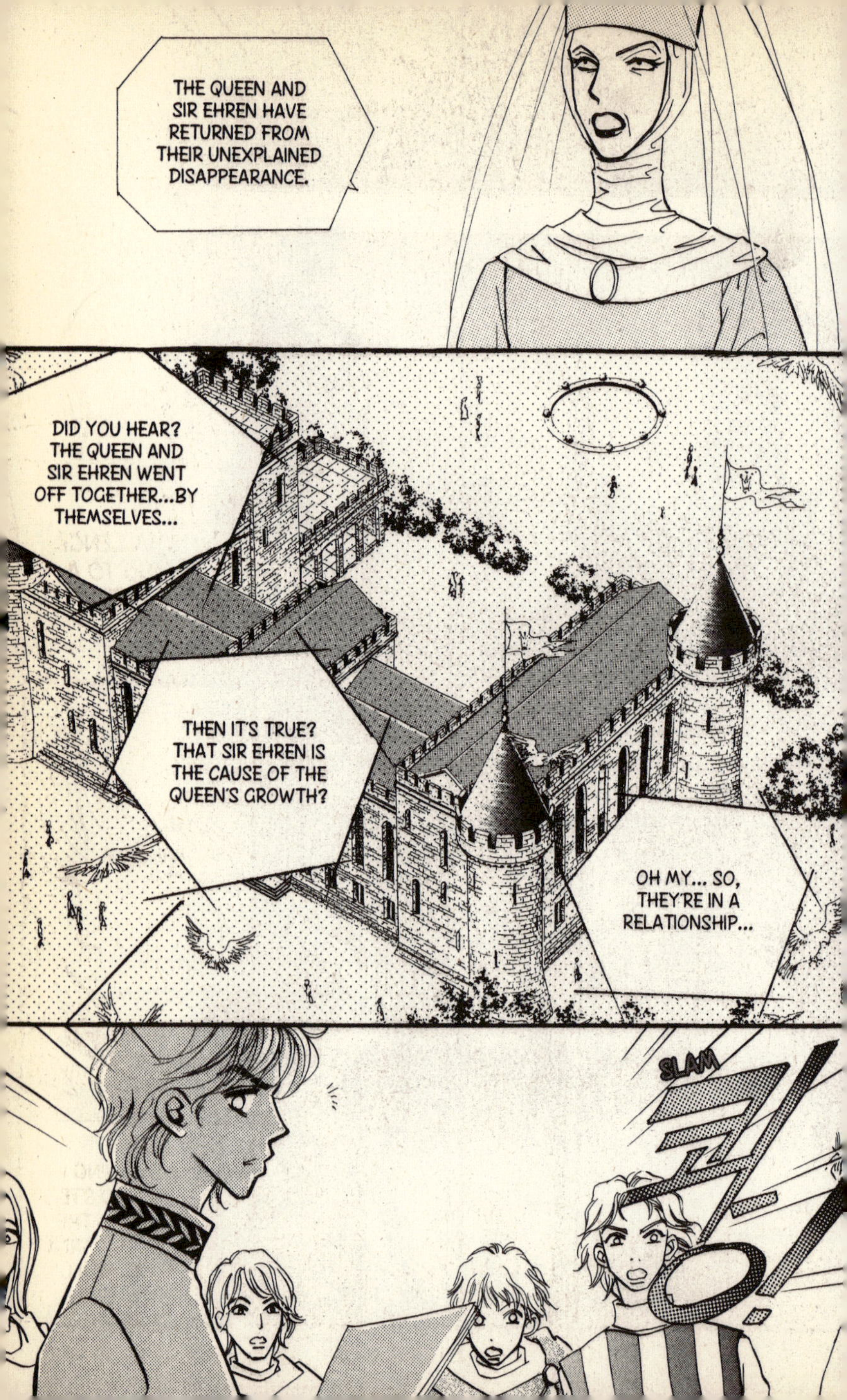
THE QUEEN AND SIR EHREN HAVE RETURNED FROM THEIR UNEXPLAINED DISAPPEARANCE.
DID YOU HEAR? THE QUEEN AND SIR EHREN WENT OFF TOGETHER...BY THEMSELVES...
THEN IT'S TRUE? THAT SIR EHREN IS THE CAUSE OF THE QUEEN'S GROWTH?
OH MY... SO, THEY'RE IN A RELATIONSHIP...
SLAM

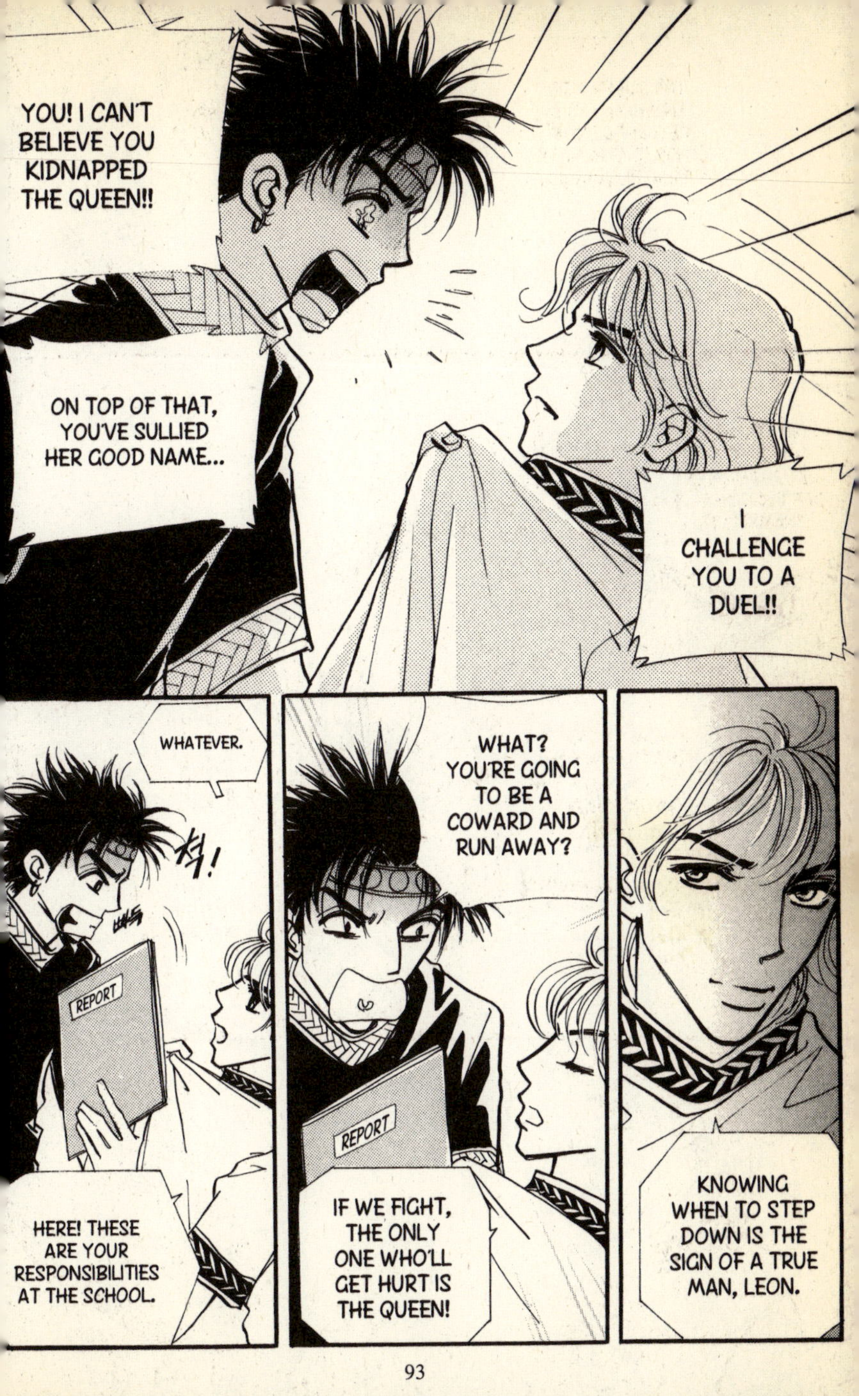
YOU! I CAN'T BELIEVE YOU KIDNAPPED THE QUEEN!!
ON TOP OF THAT, YOU'VE SULLIED HER GOOD NAME...
I CHALLENGE YOU TO A DUEL!!
WHATEVER.
척!
REPORT
HERE! THESE ARE YOUR RESPONSIBILITIES AT THE SCHOOL.
WHAT? YOU'RE GOING TO BE A COWARD AND RUN AWAY?
REPORT
IF WE FIGHT, THE ONLY ONE WHO'LL GET HURT IS THE QUEEN!
KNOWING WHEN TO STEP DOWN IS THE SIGN OF A TRUE MAN, LEON.

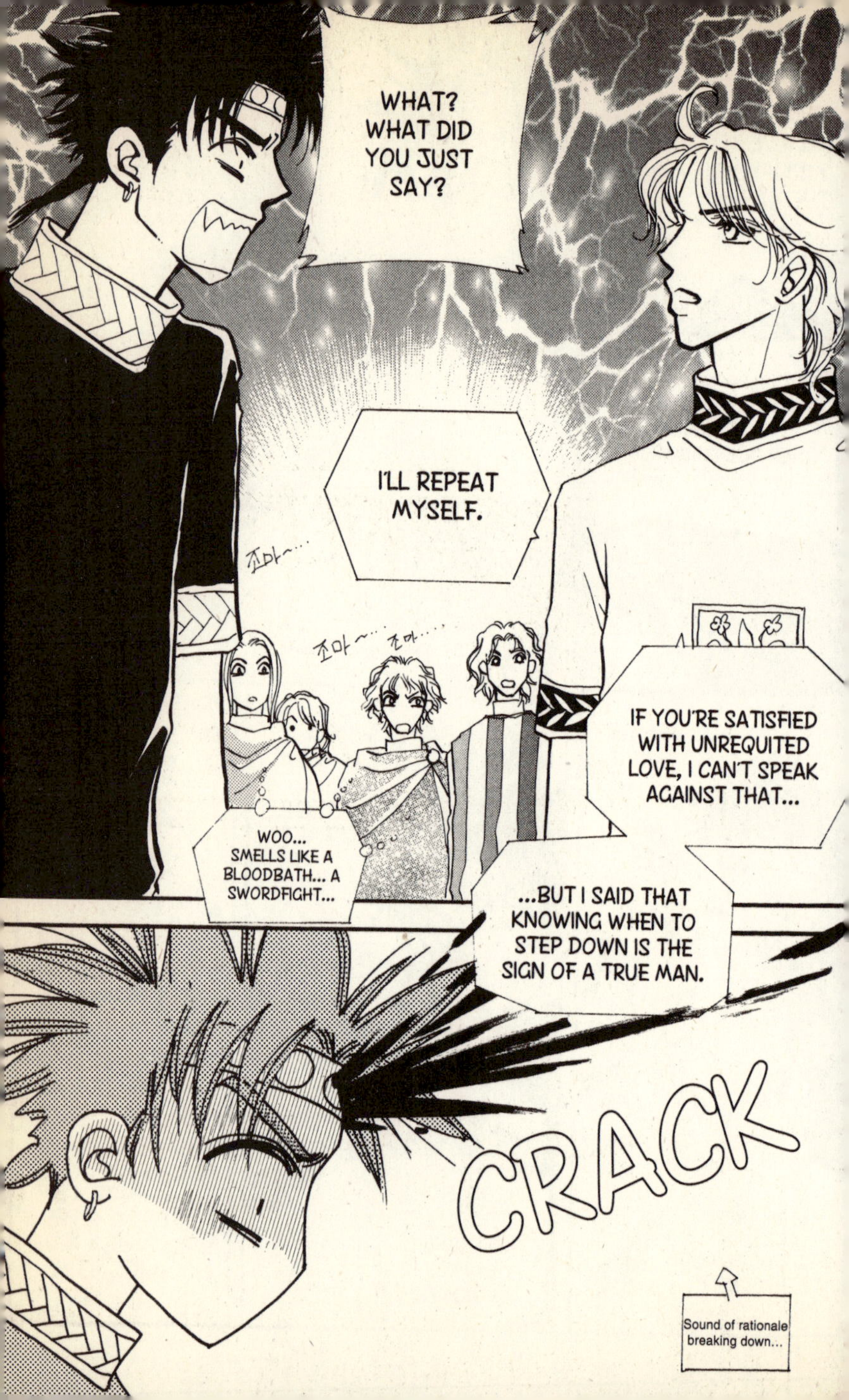
WHAT? WHAT DID YOU JUST SAY?
I'LL REPEAT MYSELF.
조마~...
조마~~...
조마...
IF YOU'RE SATISFIED WITH UNREQUITED LOVE, I CAN'T SPEAK AGAINST THAT...
WOO... SMELLS LIKE A BLOODBATH... A SWORDFIGHT...
...BUT I SAID THAT KNOWING WHEN TO STEP DOWN IS THE SIGN OF A TRUE MAN.
CRACK
Sound of rationale breaking down...

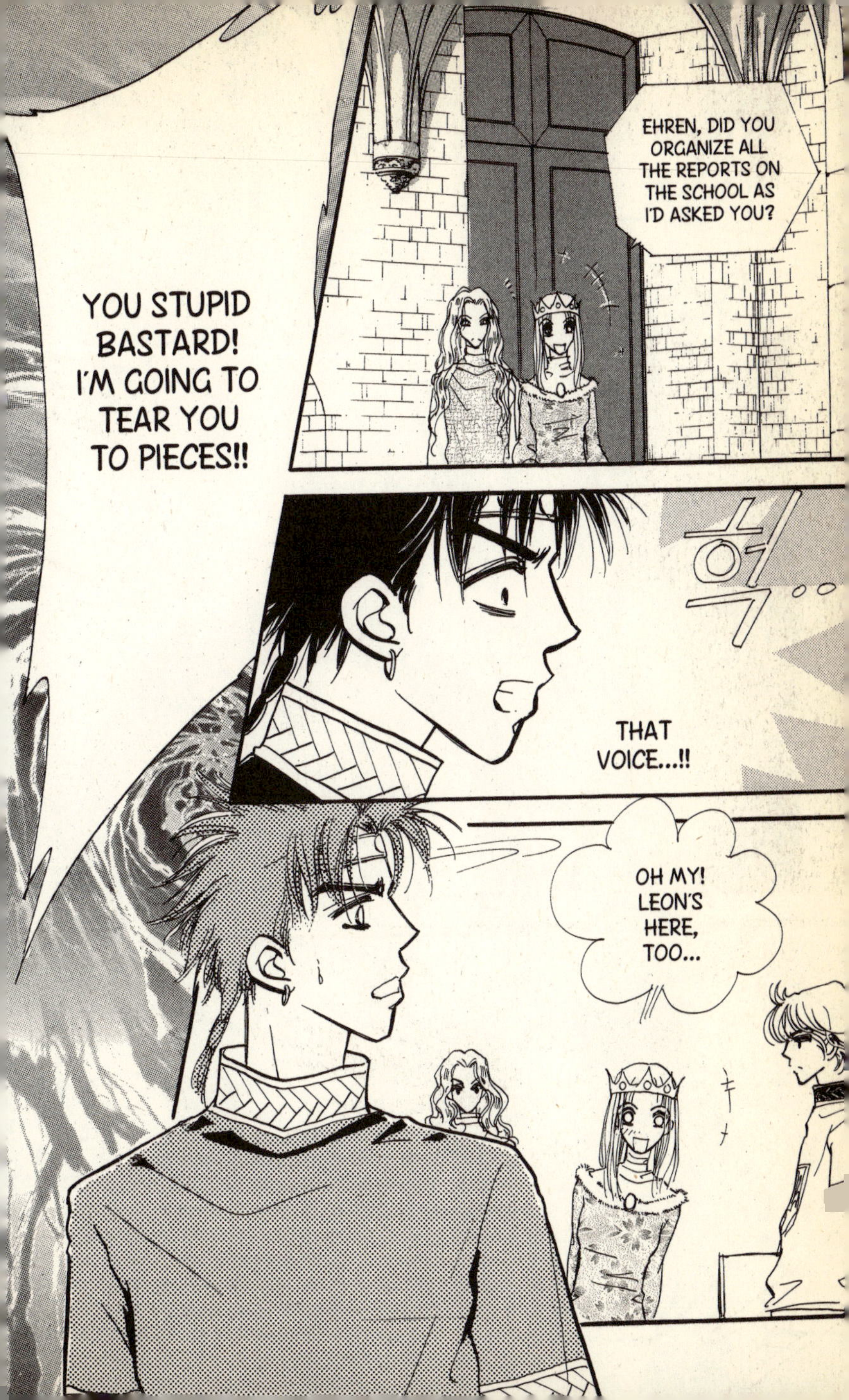
YOU STUPID BASTARD! I'M GOING TO TEAR YOU TO PIECES!!
EHREN, DID YOU ORGANIZE ALL THE REPORTS ON THE SCHOOL AS I'D ASKED YOU?
헉
THAT VOICE...!!
OH MY! LEON'S HERE, TOO...

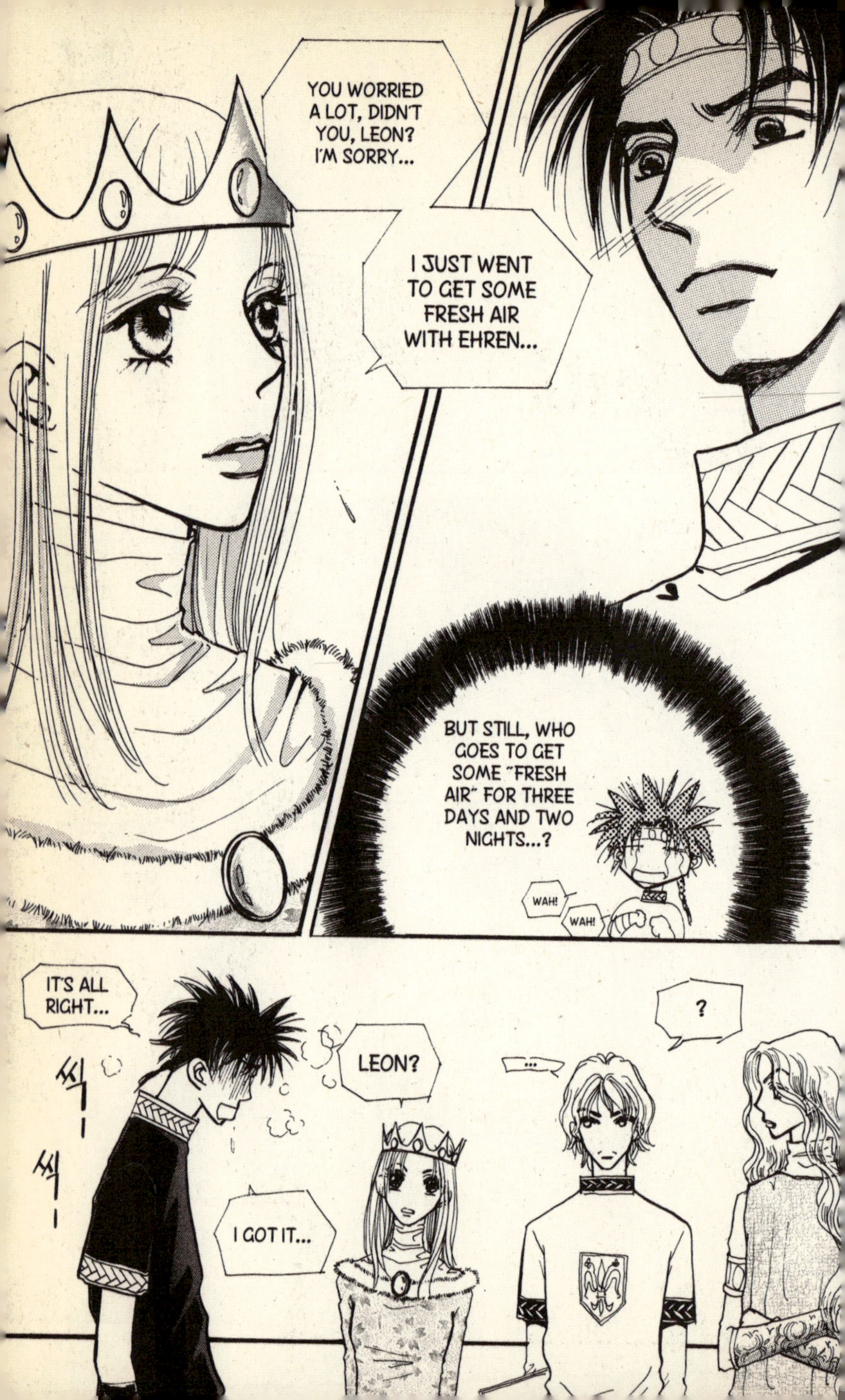
YOU WORRIED A LOT, DIDN'T YOU, LEON? I'M SORRY...
I JUST WENT TO GET SOME FRESH AIR WITH EHREN...
BUT STILL, WHO GOES TO GET SOME "FRESH AIR" FOR THREE DAYS AND TWO NIGHTS...?
WAH!
WAH!
IT'S ALL RIGHT...
씩- 씩-
LEON?
I GOT IT...
...
?

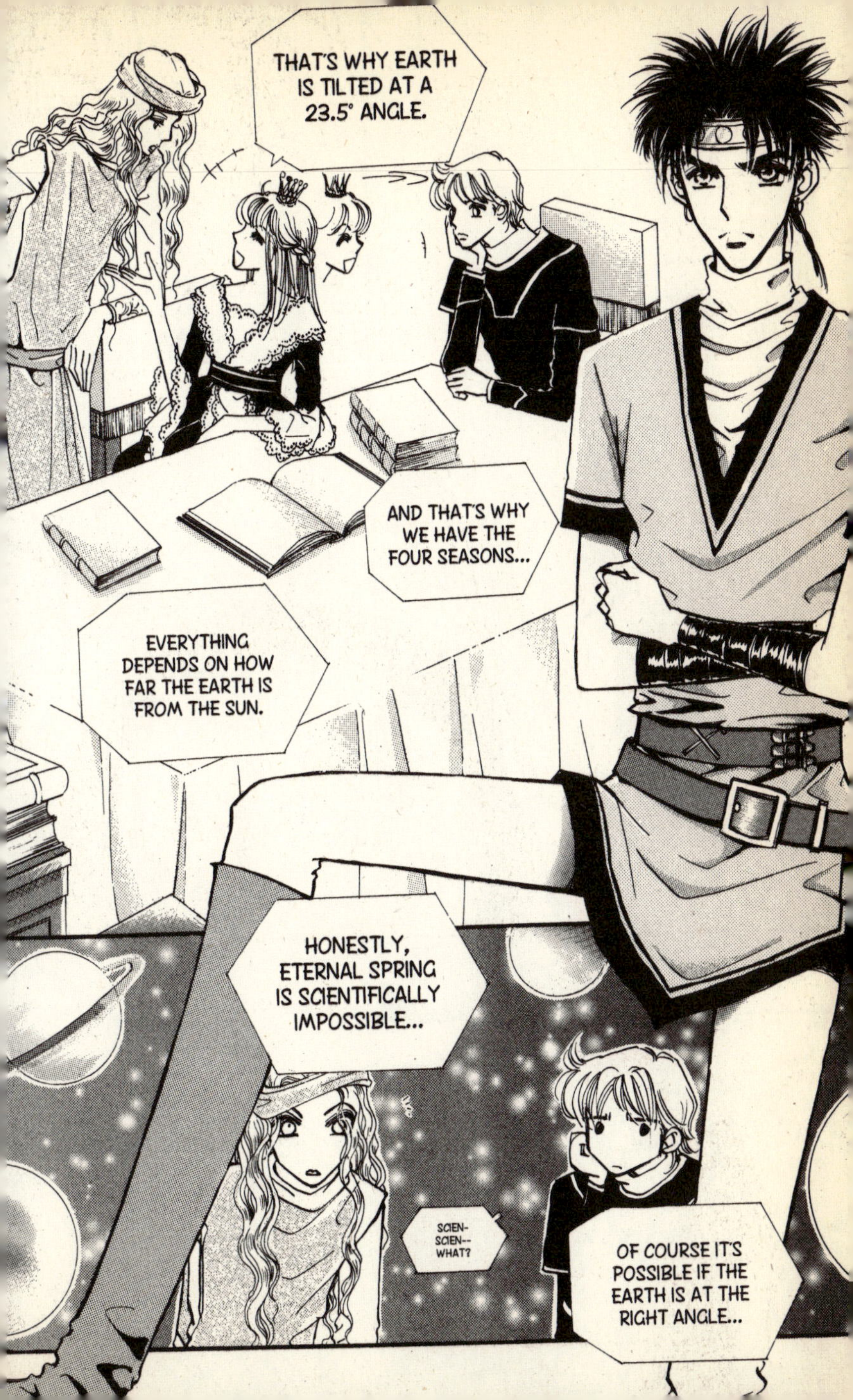
THAT'S WHY EARTH IS TILTED AT A 23.5° ANGLE.
AND THAT'S WHY WE HAVE THE FOUR SEASONS...
EVERYTHING DEPENDS ON HOW FAR THE EARTH IS FROM THE SUN.
HONESTLY, ETERNAL SPRING IS SCIENTIFICALLY IMPOSSIBLE...
SCIEN-SCIEN--WHAT?
OF COURSE IT'S POSSIBLE IF THE EARTH IS AT THE RIGHT ANGLE...

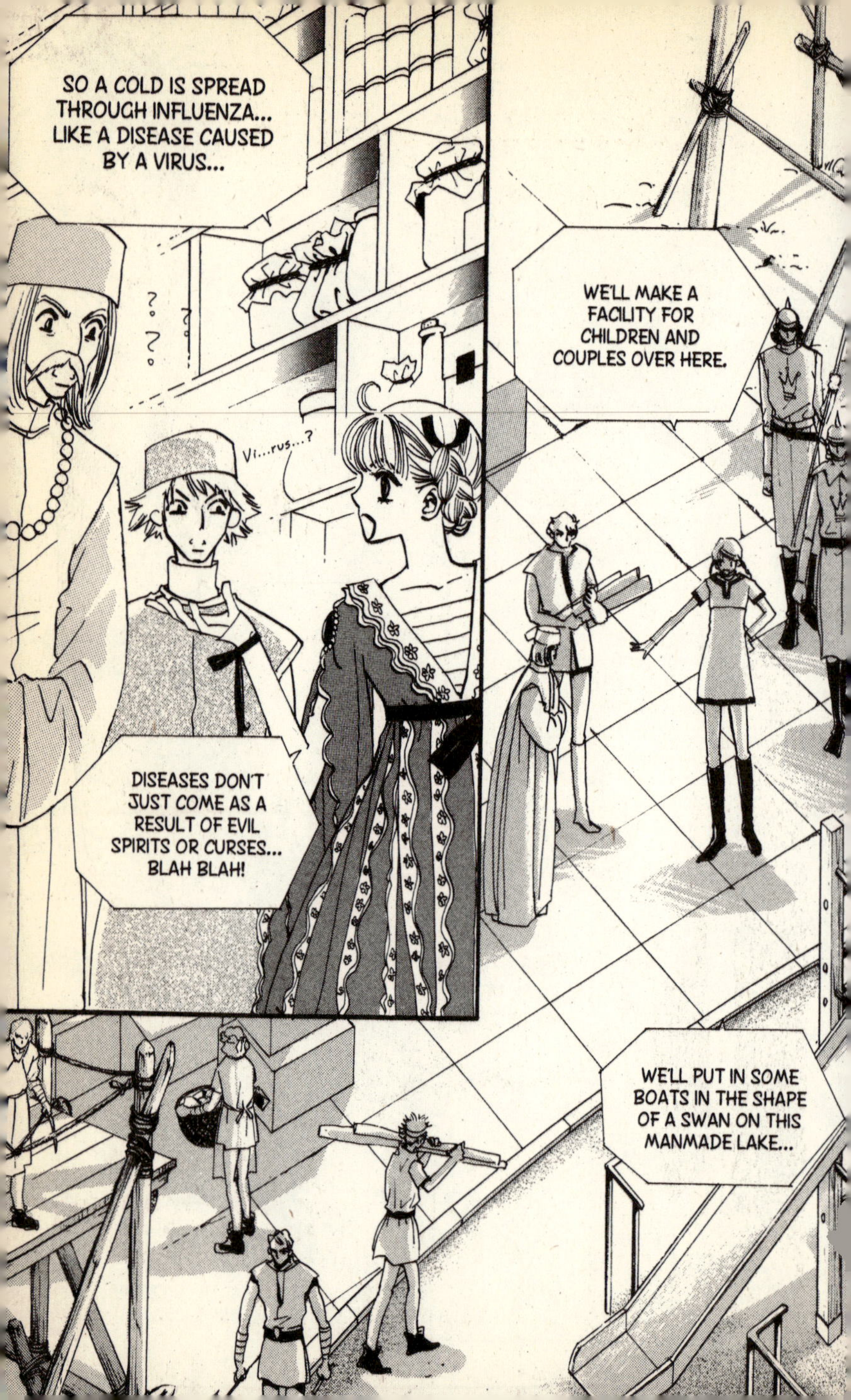
SO A COLD IS SPREAD THROUGH INFLUENZA... LIKE A DISEASE CAUSED BY A VIRUS...
?? ??
Vi...rus...?
DISEASES DON'T JUST COME AS A RESULT OF EVIL SPIRITS OR CURSES... BLAH BLAH!
WE'LL MAKE A FACILITY FOR CHILDREN AND COUPLES OVER HERE.
WE'LL PUT IN SOME BOATS IN THE SHAPE OF A SWAN ON THIS MANMADE LAKE...

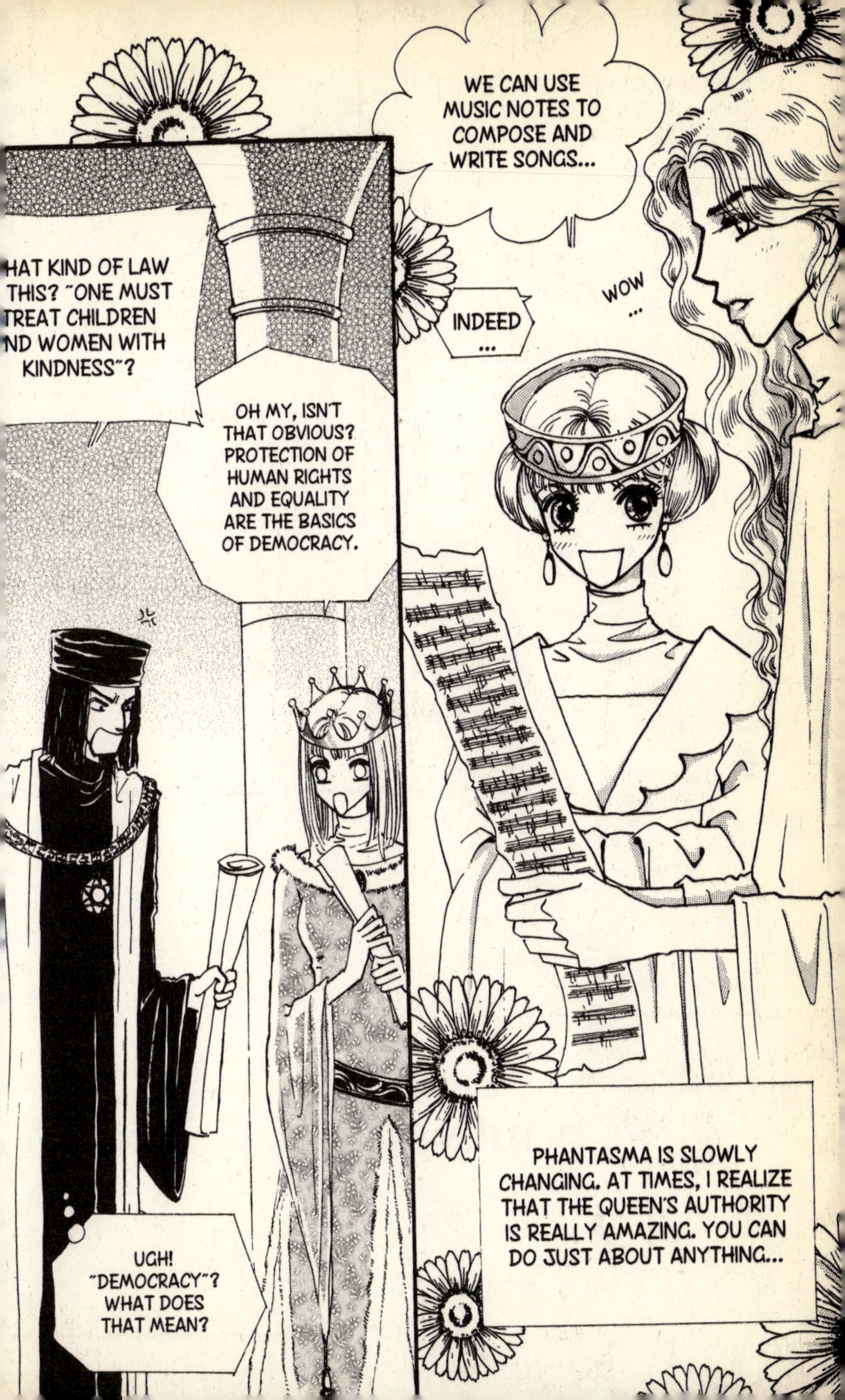
HAT KIND OF LAW THIS? "ONE MUST TREAT CHILDREN ND WOMEN WITH KINDNESS"?
OH MY, ISN'T THAT OBVIOUS? PROTECTION OF HUMAN RIGHTS AND EQUALITY ARE THE BASICS OF DEMOCRACY.
UGH! "DEMOCRACY"? WHAT DOES THAT MEAN?
WE CAN USE MUSIC NOTES TO COMPOSE AND WRITE SONGS...
INDEED ...
WOW ...
PHANTASMA IS SLOWLY CHANGING. AT TIMES, I REALIZE THAT THE QUEEN'S AUTHORITY IS REALLY AMAZING. YOU CAN DO JUST ABOUT ANYTHING...

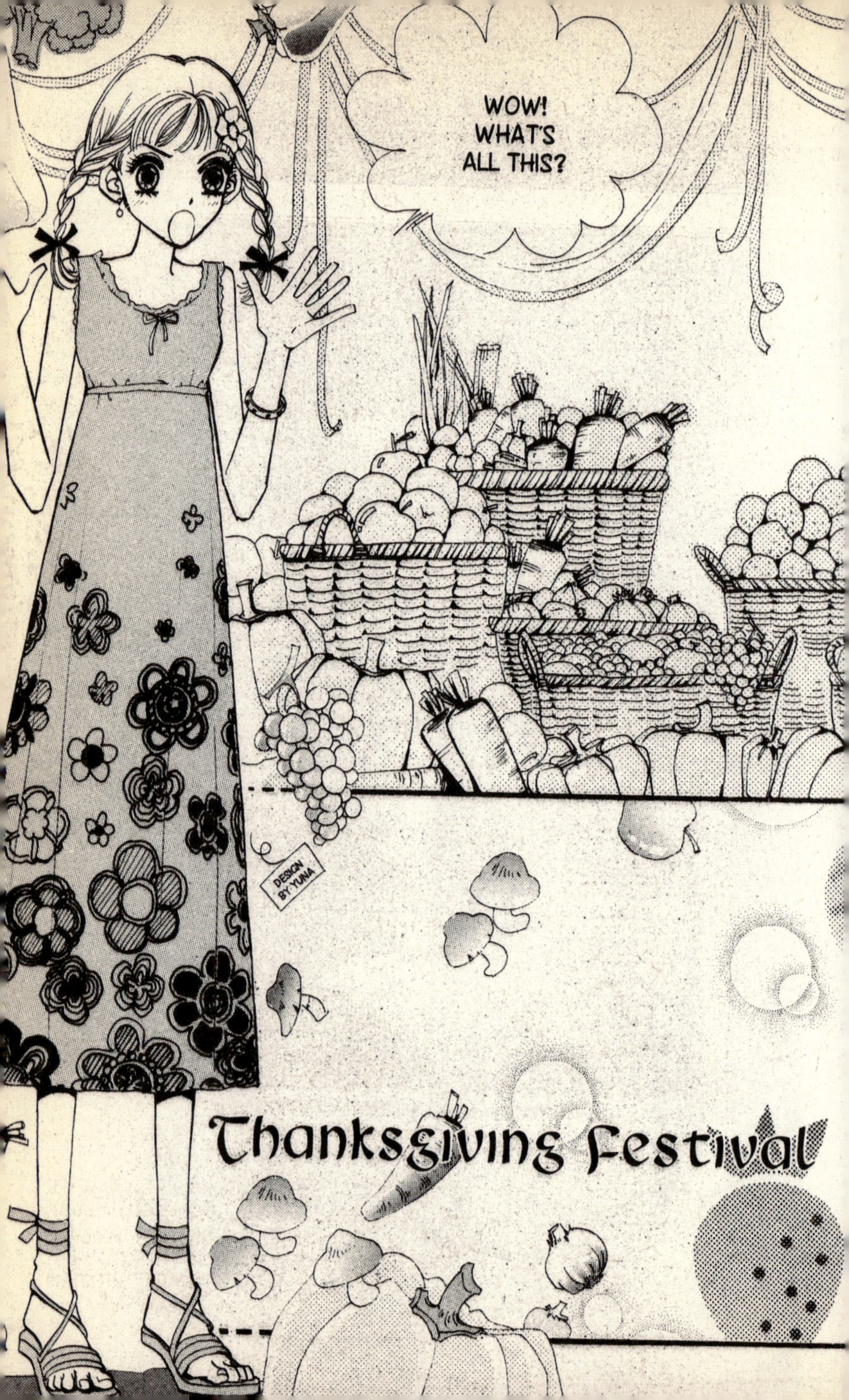
WOW! WHAT'S ALL THIS?
DESIGN BY YUNA
Thanksgiving Festival

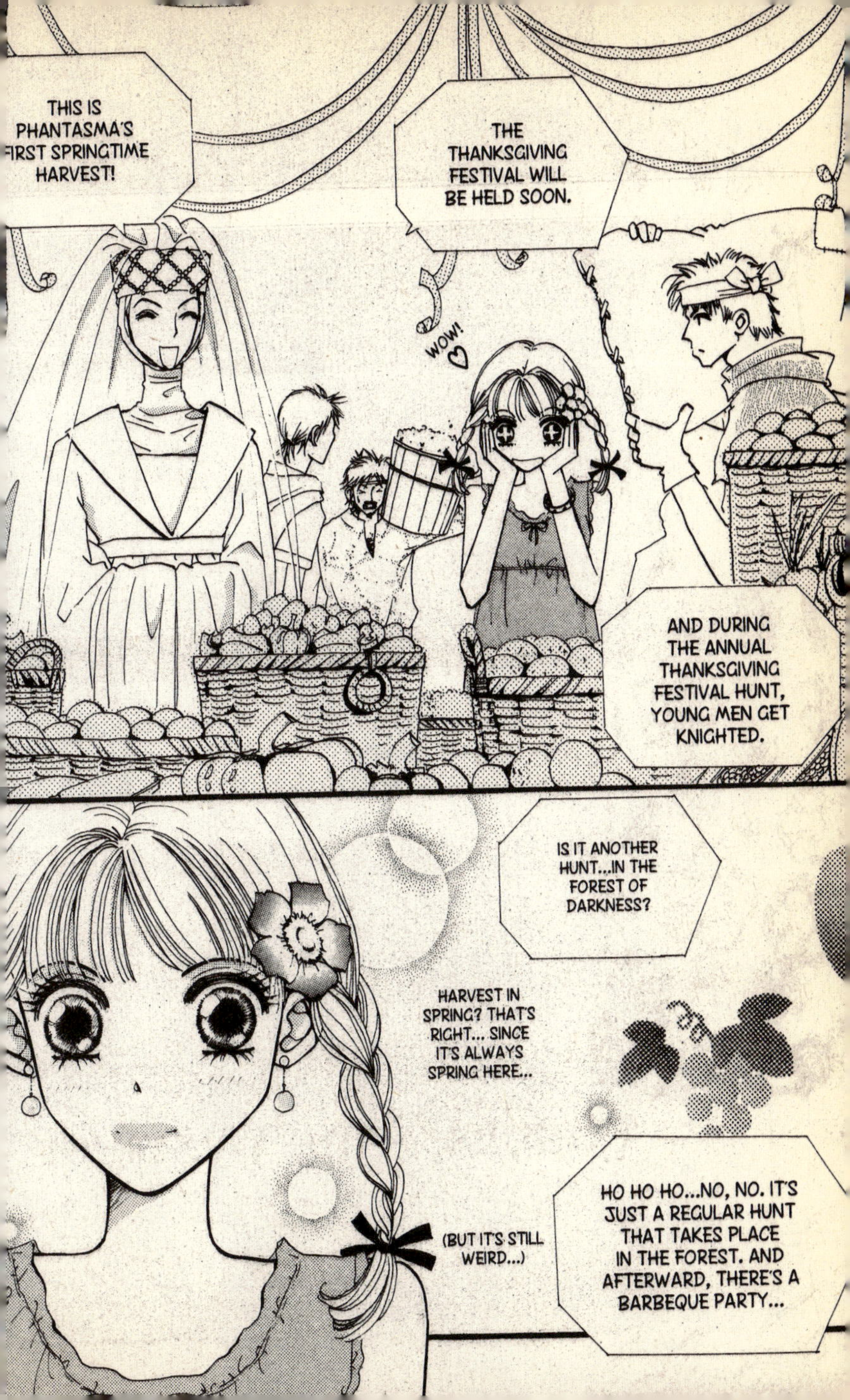
THIS IS PHANTASMA'S FIRST SPRINGTIME HARVEST!
THE THANKSGIVING FESTIVAL WILL BE HELD SOON.
WOW!
AND DURING THE ANNUAL THANKSGIVING FESTIVAL HUNT, YOUNG MEN GET KNIGHTED.
IS IT ANOTHER HUNT...IN THE FOREST OF DARKNESS?
HARVEST IN SPRING? THAT'S RIGHT... SINCE IT'S ALWAYS SPRING HERE...
(BUT IT'S STILL WEIRD...)
HO HO HO...NO, NO. IT'S JUST A REGULAR HUNT THAT TAKES PLACE IN THE FOREST. AND AFTERWARD, THERE'S A BARBEQUE PARTY...

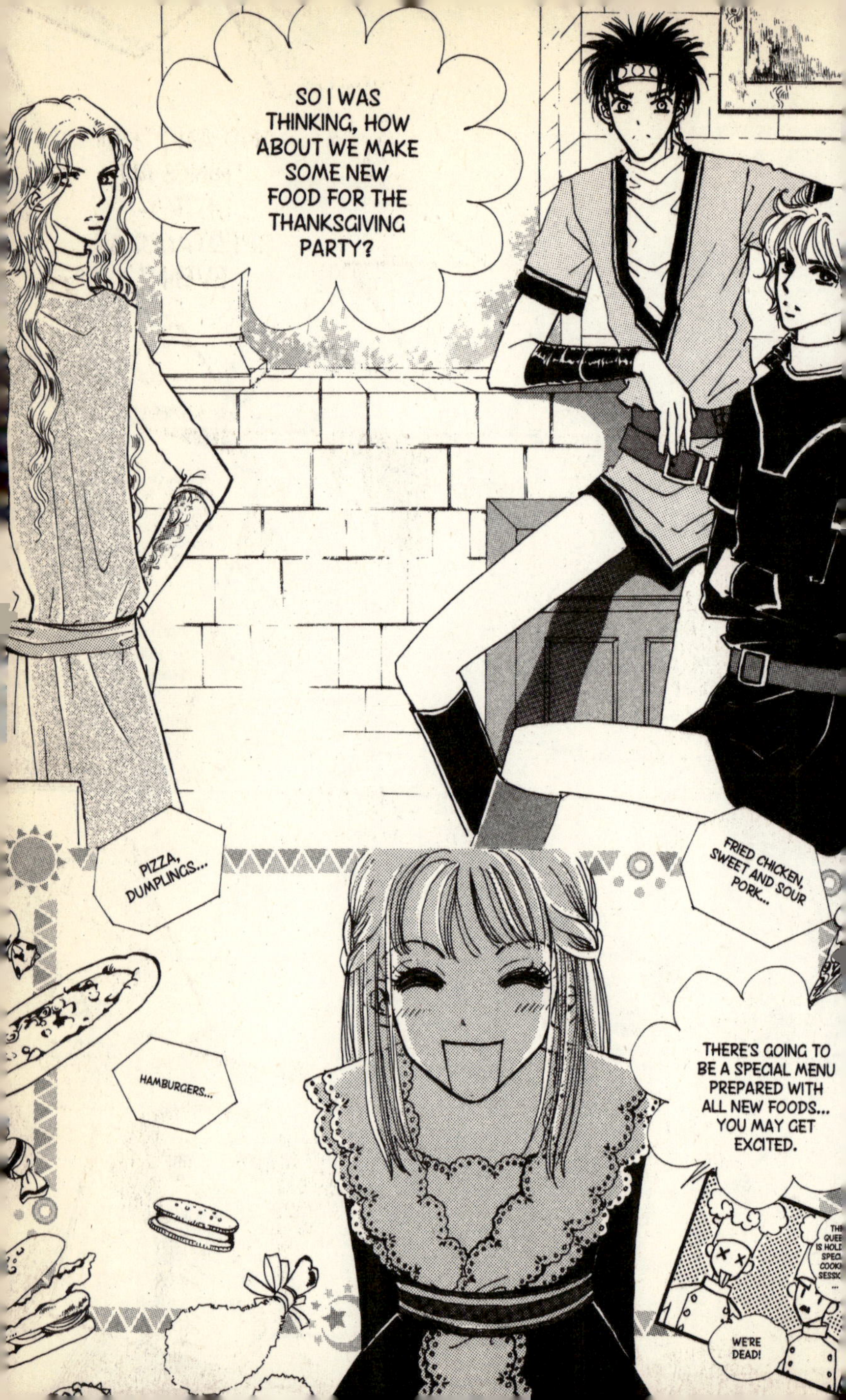
SO I WAS THINKING, HOW ABOUT WE MAKE SOME NEW FOOD FOR THE THANKSGIVING PARTY?
PIZZA, DUMPLINGS...
FRIED CHICKEN, SWEET AND SOUR PORK...
HAMBURGERS...
THERE'S GOING TO BE A SPECIAL MENU PREPARED WITH ALL NEW FOODS... YOU MAY GET EXCITED.
WE'RE DEAD!

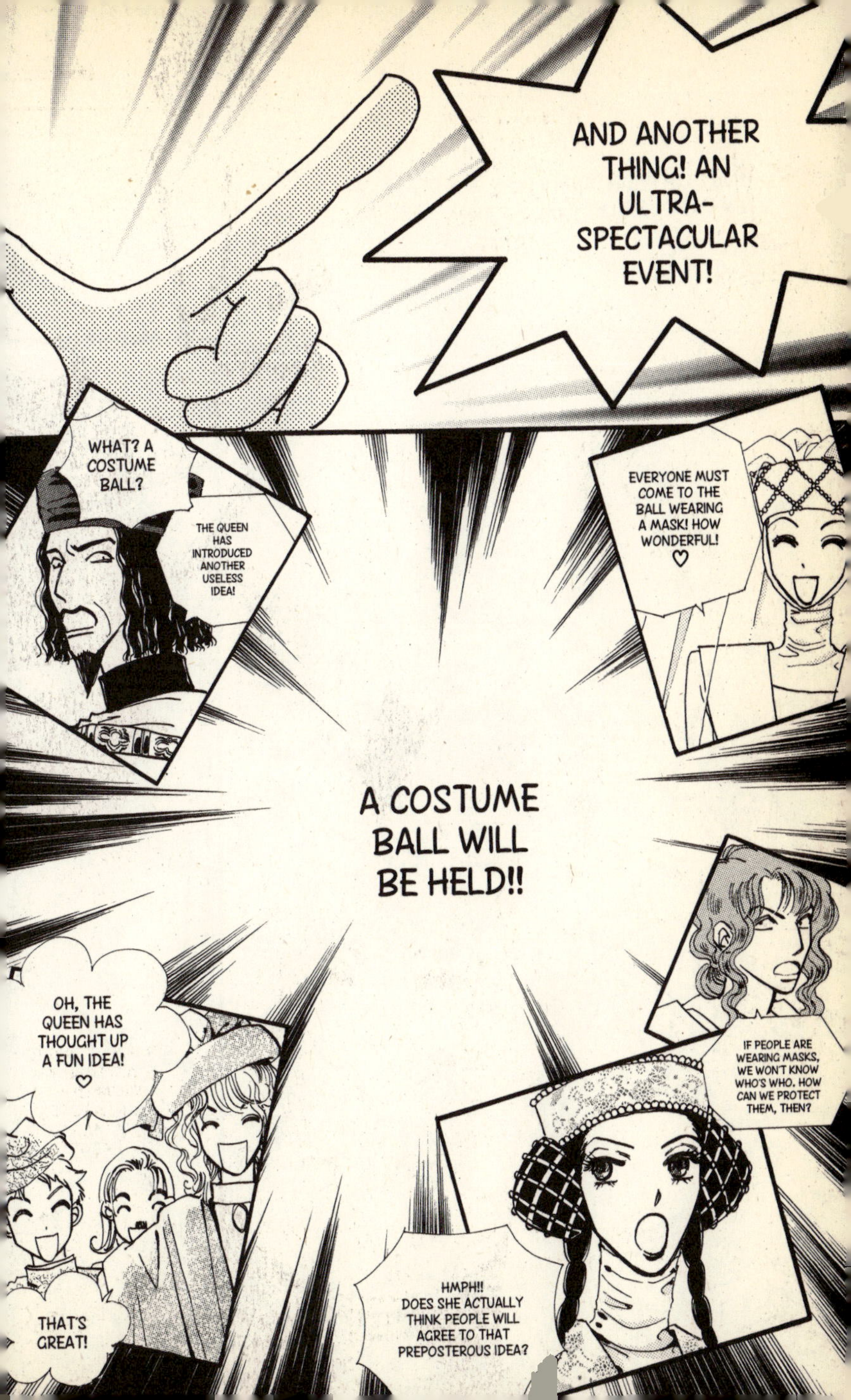
AND ANOTHER THING! AN ULTRA-SPECTACULAR EVENT!
WHAT? A COSTUME BALL?
THE QUEEN HAS INTRODUCED ANOTHER USELESS IDEA!
EVERYONE MUST COME TO THE BALL WEARING A MASK! HOW WONDERFUL! ♡
A COSTUME BALL WILL BE HELD!!
OH, THE QUEEN HAS THOUGHT UP A FUN IDEA! ♡
IF PEOPLE ARE WEARING MASKS, WE WON'T KNOW WHO'S WHO. HOW CAN WE PROTECT THEM, THEN?
THAT'S GREAT!
HMPH!! DOES SHE ACTUALLY THINK PEOPLE WILL AGREE TO THAT PREPOSTEROUS IDEA?

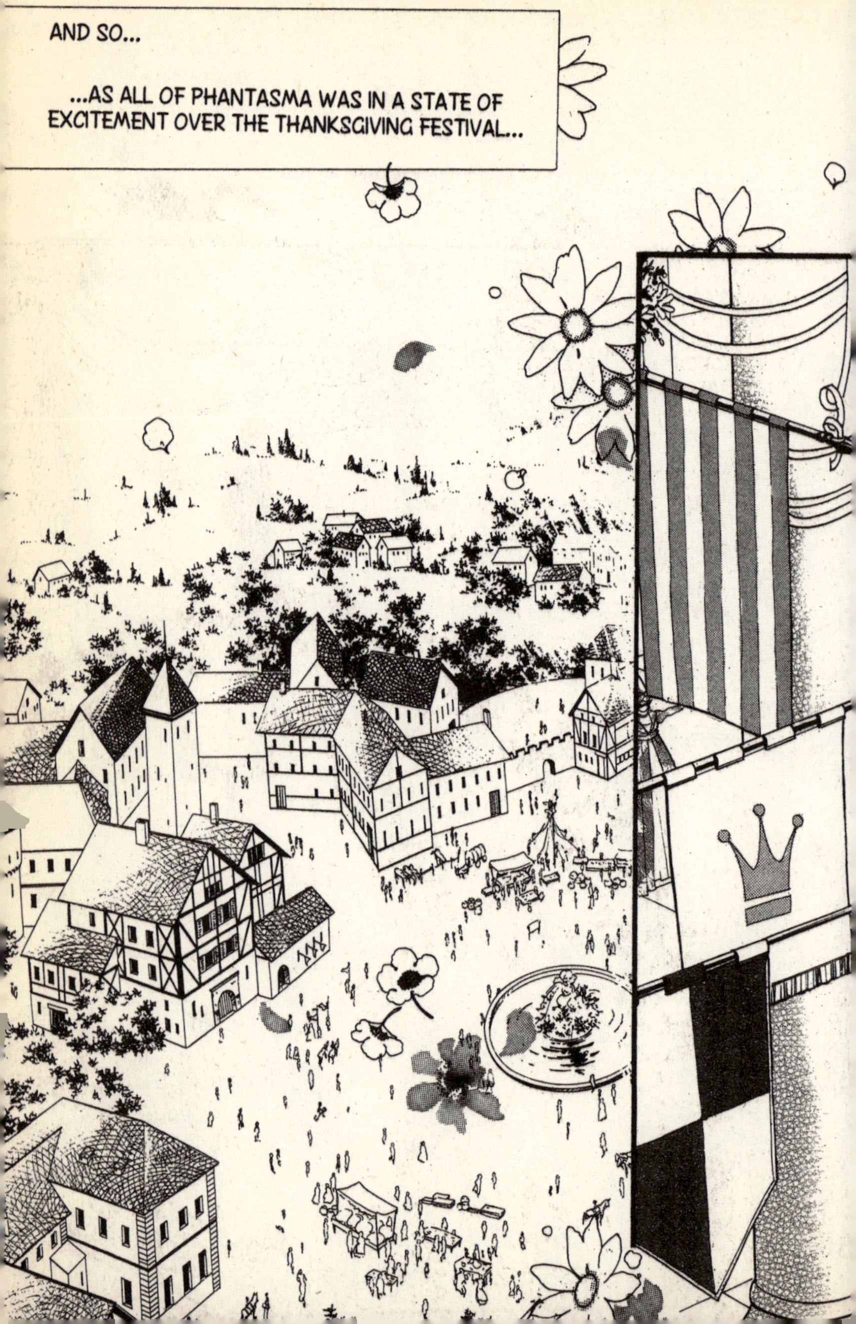
AND SO...
...AS ALL OF PHANTASMA WAS IN A STATE OF EXCITEMENT OVER THE THANKSGIVING FESTIVAL...

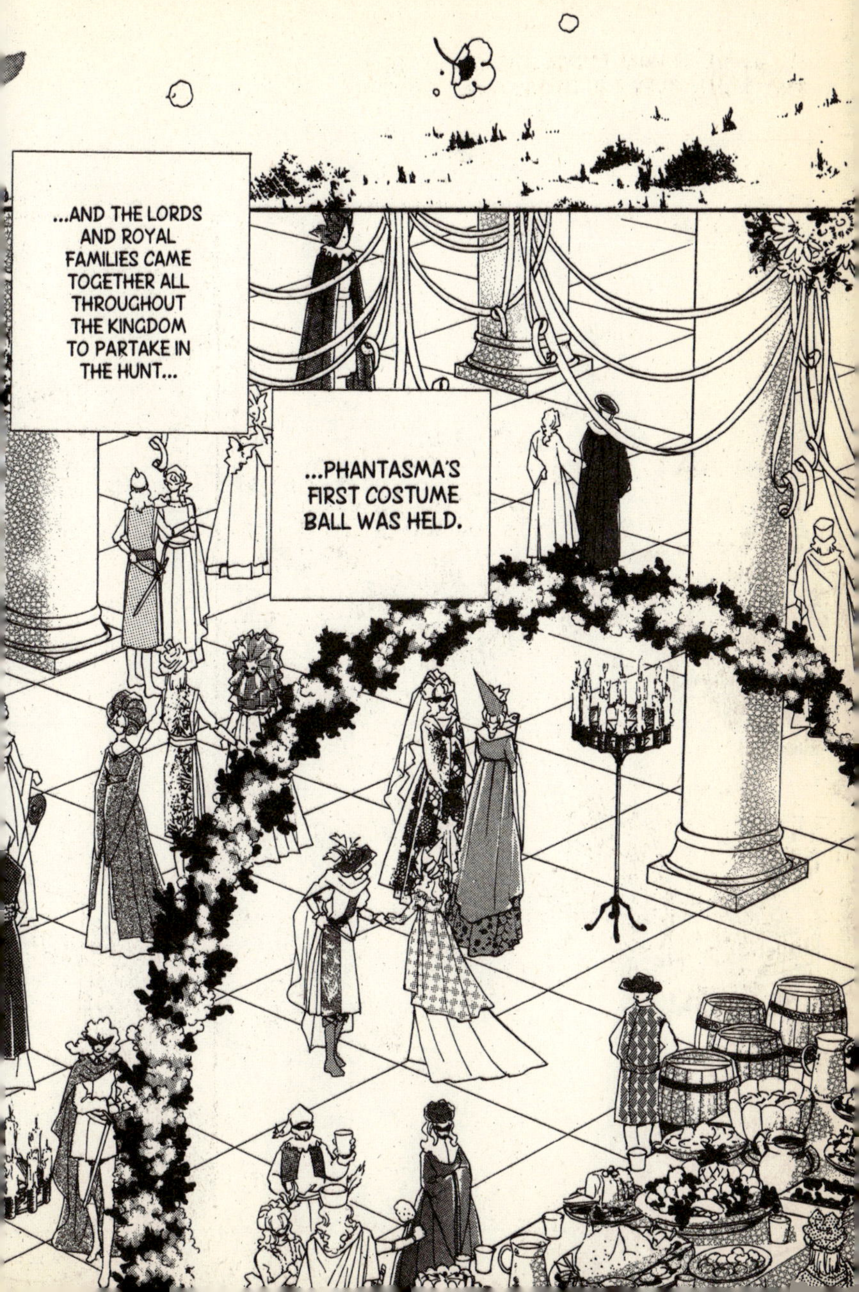
...AND THE LORDS AND ROYAL FAMILIES CAME TOGETHER ALL THROUGHOUT THE KINGDOM TO PARTAKE IN THE HUNT...
...PHANTASMA'S FIRST COSTUME BALL WAS HELD.

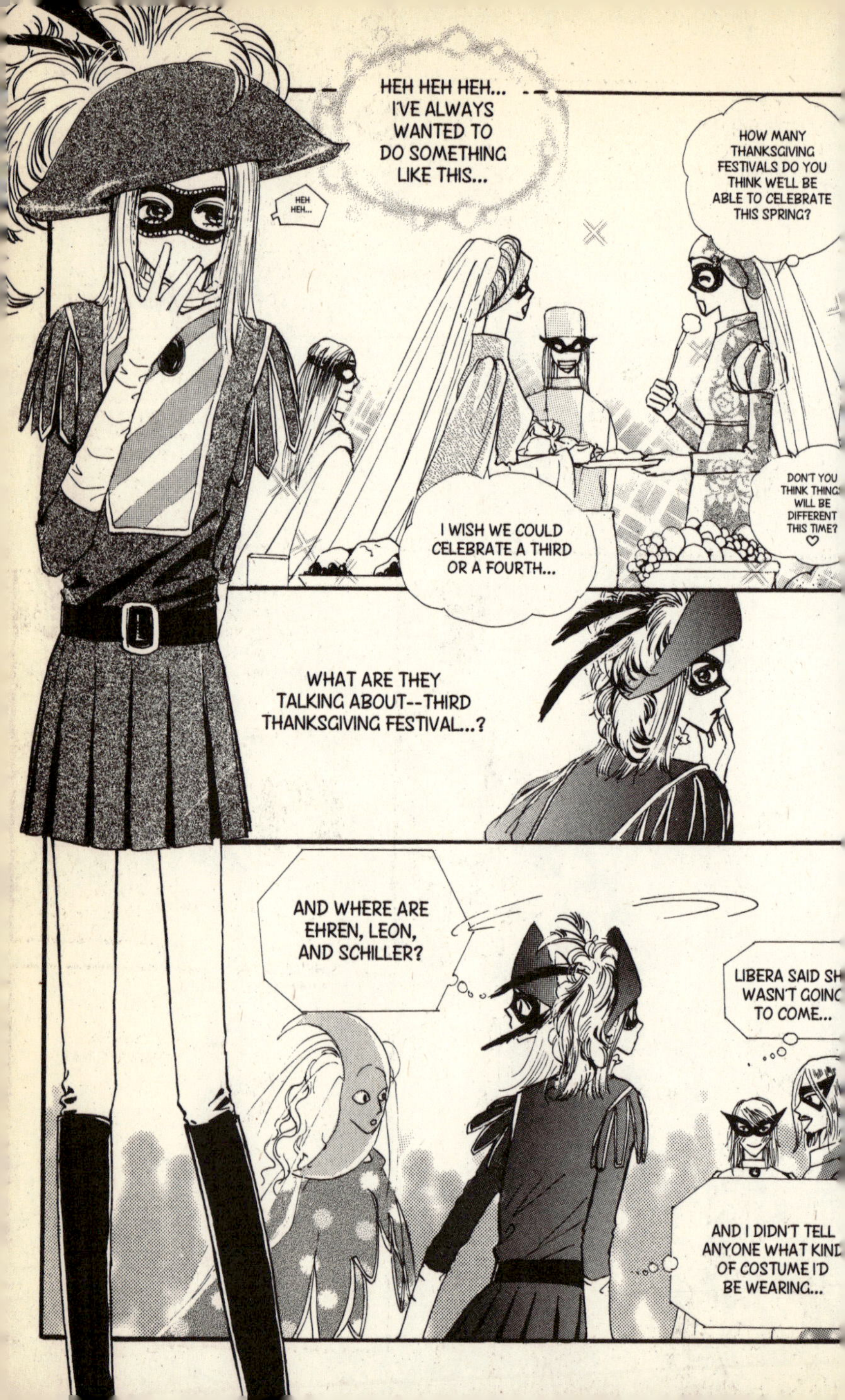
HEH HEH HEH... I'VE ALWAYS WANTED TO DO SOMETHING LIKE THIS...
HEH HEH...
HOW MANY THANKSGIVING FESTIVALS DO YOU THINK WE'LL BE ABLE TO CELEBRATE THIS SPRING?
I WISH WE COULD CELEBRATE A THIRD OR A FOURTH...
DON'T YOU THINK THINGS WILL BE DIFFERENT THIS TIME? ♡
WHAT ARE THEY TALKING ABOUT--THIRD THANKSGIVING FESTIVAL...?
AND WHERE ARE EHREN, LEON, AND SCHILLER?
LIBERA SAID SH WASN'T GOING TO COME...
AND I DIDN'T TELL ANYONE WHAT KIND OF COSTUME I'D BE WEARING...

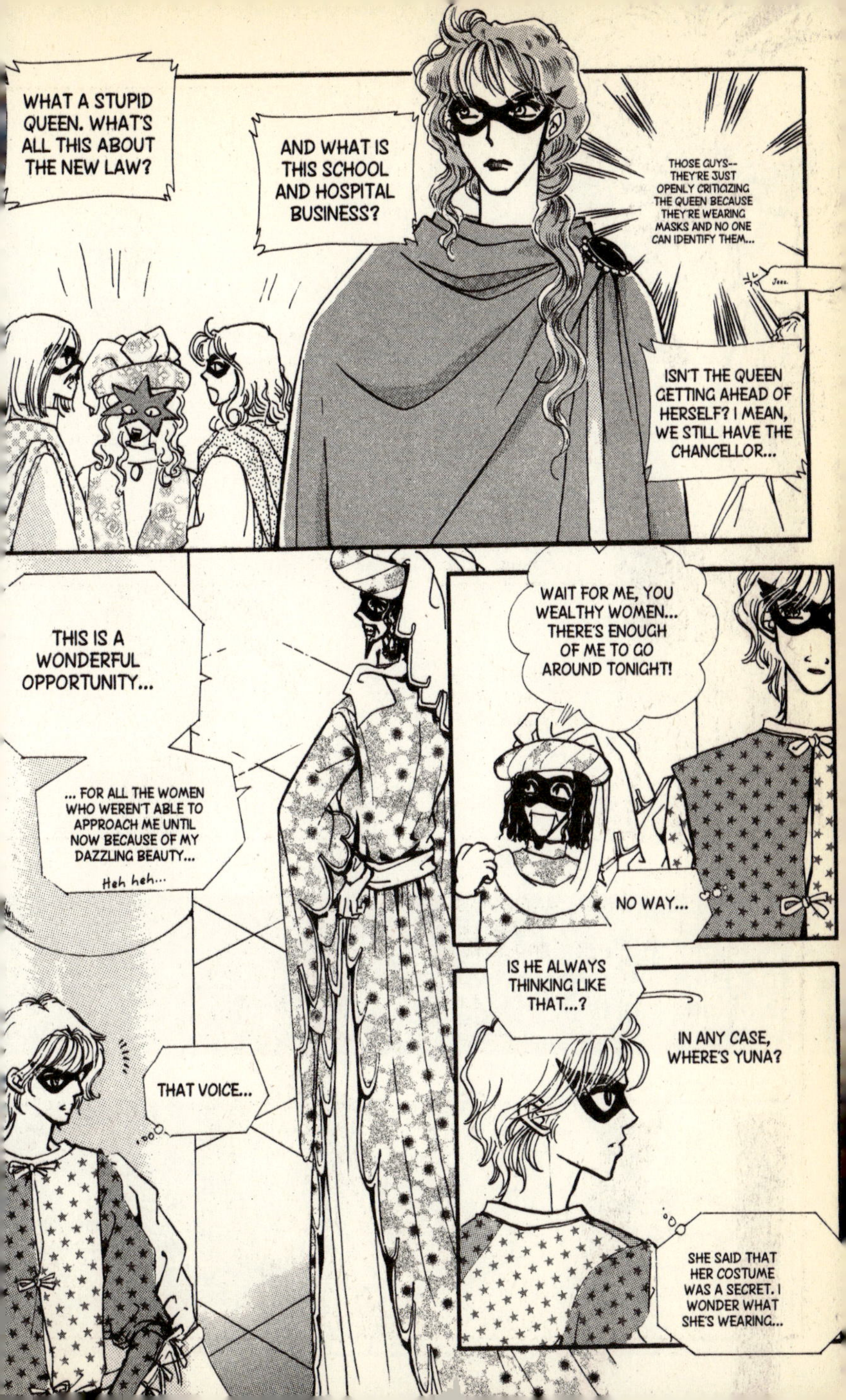
WHAT A STUPID QUEEN. WHAT'S ALL THIS ABOUT THE NEW LAW?
AND WHAT IS THIS SCHOOL AND HOSPITAL BUSINESS?
THOSE GUYS-- THEY'RE JUST OPENLY CRITICIZING THE QUEEN BECAUSE THEY'RE WEARING MASKS AND NO ONE CAN IDENTIFY THEM...
Jeez.
ISN'T THE QUEEN GETTING AHEAD OF HERSELF? I MEAN, WE STILL HAVE THE CHANCELLOR...
THIS IS A WONDERFUL OPPORTUNITY...
... FOR ALL THE WOMEN WHO WEREN'T ABLE TO APPROACH ME UNTIL NOW BECAUSE OF MY DAZZLING BEAUTY...
Heh heh...
THAT VOICE...
WAIT FOR ME, YOU WEALTHY WOMEN... THERE'S ENOUGH OF ME TO GO AROUND TONIGHT!
NO WAY...
IS HE ALWAYS THINKING LIKE THAT...?
IN ANY CASE, WHERE'S YUNA?
SHE SAID THAT HER COSTUME WAS A SECRET. I WONDER WHAT SHE'S WEARING...

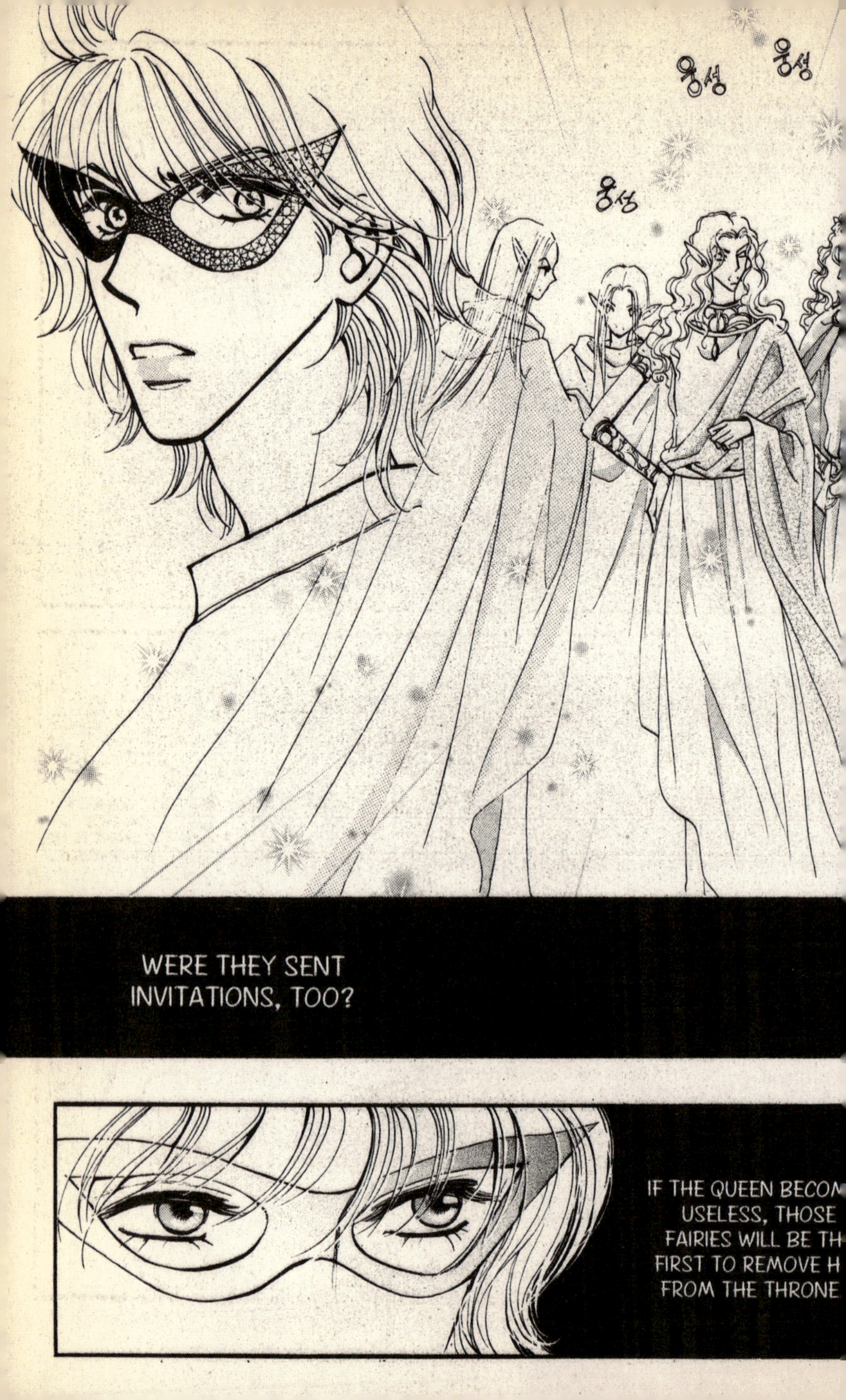
웅성 웅성
웅성
WERE THEY SENT INVITATIONS, TOO?
IF THE QUEEN BECOM USELESS, THOSE FAIRIES WILL BE TH FIRST TO REMOVE H FROM THE THRONE

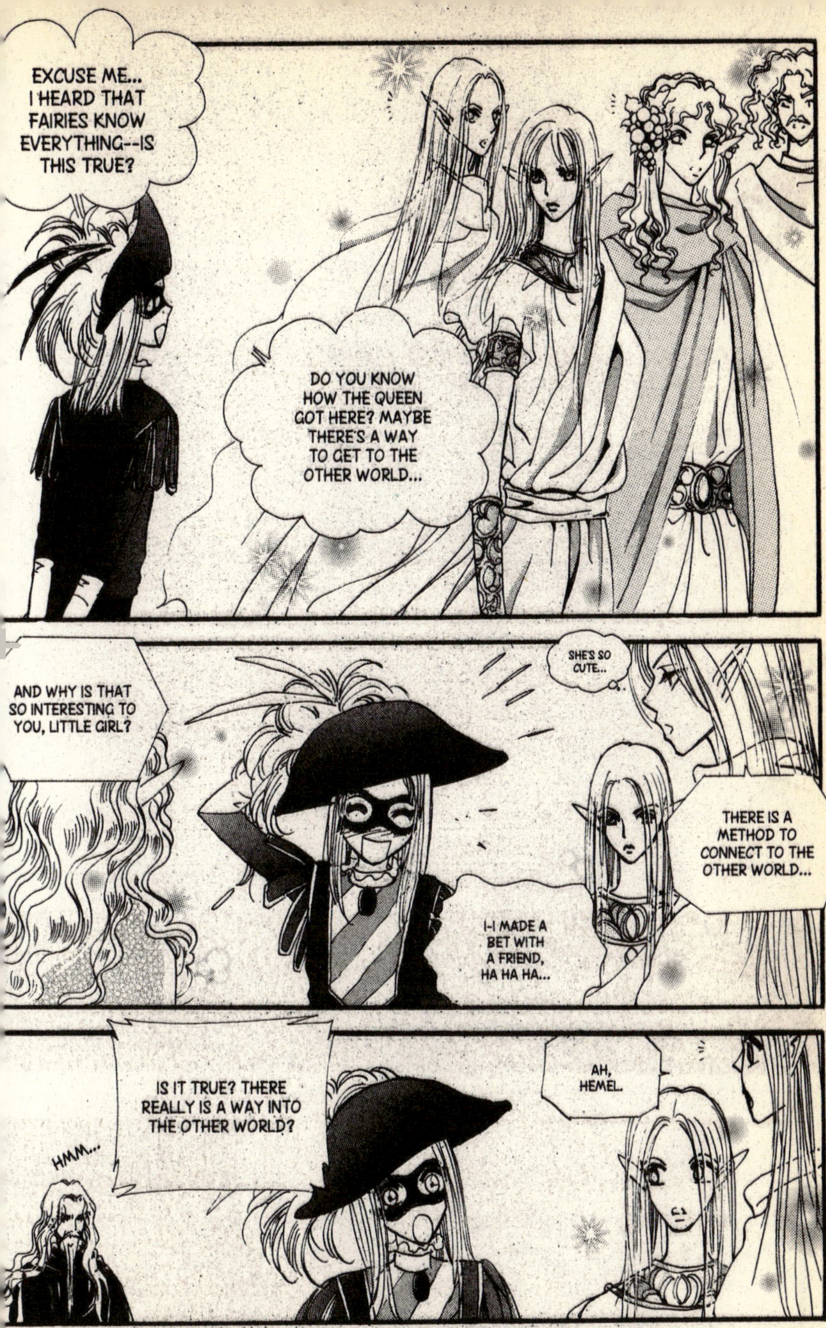
EXCUSE ME... I HEARD THAT FAIRIES KNOW EVERYTHING--IS THIS TRUE?
DO YOU KNOW HOW THE QUEEN GOT HERE? MAYBE THERE'S A WAY TO GET TO THE OTHER WORLD...
AND WHY IS THAT SO INTERESTING TO YOU, LITTLE GIRL?
SHE'S SO CUTE...
I-I MADE A BET WITH A FRIEND, HA HA HA...
THERE IS A METHOD TO CONNECT TO THE OTHER WORLD...
IS IT TRUE? THERE REALLY IS A WAY INTO THE OTHER WORLD?
HMM...
AH, HEMEL.

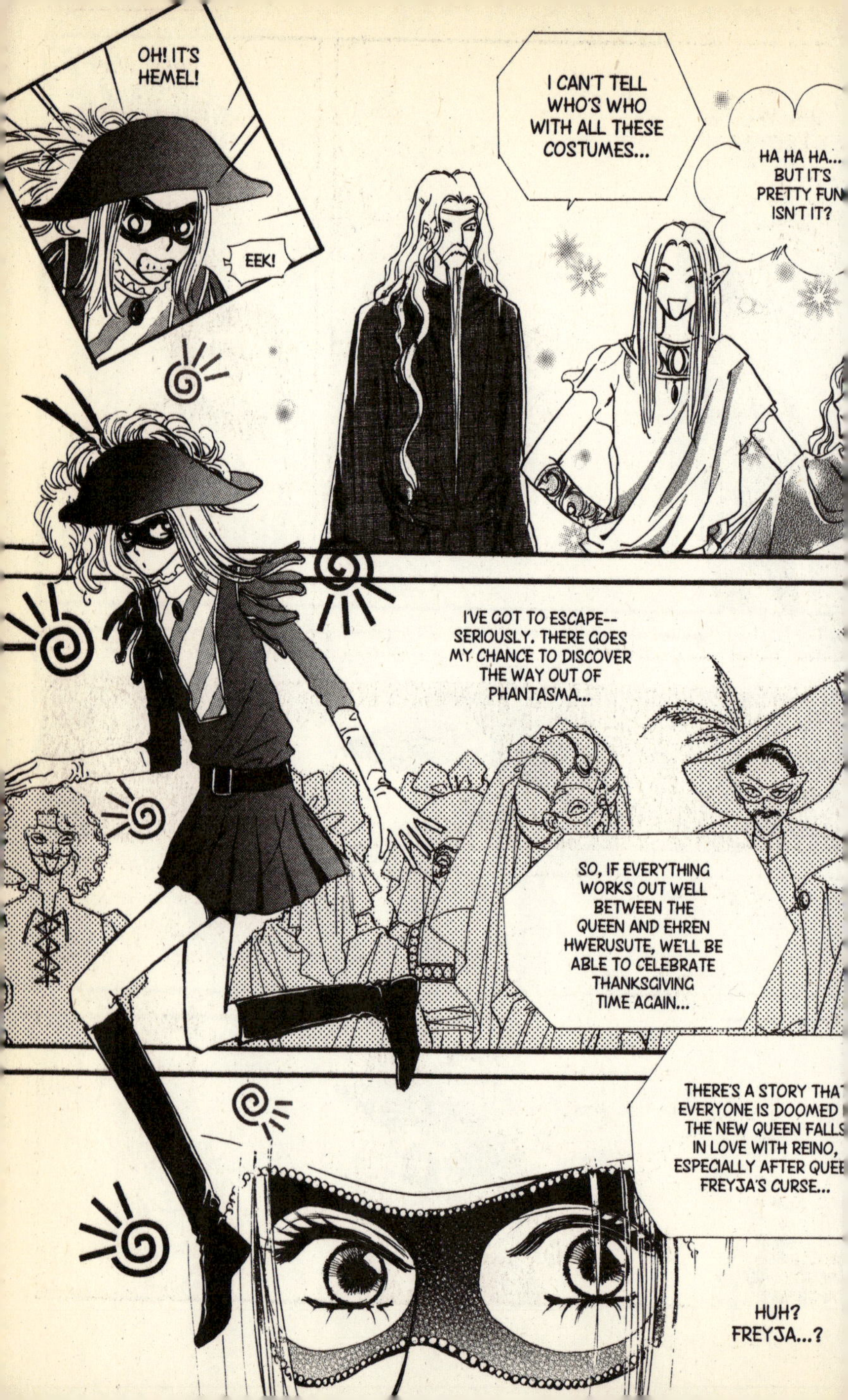
OH! IT'S HEMEL!
EEK!
I CAN'T TELL WHO'S WHO WITH ALL THESE COSTUMES...
HA HA HA... BUT IT'S PRETTY FUN ISN'T IT?
I'VE GOT TO ESCAPE-- SERIOUSLY. THERE GOES MY CHANCE TO DISCOVER THE WAY OUT OF PHANTASMA...
SO, IF EVERYTHING WORKS OUT WELL BETWEEN THE QUEEN AND EHREN HWERUSUTE, WE'LL BE ABLE TO CELEBRATE THANKSGIVING TIME AGAIN...
THERE'S A STORY THA EVERYONE IS DOOMED THE NEW QUEEN FALLS IN LOVE WITH REINO, ESPECIALLY AFTER QUEE FREYJA'S CURSE...
HUH? FREYJA...?

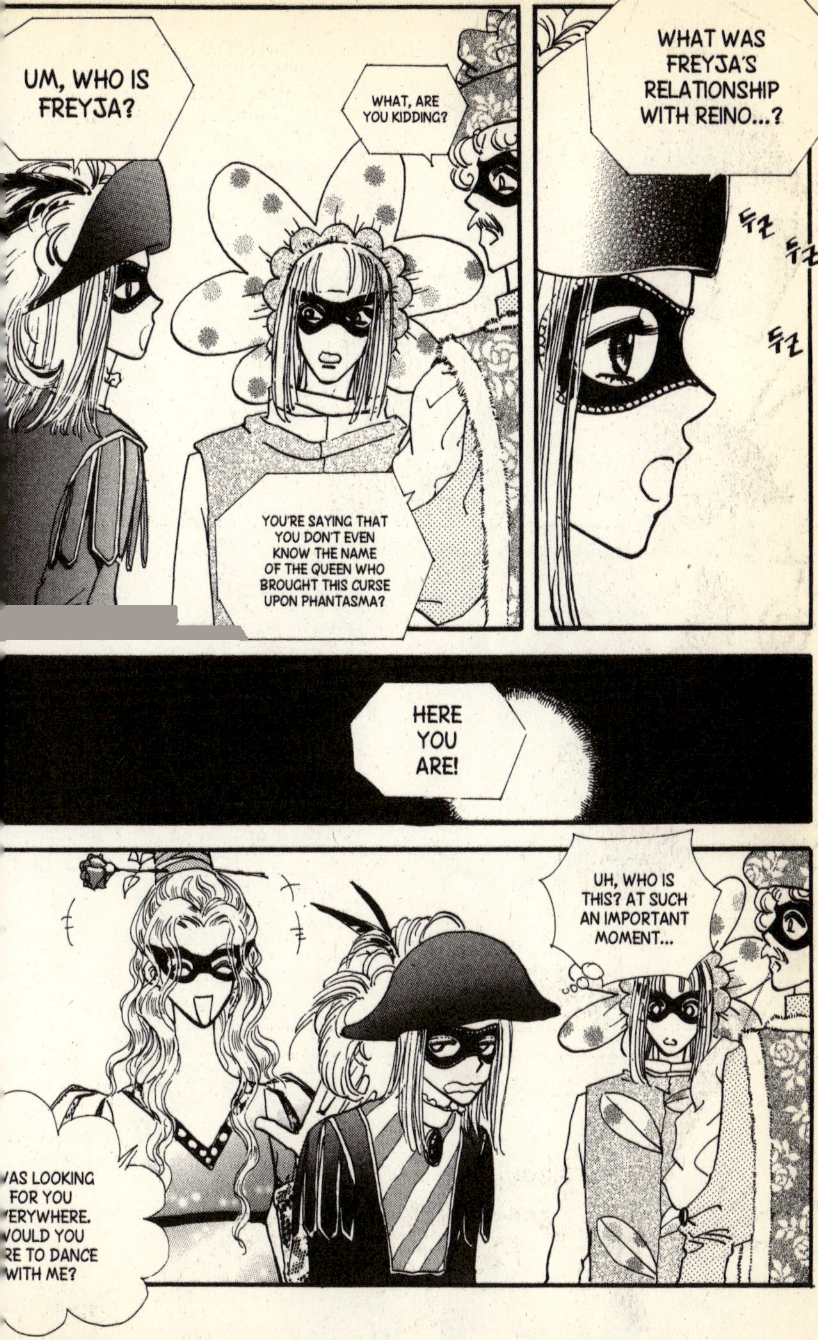
UM, WHO IS FREYJA?
WHAT, ARE YOU KIDDING?
YOU'RE SAYING THAT YOU DON'T EVEN KNOW THE NAME OF THE QUEEN WHO BROUGHT THIS CURSE UPON PHANTASMA?
WHAT WAS FREYJA'S RELATIONSHIP WITH REINO...?
두근
두근
두근
HERE YOU ARE!
AS LOOKING FOR YOU ERYWHERE. OULD YOU RE TO DANCE WITH ME?
UH, WHO IS THIS? AT SUCH AN IMPORTANT MOMENT...

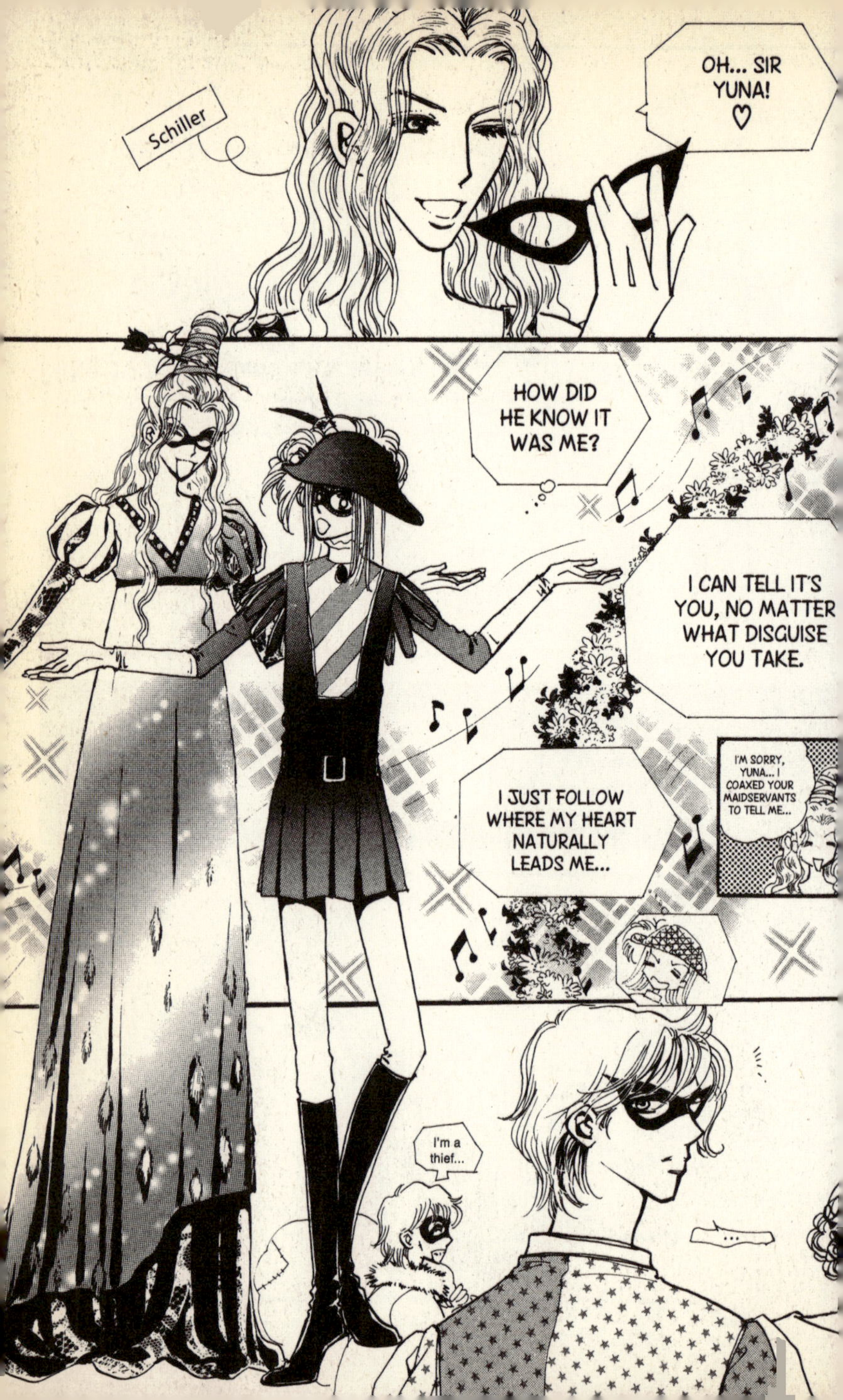
Schiller
OH... SIR YUNA! ♡
HOW DID HE KNOW IT WAS ME?
I CAN TELL IT'S YOU, NO MATTER WHAT DISGUISE YOU TAKE.
I JUST FOLLOW WHERE MY HEART NATURALLY LEADS ME...
I'M SORRY, YUNA... I COAXED YOUR MAIDSERVANTS TO TELL ME...
I'm a thief...
...

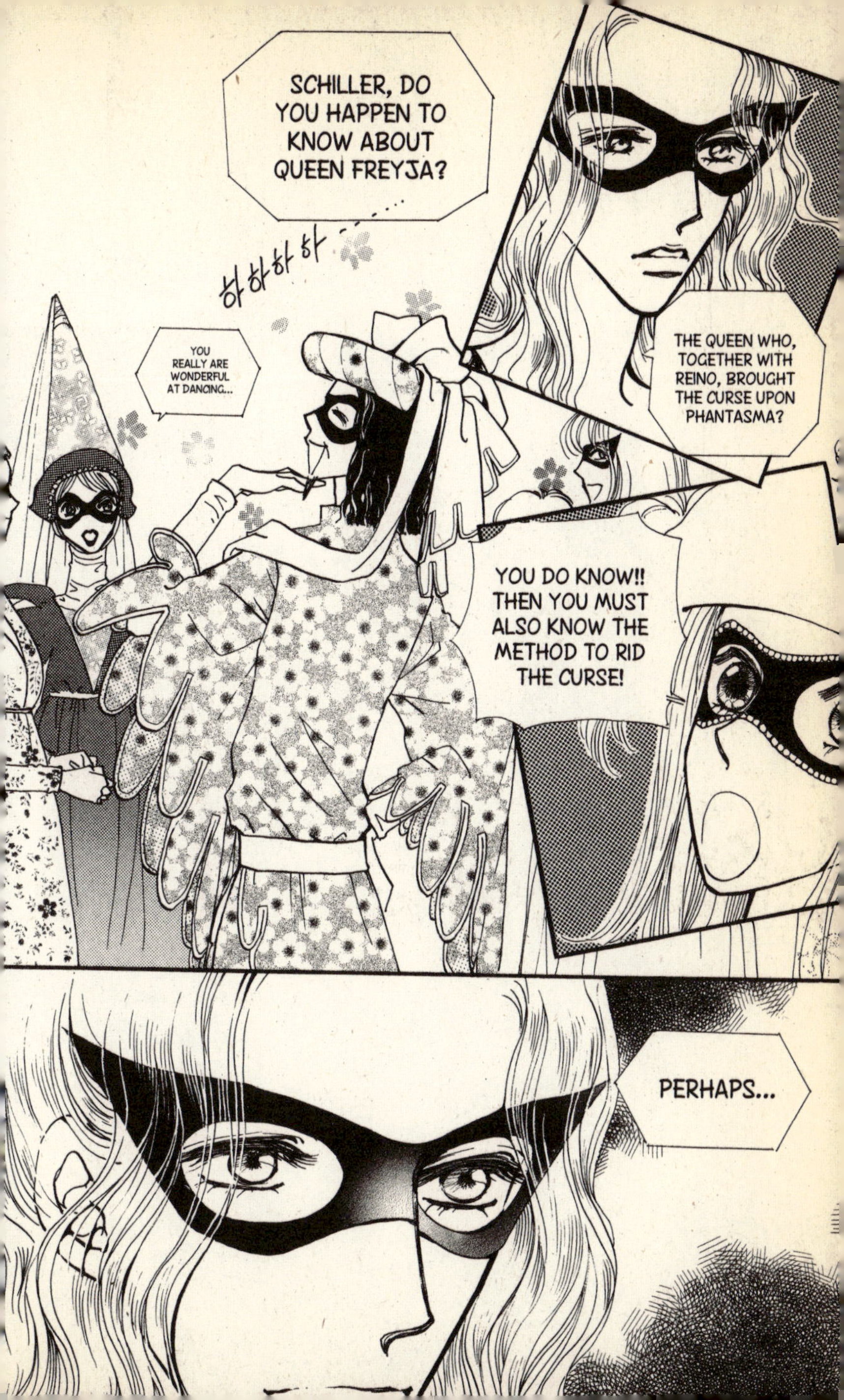
SCHILLER, DO YOU HAPPEN TO KNOW ABOUT QUEEN FREYJA?
하하하 하
YOU REALLY ARE WONDERFUL AT DANCING...
THE QUEEN WHO, TOGETHER WITH REINO, BROUGHT THE CURSE UPON PHANTASMA?
YOU DO KNOW!! THEN YOU MUST ALSO KNOW THE METHOD TO RID THE CURSE!
PERHAPS...

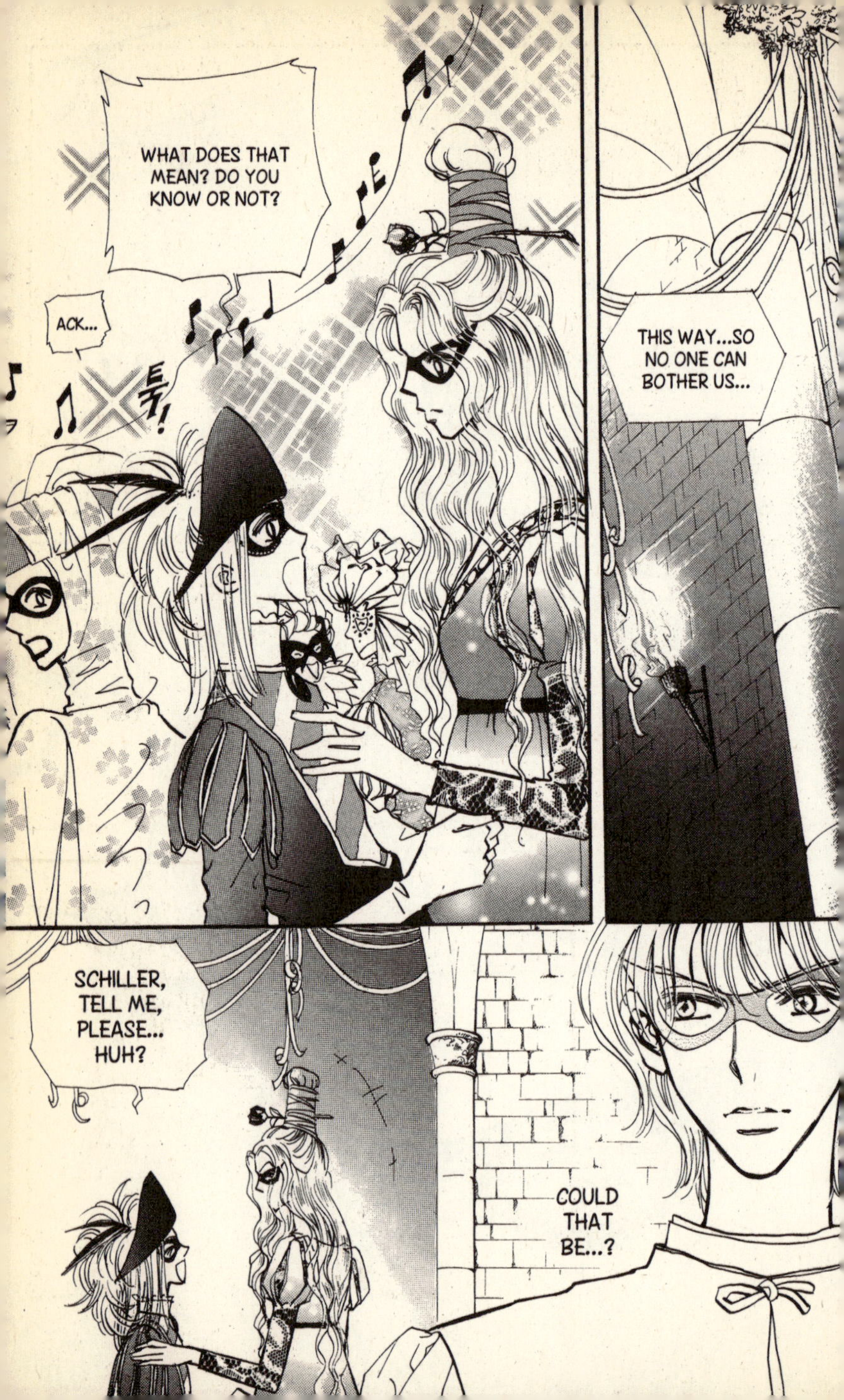
WHAT DOES THAT MEAN? DO YOU KNOW OR NOT?
ACK...
THIS WAY...SO NO ONE CAN BOTHER US...
SCHILLER, TELL ME, PLEASE... HUH?
COULD THAT BE...?

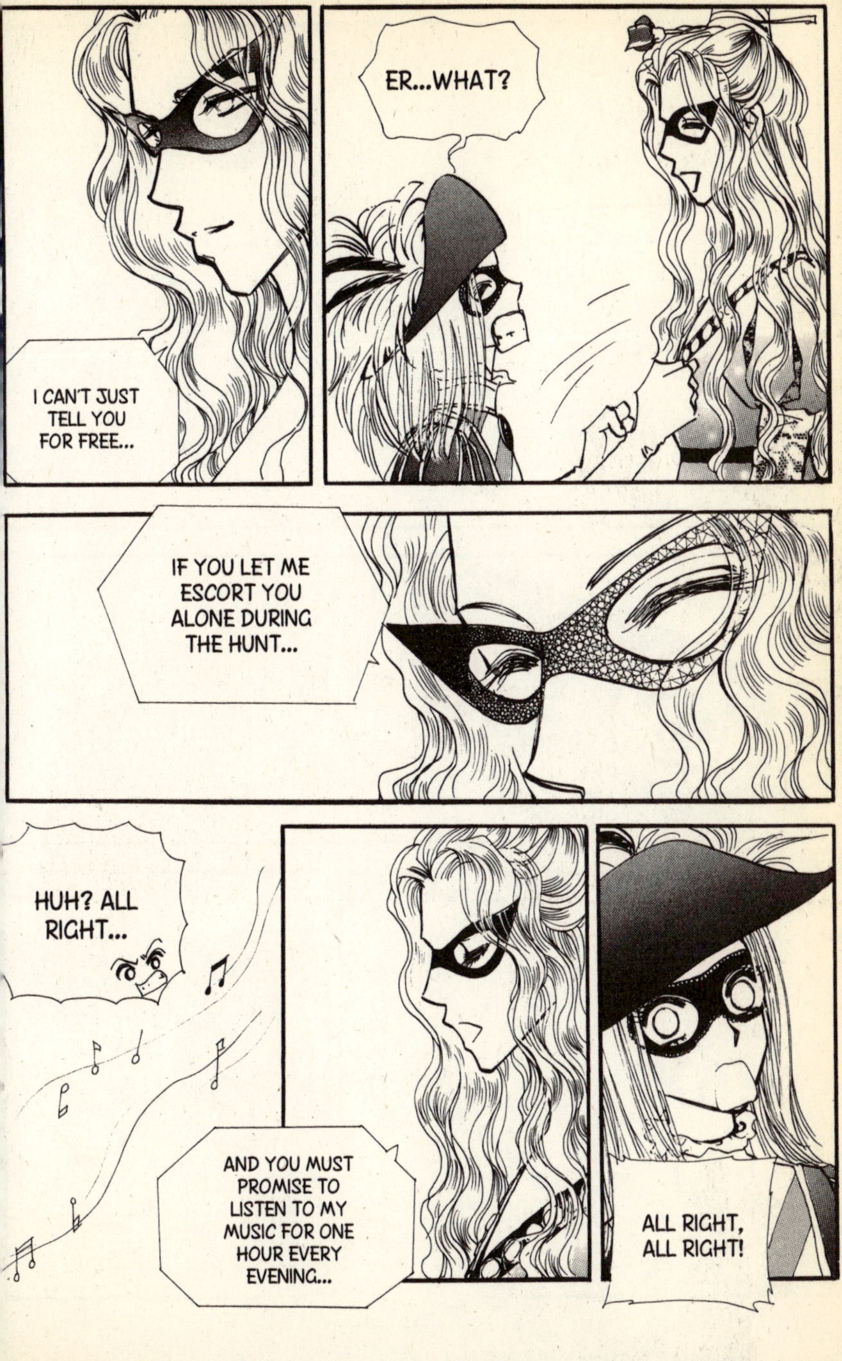
I CAN'T JUST TELL YOU FOR FREE...
ER...WHAT?
IF YOU LET ME ESCORT YOU ALONE DURING THE HUNT...
HUH? ALL RIGHT...
AND YOU MUST PROMISE TO LISTEN TO MY MUSIC FOR ONE HOUR EVERY EVENING...
ALL RIGHT, ALL RIGHT!

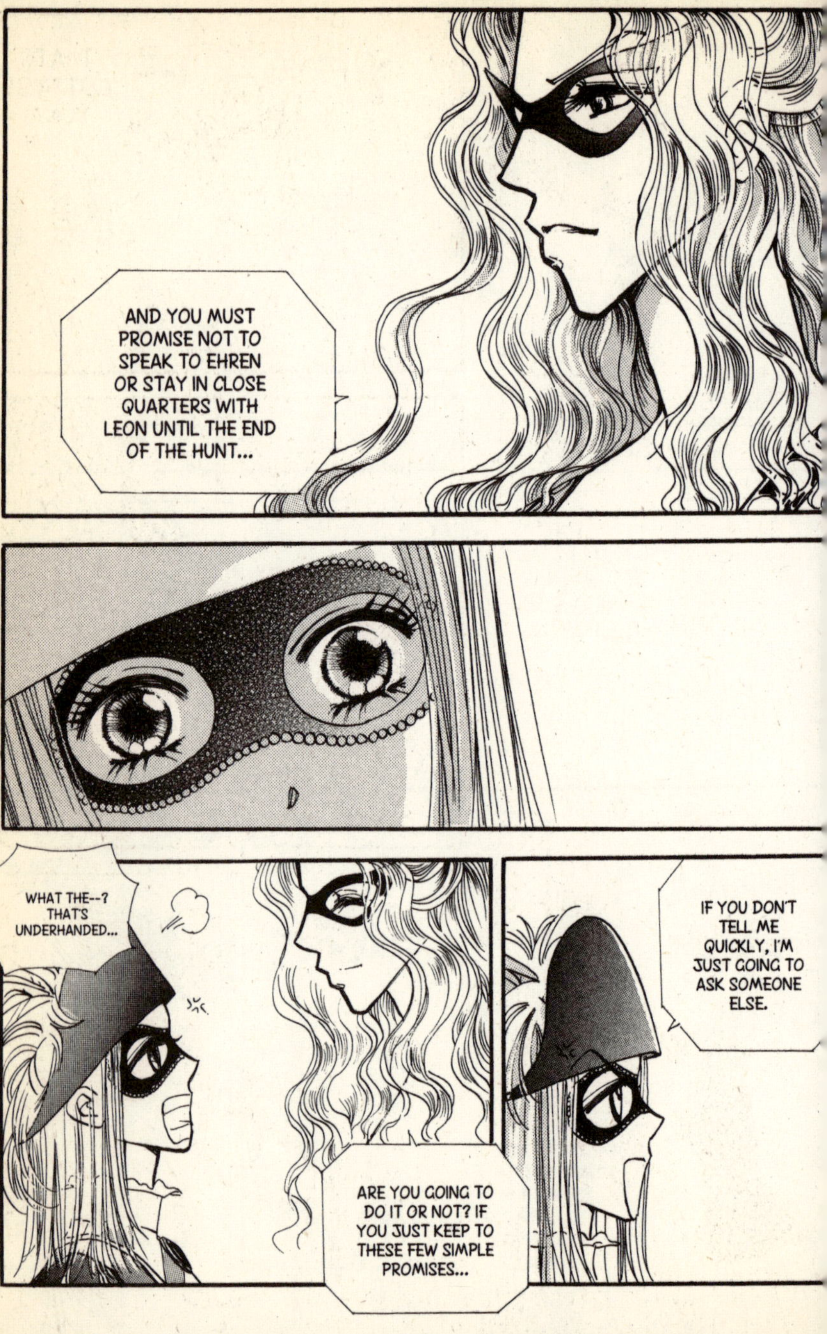
AND YOU MUST PROMISE NOT TO SPEAK TO EHREN OR STAY IN CLOSE QUARTERS WITH LEON UNTIL THE END OF THE HUNT...
WHAT THE--? THAT'S UNDERHANDED...
ARE YOU GOING TO DO IT OR NOT? IF YOU JUST KEEP TO THESE FEW SIMPLE PROMISES...
IF YOU DON'T TELL ME QUICKLY, I'M JUST GOING TO ASK SOMEONE ELSE.

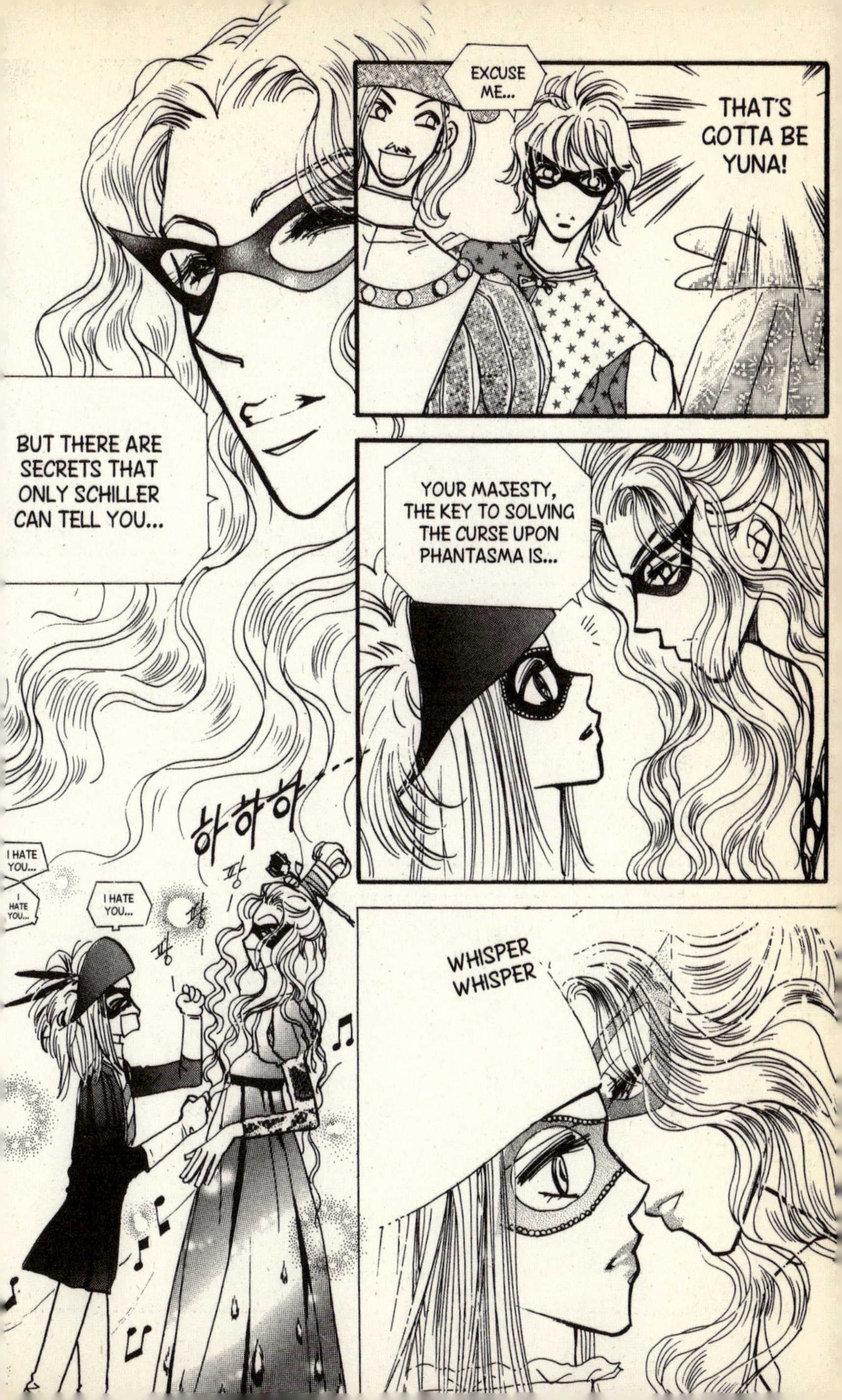
BUT THERE ARE SECRETS THAT ONLY SCHILLER CAN TELL YOU...
EXCUSE ME...
THAT'S GOTTA BE YUNA!
YOUR MAJESTY, THE KEY TO SOLVING THE CURSE UPON PHANTASMA IS...
하하하
팡
팡
팡
I HATE YOU...
I HATE YOU...
I HATE YOU...
WHISPER WHISPER

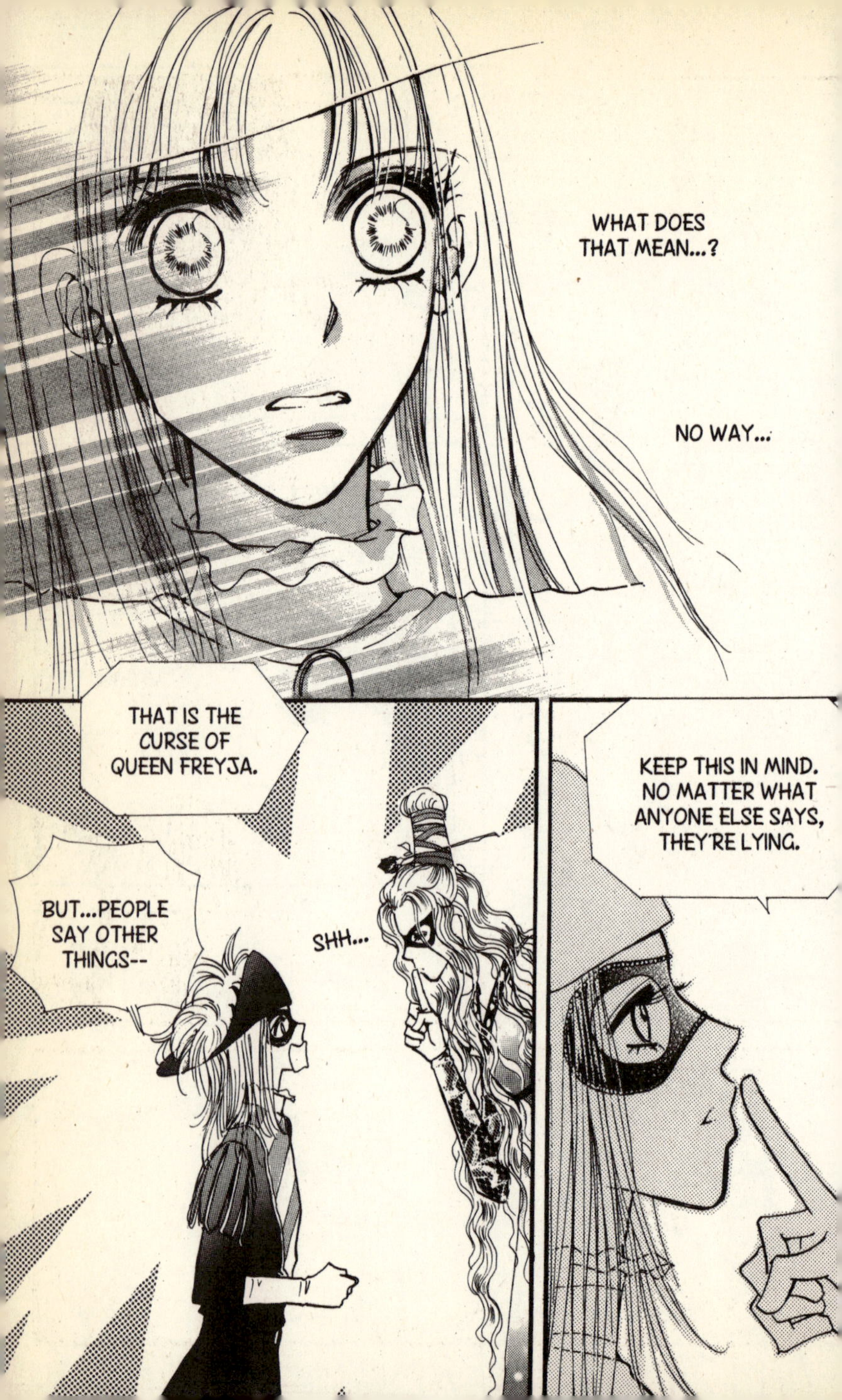
WHAT DOES THAT MEAN...?
NO WAY...
THAT IS THE CURSE OF QUEEN FREYJA.
BUT...PEOPLE SAY OTHER THINGS--
SHH...
KEEP THIS IN MIND. NO MATTER WHAT ANYONE ELSE SAYS, THEY'RE LYING.

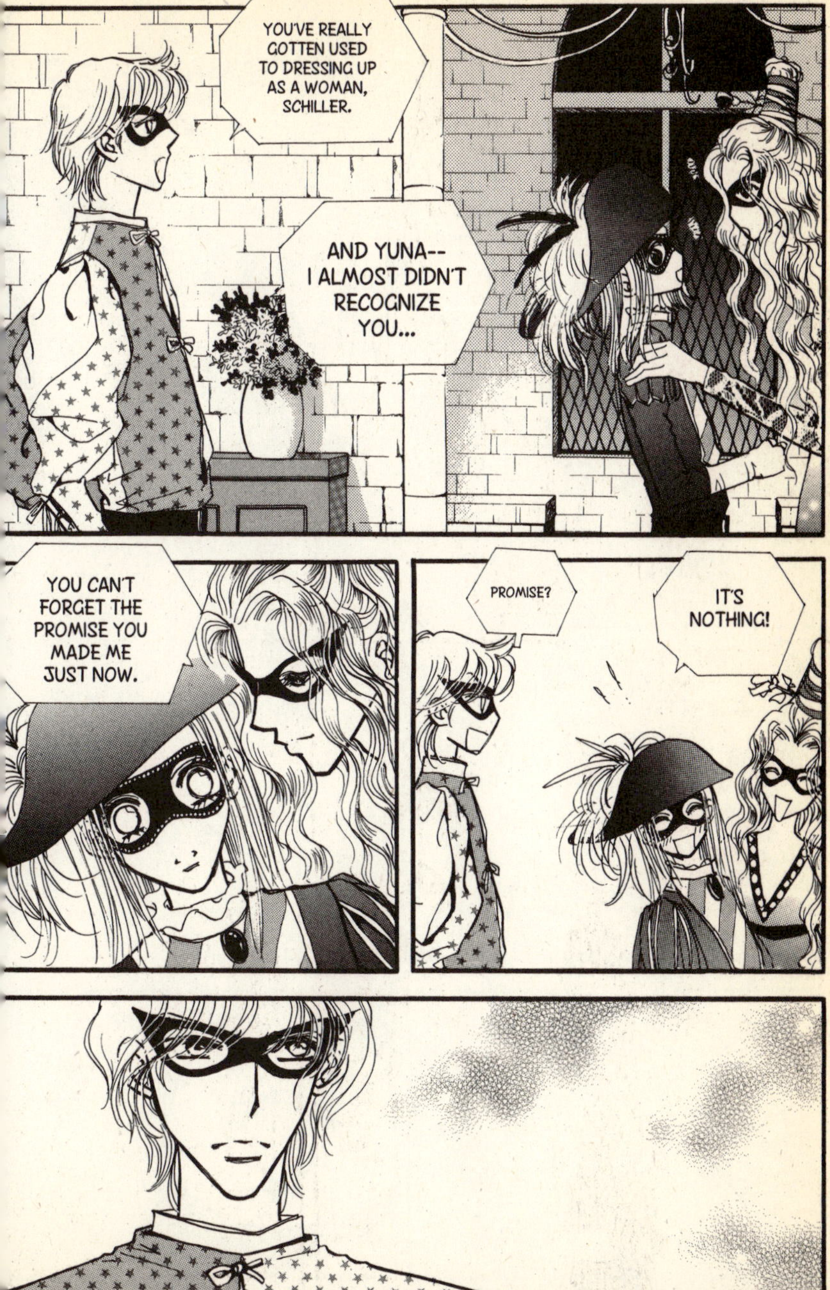
YOU'VE REALLY GOTTEN USED TO DRESSING UP AS A WOMAN, SCHILLER.
AND YUNA-- I ALMOST DIDN'T RECOGNIZE YOU...
YOU CAN'T FORGET THE PROMISE YOU MADE ME JUST NOW.
PROMISE?
IT'S NOTHING!

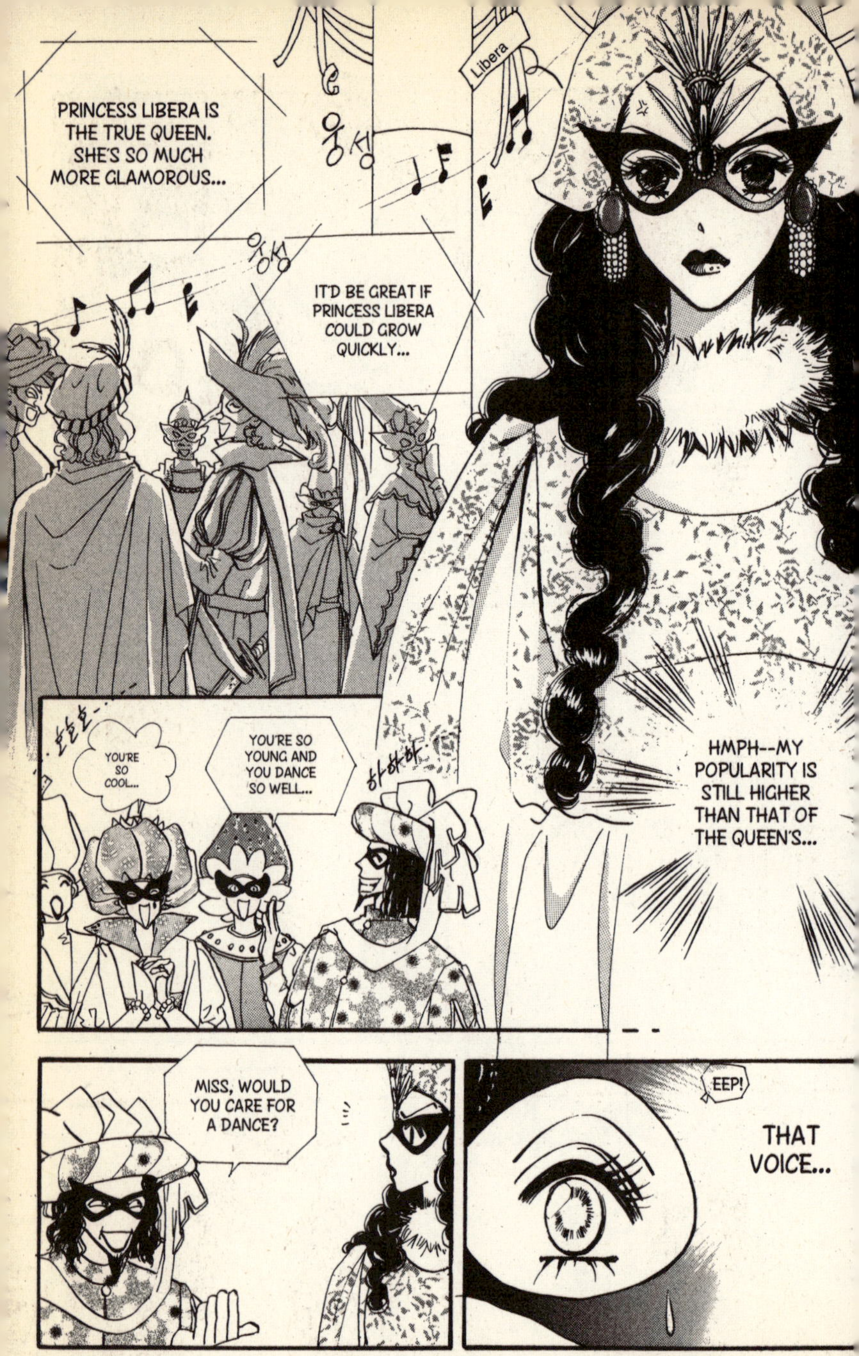

PRINCESS LIBERA IS THE TRUE QUEEN. SHE'S SO MUCH MORE GLAMOROUS...
웅성
Libera
웅성
IT'D BE GREAT IF PRINCESS LIBERA COULD GROW QUICKLY...
YOU'RE SO COOL...
YOU'RE SO YOUNG AND YOU DANCE SO WELL...
HMPH--MY POPULARITY IS STILL HIGHER THAN THAT OF THE QUEEN'S...
MISS, WOULD YOU CARE FOR A DANCE?
EEP!
THAT VOICE...

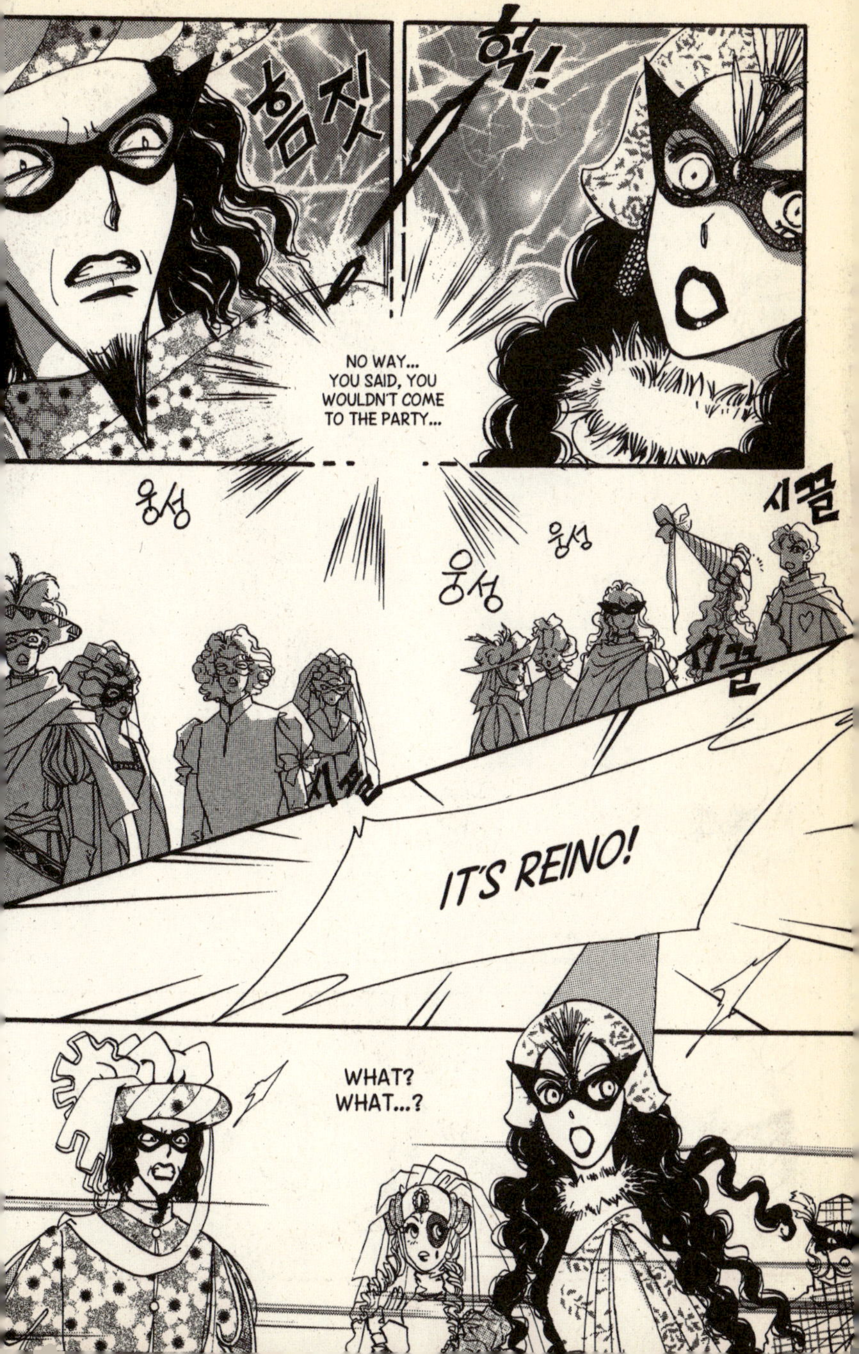
흠칫
헉!
NO WAY... YOU SAID, YOU WOULDN'T COME TO THE PARTY...
웅성
웅성
웅성
시끌
시끌
IT'S REINO!
WHAT? WHAT...?

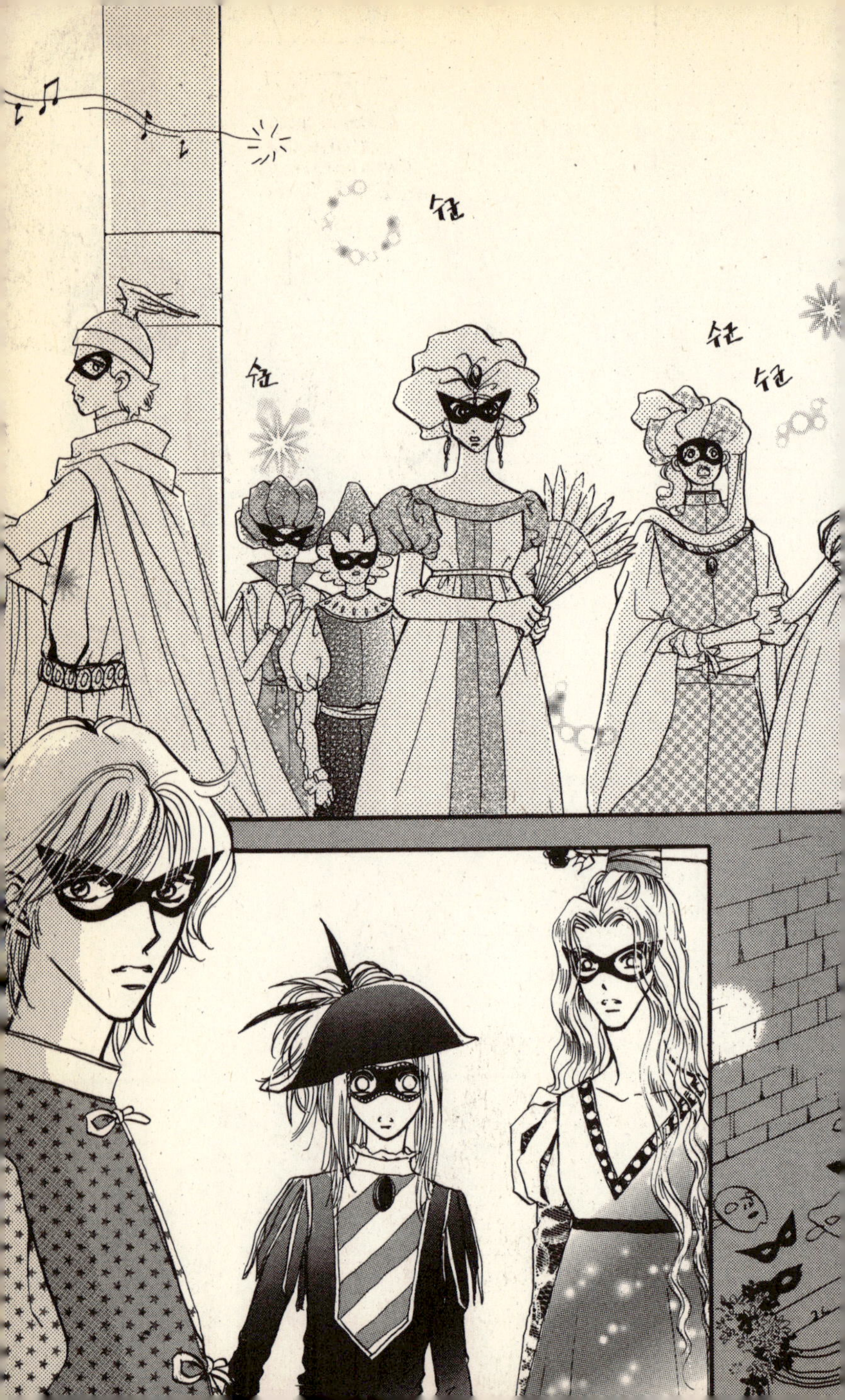
수군
수군
수군
수군

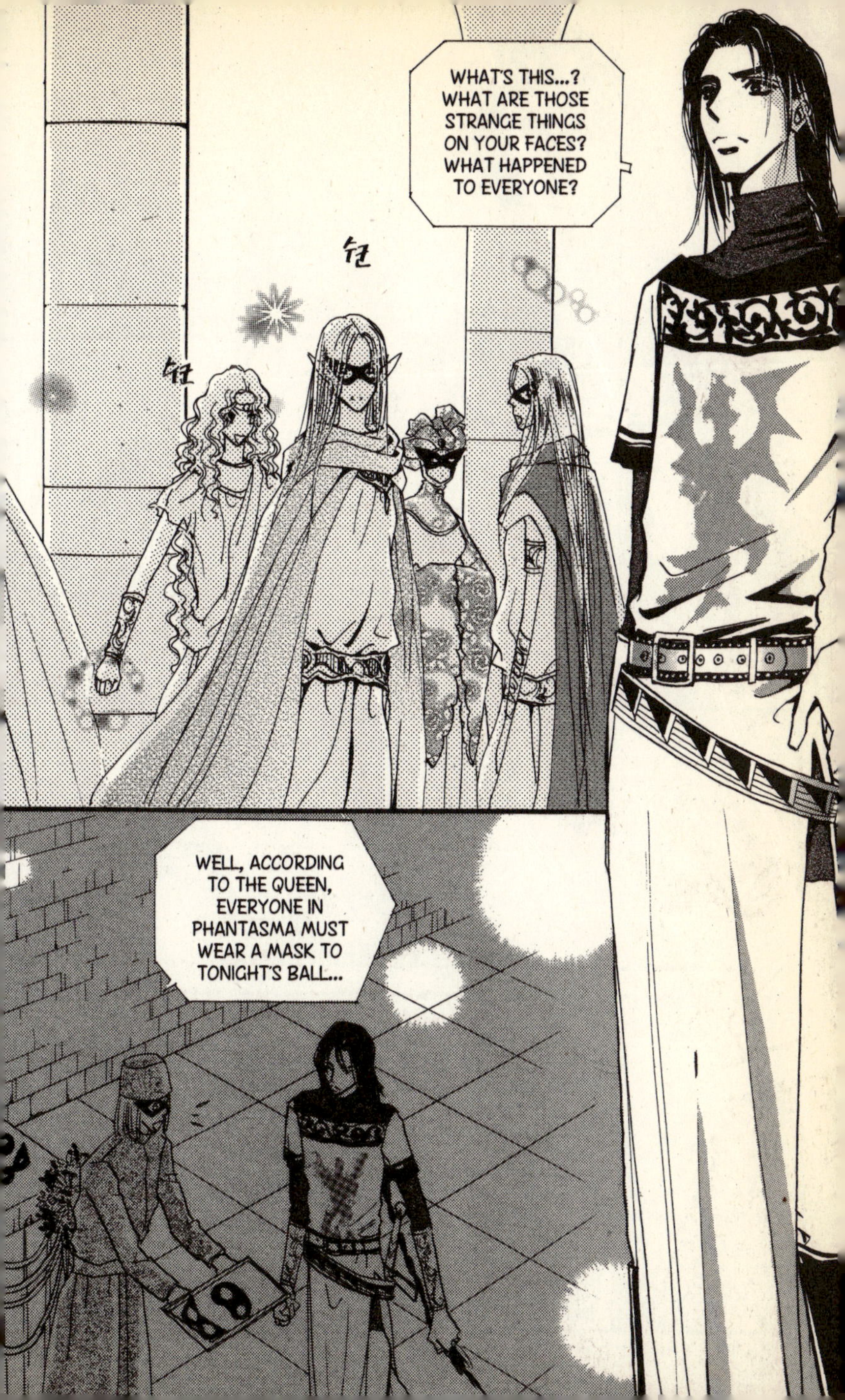
WHAT'S THIS...? WHAT ARE THOSE STRANGE THINGS ON YOUR FACES? WHAT HAPPENED TO EVERYONE?
WELL, ACCORDING TO THE QUEEN, EVERYONE IN PHANTASMA MUST WEAR A MASK TO TONIGHT'S BALL...

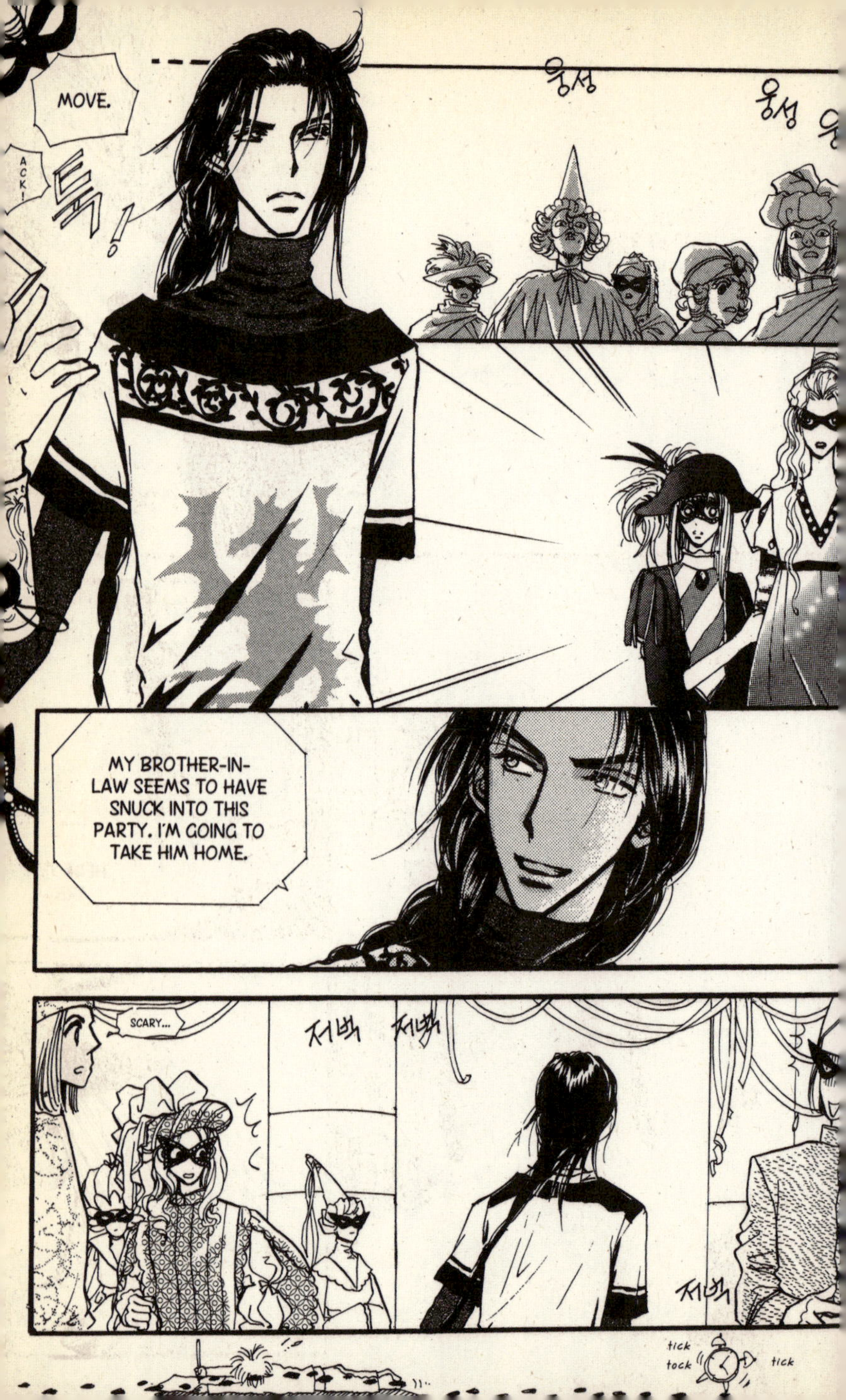
MOVE.
ACK!
툭!
웅성
웅성
MY BROTHER-IN-LAW SEEMS TO HAVE SNUCK INTO THIS PARTY. I'M GOING TO TAKE HIM HOME.
SCARY...
저벅 저벅
저벅
tick
tock
tick

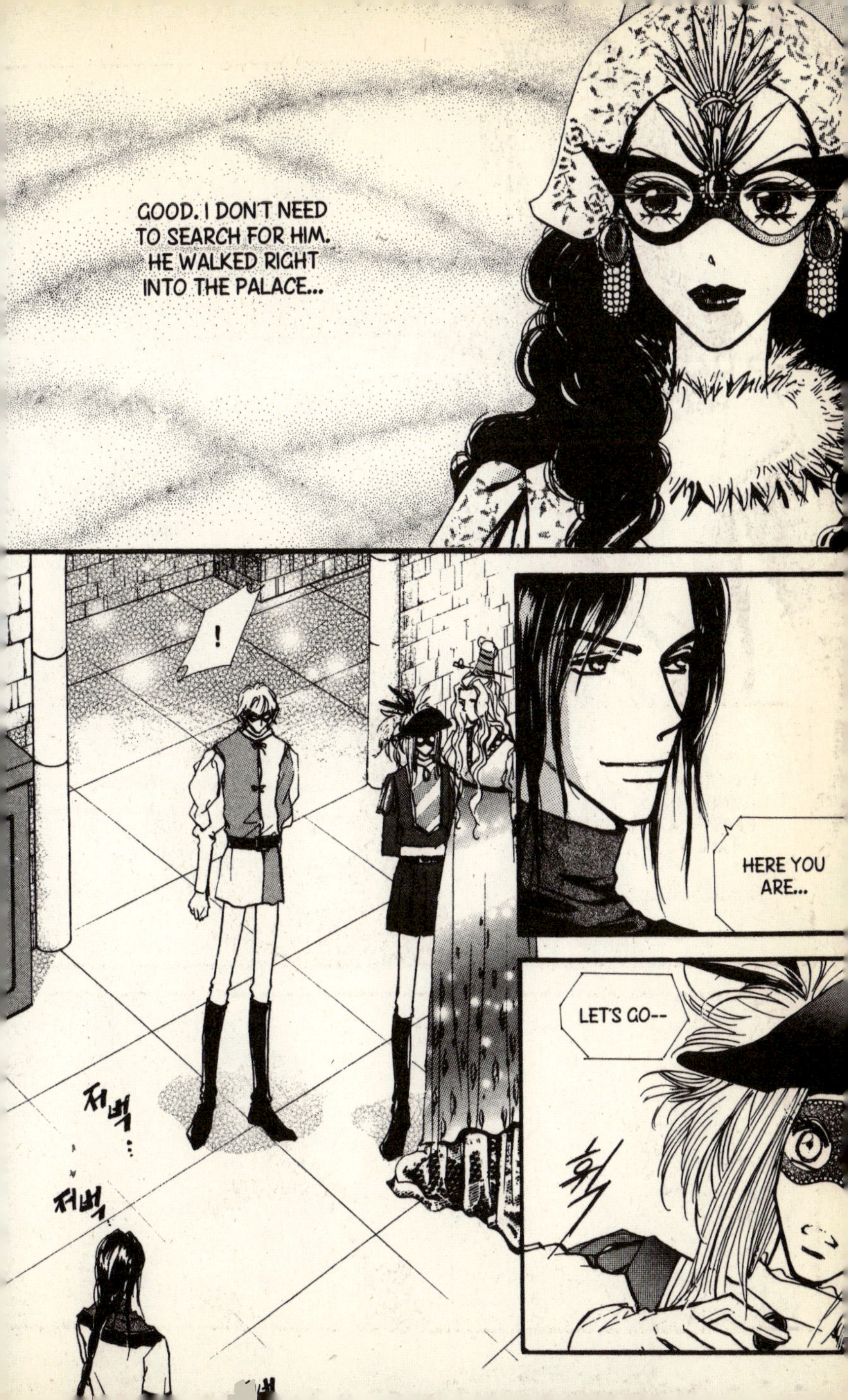

GOOD. I DON'T NEED TO SEARCH FOR HIM. HE WALKED RIGHT INTO THE PALACE...
!
저벅...
저벅
HERE YOU ARE...
LET'S GO--
휙

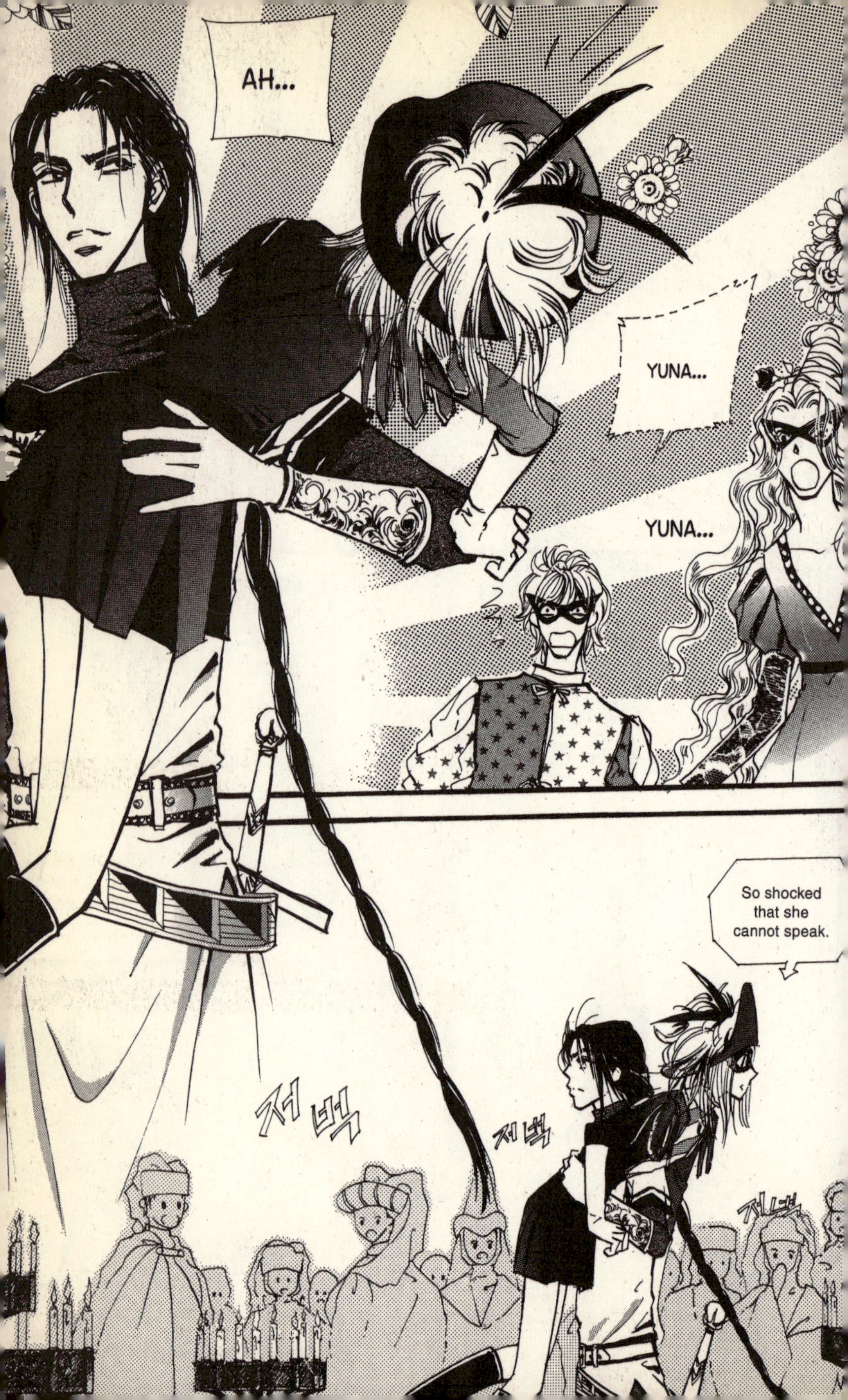
AH...
YUNA...
YUNA...
So shocked that she cannot speak.
저벅
저벅
저벅

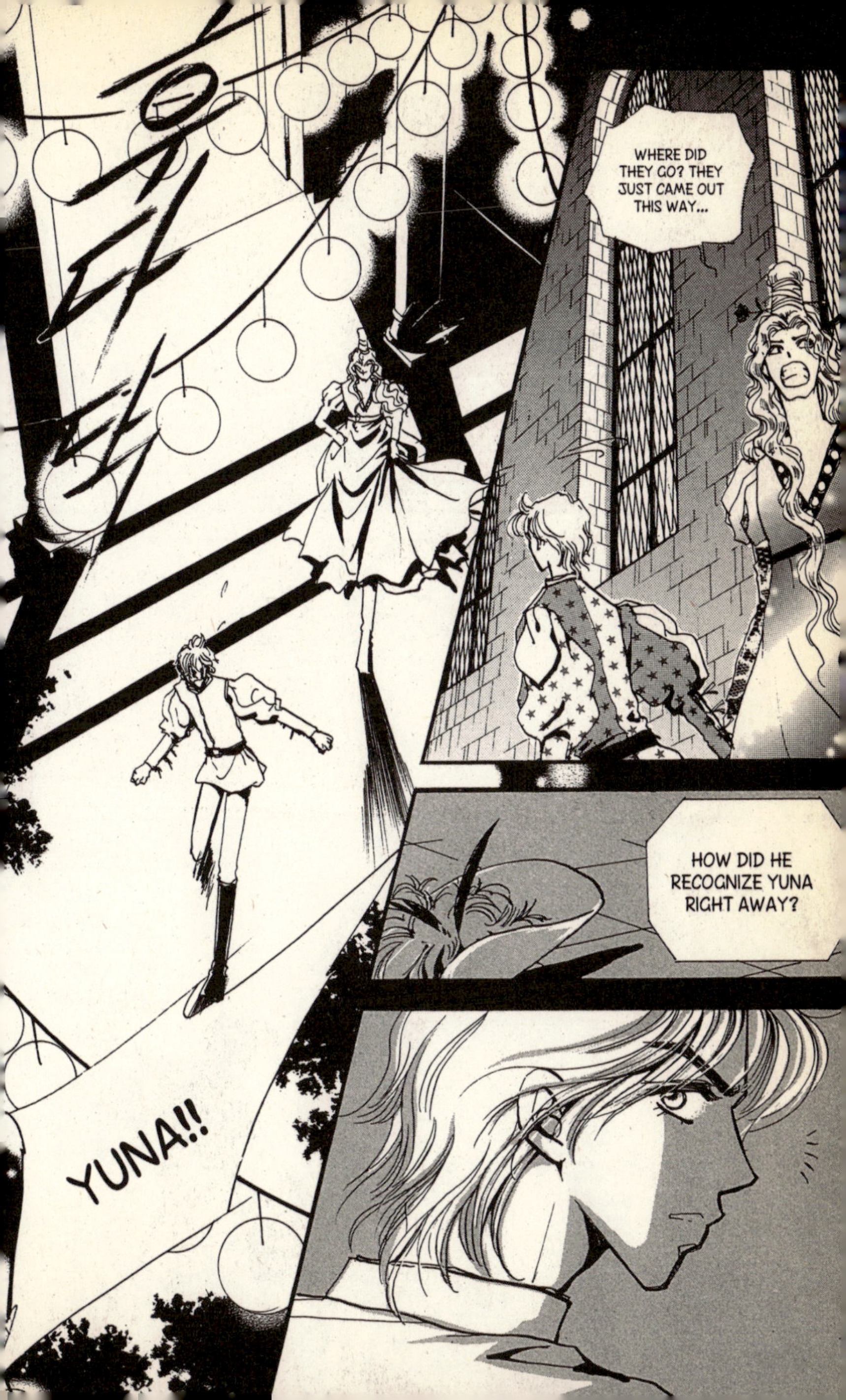
YUNA!!
WHERE DID THEY GO? THEY JUST CAME OUT THIS WAY...
HOW DID HE RECOGNIZE YUNA RIGHT AWAY?

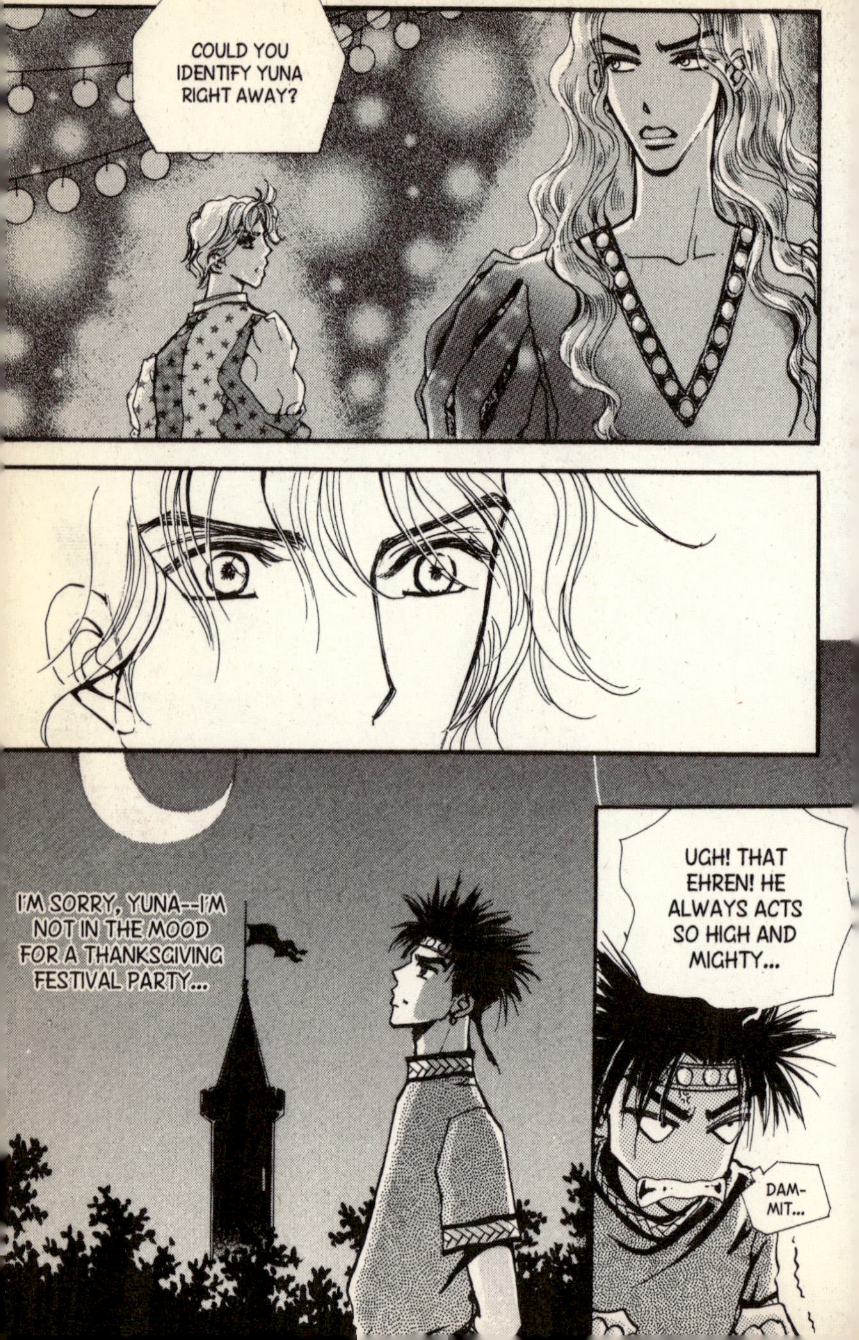
COULD YOU IDENTIFY YUNA RIGHT AWAY?
I'M SORRY, YUNA--I'M NOT IN THE MOOD FOR A THANKSGIVING FESTIVAL PARTY...
UGH! THAT EHREN! HE ALWAYS ACTS SO HIGH AND MIGHTY...
DAM-MIT...

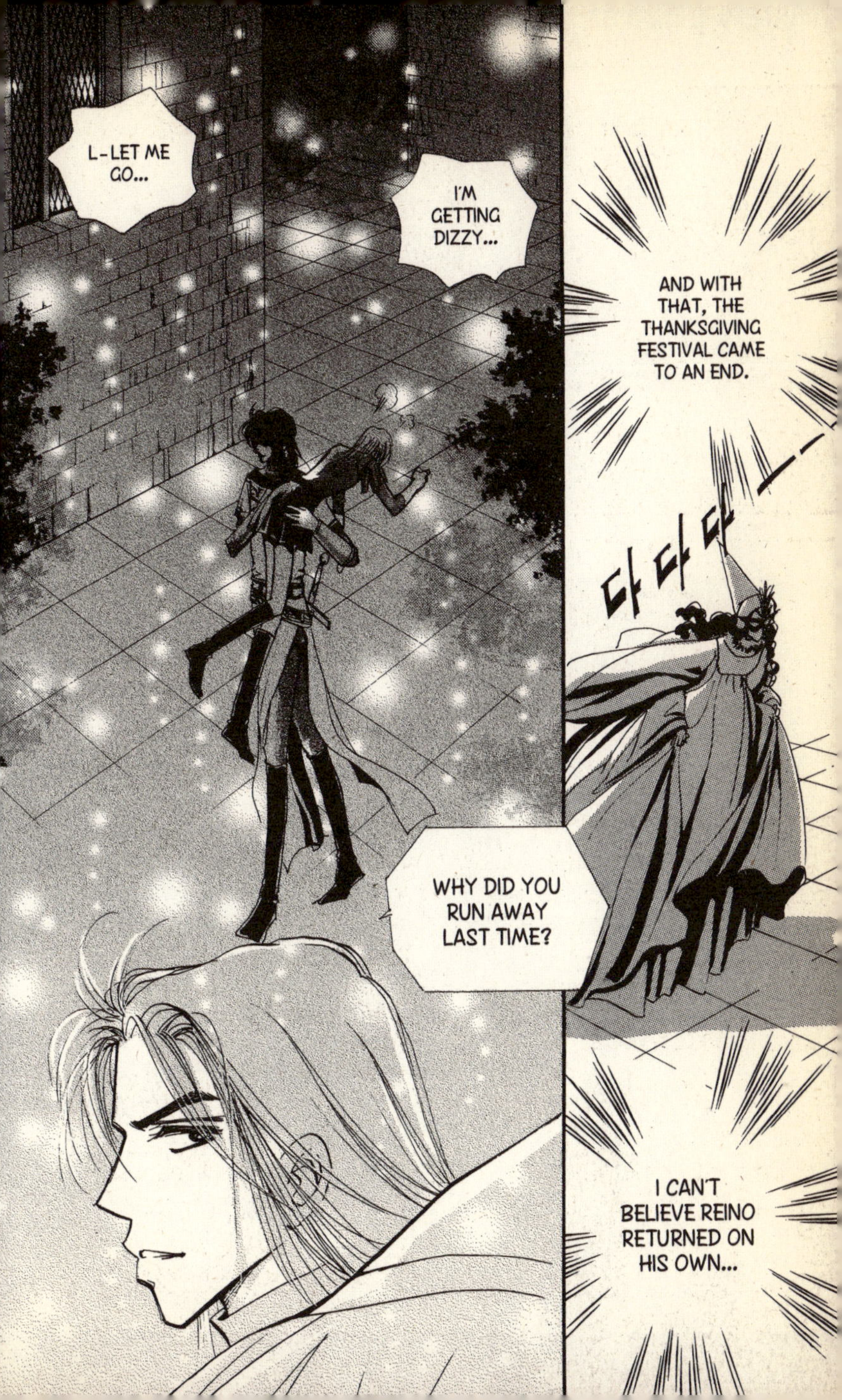
L-LET ME GO...
I'M GETTING DIZZY...
WHY DID YOU RUN AWAY LAST TIME?
AND WITH THAT, THE THANKSGIVING FESTIVAL CAME TO AN END.
다다다
I CAN'T BELIEVE REINO RETURNED ON HIS OWN...

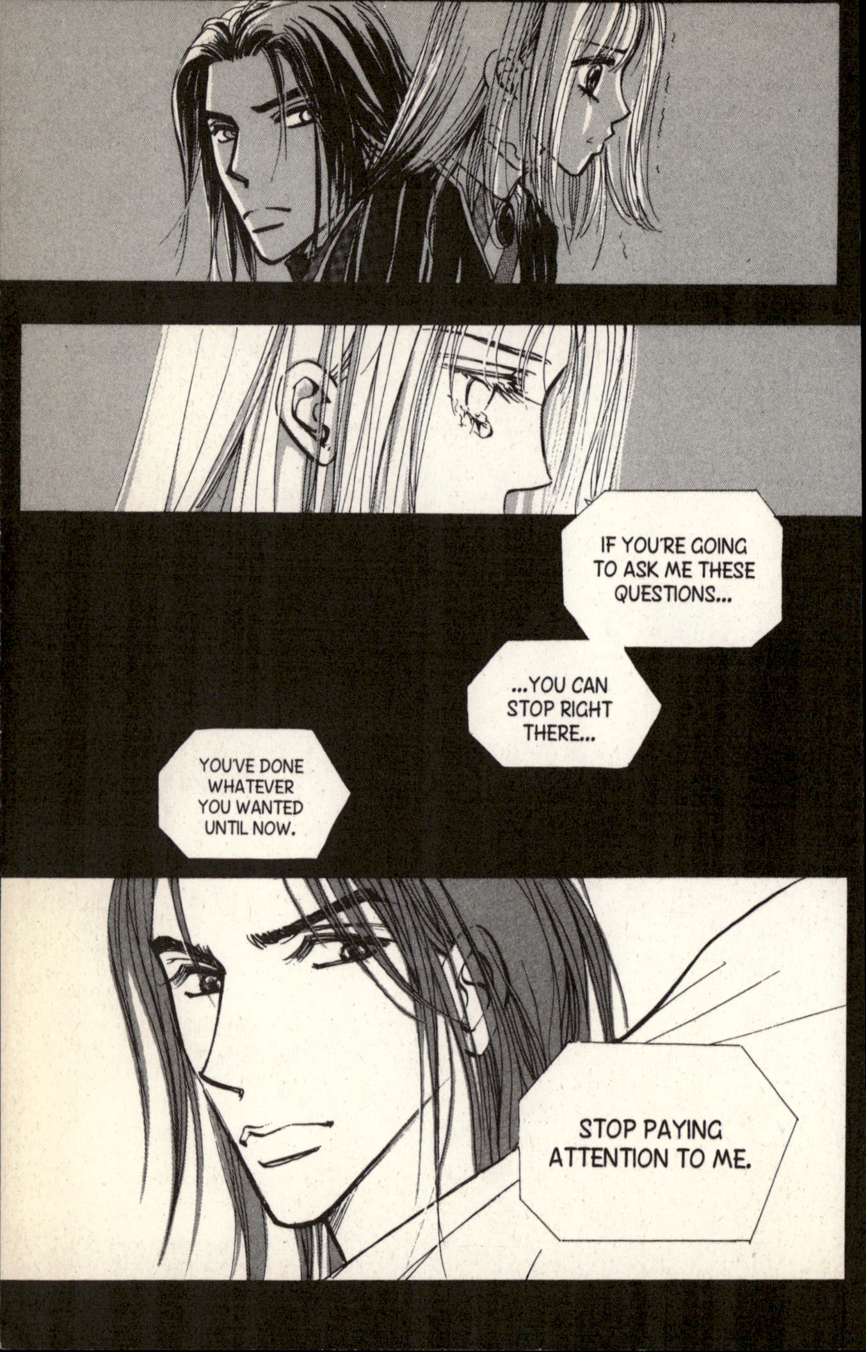
IF YOU'RE GOING TO ASK ME THESE QUESTIONS...
...YOU CAN STOP RIGHT THERE...
YOU'VE DONE WHATEVER YOU WANTED UNTIL NOW.
STOP PAYING ATTENTION TO ME.

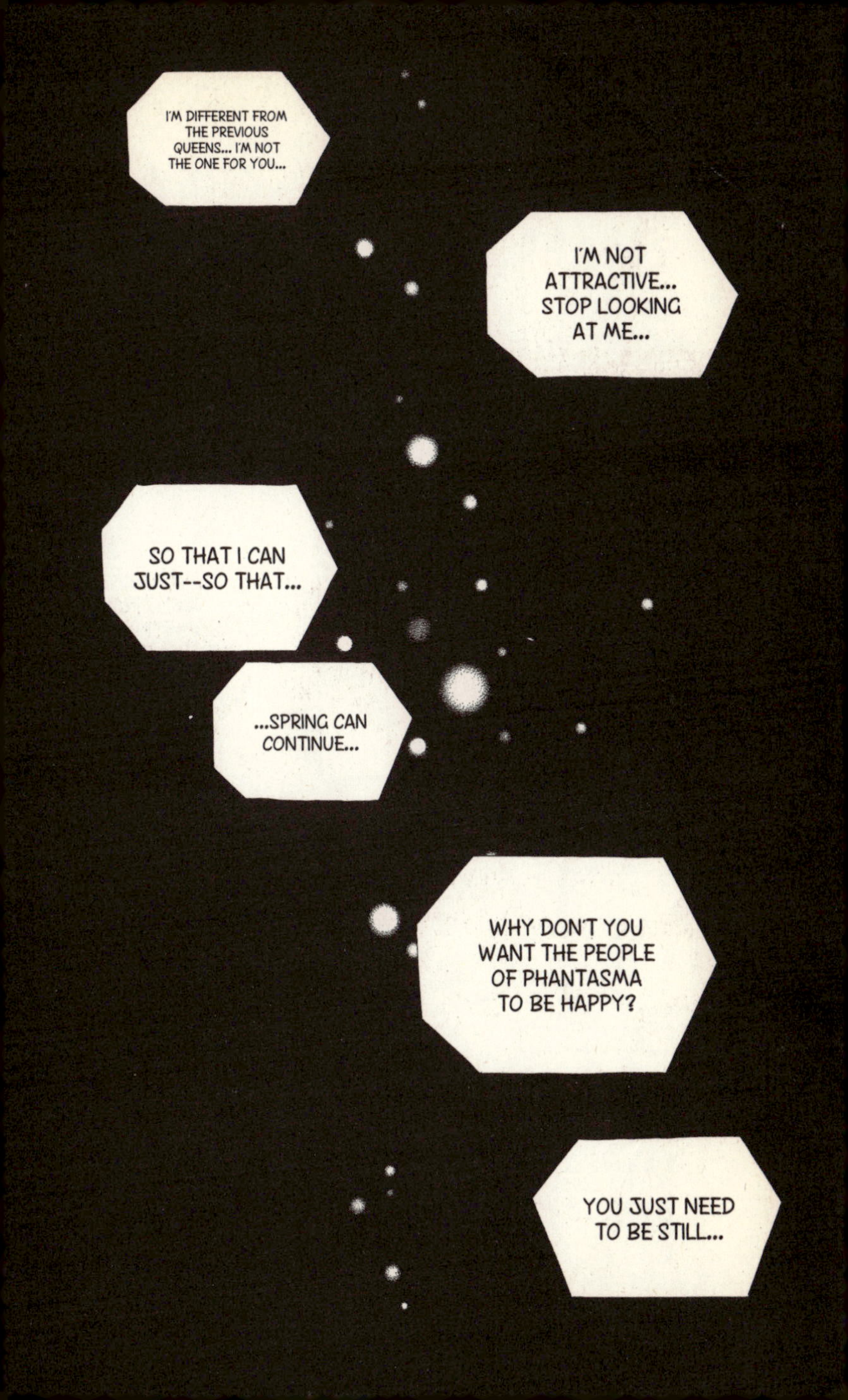
I'M DIFFERENT FROM THE PREVIOUS QUEENS... I'M NOT THE ONE FOR YOU...
I'M NOT ATTRACTIVE... STOP LOOKING AT ME...
SO THAT I CAN JUST--SO THAT...
...SPRING CAN CONTINUE...
WHY DON'T YOU WANT THE PEOPLE OF PHANTASMA TO BE HAPPY?
YOU JUST NEED TO BE STILL...

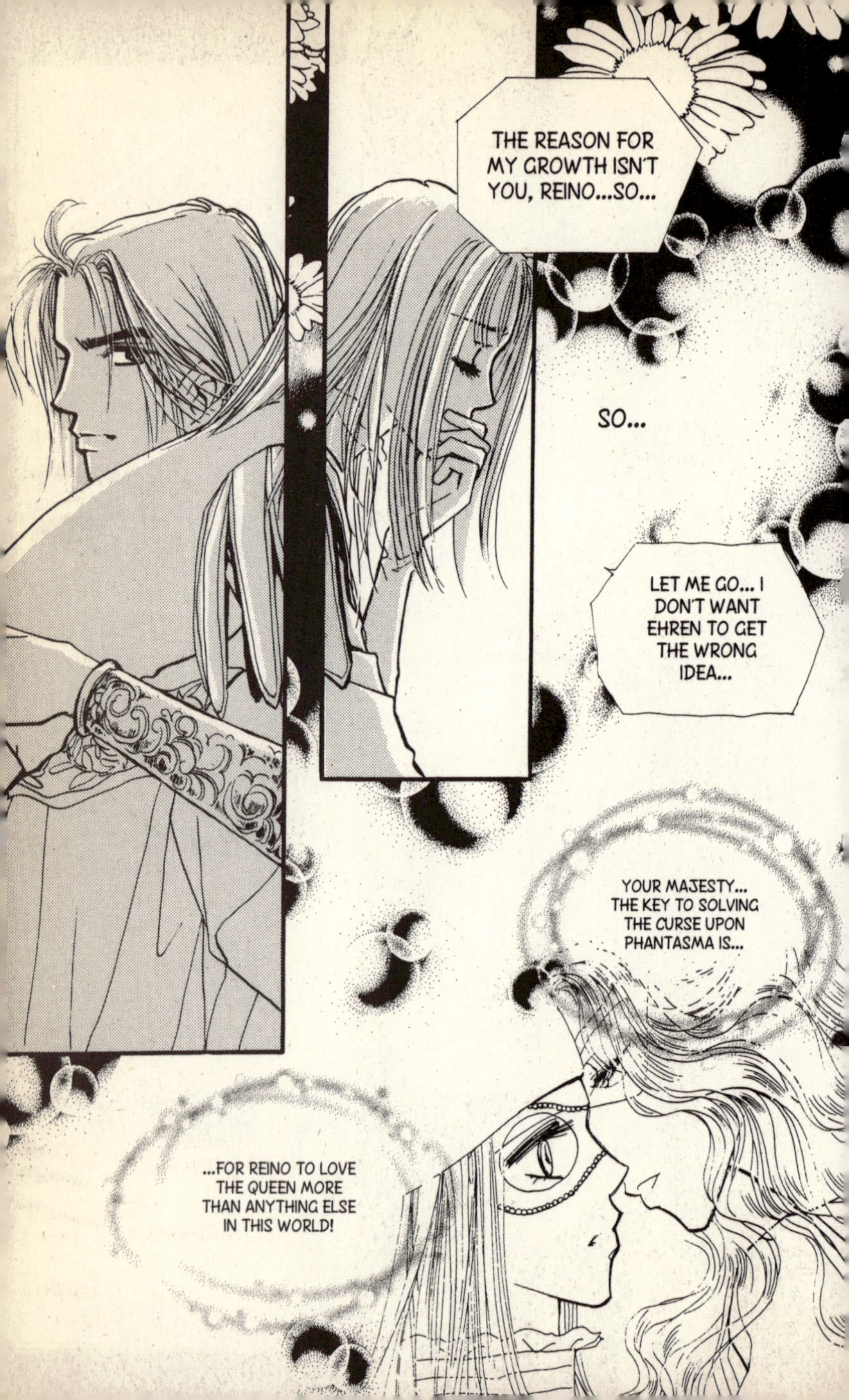
THE REASON FOR MY GROWTH ISN'T YOU, REINO...SO...
SO...
LET ME GO... I DON'T WANT EHREN TO GET THE WRONG IDEA...
YOUR MAJESTY... THE KEY TO SOLVING THE CURSE UPON PHANTASMA IS...
...FOR REINO TO LOVE THE QUEEN MORE THAN ANYTHING ELSE IN THIS WORLD!

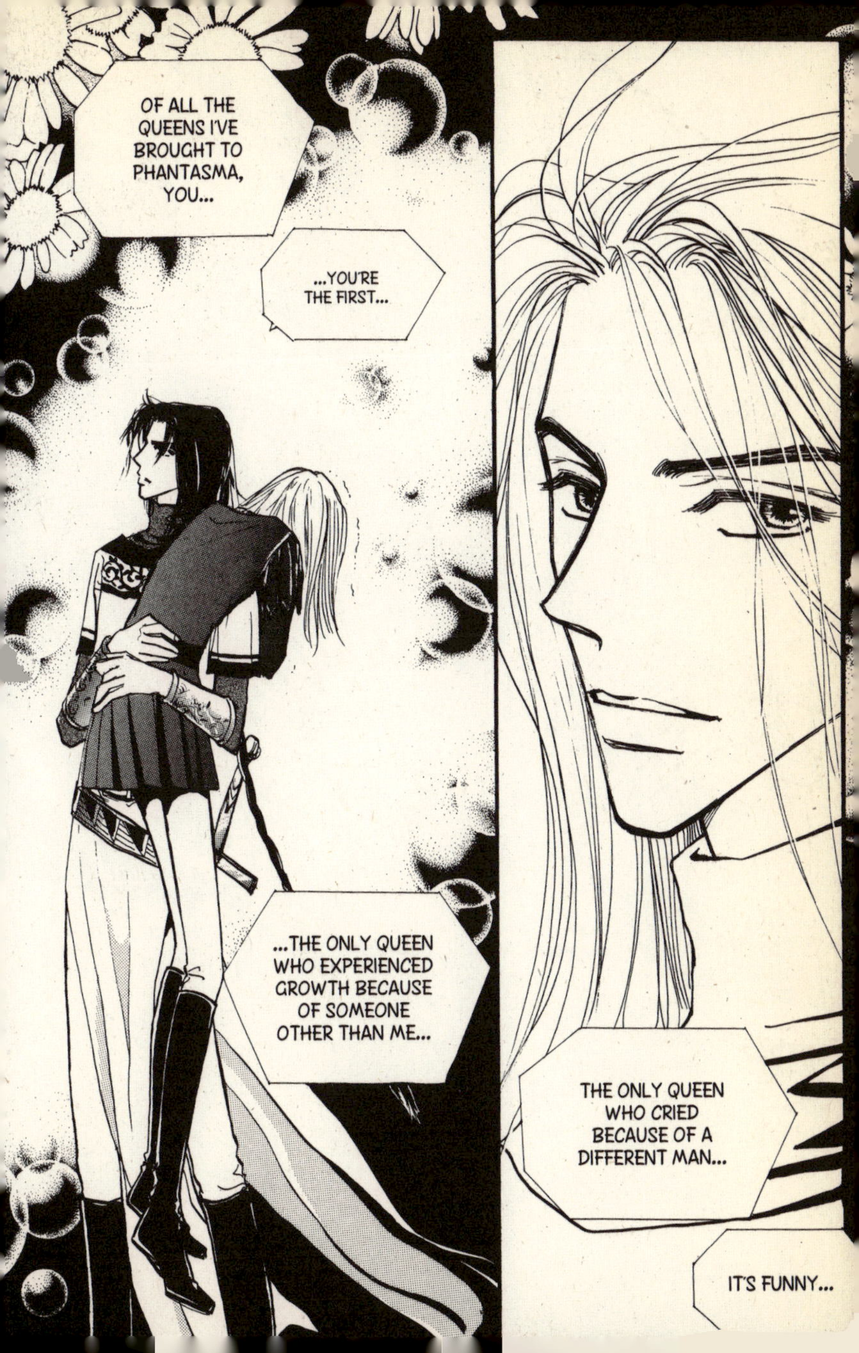
OF ALL THE QUEENS I'VE BROUGHT TO PHANTASMA, YOU...
...YOU'RE THE FIRST...
...THE ONLY QUEEN WHO EXPERIENCED GROWTH BECAUSE OF SOMEONE OTHER THAN ME...
THE ONLY QUEEN WHO CRIED BECAUSE OF A DIFFERENT MAN...
IT'S FUNNY...

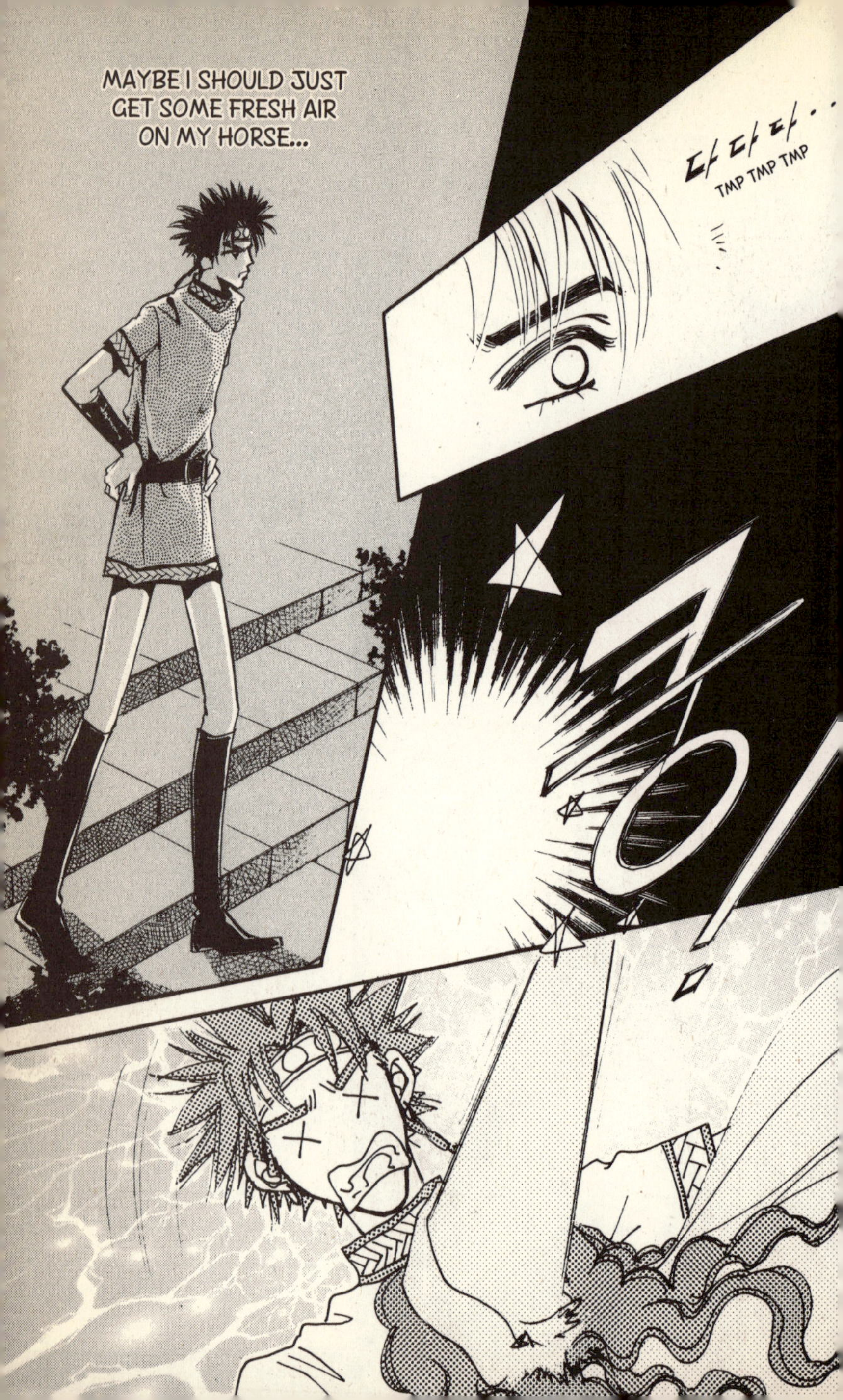
MAYBE I SHOULD JUST GET SOME FRESH AIR ON MY HORSE...
다다다..
TMP TMP TMP

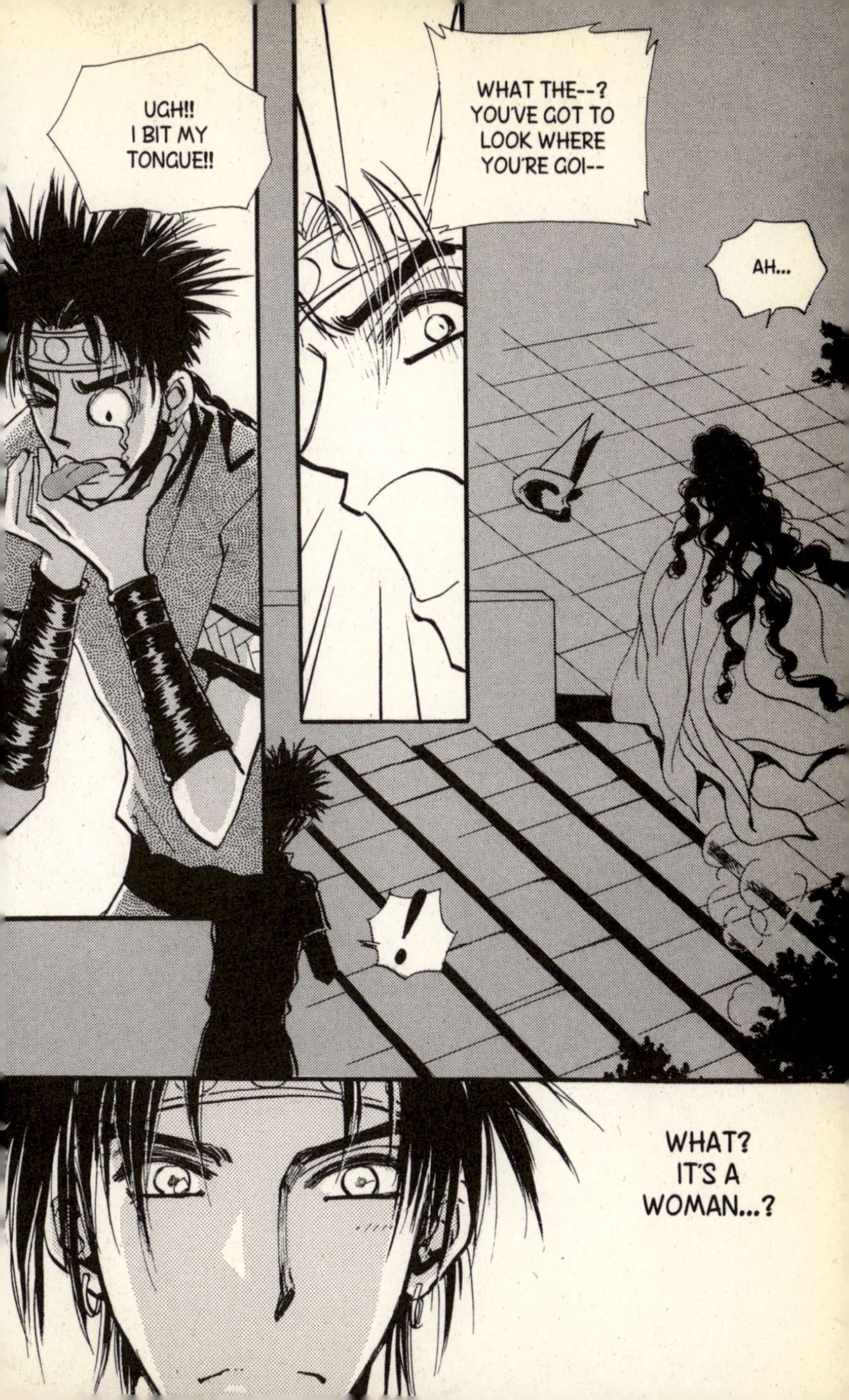
UGH!! I BIT MY TONGUE!!
WHAT THE--? YOU'VE GOT TO LOOK WHERE YOU'RE GOI--
AH...
!
WHAT? IT'S A WOMAN...?

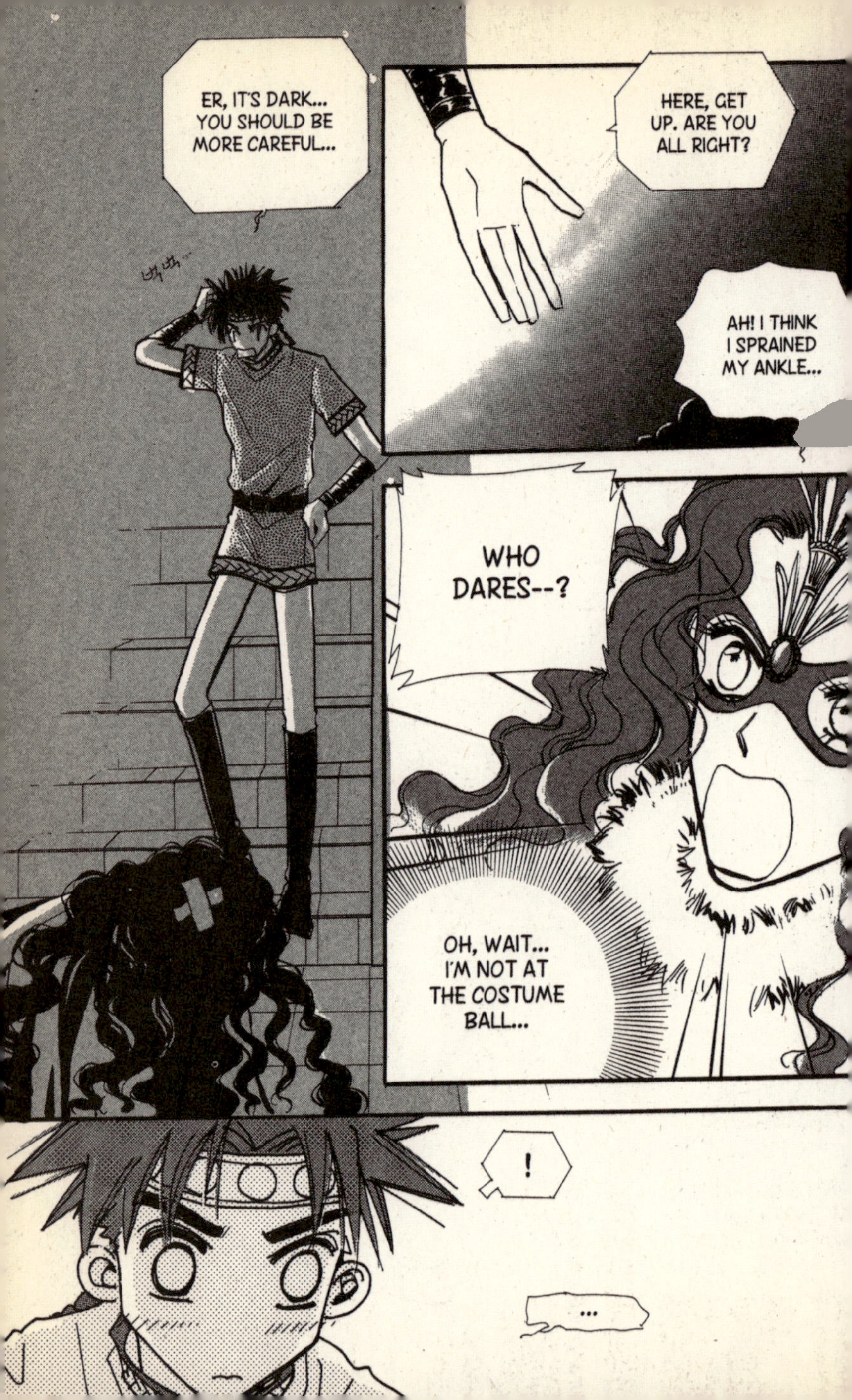
ER, IT'S DARK... YOU SHOULD BE MORE CAREFUL...
HERE, GET UP. ARE YOU ALL RIGHT?
AH! I THINK I SPRAINED MY ANKLE...
WHO DARES--?
OH, WAIT... I'M NOT AT THE COSTUME BALL...
!
...

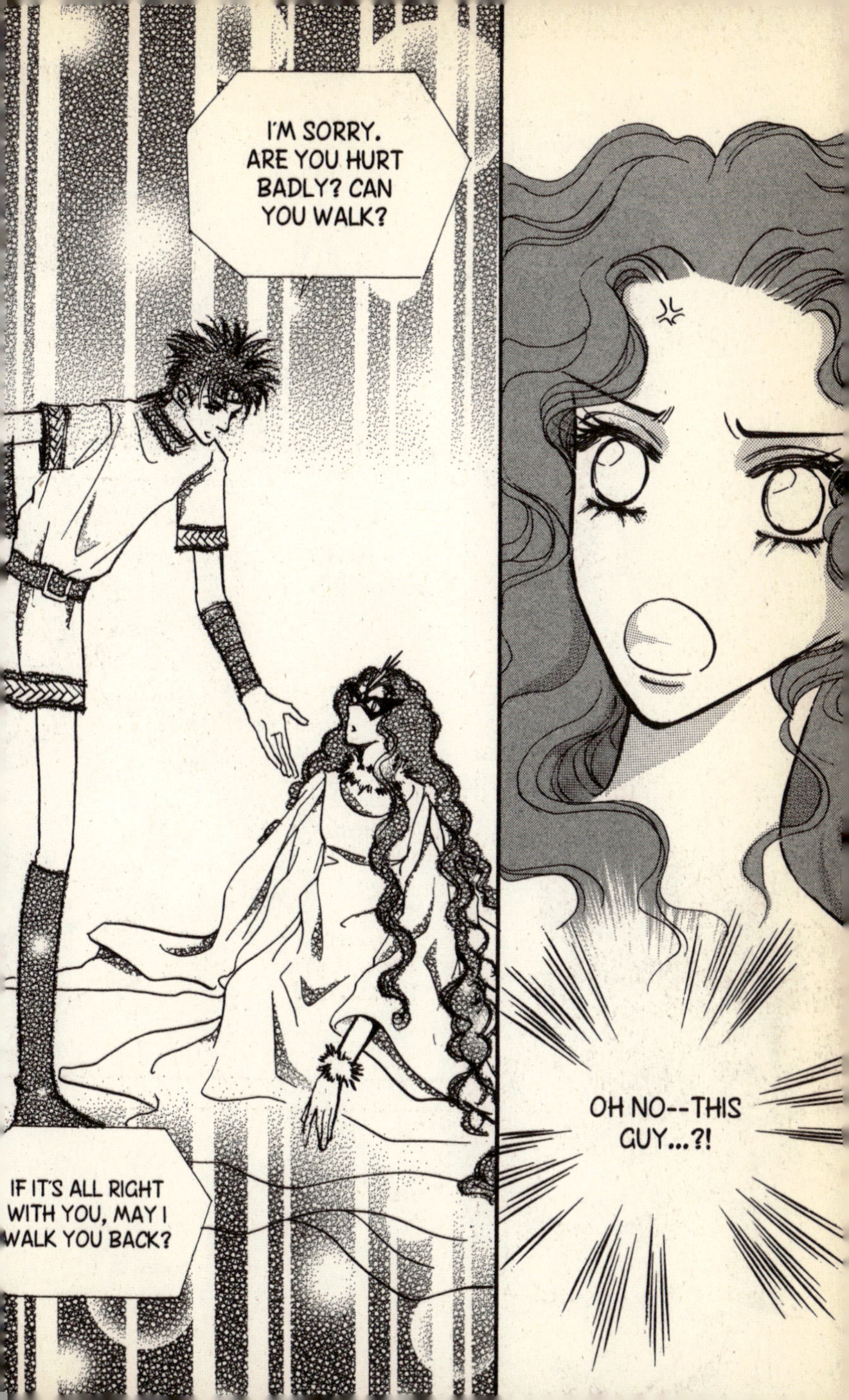
I'M SORRY. ARE YOU HURT BADLY? CAN YOU WALK?
IF IT'S ALL RIGHT WITH YOU, MAY I WALK YOU BACK?
OH NO--THIS GUY...?!

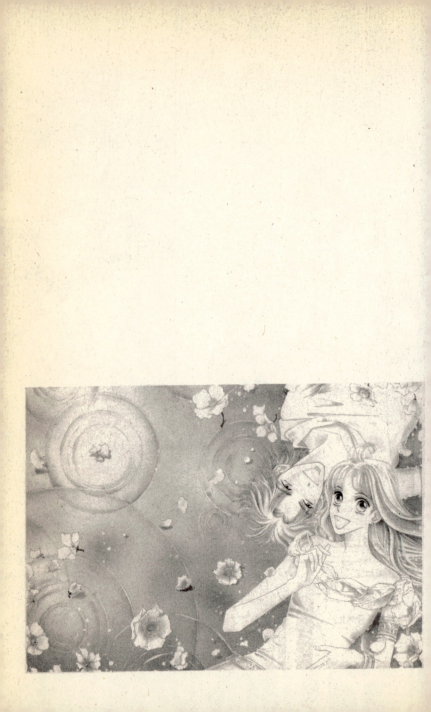

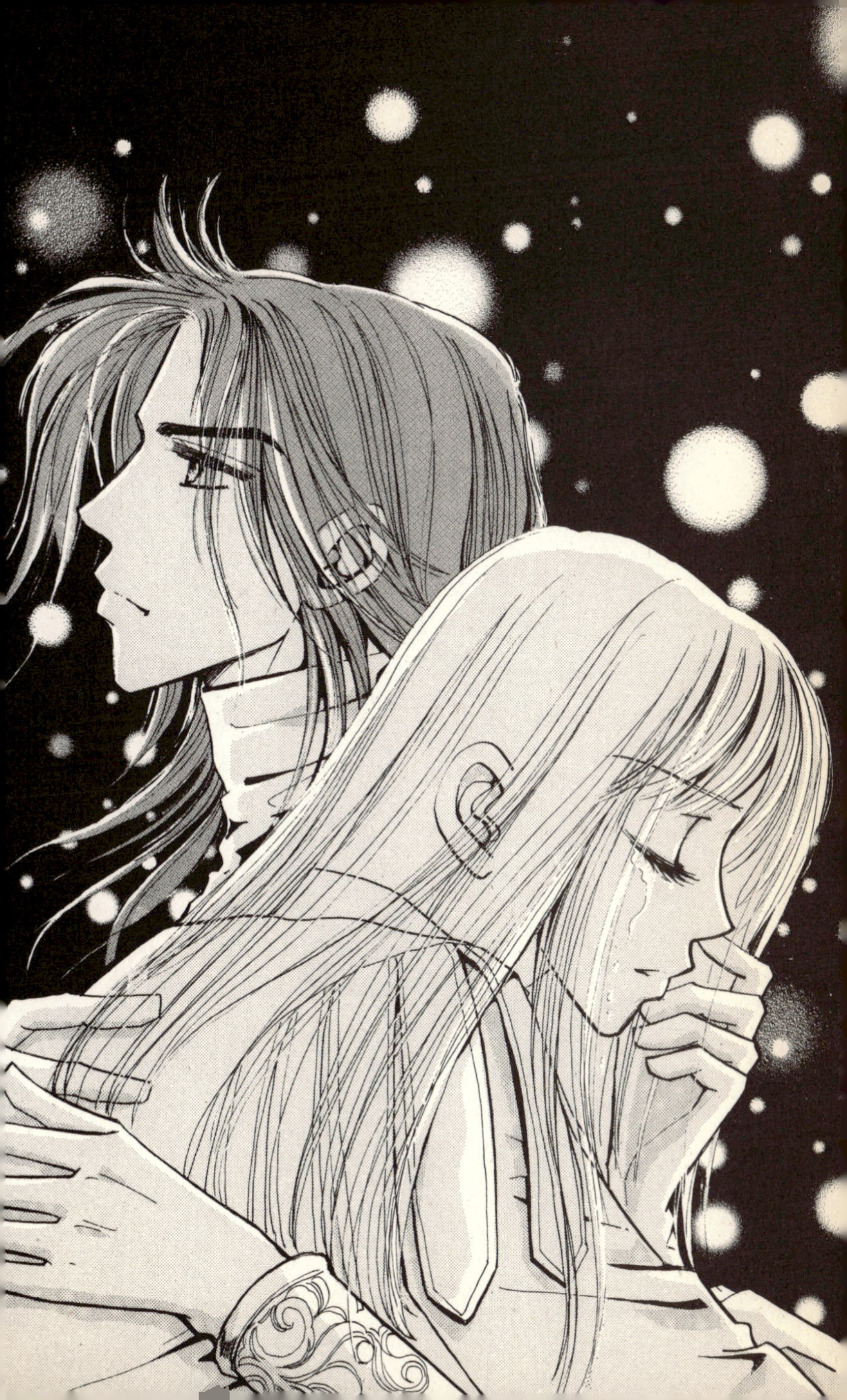

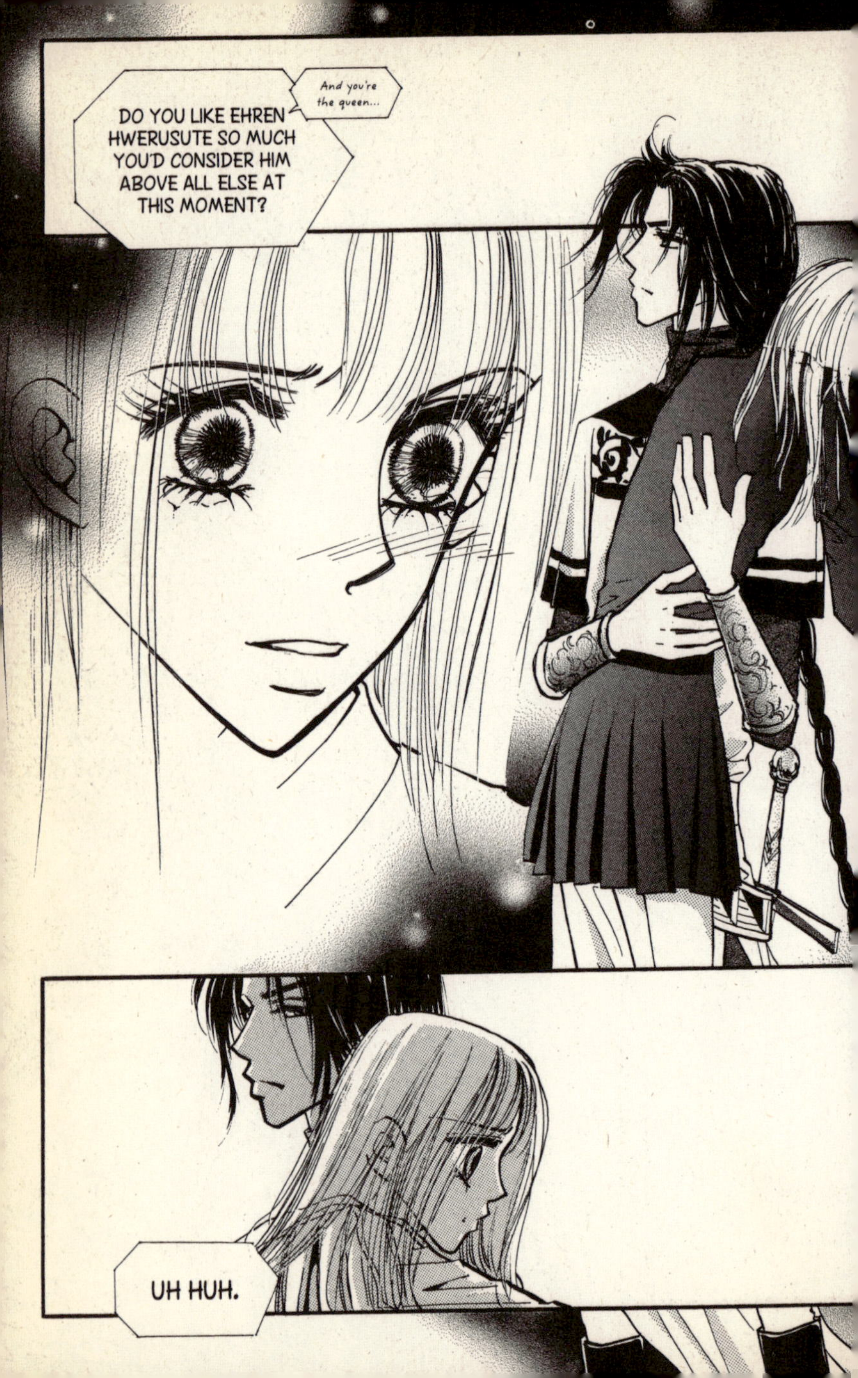
DO YOU LIKE EHREN HWERUSUTE SO MUCH YOU'D CONSIDER HIM ABOVE ALL ELSE AT THIS MOMENT?
And you're the queen...
UH HUH.

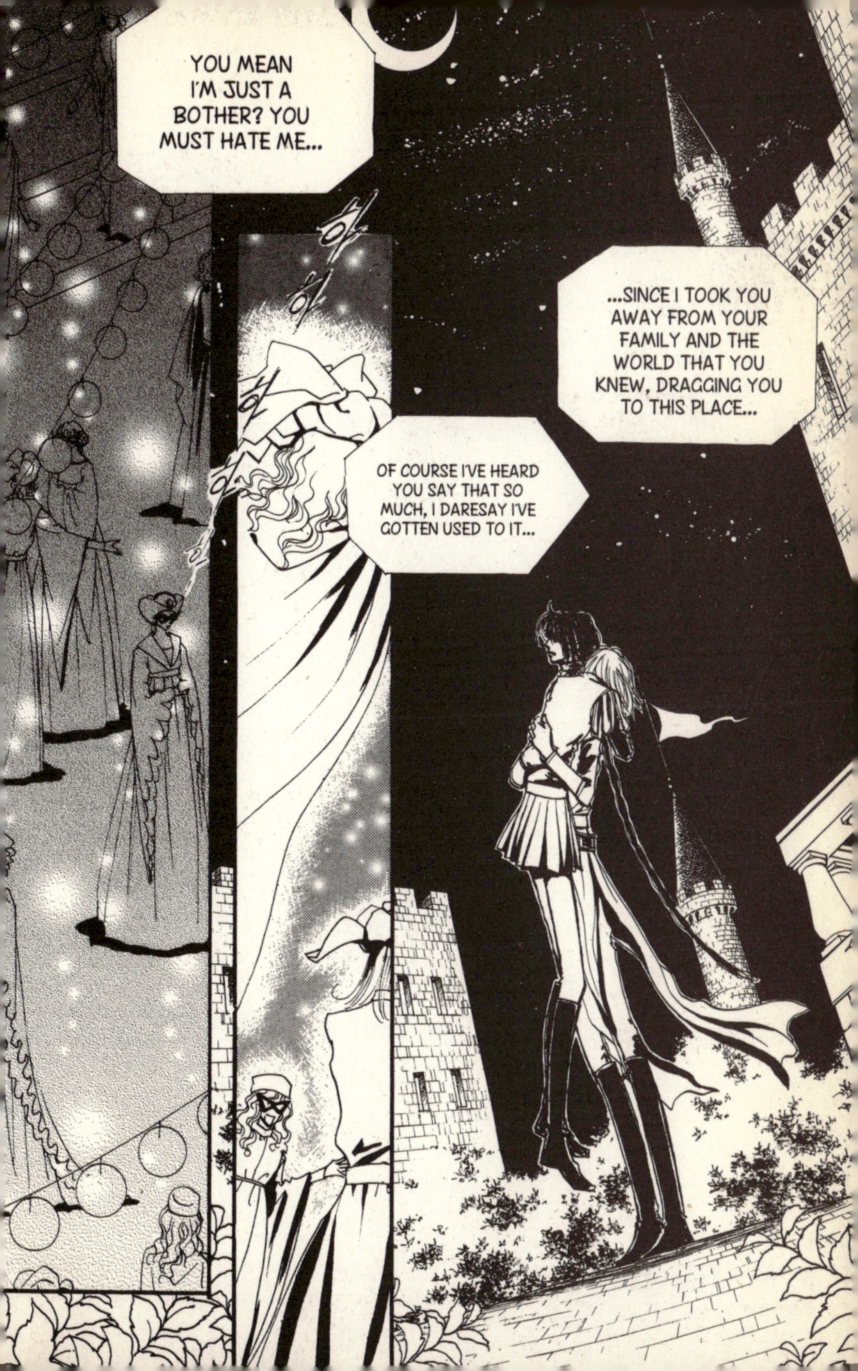
YOU MEAN I'M JUST A BOTHER? YOU MUST HATE ME...
...SINCE I TOOK YOU AWAY FROM YOUR FAMILY AND THE WORLD THAT YOU KNEW, DRAGGING YOU TO THIS PLACE...
OF COURSE I'VE HEARD YOU SAY THAT SO MUCH, I DARESAY I'VE GOTTEN USED TO IT...

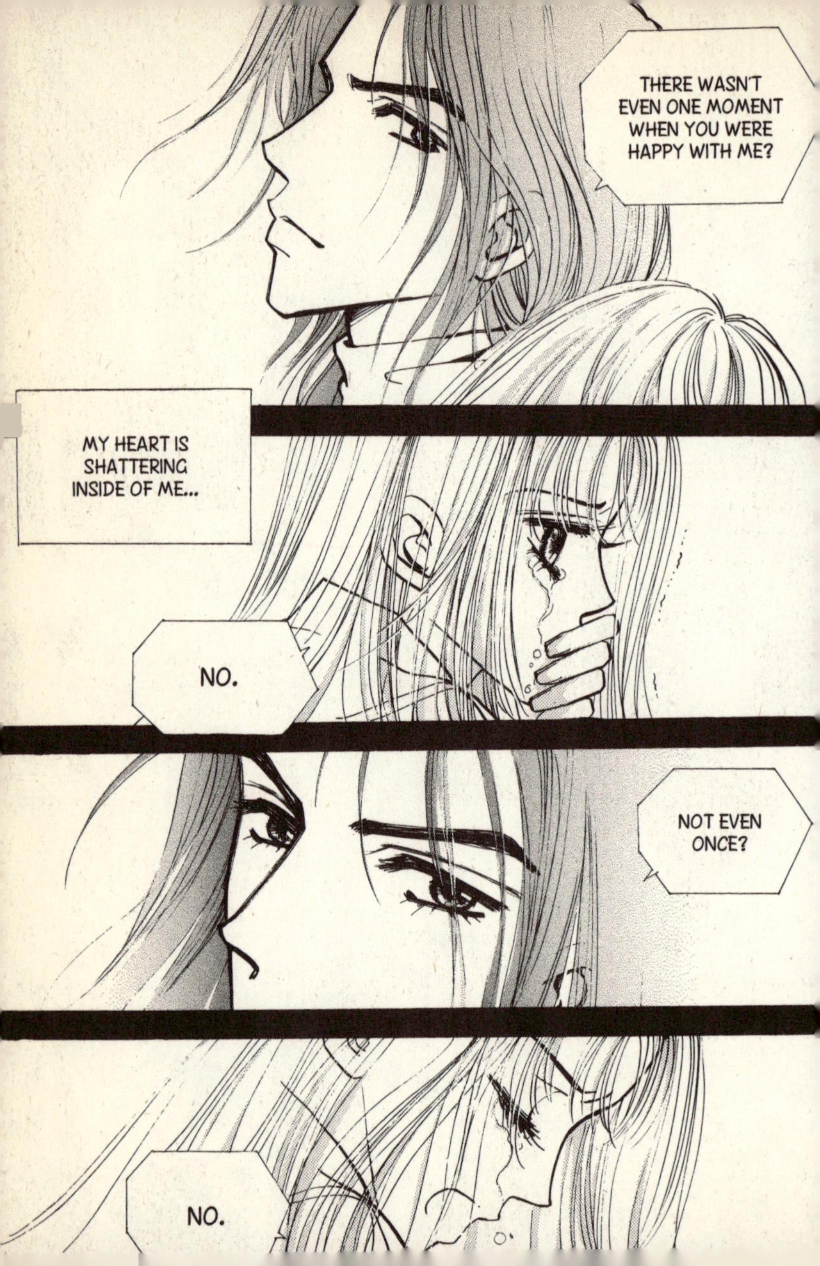
THERE WASN'T EVEN ONE MOMENT WHEN YOU WERE HAPPY WITH ME?
MY HEART IS SHATTERING INSIDE OF ME...
NO.
NOT EVEN ONCE?
NO.

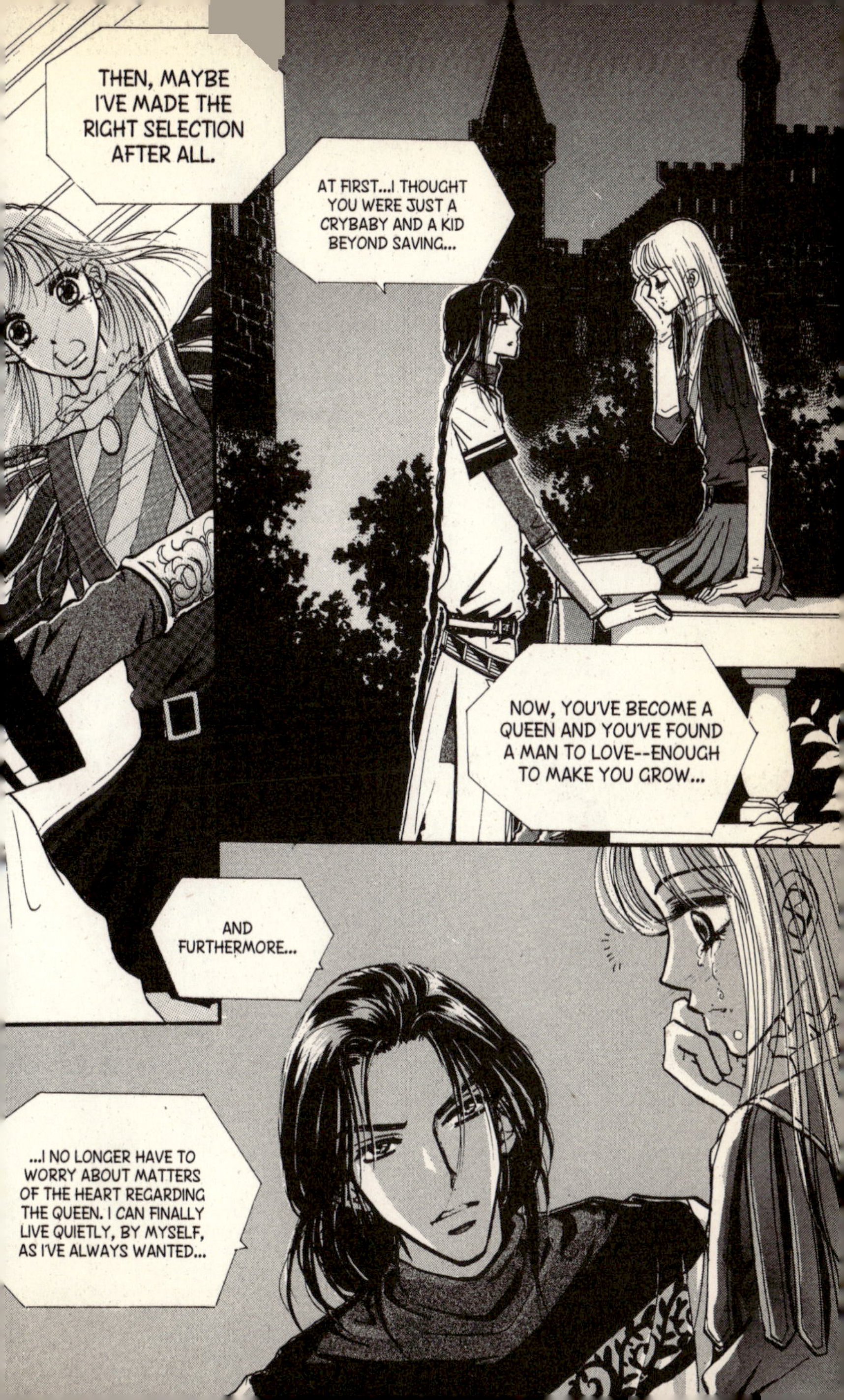
THEN, MAYBE I'VE MADE THE RIGHT SELECTION AFTER ALL.
AT FIRST...I THOUGHT YOU WERE JUST A CRYBABY AND A KID BEYOND SAVING...
NOW, YOU'VE BECOME A QUEEN AND YOU'VE FOUND A MAN TO LOVE--ENOUGH TO MAKE YOU GROW...
AND FURTHERMORE...
...I NO LONGER HAVE TO WORRY ABOUT MATTERS OF THE HEART REGARDING THE QUEEN. I CAN FINALLY LIVE QUIETLY, BY MYSELF, AS I'VE ALWAYS WANTED...

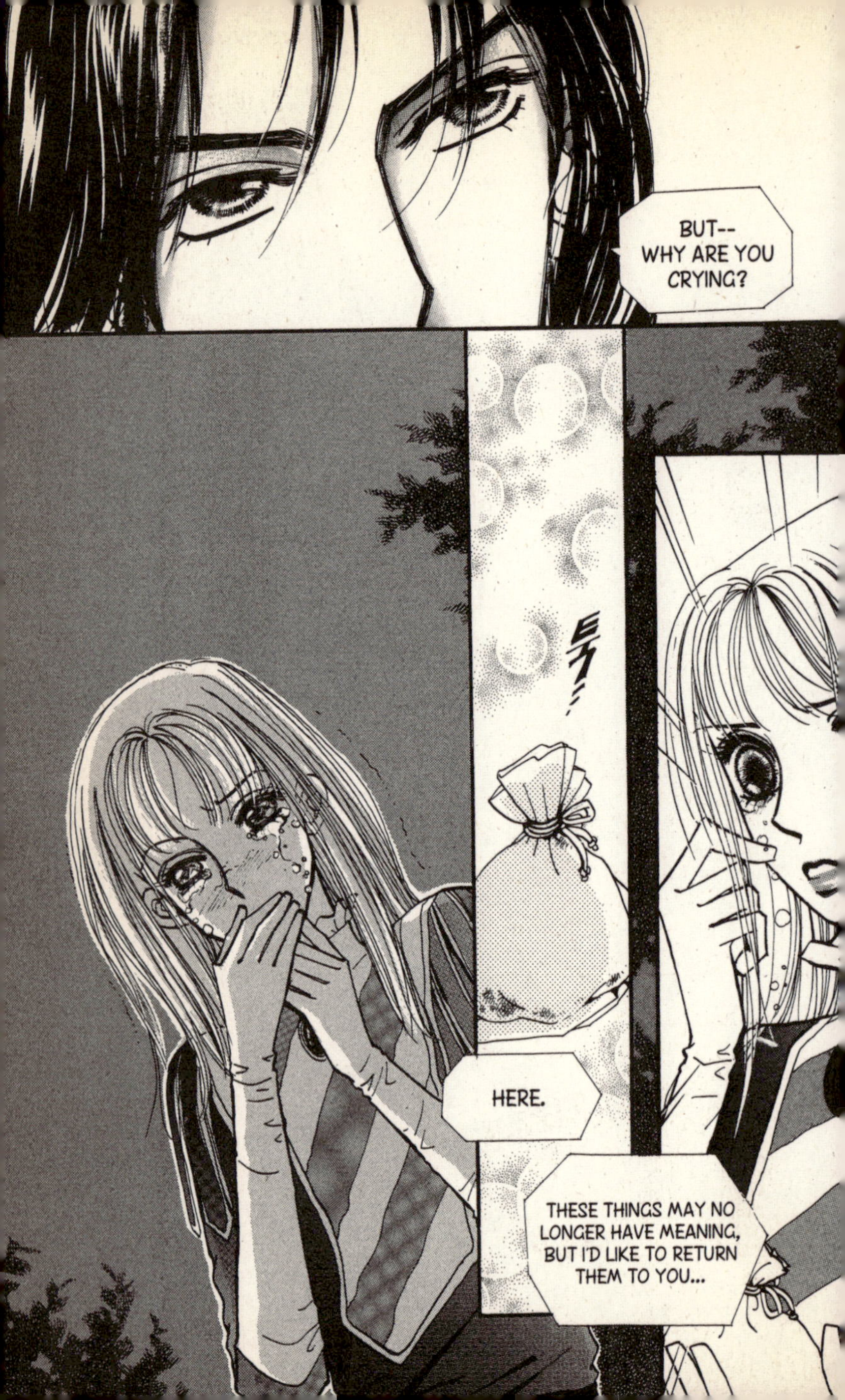
BUT-- WHY ARE YOU CRYING?
HERE.
THESE THINGS MAY NO LONGER HAVE MEANING, BUT I'D LIKE TO RETURN THEM TO YOU...

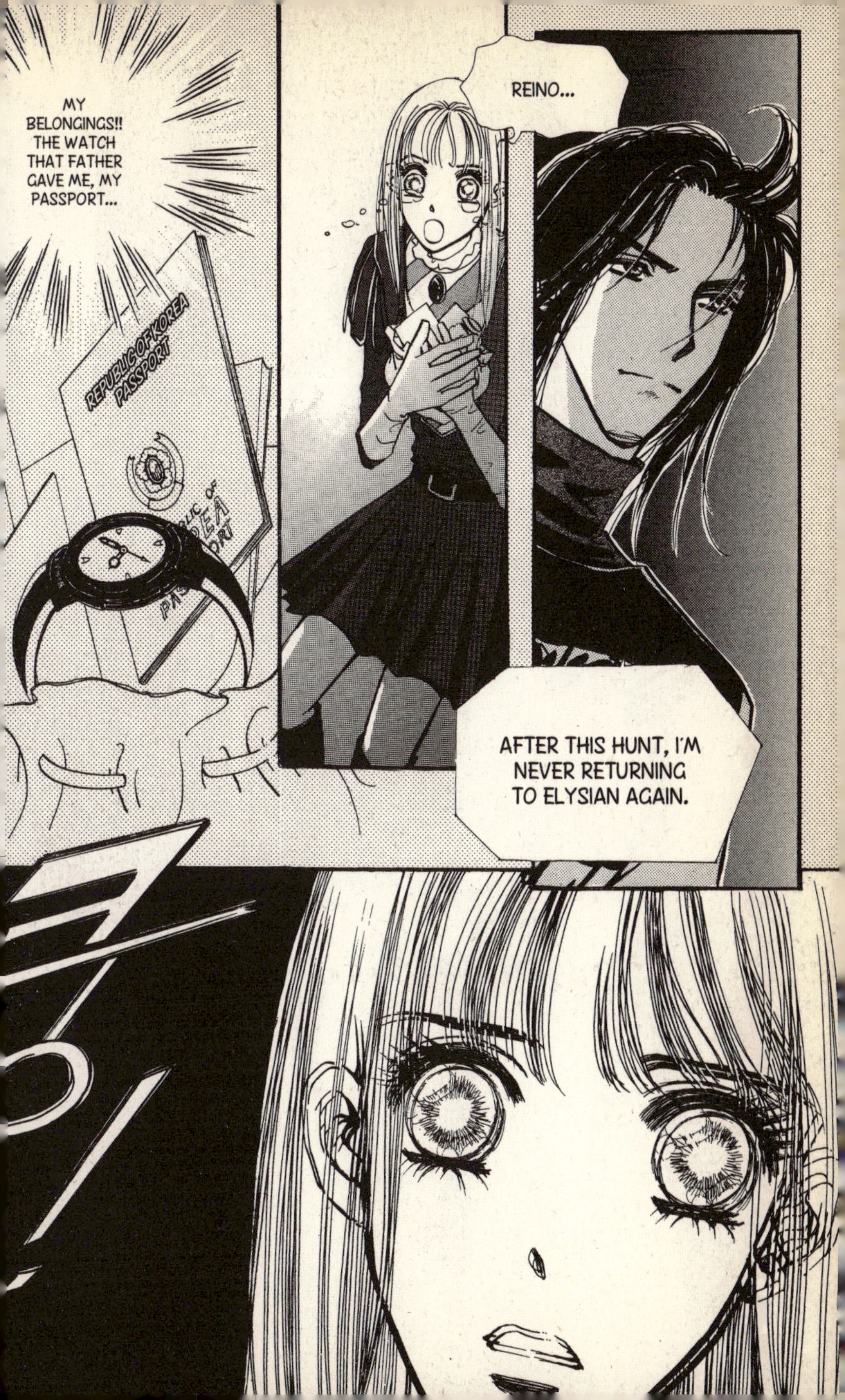
MY BELONGINGS!! THE WATCH THAT FATHER GAVE ME, MY PASSPORT...
REPUBLIC OF KOREA PASSPORT
REINO...
AFTER THIS HUNT, I'M NEVER RETURNING TO ELYSIAN AGAIN.

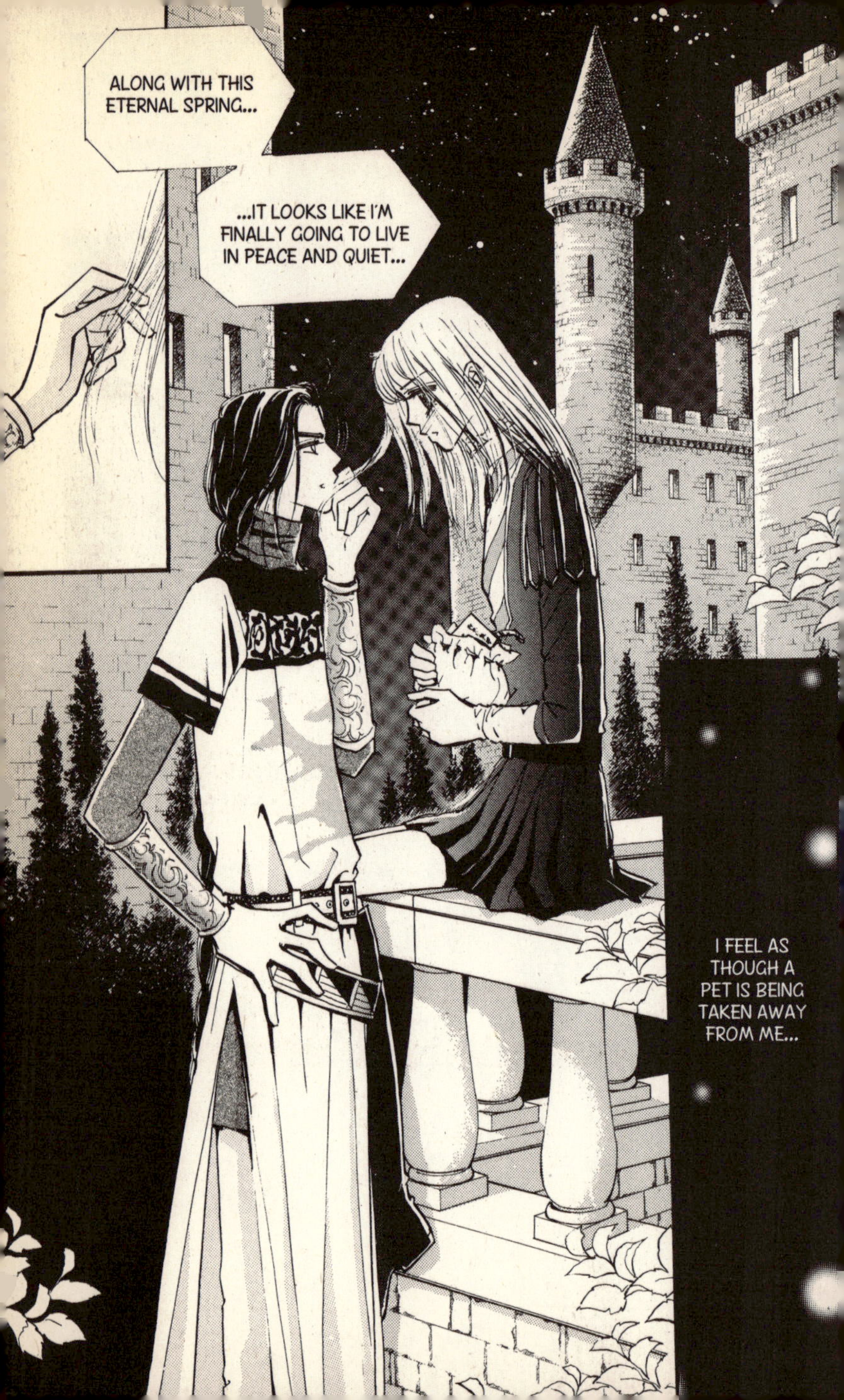
ALONG WITH THIS ETERNAL SPRING...
...IT LOOKS LIKE I'M FINALLY GOING TO LIVE IN PEACE AND QUIET...
I FEEL AS THOUGH A PET IS BEING TAKEN AWAY FROM ME...

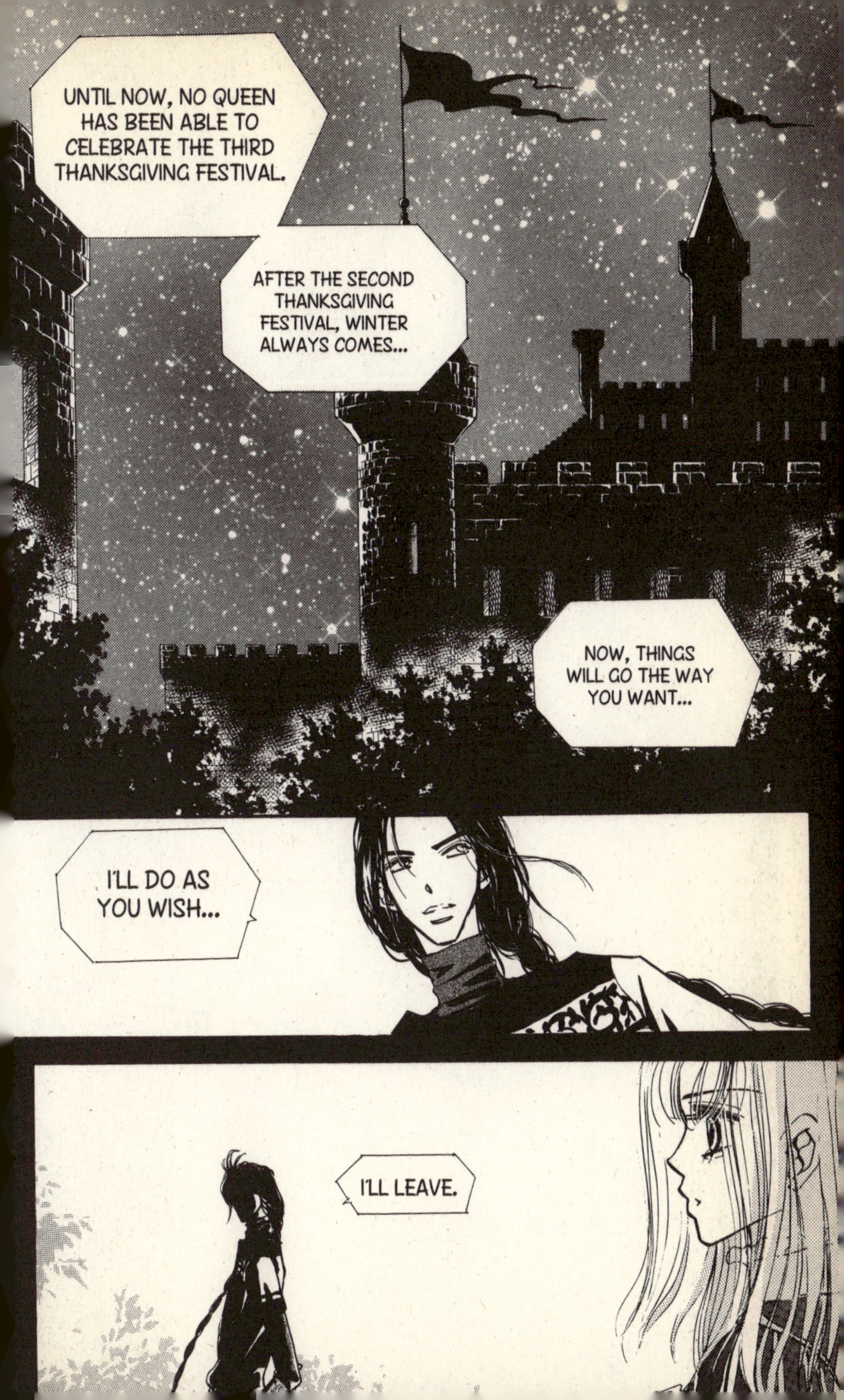
UNTIL NOW, NO QUEEN HAS BEEN ABLE TO CELEBRATE THE THIRD THANKSGIVING FESTIVAL.
AFTER THE SECOND THANKSGIVING FESTIVAL, WINTER ALWAYS COMES...
NOW, THINGS WILL GO THE WAY YOU WANT...
I'LL DO AS YOU WISH...
I'LL LEAVE.

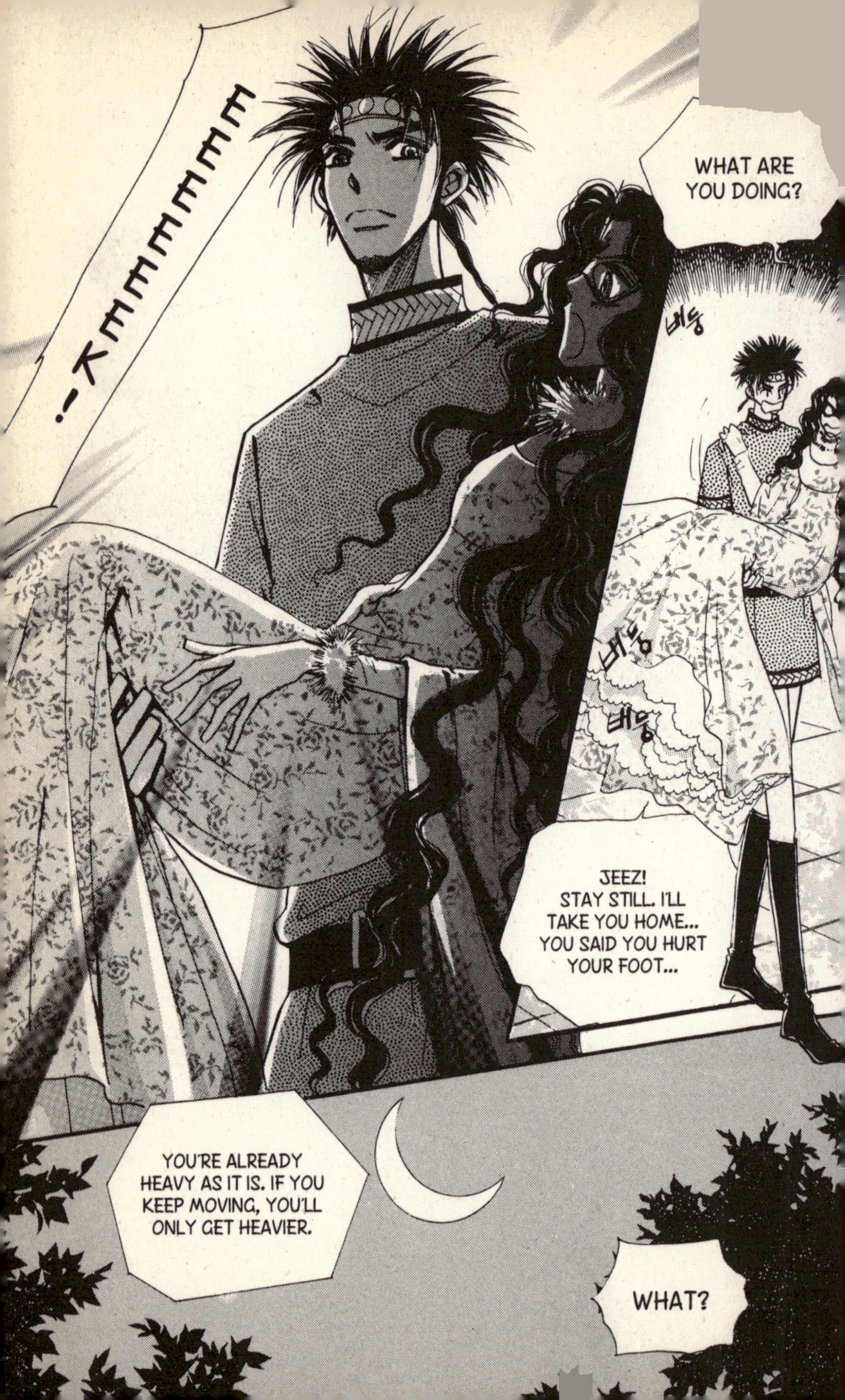
EEEEEEEEK!
WHAT ARE YOU DOING?
버둥
버둥
버둥
JEEZ! STAY STILL. I'LL TAKE YOU HOME... YOU SAID YOU HURT YOUR FOOT...
YOU'RE ALREADY HEAVY AS IT IS. IF YOU KEEP MOVING, YOU'LL ONLY GET HEAVIER.
WHAT?

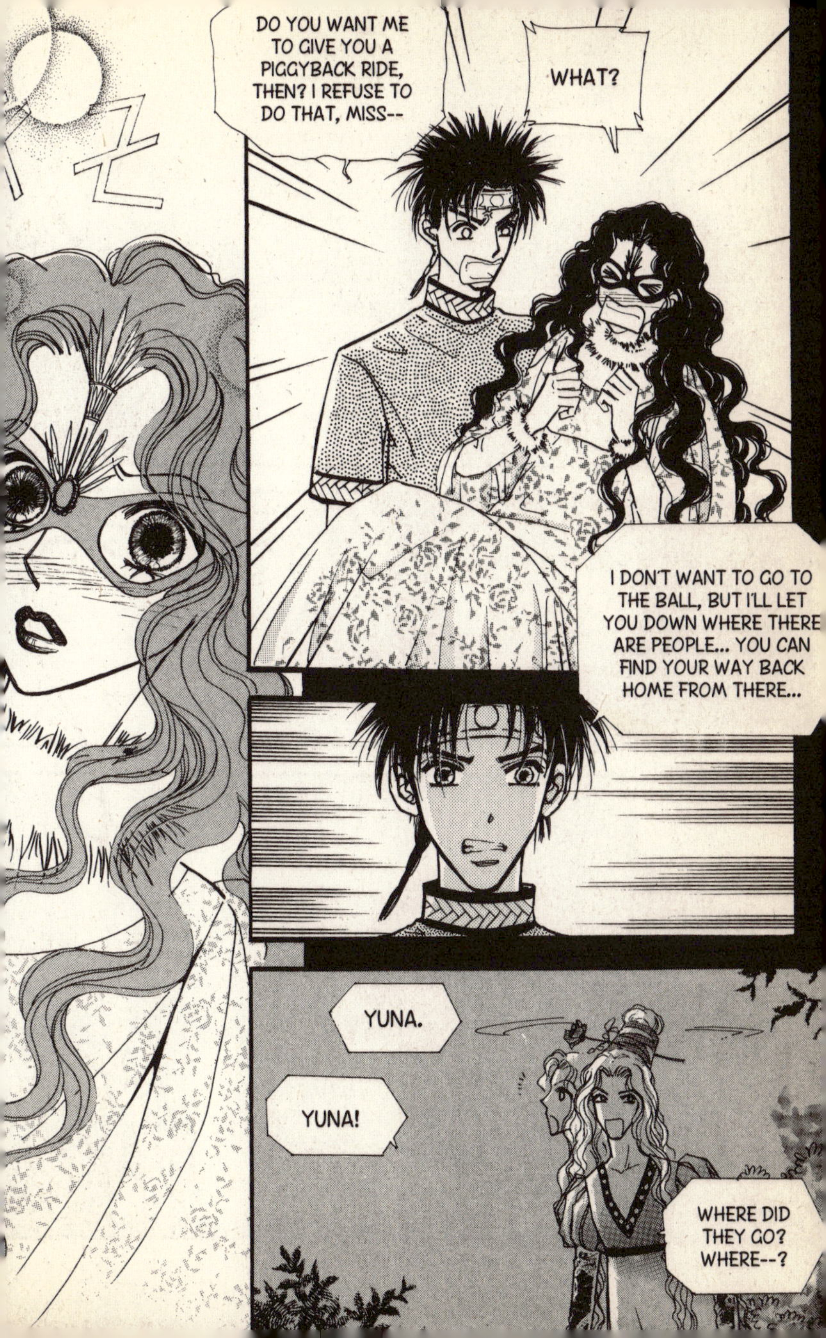
DO YOU WANT ME TO GIVE YOU A PIGGYBACK RIDE, THEN? I REFUSE TO DO THAT, MISS--
WHAT?
I DON'T WANT TO GO TO THE BALL, BUT I'LL LET YOU DOWN WHERE THERE ARE PEOPLE... YOU CAN FIND YOUR WAY BACK HOME FROM THERE...
YUNA.
YUNA!
WHERE DID THEY GO? WHERE--?

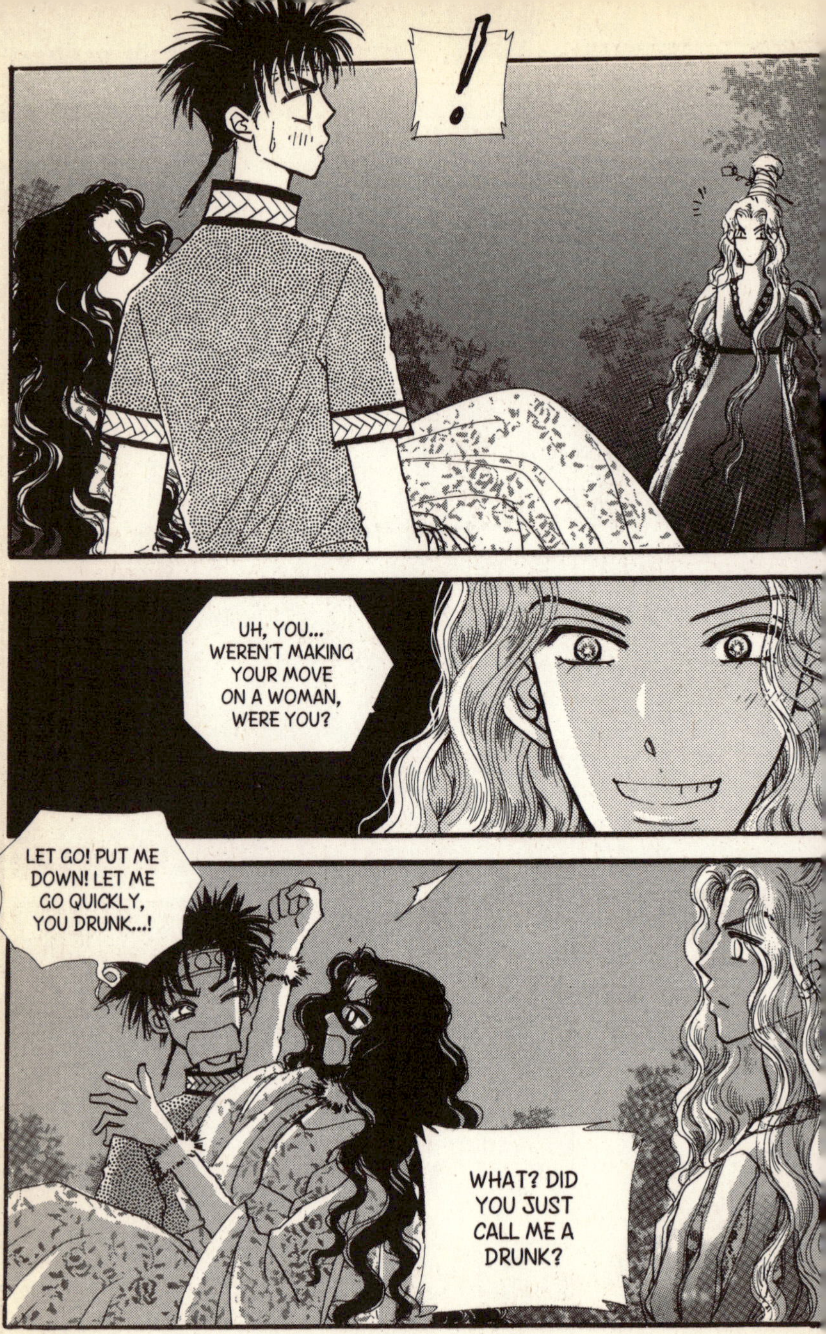
!
UH, YOU... WEREN'T MAKING YOUR MOVE ON A WOMAN, WERE YOU?
LET GO! PUT ME DOWN! LET ME GO QUICKLY, YOU DRUNK...!
WHAT? DID YOU JUST CALL ME A DRUNK?

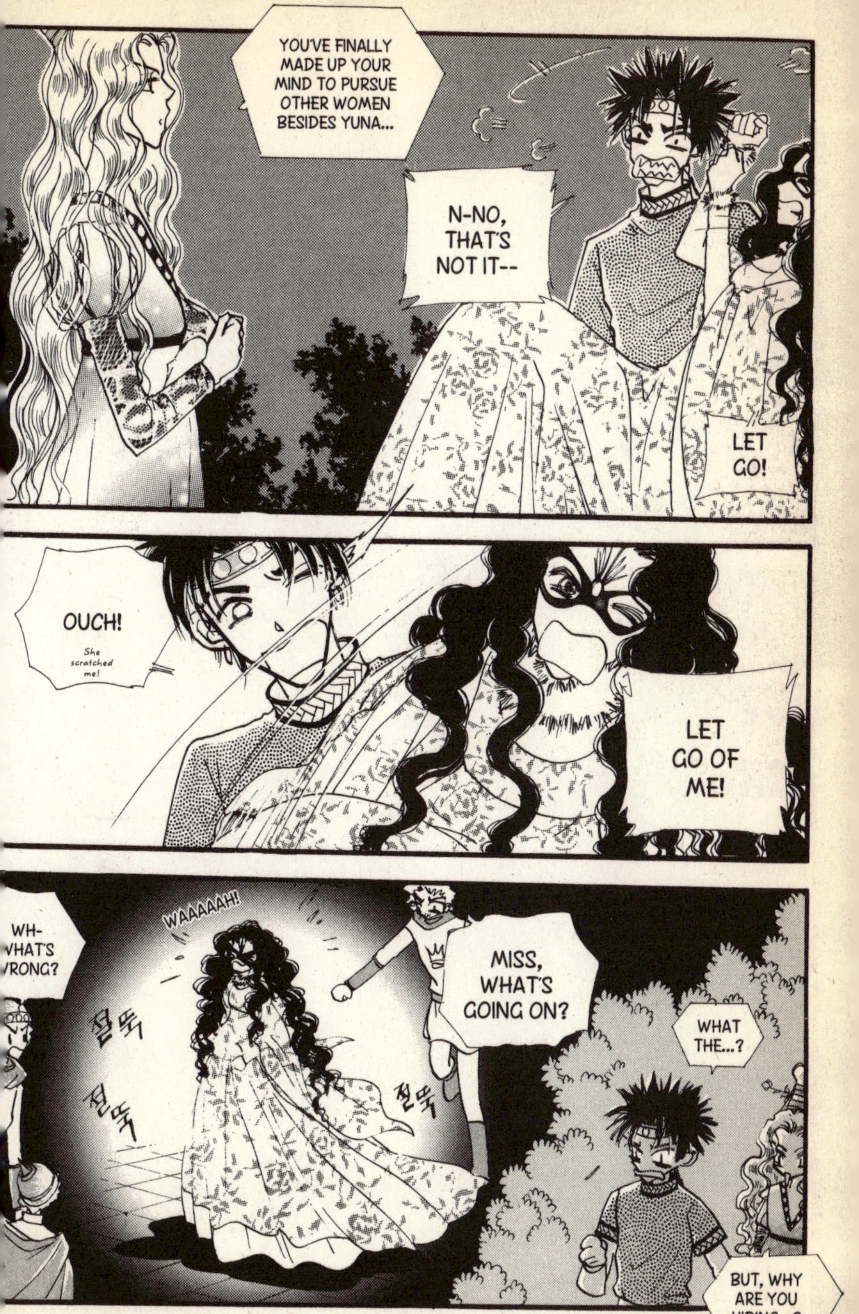
YOU'VE FINALLY MADE UP YOUR MIND TO PURSUE OTHER WOMEN BESIDES YUNA...
N-NO, THAT'S NOT IT--
LET GO!
OUCH!
She scratched me!
LET GO OF ME!
WH- WHAT'S WRONG?
WAAAAAH!
절뚝
절뚝
MISS, WHAT'S GOING ON?
절뚝
WHAT THE...?
BUT, WHY ARE YOU HIDING...?

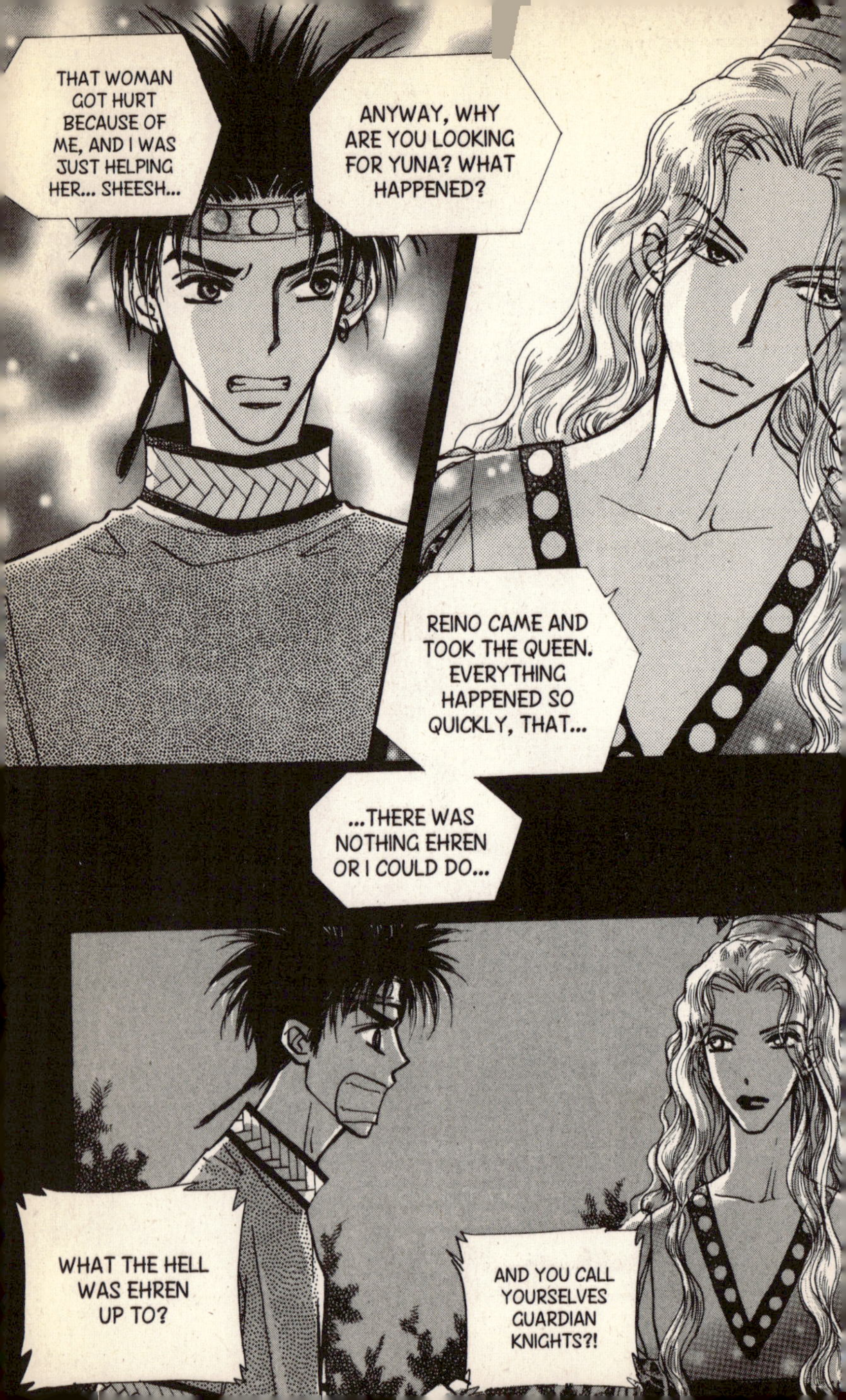
THAT WOMAN GOT HURT BECAUSE OF ME, AND I WAS JUST HELPING HER... SHEESH...
ANYWAY, WHY ARE YOU LOOKING FOR YUNA? WHAT HAPPENED?
REINO CAME AND TOOK THE QUEEN. EVERYTHING HAPPENED SO QUICKLY, THAT...
...THERE WAS NOTHING EHREN OR I COULD DO...
WHAT THE HELL WAS EHREN UP TO?
AND YOU CALL YOURSELVES GUARDIAN KNIGHTS?!

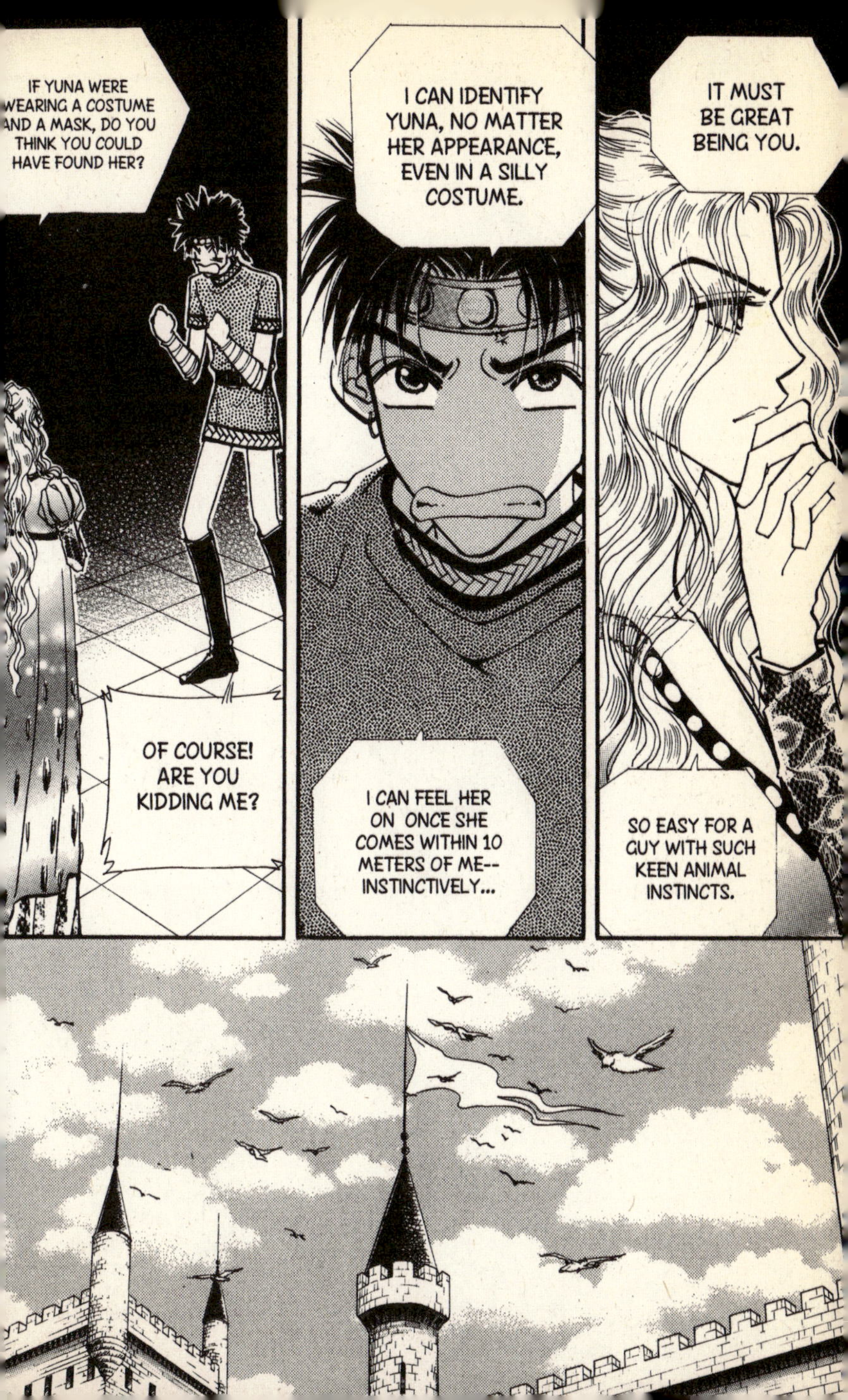
IF YUNA WERE WEARING A COSTUME AND A MASK, DO YOU THINK YOU COULD HAVE FOUND HER?
OF COURSE! ARE YOU KIDDING ME?
I CAN IDENTIFY YUNA, NO MATTER HER APPEARANCE, EVEN IN A SILLY COSTUME.
I CAN FEEL HER ON ONCE SHE COMES WITHIN 10 METERS OF ME-- INSTINCTIVELY...
IT MUST BE GREAT BEING YOU.
SO EASY FOR A GUY WITH SUCH KEEN ANIMAL INSTINCTS.

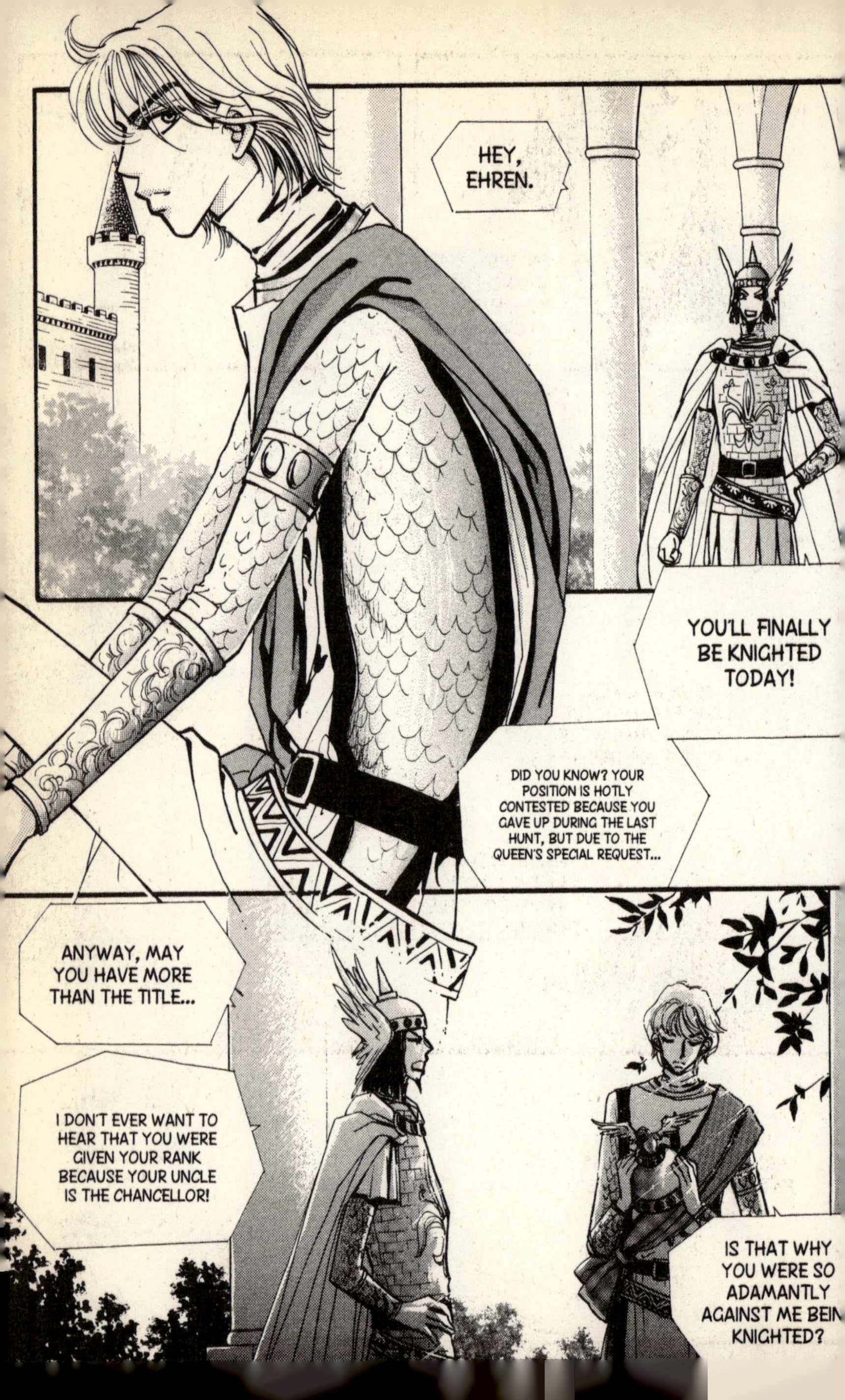
HEY, EHREN.
YOU'LL FINALLY BE KNIGHTED TODAY!
DID YOU KNOW? YOUR POSITION IS HOTLY CONTESTED BECAUSE YOU GAVE UP DURING THE LAST HUNT, BUT DUE TO THE QUEEN'S SPECIAL REQUEST...
ANYWAY, MAY YOU HAVE MORE THAN THE TITLE...
I DON'T EVER WANT TO HEAR THAT YOU WERE GIVEN YOUR RANK BECAUSE YOUR UNCLE IS THE CHANCELLOR!
IS THAT WHY YOU WERE SO ADAMANTLY AGAINST ME BEIN KNIGHTED?

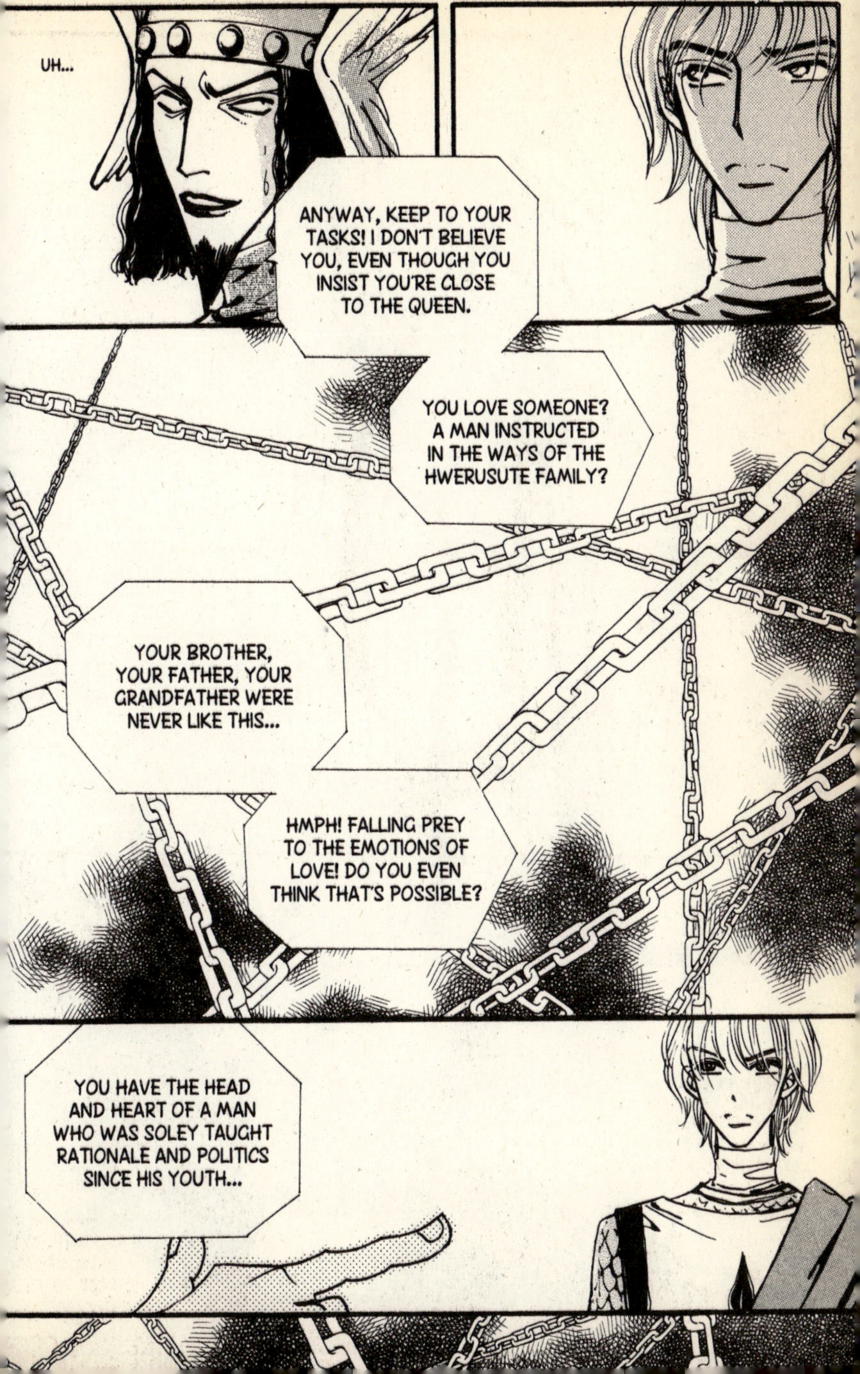
UH...
ANYWAY, KEEP TO YOUR TASKS! I DON'T BELIEVE YOU, EVEN THOUGH YOU INSIST YOU'RE CLOSE TO THE QUEEN.
YOU LOVE SOMEONE? A MAN INSTRUCTED IN THE WAYS OF THE HWERUSUTE FAMILY?
YOUR BROTHER, YOUR FATHER, YOUR GRANDFATHER WERE NEVER LIKE THIS...
HMPH! FALLING PREY TO THE EMOTIONS OF LOVE! DO YOU EVEN THINK THAT'S POSSIBLE?
YOU HAVE THE HEAD AND HEART OF A MAN WHO WAS SOLEY TAUGHT RATIONALE AND POLITICS SINCE HIS YOUTH...

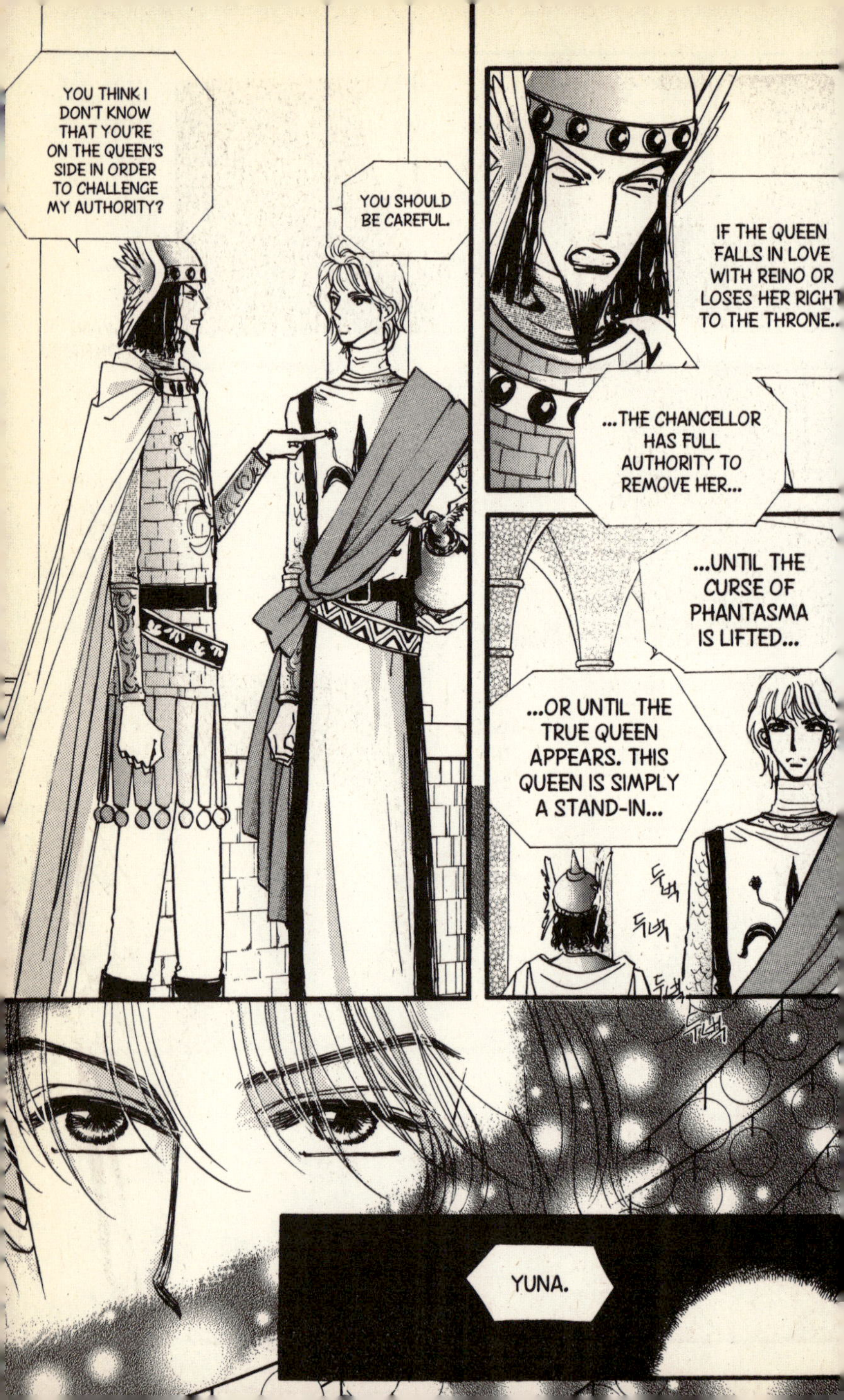
YOU THINK I DON'T KNOW THAT YOU'RE ON THE QUEEN'S SIDE IN ORDER TO CHALLENGE MY AUTHORITY?
YOU SHOULD BE CAREFUL.
IF THE QUEEN FALLS IN LOVE WITH REINO OR LOSES HER RIGHT TO THE THRONE...
...THE CHANCELLOR HAS FULL AUTHORITY TO REMOVE HER...
...UNTIL THE CURSE OF PHANTASMA IS LIFTED...
...OR UNTIL THE TRUE QUEEN APPEARS. THIS QUEEN IS SIMPLY A STAND-IN...
YUNA.

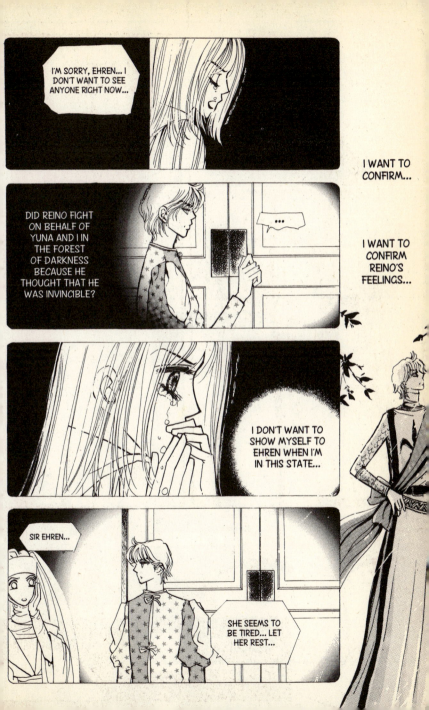

I'M SORRY, EHREN... I DON'T WANT TO SEE ANYONE RIGHT NOW...

I WANT TO CONFIRM...

DID REINO FIGHT ON BEHALF OF YUNA AND I IN THE FOREST OF DARKNESS BECAUSE HE THOUGHT THAT HE WAS INVINCIBLE?

...

I WANT TO CONFIRM REINO'S FEELINGS...

I DON'T WANT TO SHOW MYSELF TO EHREN WHEN I'M IN THIS STATE...

SIR EHREN...

SHE SEEMS TO BE TIRED... LET HER REST...

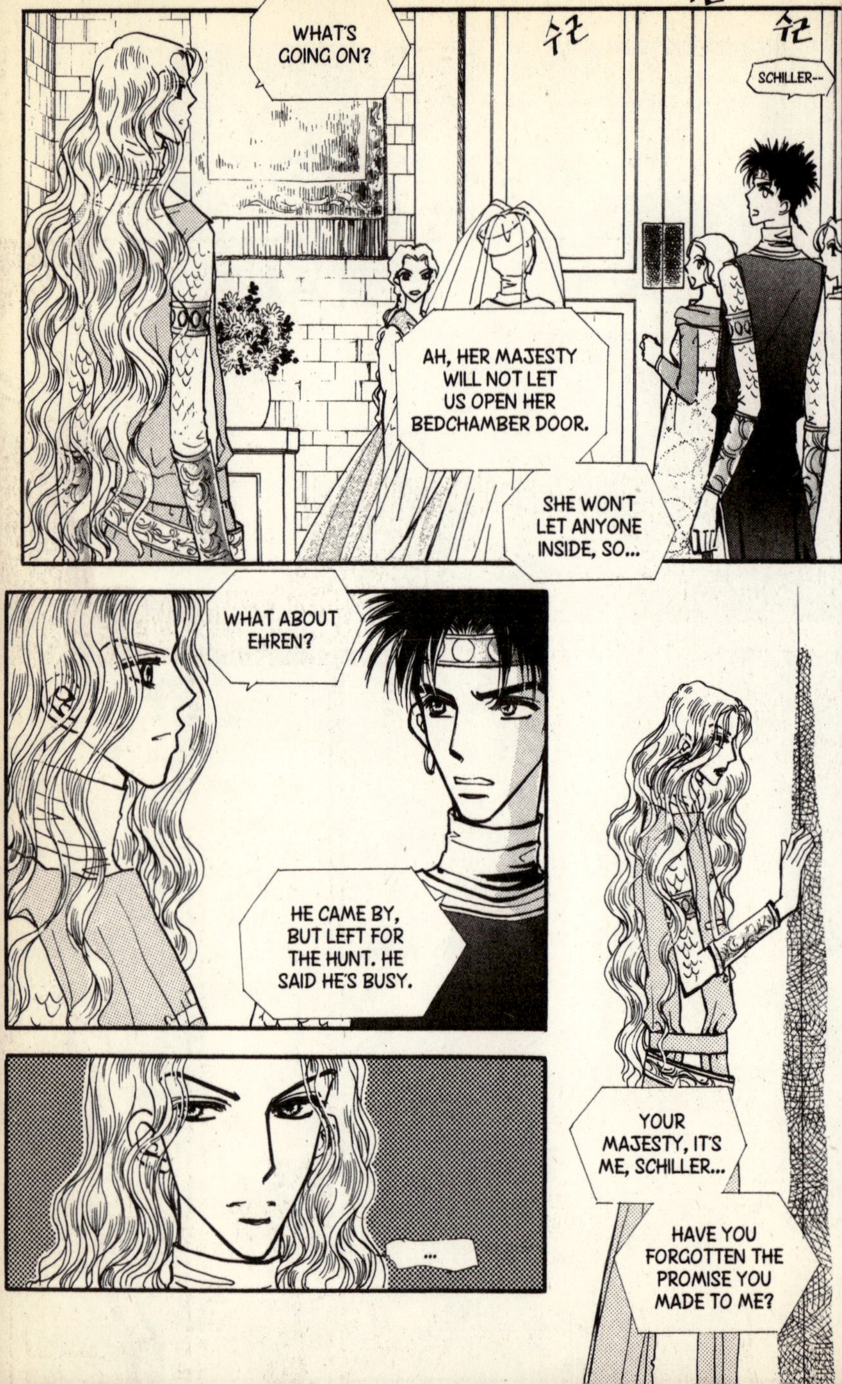
WHAT'S GOING ON?
SCHILLER--
AH, HER MAJESTY WILL NOT LET US OPEN HER BEDCHAMBER DOOR.
SHE WON'T LET ANYONE INSIDE, SO...
WHAT ABOUT EHREN?
HE CAME BY, BUT LEFT FOR THE HUNT. HE SAID HE'S BUSY.
...
YOUR MAJESTY, IT'S ME, SCHILLER...
HAVE YOU FORGOTTEN THE PROMISE YOU MADE TO ME?

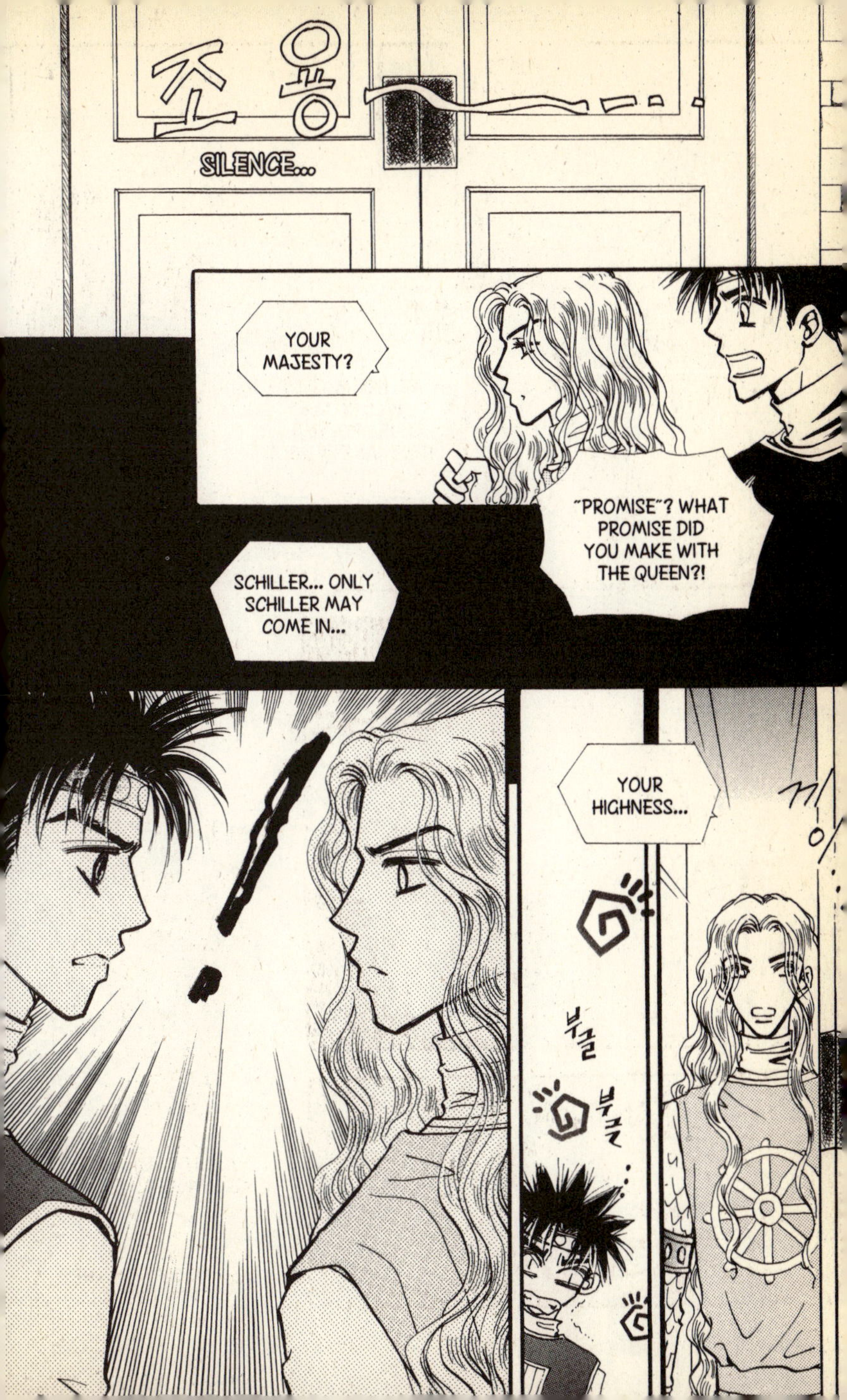
조용—...
SILENCE...
YOUR MAJESTY?
"PROMISE"? WHAT PROMISE DID YOU MAKE WITH THE QUEEN?!
SCHILLER... ONLY SCHILLER MAY COME IN...
YOUR HIGHNESS...
끼이...
부글
부글

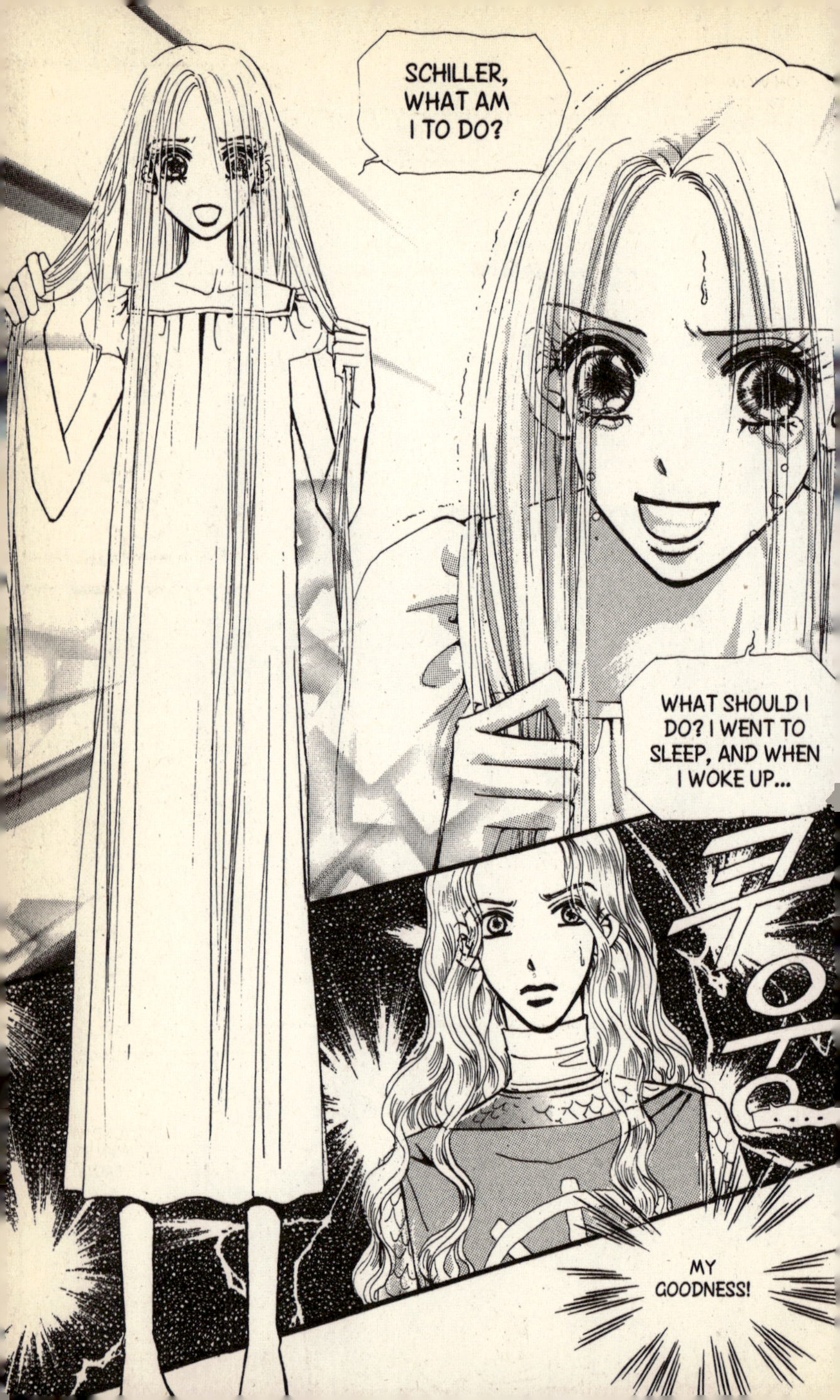
SCHILLER, WHAT AM I TO DO?
WHAT SHOULD I DO? I WENT TO SLEEP, AND WHEN I WOKE UP...
MY GOODNESS!

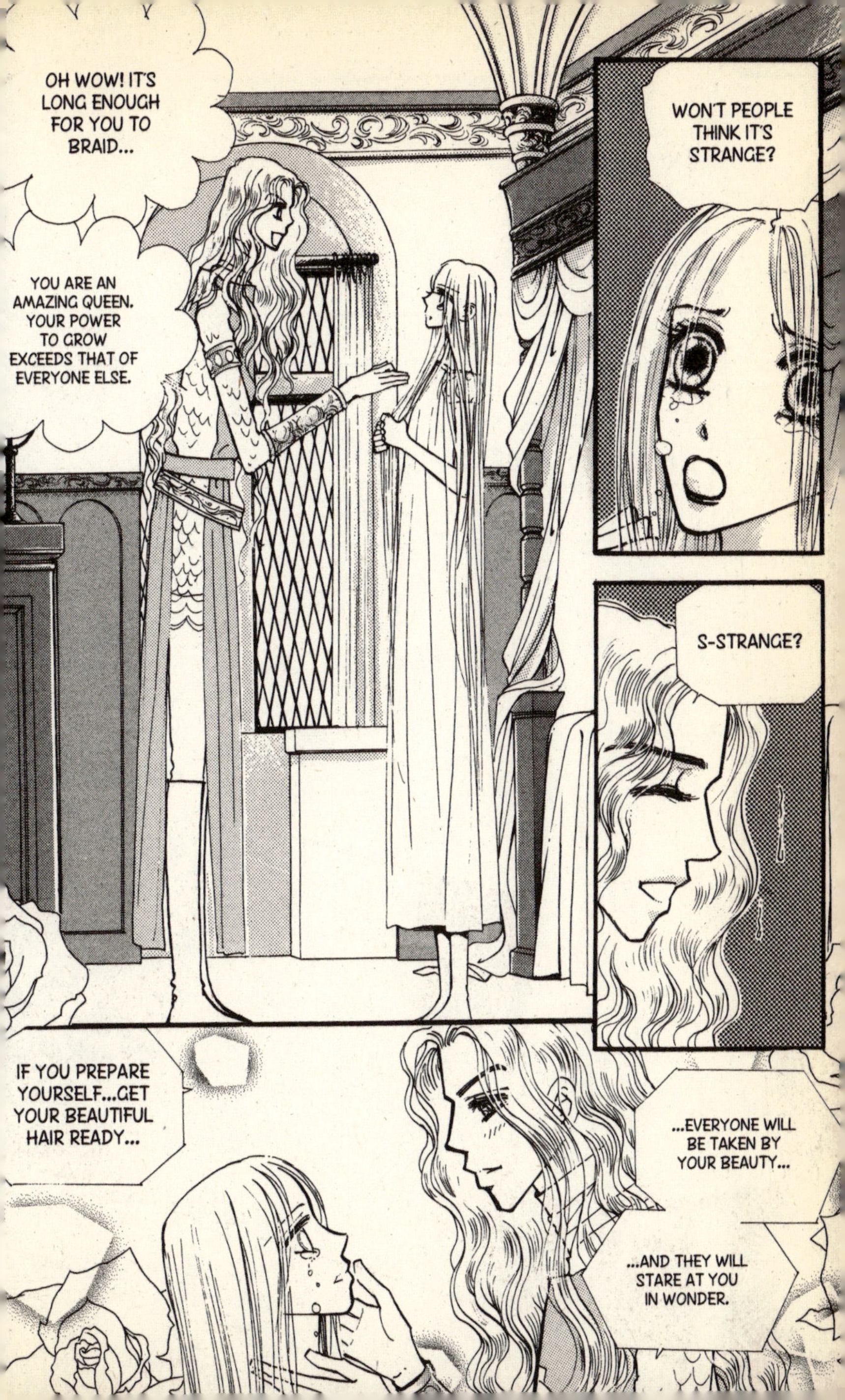
OH WOW! IT'S LONG ENOUGH FOR YOU TO BRAID...
YOU ARE AN AMAZING QUEEN. YOUR POWER TO GROW EXCEEDS THAT OF EVERYONE ELSE.
WON'T PEOPLE THINK IT'S STRANGE?
S-STRANGE?
IF YOU PREPARE YOURSELF...GET YOUR BEAUTIFUL HAIR READY...
...EVERYONE WILL BE TAKEN BY YOUR BEAUTY...
...AND THEY WILL STARE AT YOU IN WONDER.

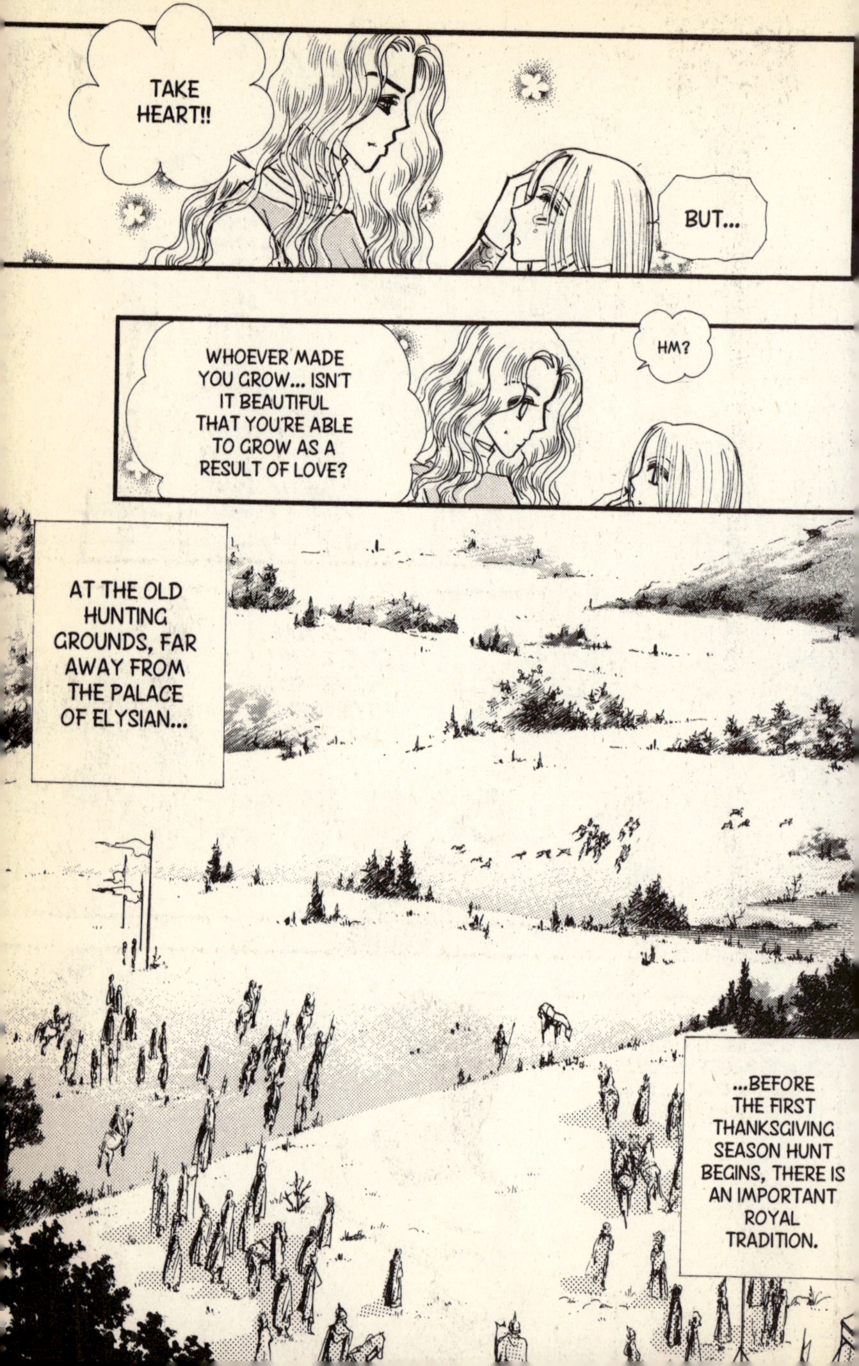
TAKE HEART!!
BUT...
WHOEVER MADE YOU GROW... ISN'T IT BEAUTIFUL THAT YOU'RE ABLE TO GROW AS A RESULT OF LOVE?
HM?
AT THE OLD HUNTING GROUNDS, FAR AWAY FROM THE PALACE OF ELYSIAN...
...BEFORE THE FIRST THANKSGIVING SEASON HUNT BEGINS, THERE IS AN IMPORTANT ROYAL TRADITION.

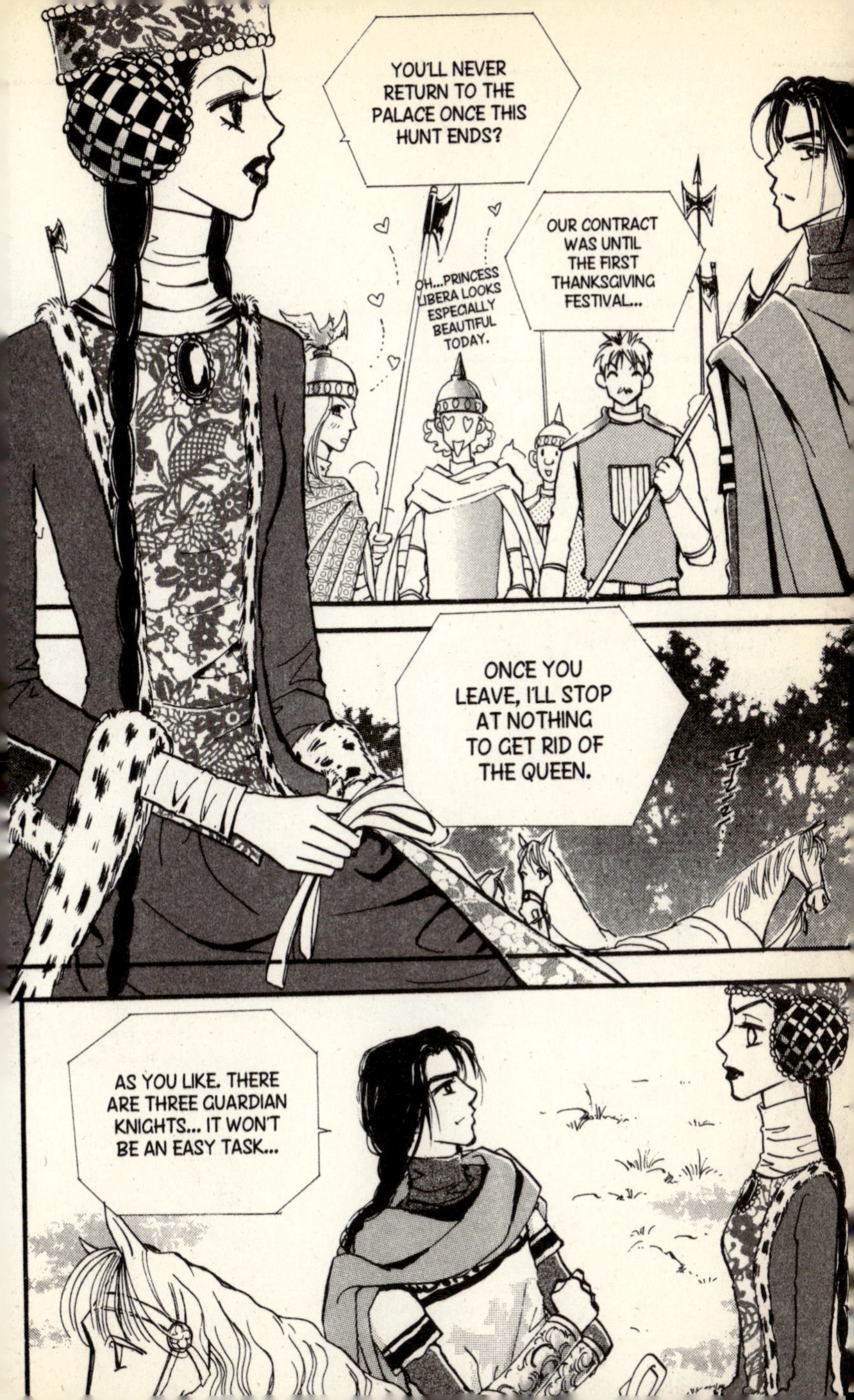
YOU'LL NEVER RETURN TO THE PALACE ONCE THIS HUNT ENDS?
OH...PRINCESS LIBERA LOOKS ESPECIALLY BEAUTIFUL TODAY.
OUR CONTRACT WAS UNTIL THE FIRST THANKSGIVING FESTIVAL...
ONCE YOU LEAVE, I'LL STOP AT NOTHING TO GET RID OF THE QUEEN.
AS YOU LIKE. THERE ARE THREE GUARDIAN KNIGHTS... IT WON'T BE AN EASY TASK...

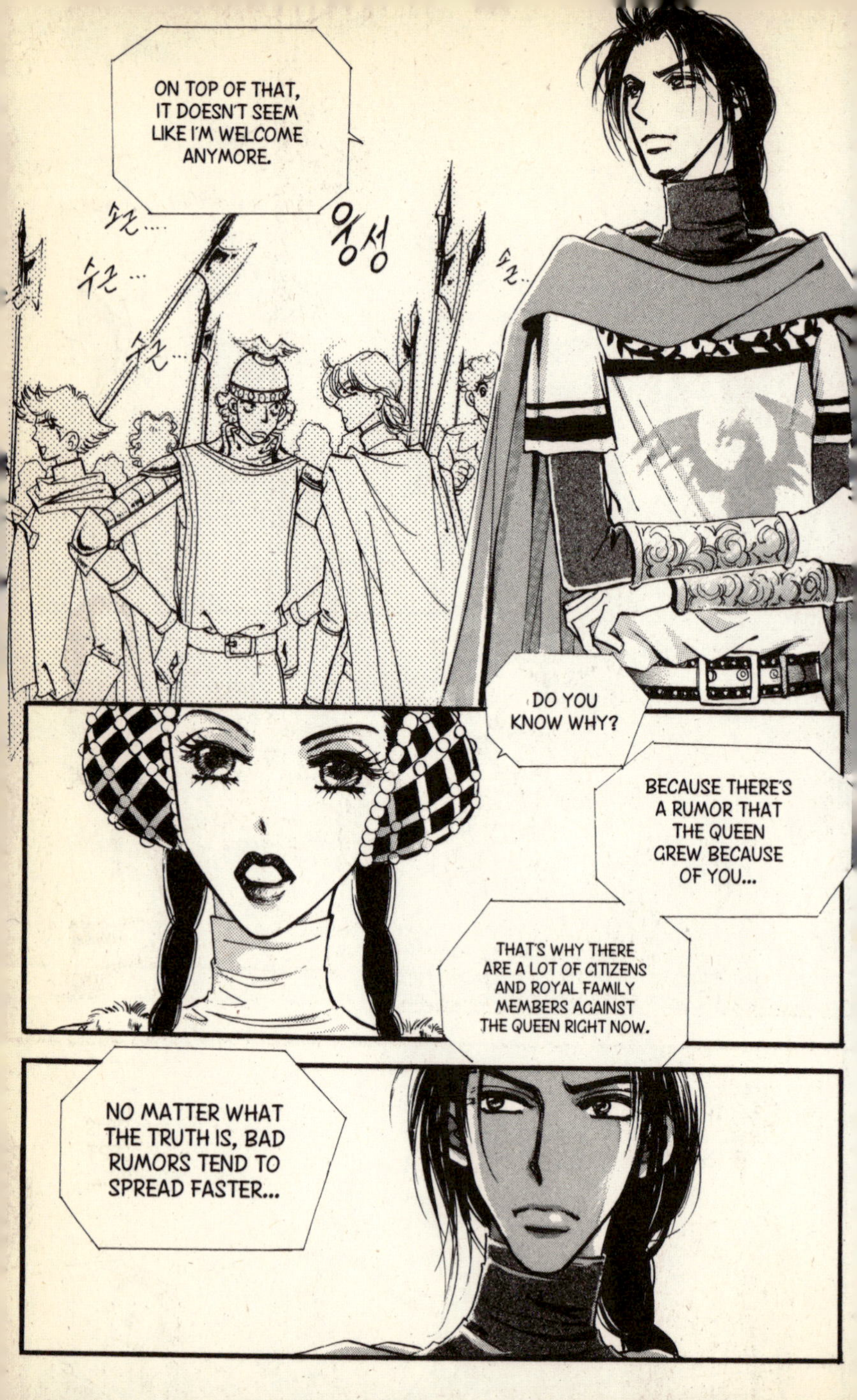
ON TOP OF THAT, IT DOESN'T SEEM LIKE I'M WELCOME ANYMORE.
소곤....
수군...
수군...
웅성
소곤...
DO YOU KNOW WHY?
BECAUSE THERE'S A RUMOR THAT THE QUEEN GREW BECAUSE OF YOU...
THAT'S WHY THERE ARE A LOT OF CITIZENS AND ROYAL FAMILY MEMBERS AGAINST THE QUEEN RIGHT NOW.
NO MATTER WHAT THE TRUTH IS, BAD RUMORS TEND TO SPREAD FASTER...

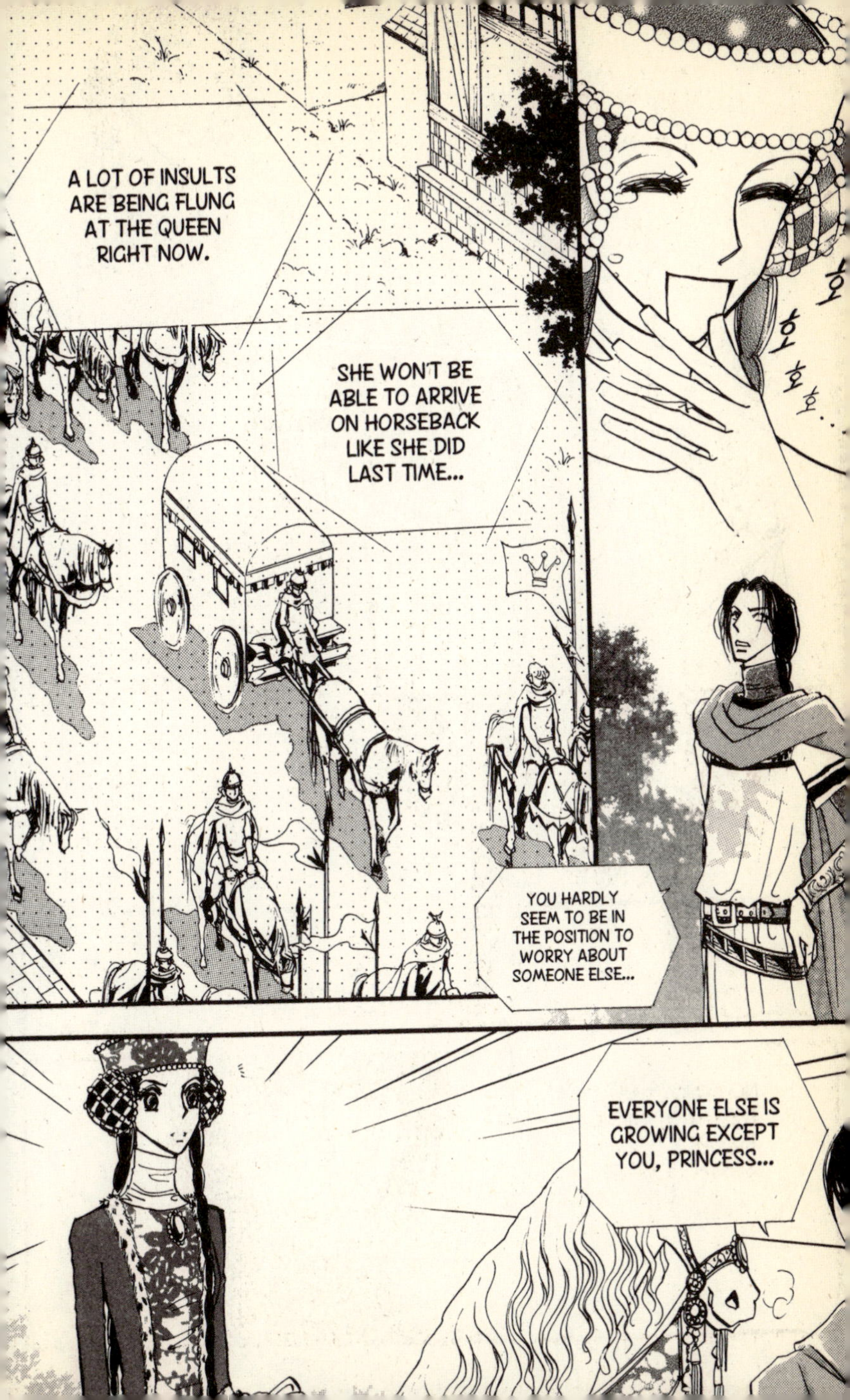
A LOT OF INSULTS ARE BEING FLUNG AT THE QUEEN RIGHT NOW.
SHE WON'T BE ABLE TO ARRIVE ON HORSEBACK LIKE SHE DID LAST TIME...
호호호호...
YOU HARDLY SEEM TO BE IN THE POSITION TO WORRY ABOUT SOMEONE ELSE...
EVERYONE ELSE IS GROWING EXCEPT YOU, PRINCESS...

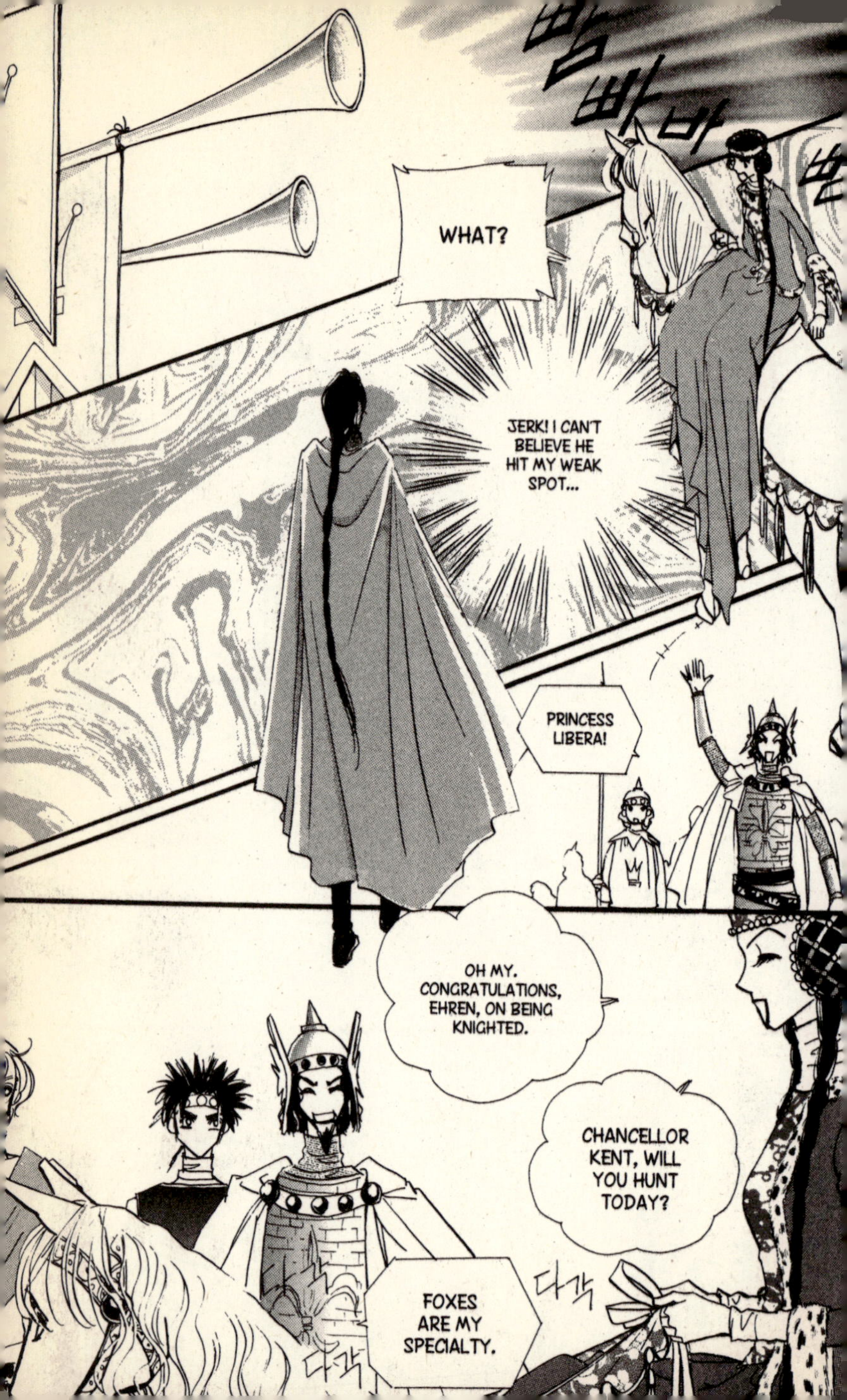

빰빠바
WHAT?
JERK! I CAN'T BELIEVE HE HIT MY WEAK SPOT...
PRINCESS LIBERA!
OH MY. CONGRATULATIONS, EHREN, ON BEING KNIGHTED.
CHANCELLOR KENT, WILL YOU HUNT TODAY?
FOXES ARE MY SPECIALTY.
다각
다각

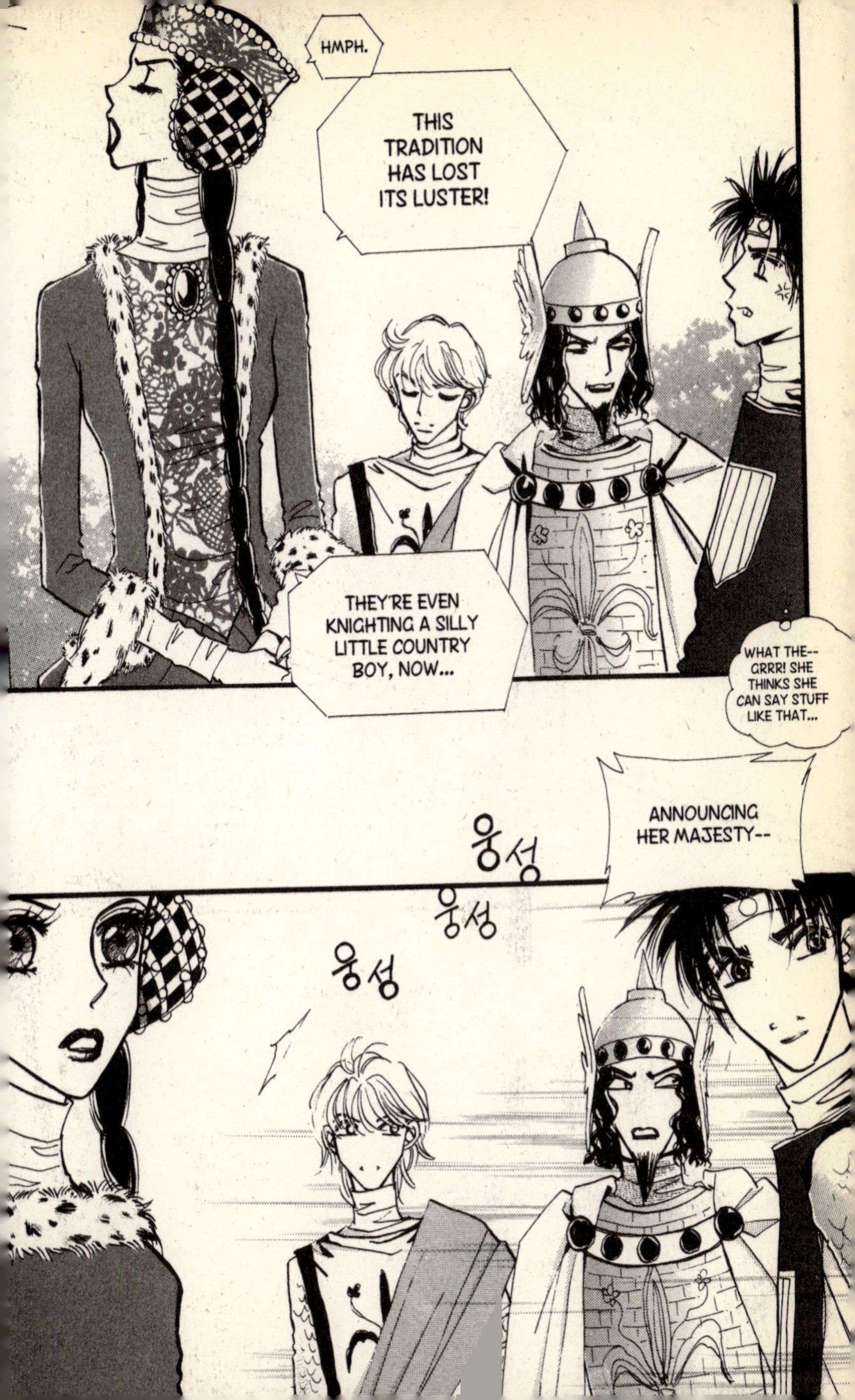
HMPH.
THIS TRADITION HAS LOST ITS LUSTER!
THEY'RE EVEN KNIGHTING A SILLY LITTLE COUNTRY BOY, NOW...
WHAT THE-- GRRR! SHE THINKS SHE CAN SAY STUFF LIKE THAT...
웅성
웅성
웅성
ANNOUNCING HER MAJESTY--

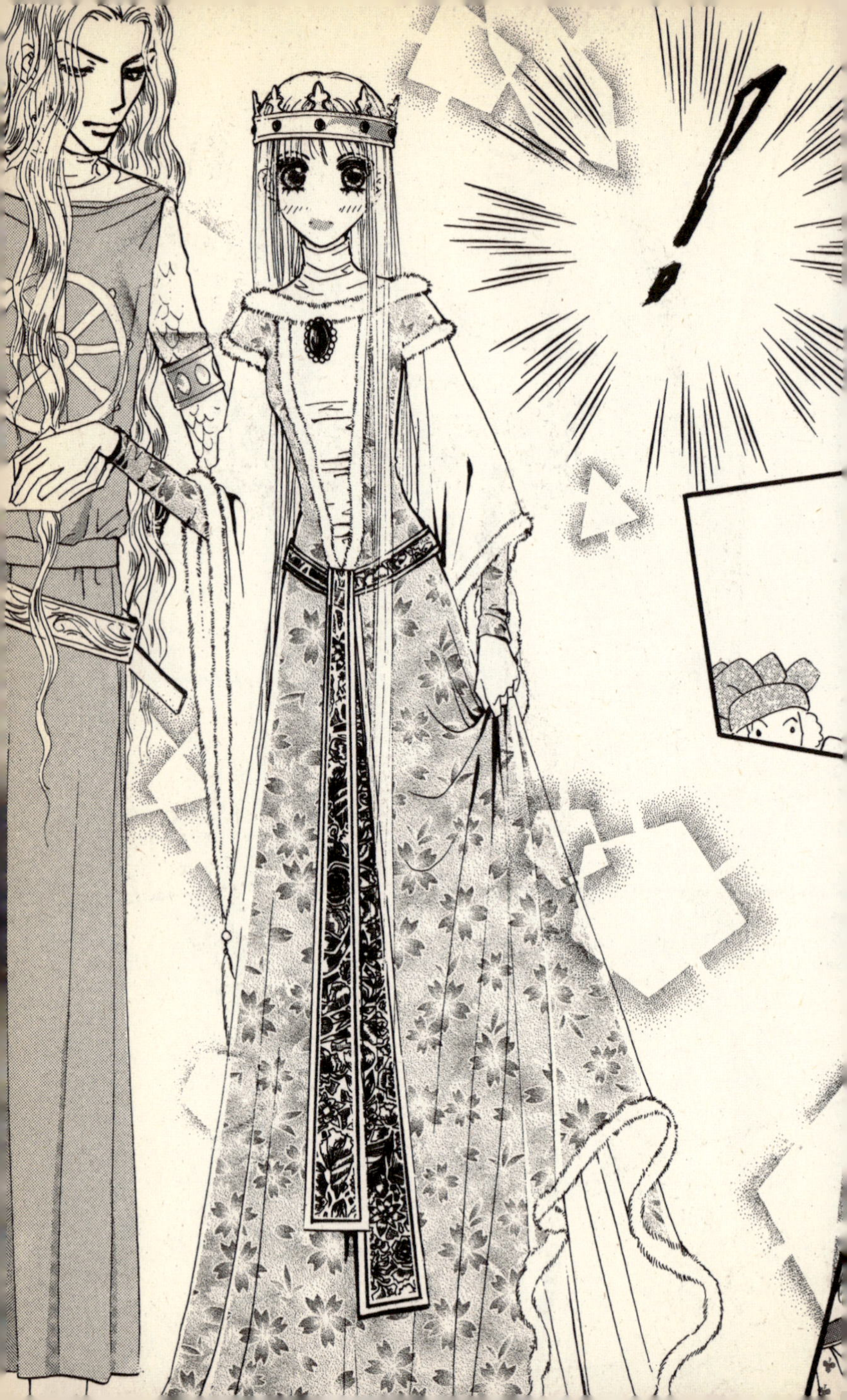

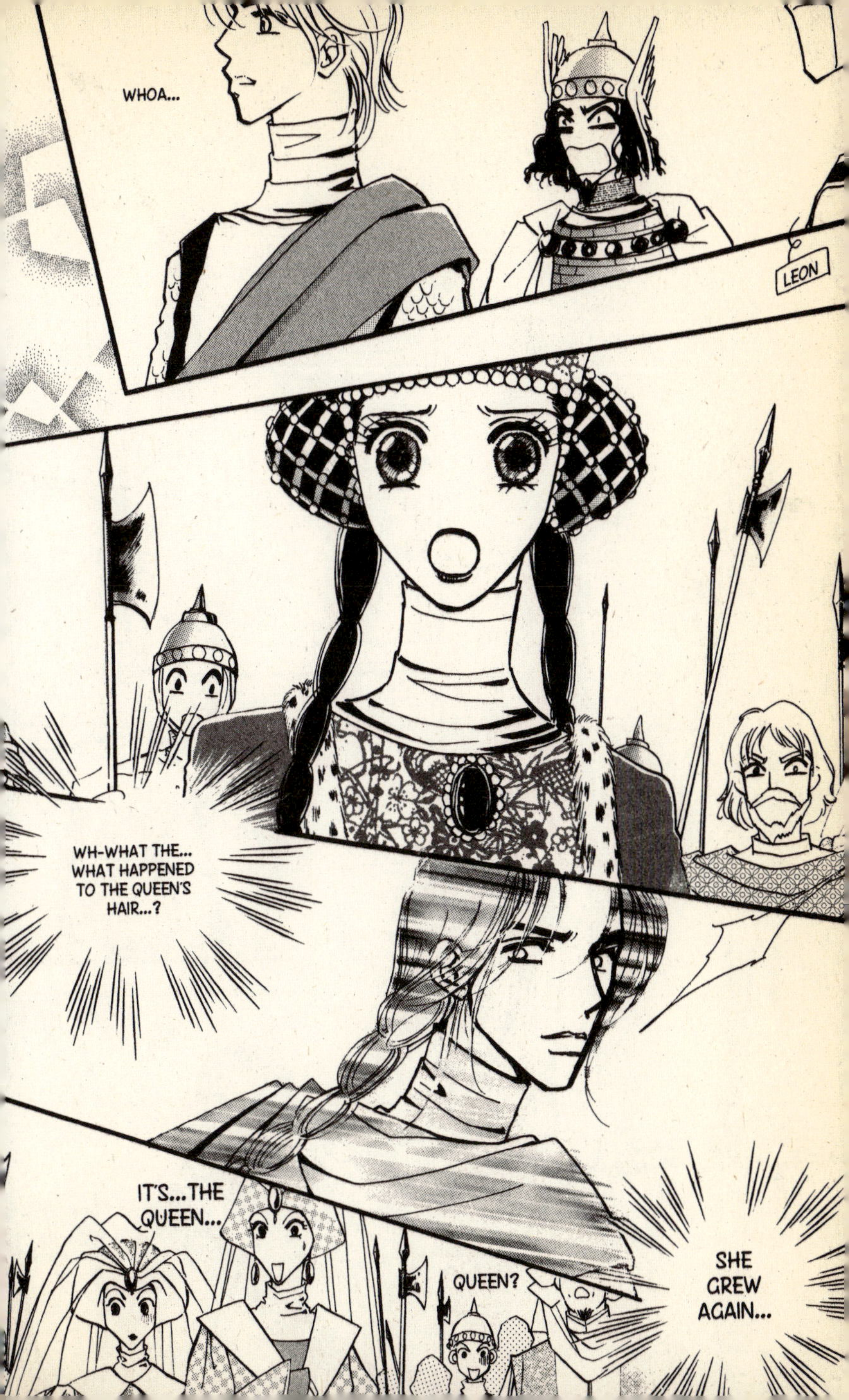
WHOA...
LEON
WH-WHAT THE... WHAT HAPPENED TO THE QUEEN'S HAIR...?
IT'S...THE QUEEN...
QUEEN?
SHE GREW AGAIN...

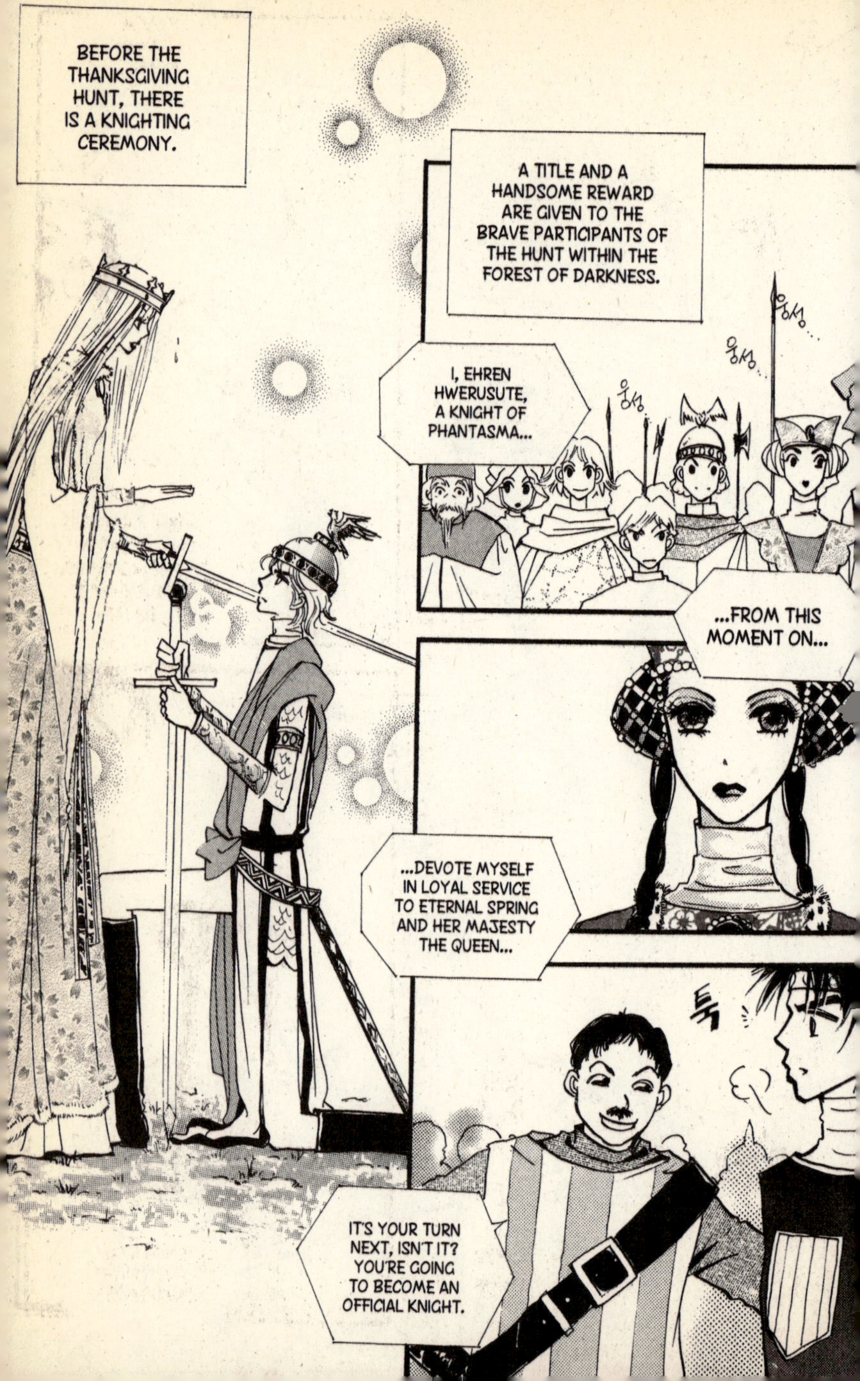
BEFORE THE THANKSGIVING HUNT, THERE IS A KNIGHTING CEREMONY.
A TITLE AND A HANDSOME REWARD ARE GIVEN TO THE BRAVE PARTICIPANTS OF THE HUNT WITHIN THE FOREST OF DARKNESS.
I, EHREN HWERUSUTE, A KNIGHT OF PHANTASMA...
웅성
웅성...
웅성...
...FROM THIS MOMENT ON...
...DEVOTE MYSELF IN LOYAL SERVICE TO ETERNAL SPRING AND HER MAJESTY THE QUEEN...
툭
IT'S YOUR TURN NEXT, ISN'T IT? YOU'RE GOING TO BECOME AN OFFICIAL KNIGHT.

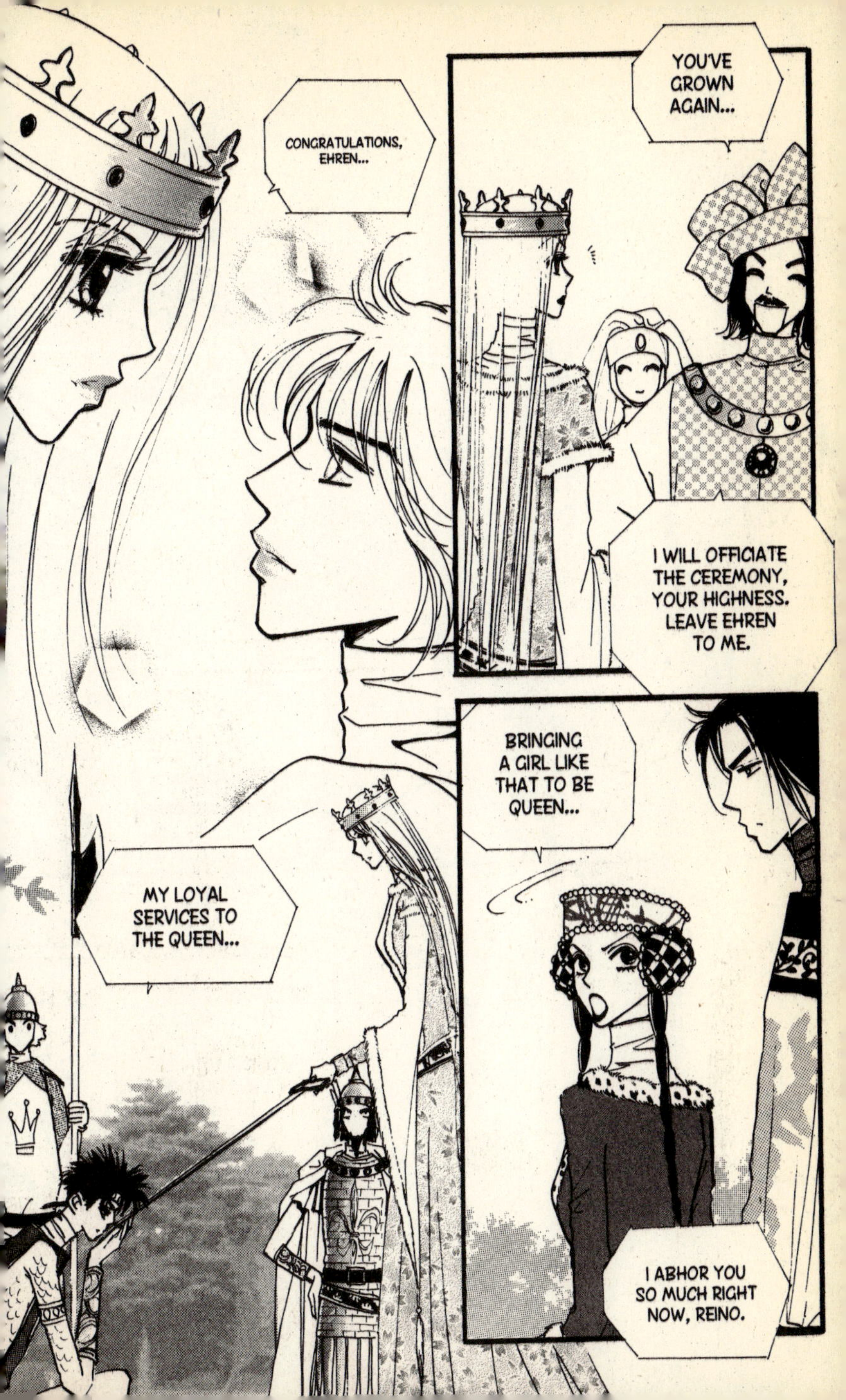
CONGRATULATIONS, EHREN...
MY LOYAL SERVICES TO THE QUEEN...
YOU'VE GROWN AGAIN...
I WILL OFFICIATE THE CEREMONY, YOUR HIGHNESS. LEAVE EHREN TO ME.
BRINGING A GIRL LIKE THAT TO BE QUEEN...
I ABHOR YOU SO MUCH RIGHT NOW, REINO.

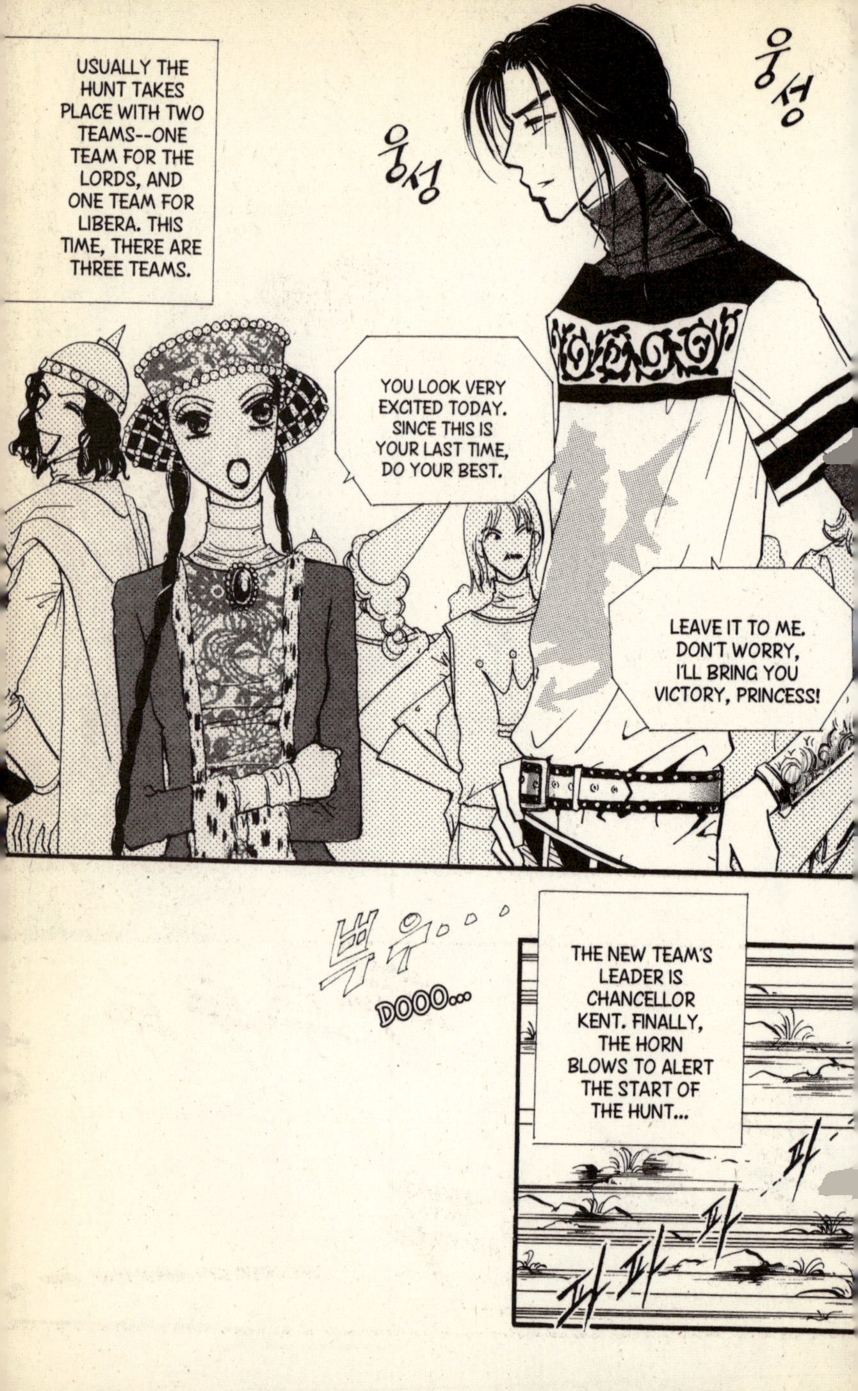
USUALLY THE HUNT TAKES PLACE WITH TWO TEAMS--ONE TEAM FOR THE LORDS, AND ONE TEAM FOR LIBERA. THIS TIME, THERE ARE THREE TEAMS.
웅성
웅성
YOU LOOK VERY EXCITED TODAY. SINCE THIS IS YOUR LAST TIME, DO YOUR BEST.
LEAVE IT TO ME. DON'T WORRY, I'LL BRING YOU VICTORY, PRINCESS!
뿌우
DOOO...
THE NEW TEAM'S LEADER IS CHANCELLOR KENT. FINALLY, THE HORN BLOWS TO ALERT THE START OF THE HUNT...
파
파
파
파

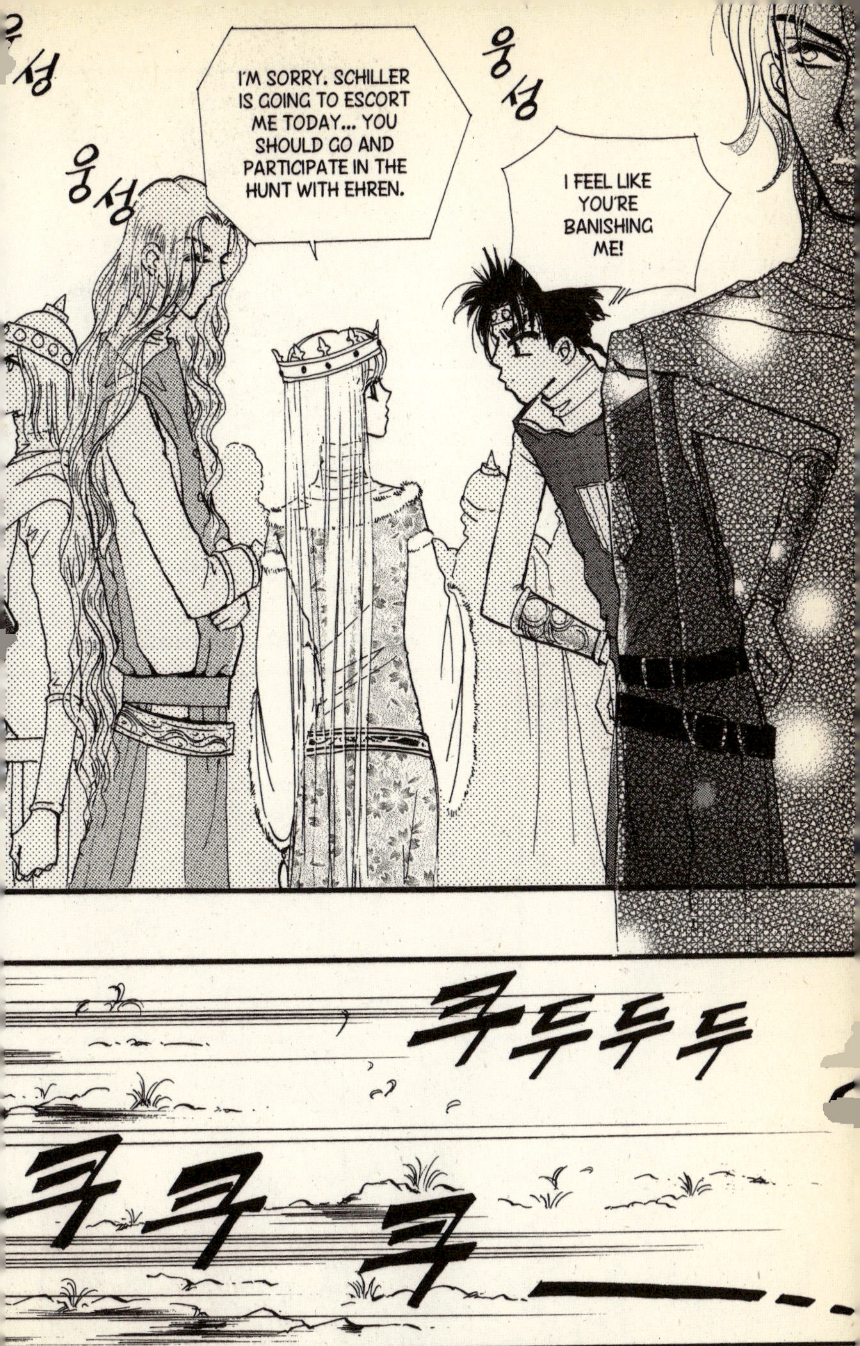
웅성
I'M SORRY. SCHILLER IS GOING TO ESCORT ME TODAY... YOU SHOULD GO AND PARTICIPATE IN THE HUNT WITH EHREN.
웅성
I FEEL LIKE YOU'RE BANISHING ME!
쿠두두두
쿠 쿠 쿠—...

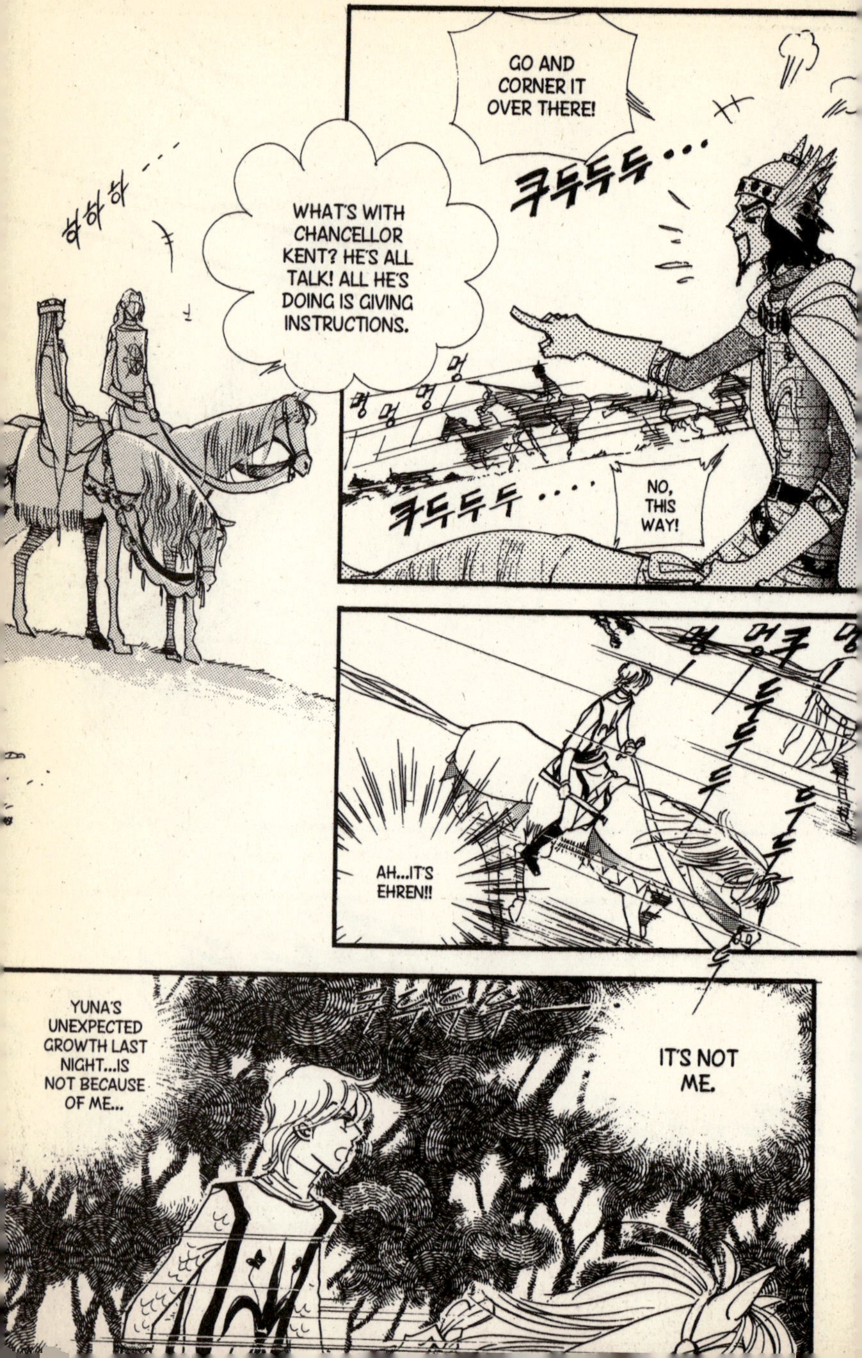

하하하 ...
WHAT'S WITH CHANCELLOR KENT? HE'S ALL TALK! ALL HE'S DOING IS GIVING INSTRUCTIONS.
GO AND CORNER IT OVER THERE!
쿠두두두 ...
쿠두두두 ....
NO, THIS WAY!
AH...IT'S EHREN!!
YUNA'S UNEXPECTED GROWTH LAST NIGHT...IS NOT BECAUSE OF ME...
IT'S NOT ME.

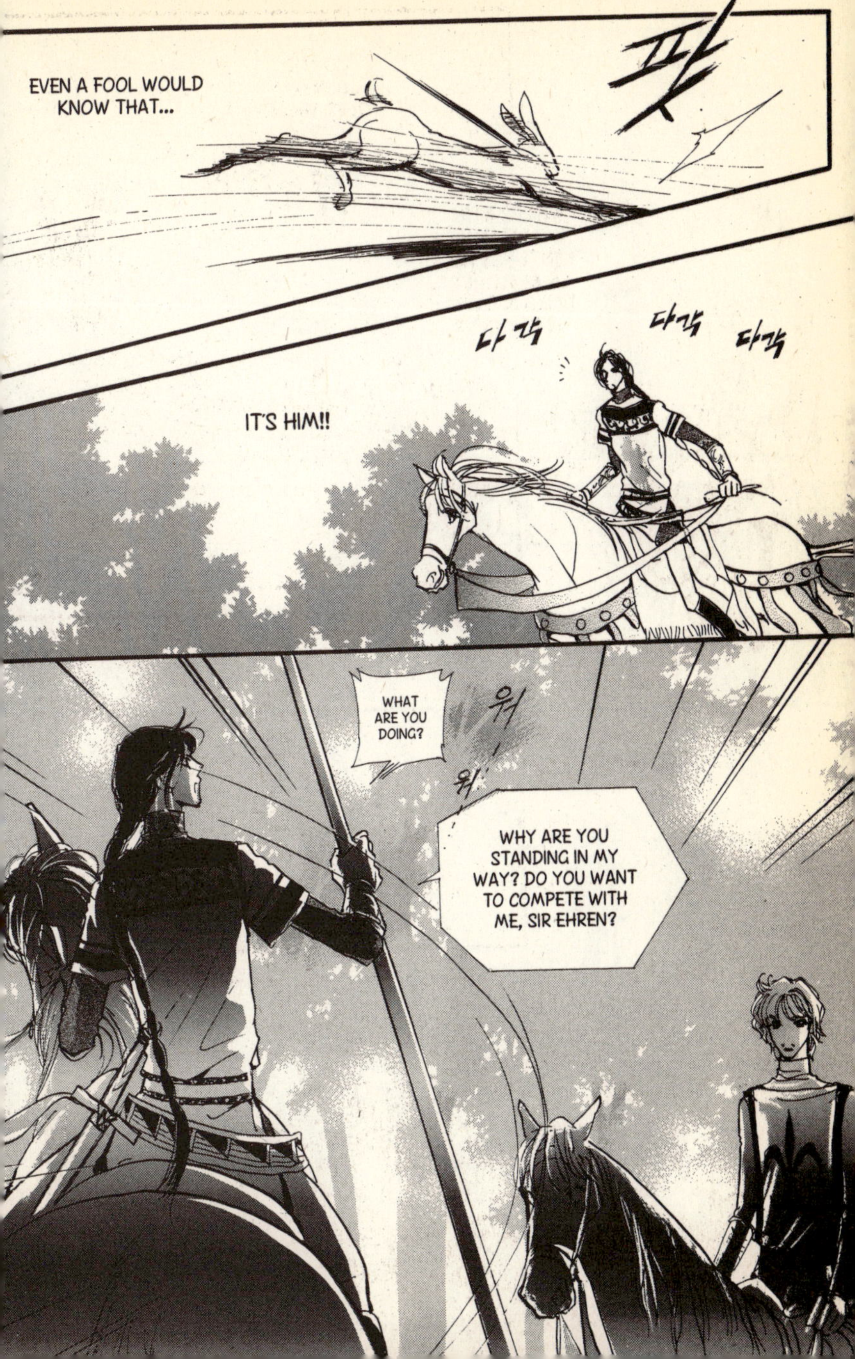
EVEN A FOOL WOULD KNOW THAT...
팍
다각
다각
다각
IT'S HIM!!
WHAT ARE YOU DOING?
워
워
WHY ARE YOU STANDING IN MY WAY? DO YOU WANT TO COMPETE WITH ME, SIR EHREN?

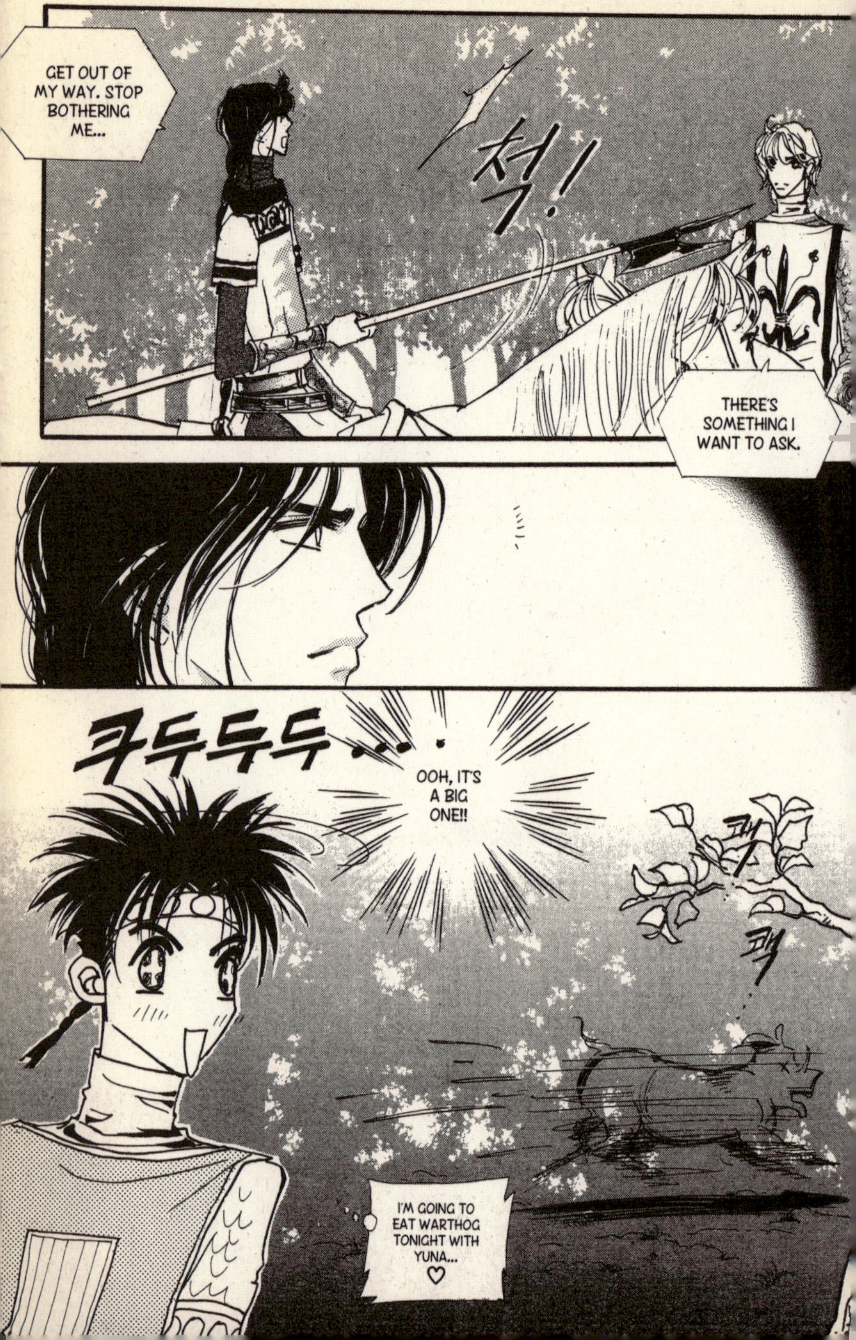
GET OUT OF MY WAY. STOP BOTHERING ME...
척!
THERE'S SOMETHING I WANT TO ASK.
쿠두두두...
OOH, IT'S A BIG ONE!!
꽥
꽥
I'M GOING TO EAT WARTHOG TONIGHT WITH YUNA... ♡

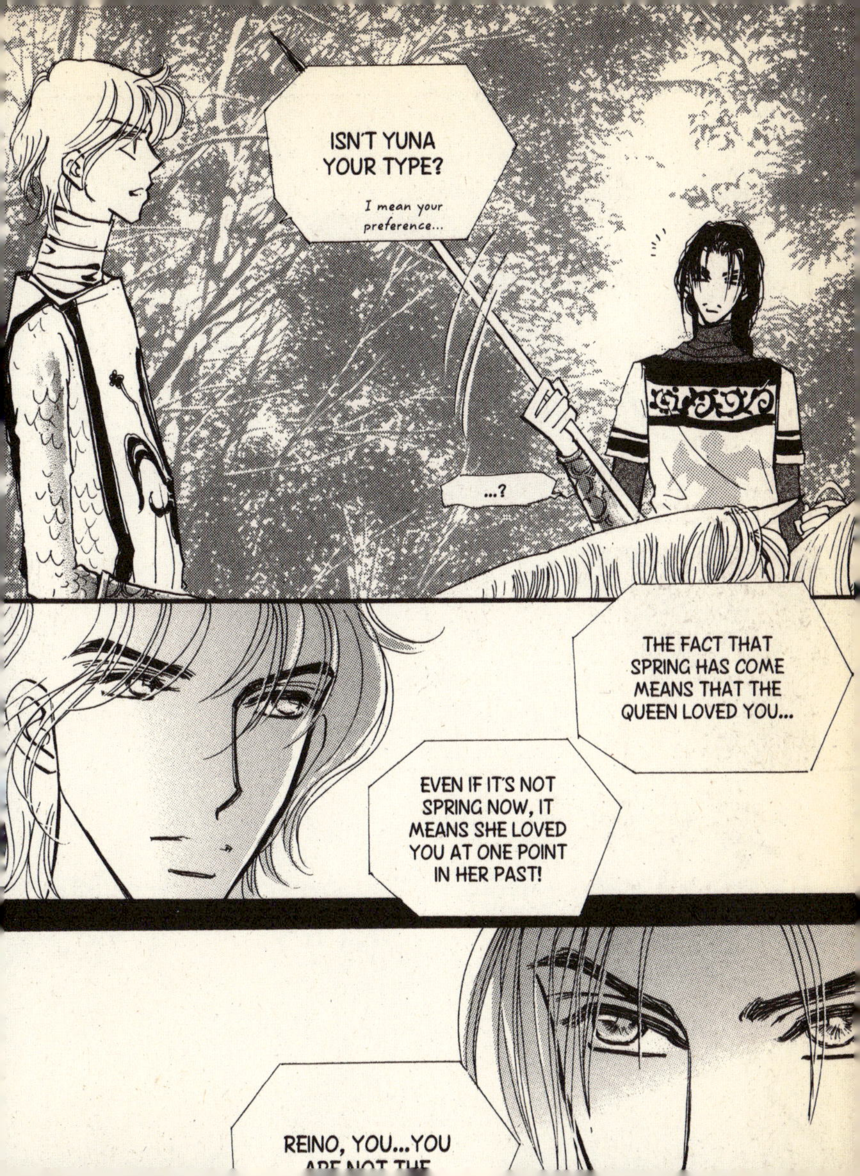
ISN'T YUNA YOUR TYPE?
I mean your preference...
...?
THE FACT THAT SPRING HAS COME MEANS THAT THE QUEEN LOVED YOU...
EVEN IF IT'S NOT SPRING NOW, IT MEANS SHE LOVED YOU AT ONE POINT IN HER PAST!
REINO, YOU...YOU

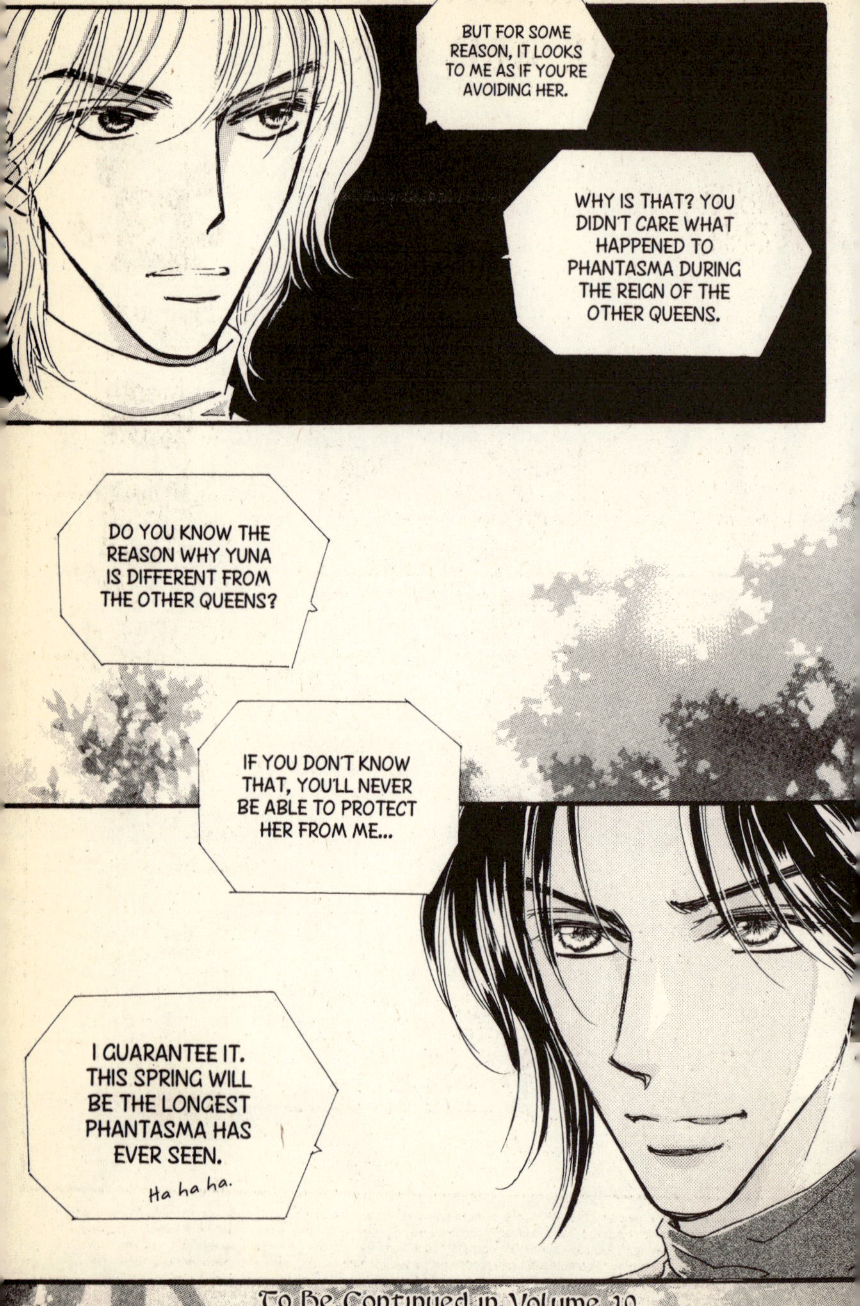
BUT FOR SOME REASON, IT LOOKS TO ME AS IF YOU'RE AVOIDING HER.
WHY IS THAT? YOU DIDN'T CARE WHAT HAPPENED TO PHANTASMA DURING THE REIGN OF THE OTHER QUEENS.
DO YOU KNOW THE REASON WHY YUNA IS DIFFERENT FROM THE OTHER QUEENS?
IF YOU DON'T KNOW THAT, YOU'LL NEVER BE ABLE TO PROTECT HER FROM ME...
I GUARANTEE IT. THIS SPRING WILL BE THE LONGEST PHANTASMA HAS EVER SEEN.
Ha ha ha.

To Be Continued in Volume 10

Congratulations on your 9th book!!

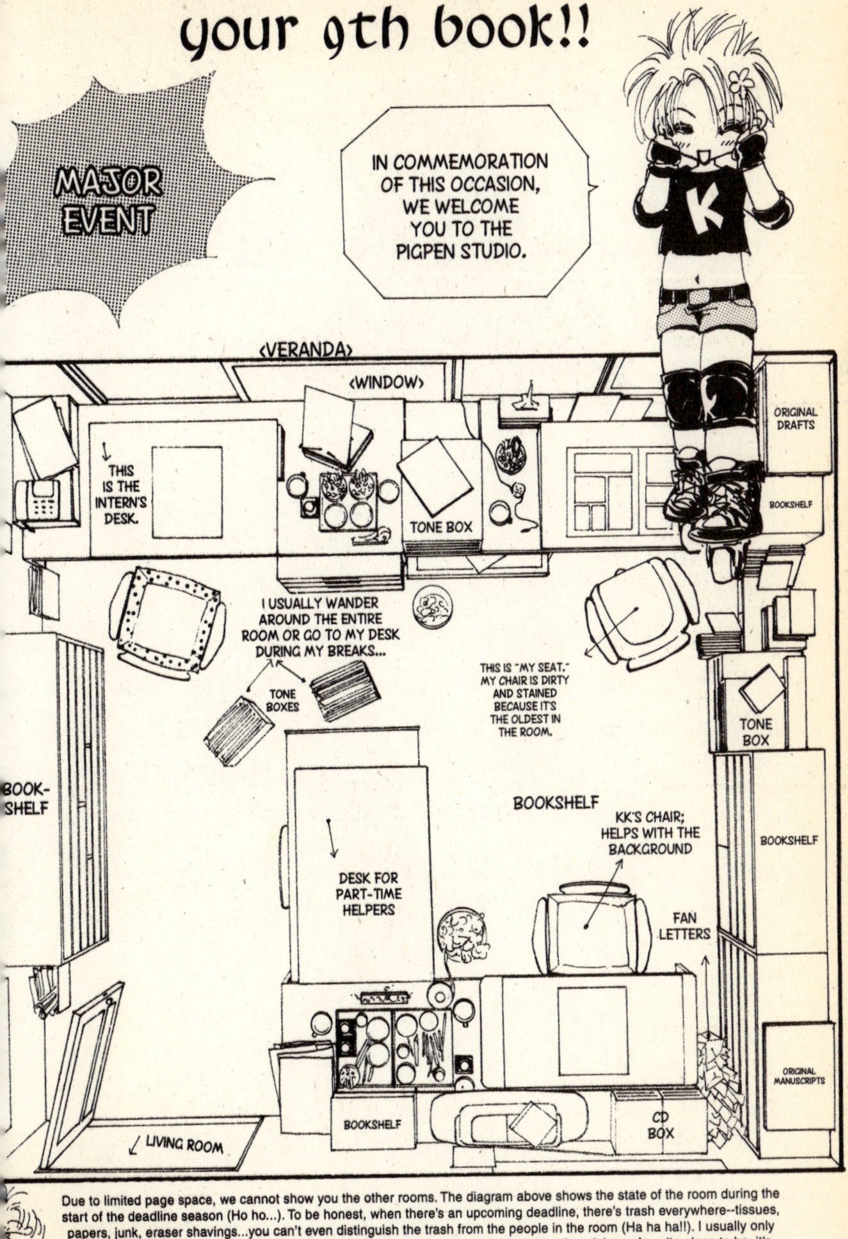
MAJOR EVENT
IN COMMEMORATION OF THIS OCCASION, WE WELCOME YOU TO THE PIGPEN STUDIO.
<VERANDA>
<WINDOW>
ORIGINAL DRAFTS
THIS IS THE INTERN'S DESK.
TONE BOX
BOOKSHELF
I USUALLY WANDER AROUND THE ENTIRE ROOM OR GO TO MY DESK DURING MY BREAKS...
TONE BOXES
THIS IS "MY SEAT." MY CHAIR IS DIRTY AND STAINED BECAUSE IT'S THE OLDEST IN THE ROOM.
TONE BOX
BOOK-SHELF
BOOKSHELF
KK'S CHAIR; HELPS WITH THE BACKGROUND
BOOKSHELF
DESK FOR PART-TIME HELPERS
FAN LETTERS
ORIGINAL MANUSCRIPTS
BOOKSHELF
CD BOX
LIVING ROOM

Due to limited page space, we cannot show you the other rooms. The diagram above shows the state of the room during the start of the deadline season (Ho ho...). To be honest, when there's an upcoming deadline, there's trash everywhere--tissues, papers, junk, eraser shavings...you can't even distinguish the trash from the people in the room (Ha ha ha!!). I usually only use this room to work. Whenever I come here, I feel tense and nervous. At the same time, it is my favorite place to be; it's warm and comfortable like a mother's embrace. (The above diagram is the product of KK, who is my background artist.)

IN THE NEXT VOLUME OF...

THE QUEEN's KNIGHT

WHILE YUNA CONTINUES TO BE AT A LOSS AS TO THE IDENTITY OF THE PERSON OF HER AFFECTIONS, SHE IS BRIEFLY ABLE TO FORGET HER WOES VIA A COSTUME BALL. HOWEVER, WHEN REINO STORMS IN AND CARRIES HER AWAY, IT WORKS THE KNIGHTS INTO A FRENZY... BUT EVEN MORE UPSETTING FOR YUNA IS THAT SOON AFTER THIS EVENT HER HAIR GROWS YET AGAIN. THIS ALL SUGGESTS THAT PERHAPS REINO IS INDEED HER HEART'S DESIRE...BUT AT WHAT COST?

COMING SOON!

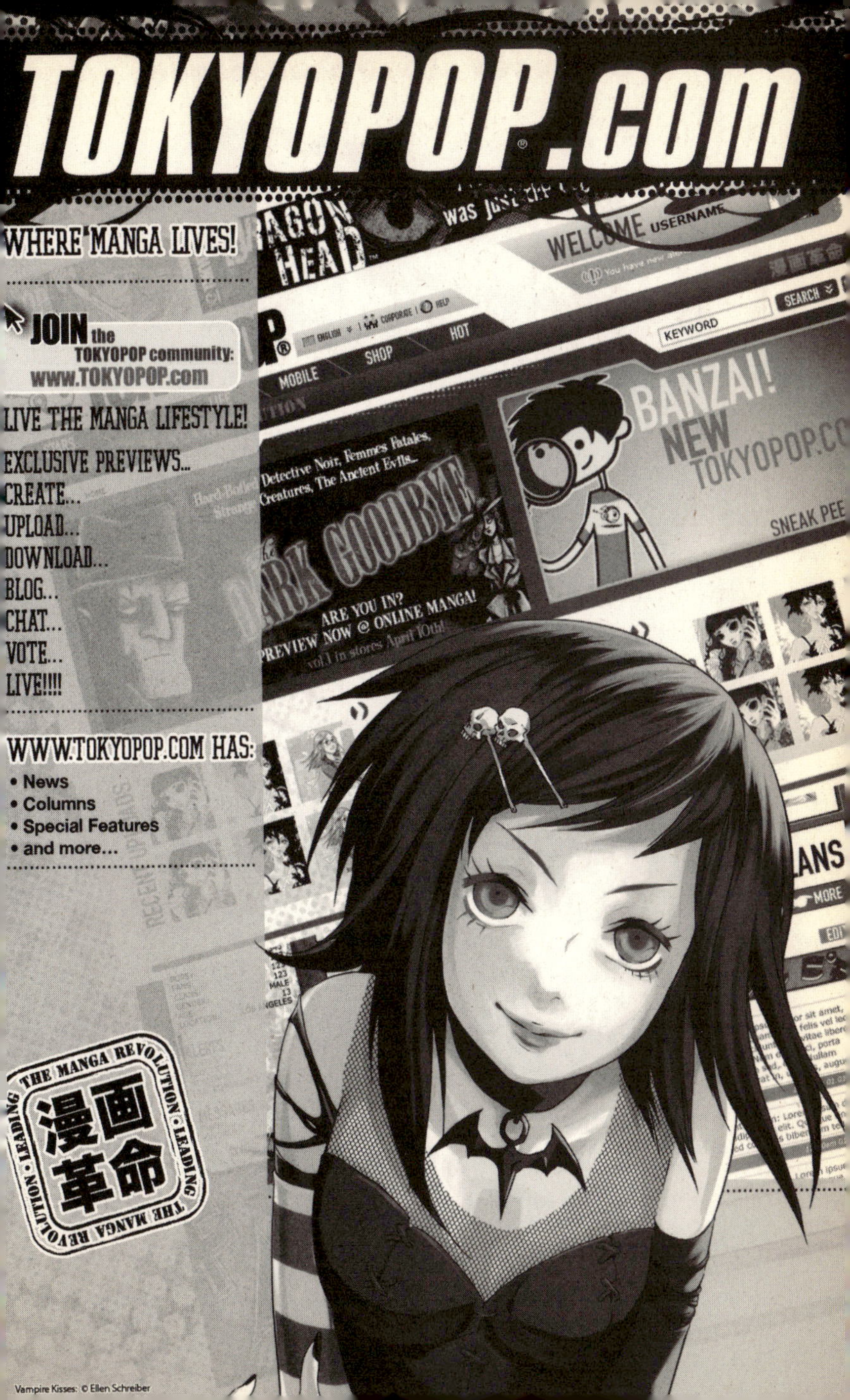
TOKYOPOP.com
WHERE MANGA LIVES!
JOIN the TOKYOPOP community: www.TOKYOPOP.com
LIVE THE MANGA LIFESTYLE!
EXCLUSIVE PREVIEWS...
CREATE...
UPLOAD...
DOWNLOAD...
BLOG...
CHAT...
VOTE...
LIVE!!!!
WWW.TOKYOPOP.COM HAS:
• News
• Columns
• Special Features
• and more...
THE MANGA REVOLUTION • LEADING • LEADING THE MANGA REVOLUTION
漫画革命
Vampire Kisses: © Ellen Schreiber